SIKH SOLDIER

VOLUME THREE

Policing the Empire

Shaheed Baba Deep Singh Ji (1684-1757)

NARINDAR SINGH DHESI

With the assistance of:
GRAHAM WATKINS B.Sc. (Hons)

Published by

The Naval & Military Press Ltd
Unit 10 Ridgewood Industrial Park,
Uckfield, East Sussex,
TN22 5QE England
Tel: + 44 (0) 1825 749494
Fax: + 44 (0) 1825 765701
www.naval-military-press.com

The Awakening

CONTENTS

Contents

MAPS

'Motor Muscle' of the British Empire

ILLUSTRATIONS

Illustrations

Illustrations

Illustrations

ACKNOWLEDGEMENTS

My profound thanks to the descendants of Sardar Karam Singh for permission to quote and use the photographs from Sardar Karam Singh's book; The Sikh Police Contingent (Custodians of the Empire) ISBN: 978-981-08-3148-6

I am deeply grateful to fellow Kenyan Diljit Singh Bahra for contributing the articles on Kenya Police, Uganda Police, Tanzania Police, and the British Police.

Thanks to Singapore Khalsa Association in providing the Photos and details about Singaporean Sikhs in the Singapore Armed Forces.

Thanks to Harjinder Singh Kanwal, for contributing a Sketch of Kenya Police.

I must express my warmest thanks to Colonel (Retired) Baldev Singh Johl for providing the profiles of Malaysian Sikhs in uniform and for writing the foreward to this book. May you always stay in chardikala!

My special thanks to my family, Beverley, Surindar, Jodh, Jassa and Sher.

And final thanks to long-suffering Hon. Prof. Graham Watkins, who helped to make the manuscript ready for publication.

Maharajah Ranjit Singh
(1780-1839)
The Sikh Emperor

FOREWORD

Narindar Singh Dhesi examines in successive chapters the Indian Army's role in extending and securing the British Empire, especially the employment of Sikh soldiers to be in the vanguard of military operations, and as the Sentinels of the Empire. The structure of this work is not that of conventional narrative history. The individual chapters are organized around selected topics. It is best considered as a set of essays that together offer us a view into the martial traditions of the Sikh soldier. Narindar Singh takes us from the fall of the Sikh kingdom to the horrors of the Sepoy mutiny. He takes us to the North West Frontier of India, the most sensitive strategic frontier of the British Empire, as the British feared a Russian invasion of India through the Khyber and Bolan Passes as the Russian Empire had expanded towards India. The military operations on the Frontier tied down large numbers of Sikh soldiers in a long series of inconclusive skirmishes and major campaigns. The British military success over Burma in 1826 and the annexation of the Ahom kingdom of Assam marked the entry of the British to the Northeastern region of India. The right of conquest brought these territories directly under the control of the British government. The steady annexation of Chinese territory by Europeans led to British occupation of Hong Kong and Shanghai. This led to extensive recruitment of Sikh soldiers for paramilitary forces of these territories. The same tale of recruitment and policing is told of the Straits Settlements, Especially the Sikhs of Singapore and Malaysia, who carry on the martial traditions of their forefathers in their respective countries. After the Indian Army's conquest of East and Central Africa, Kenya, Uganda, and Somaliland, the Sikh soldier policed the forests and barren lands of these countries. Narindar tells us how the Sikh soldiers were especially recruited to fight the slave hunters in Nyasaland and after defeating them went on to fight in the Ashanti war and in Somaliland. And finally, we see the Sikh soldier's gallantry in the bloodletting of the two world wars.*

This is an extensively researched sequel to the author's earlier publications on the gallantry awards and battle honours of the Sikh soldier. Hitherto, no chronicle existed that had been so exhaustively and painstakingly researched in a single publication. Often Sikh historians have distorted or excised relevant portions. These texts bare the original version. They belong to the class of lexicons, concordances, and reference books that are so lacking in Sikh military history. Any serious scholar should use these as the starting point for further research. I take this opportunity to compliment Narindar Singh Dhesi on his book *Sikh Soldier: Policing the Empire*. A well researched and well-written book will be of great interest and use to those who wish to increase their knowledge of that particular part of Sikh military history.

Lieutenant Colonel (Retd) Baldev Singh Johl
Malaysian Armed Forces

*Most of the Gallantry award citations in this volume are taken from the sister volume: *Sikh Soldier: Gallantry Awards*, by the same author.

PREFACE

This book is an attempt to tell something about the use of the Indian Army to extend and secure the British Empire. The Sikh soldiers were the cutting edge of the Indian Army; their endeavours have gone virtually unnoticed despite many books written on British colonial military history. This book does not endeavour to remedy that shortcoming. Rather, by selecting several overseas campaigns, it illuminates the ways in which the Sikh soldier secured and sustained the British Colonial Empire. A particular effort has been made to cover the overlooked gallantry awards made to the Sikh soldiers during all the major and minor conflicts of the British Empire. Sikh soldiers were able to entrench themselves in Malaya and Singapore largely because of the para-military nature of the early Colonial Police Forces. An effort has been made to provide profiles of these soldiers who served, and are currently serving in the armed forces of their respective countries. If there was a single inspiration behind the book, it was admiration and fascination for the soldiers of these diverse formations, who soldiered in all climes and terrains of the world. That regard has increased many times over in the course of researching and writing this book. I am aware of the book's shortcomings, with errors and unintentional oversights. Nonetheless, it is hoped the book is a start on telling the story in part of Sikh soldier's martial history.

N.S. Dhesi

Maharajah Duleep Singh
(1838-1893)
The Last Sikh Emperor

INTRODUCTION

At the fall of the Sikh Kingdom and its annexation to British India, the Sikh soldier went soldiering to the far corners of the British Empire. He found employment overseas in two related kinds of imperial enterprise: the initial conquest of new territories and subsequent suppression of rebellions, when reliable local forces did not exist or were insufficient for the task. The structure of colonial forces, especially in initial stages after colonization or British intervention, was focused on military muscle and organization, as the British felt that they needed to protect their own interests against possible internal and external threats against their rule.

The reputation of the Sikh soldier as the premier colonial soldier was so great that from the outset the colonial administrators insisted that Sikhs, and Sikhs alone, must be supplied to them for the paramilitary policing needs of the colonial forces. They were extensively used as the 'Motor Muscle' of imperial authority. During the initial period of pacification, the Sikhs performed the role of shock troops, leading attacks against various hostile elements. Subsequently they did garrison duties and trained the native soldiers to meet the requirements of their respective territories.

The Sikhs had become such an entrenched aspect of colonial policing that even when the colonies became sovereign states, the Sikhs retained their employment in the police forces of their respective countries. Their descendants carry on the martial traditions to this day.

'Tall, well built and upright, with a dignified demeanour, long hair tied under a tight turban, beard and whiskers curled up, the Sikh soldier looks the very picture and personification of a warrior with a vivid and forceful personality!' (Sharma, 1989, p181)

'By the end of nineteenth century, across a great arc ranging from Zomba to Tientsin, Indian, predominately Sikh contingents patrolled and policed the British Empire.' (Metcalf, 2008, p102)

DEDICATION

This collection endeavours to celebrate the heroic Sikh military tradition of individual bravery, of undying loyalty, of courage and dedication to duty in virtually every field of battle. The Sikh soldier asked for no nobler end than a death on the battlefield:

O Lord, these boons of Thee I ask,
Let me never shun a righteous task,
Let me be fearless when I go to battle,
Give me faith that victory will be mine,
Give me power to sing Thy praise,
And when it comes the time to end my life,
Let me fall in mighty strife.

The Ghorchurras
(Sikh Light Cavalry)

(Francois Balthazar Solvyns)

SIKH EMPIRE

Punjab was the main gateway and the first home of all conquerors coming into India from the northwest of India. It was fated to be a 'perpetual field of battle'. The close of the eighteenth century was a highly turbulent time politically and militarily in the Punjab. This was caused by the overall decline of the Mughal control from repeated Afghan invasions. The need to protect the Punjab from further Afghan invasions and the desire to make it independent of Mughal rule led to the growth of Sikh power in the Punjab. Sikh warlords, with their strong arms, overthrew Muslim authority and carved out their own independent principalities, which formed the Sikh Confederacy. An ambitious young 'Baron of the Horse', Ranjit Singh of the Sukkarchakkia Misl, by welding together the rude Barons of the Sikh Confederacy, forged a powerful military machine that would not only overpower the outmoded and feudal armies of the petty principalities, but also contain the British, who were relentlessly expanding their Indian Empire. He created and consolidated the most awesome military muscle ever seen in India and became King of an Empire extending from Tibet to the deserts of Sindh and from the Khyber Pass to the River Satluj. The rule of Maharaja Ranjit Singh will ever remain a watershed in the annals of the Trans-Indus regions, especially Peshawar and Bannu, as well as Hazara. All these areas were part of Afghanistan. "Ranjit Singh had wrested from Afghans their fairest provinces, not only those east of Indus where Kabul rulers could claim no racial affinity, but Peshawar itself and Bannu, fertile gardens inhabited by proud people of Afghan and Pathan stock". (Caroe, 1964, p317). After the conquest of the Afghan principalities of Kasur, Kashmir, and Multan, Ranjit Singh led his legions across the Indus and conquered Peshawar and its surrounding areas. Peshawar was annexed to the Sikh kingdom and Hari Singh Nalwa, the most dashing of the Kingdom's generals, was appointed as its Governor. Nalwa set up a very strong administration in the Peshawar valley and constructed forts on all the strategic points of the mountain passes to check any Afghan incursions into the Sikh Kingdom. All these measures alarmed the Afghans; they apprehended that their dangerous neighbours would make an inroad beyond the formidable defiles and conquer Afghanistan. They, therefore, resolved to put a stop to any further advance of Sikhs into Afghanistan. At Jamrud, Sardar Hari Singh built a massive fort, which was quite impregnable to artillery fire and could hold on for several weeks of pounding. The Emir of Afghanistan, Dost Mohammad, advanced on Jamrud with 7,000 horsemen, 2,000 matchlock men and 18 guns. His three sons, with their forces and a force of 12,000 to 15,000 Khaibiris, joined the main force and started pounding Jamrud fort but could not make any headway; eventually they were forced to lift the siege and retreat into the Khyber Pass. The Sikhs pursued the retreating Afghans and after heavy fighting captured the pass. As a result of this battle, Jamrud and the Khyber Pass became the western limits of Sikh Empire. Thus, the Sikhs closed the invader's gateway of India, through which, until it was bolted and barred by them, successive waves of invaders have from time immemorial poured into India.

Sikh Empire

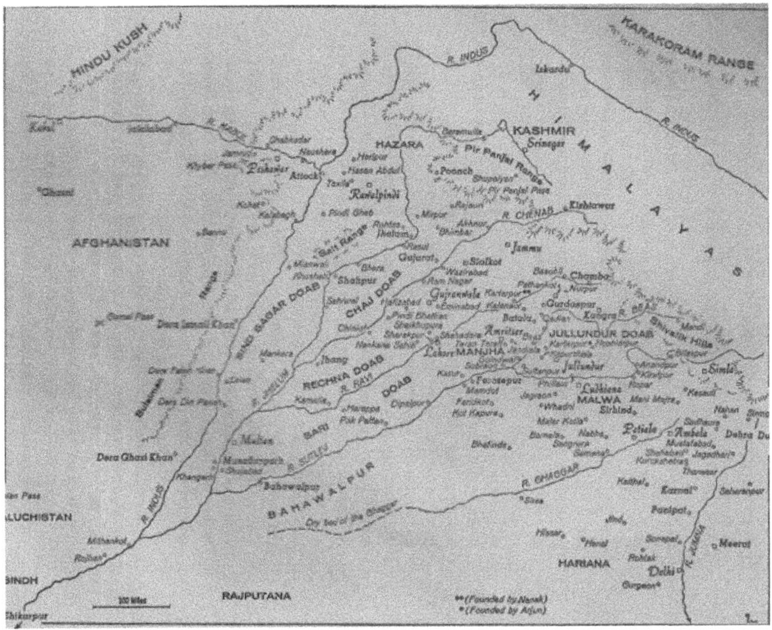

Sikh Empire with Cis Satluj towns

General Hari Singh Nalwa.

The most dashing champion of the Khalsa

(Lahore Museum)

Sikh Empire

Jamrud Fort

Jamrud Fort, between Peshawar and Khyber Pass, built by the Sikh Governor of Peshawar, Hari Singh Nalwa in 1823
(National Army Museum)

Bala Hissar Fort

Bala Hissar Fort at Peshawar, originally built by the Emperor Babur in 1526 but rebuilt by the Sikhs in 1830
(National Army Museum)

Sikh Empire

Tribesmen on the North-West Frontier, 1840
(National Army Museum)

Sikh regular infantryman, 1845
(By Richard Scollins)

BRITISH EMPIRE

The British Empire was the largest empire in history and for over a century the foremost global power. The British established and directed this vast imperial enterprise and they did so to secure wealth and advantage for themselves. The East India Company drove the expansion of the British Empire in India, taking over the lands of the Mughal Empire. However, the Sikh Kingdom of Maharajah Ranjit Singh checked its expansion to the North of India.

Fall of Sikh Empire

At the death of Maharajah Ranjit Singh and the ensuing bloodletting between various factions competing for power, the Khalsa (Sikh Army) assumed control of the State. They had created the Sikh State and Kingdom. They were the State's defenders and preservers and became an executive sovereign of the State. The Khalsa ruled through regimental committees. They could decide succession and proclaim a new sovereign; appoint Viziers and dismiss them; declare war or peace and keep the provincial satraps obedient. Deliberations of the Khalsa were often public, its decisions precise and their execution firm and instantaneous. Those in power feared the Khalsa and it seemed to them that their only chance of retaining power and safeguarding their estates and privileges was to destroy it in contest with the British. Thus, they frantically sought British intervention. With the turmoil in the Punjab and their underestimation of the fighting qualities of the Sikh soldier, the British started massing their armies, the largest force ever assembled in India, on the Kingdom's borders. The British also had an understanding of co-operation with the Sikh Government's leading ministers. Minister Gulab Singh Dogra, Chief Minister Lal Singh, and the Commander-in-Chief Tej Singh, whose intention was to shatter the Khalsa on the British bayonets. As the British advanced on the Punjab, the Khalsa prepared for war. Matters came to a head in December 1845 when they sighted the British forces near the villages of Mudki. The Sikhs attacked immediately while their commander Lal Singh fled the battlefield. Though outnumbered, the Sikhs fought the enemy to a standstill. General Wheeler's brigade, so terrified at the sight of the Sikh cavalry, formed squares and would not obey orders to reform and advance. In the fierce encounter, having lost almost half of their force and fifteen guns, the leaderless Khalsa withdrew back to the main force at Ferozeshah. The British had lost 872 dead and wounded. They were shaken by the fighting qualities of the Khalsa, the likes of which they had never encountered in India. They licked their wounds and frantically waited for reinforcements to arrive from Ambala, Meerut, and Delhi. With his army reinforced, General Gough, the British commander, pressed on to attack the Sikhs around Ferozeshah. The Sikhs repulsed every British charge and decimated their attacking parties, which had penetrated their lines. On that night, the British were a spent force.

British Empire

Fall of Sikh Empire (Cont.)

The next morning, as the battered British force gathered itself, battalions and battalions of Khalsa with heavy guns appeared on the battlefield. The Sikh guns opened fire; there was no reply from the British artillery. As the British steeled themselves to be slaughtered, Tej Singh wheeled away the Sikh army and abandoned the battlefield. The shattered British ranks immediately retreated to Ferozepore. The climax of the campaign came on 10TH February when the British carried the war back across the Satluj and defeated the Sikhs at Sobraon. At the conclusion of the First Anglo-Sikh War, the British methodically destroyed the military power of the Sikhs and declared a Protectorate over the Punjab. The Sikh soldiers were disarmed, disbanded, and dispersed. The pride of the Khalsa, the guns, were dismantled and taken away. What remained was but a shadow of the colossal military machine of Maharajah Ranjit Singh.

The district of Multan was a tributary of the Sikh Kingdom and the revolt of the governor of Multan against the Kingdom's authority provided the excuse for the British annexation of the Punjab. As the remnants of the Khalsa rallied around the city of Multan, the British declared war on the Sikh Nation. The major battle of the Second Sikh War was fought near Chillianwala. The British casualties amounted to 2,446 men, with 132 officers killed and 4 guns lost. Chillianwala was the worst defeat the British had suffered in the annals of Indian warfare. However, reinforced with fresh forces, they turned defeat into victory at the battle of Gujarat. On 29TH March 1849, Maharajah Dalip Singh took his seat on the throne for the last time. The Sikh Kingdom ended and Dalip Singh was pensioned off to England. With the annexation of the Punjab, some 80,000 square miles were added to British India, whose western boundary now marked the mountain ranges of the Hindu Kush to the deserts of Sind. The problem of guarding the North-West Frontier of the empire was finally in British hands. The British had the right material at hand: the disbanded soldiers of the Khalsa, who had subdued and ruled the same territories with an iron hand. The Sikhs were considered the finest soldiers in the East. "If I had anything to say to annexation," Sir Henry Harding the Governor–General of India had commented: "I should enlist whole regiments of Sikhs into our service." The Sikh soldiers saw the Sikh dominions overrun and their leaders surrendering their swords. They were trained soldiers and knew no other calling and, when the offer came, flocked to the British standards, and became the Sentinels of guarding the North West Frontier of British India.

The two main gateways to India on the Frontier are the Khyber and Bolan Passes. Since ancient times India has been invaded by these routes. With the expansion of the Russian Empire into Central Asia, control of Afghanistan and stability of the Frontier became cornerstones of defensive strategy for British India. Military history of guarding the frontier of this region of the British Empire had been a succession of punitive expeditions against offending Pakhtun (or *Pathan*) tribes, punctuated by three wars against Afghanistan.

British Empire

The end of British East India Company was precipitated by a mutiny of Sepoys against their British commanders, which spilled over into widespread civil unrest. The Rebellion took six months to suppress, with heavy loss of life on both sides. It was at this point the Sikhs came to the rescue of the British. They could not become enthusiastic about either the Hindu aspiration of a Maratha Emperor in Delhi or the Muslim hope of the restoration of Mughal glory. Sikhs fought to save the British in the principal centres of the revolt and led the British to recruit them in all arms of the armed forces. Sikhs started enlisting heavily in the British forces and were thus back to the profession of their liking, the military services. After the Mutiny, the British government assumed direct control over India, ushering in the period known as the British Raj, where an appointed Governor-General administered India and Queen Victoria was crowned the Empress of India. The Indian Empire had to be supplied by a sea route. This led to a series of bases along the route to India. After the Suez Canal was built in Egypt, the Canal Zone became a British base to protect it, and Egypt itself became a protectorate. Aden at the southern tip of Arabia was a fuelling point for steam ships passing from Suez to India and a naval base for patrolling the Red Sea and Indian Ocean. To protect Aden a protectorate was declared over the surrounding area, which became the Aden Protectorate. The government of India was also interested in keeping order in the borders of India. To the west, they exercised control over both shores of the Arabian Gulf, Baluchistan to the north and Trucial Oman to the south. To the north, they policed and secured the borders and influenced the affairs of Afghanistan. They annexed the fringe states of India to their Indian Empire. To the east, British conquest and annexation extended into Burma, a kingdom of people with a different culture and language. To the southeast, they also extended to Singapore, where a trading post was built that became a city. From here, British traders extended to the island of Borneo where two colonies were formed in the north, one the quasi-feudal state of Sarawak, ruled by the so-called White Rajahs of the Brooks family on behalf of the Sultan of Brunei, the other North Borneo (now Sabah). North of Singapore the British came to rule the Malayan peninsula. A colony in Hong Kong grew out of the opium wars with China. China was not formally ruled as a colony but British and other European traders forced immunity from Chinese courts and controlled such governmental functions as the Customs and the navigation on the Yangtze.

The British Empire in Africa started as slave trading depots in Ghana (Gold Coast) and other parts of the West African coast. Then when Britain ended its slave trade - having become rich enough to do without its profits - there was a need for bases for the naval patrols trying to prevent other countries carrying on a slave trade. In Sierra Leone, there was also a base at Freetown to land freed ex-slaves. Then there were bases for "legitimate" trade. These grew from Lagos in Nigeria (a former Portuguese base), Accra in Ghana and Gambia. In many cases the coastal base was declared a Colony (sovereign British territory), and the interior lands were declared a Protectorate.

British Empire

In the 1890s British troops pushed inland in Africa using the new technologies of steam, telegraphs and machine guns (and quinine to prevent malaria) until they reached the borders of the French colonial territories. The Berlin Conference (1884) on Colonial matters carved up Africa and gave each of the European powers their own sections. Thus, Britain ended with territories in East, West, and Southern Africa. The conquest of the Sudan in 1895 was one of the last wars of expansion. This war derived from Britain's control of Egypt. The Egyptian ruler claimed Sudan and Britain was making good that claim. Sudan subsequently became a joint British-Egyptian territory - a Condominium.

The Sikh soldier was in the vanguard of extending and securing Britain's Empire and established his authority as the foremost Imperial 'Motor Muscle.'

On the following pages are listed galaxies of Sikh soldiers who were awarded the Indian Order of Merit for their conspicuous gallantry in battle during the Empire period.

INDIAN ORDER OF MERIT

The East India Company first introduced this medal in 1837 and it was proposed for "conspicuous gallantry in the field". The Indian Order of Merit was the highest gallantry award available to Indian soldiers between 1837 and 1911, when the eligibility for the Victoria Cross was extended to Indian officers and men. The Indian Order of Merit ranks high among the oldest and most venerable of decorations for bravery, pre-dating the Victoria Cross by nineteen years and the United State's Medal of Honour by twenty-four years. The order was removed when India became indenendent in 1947.

Subedar Major Sarwan Singh, IOM, 1917.

NORTH-WEST FRONTIER, 1849-1857

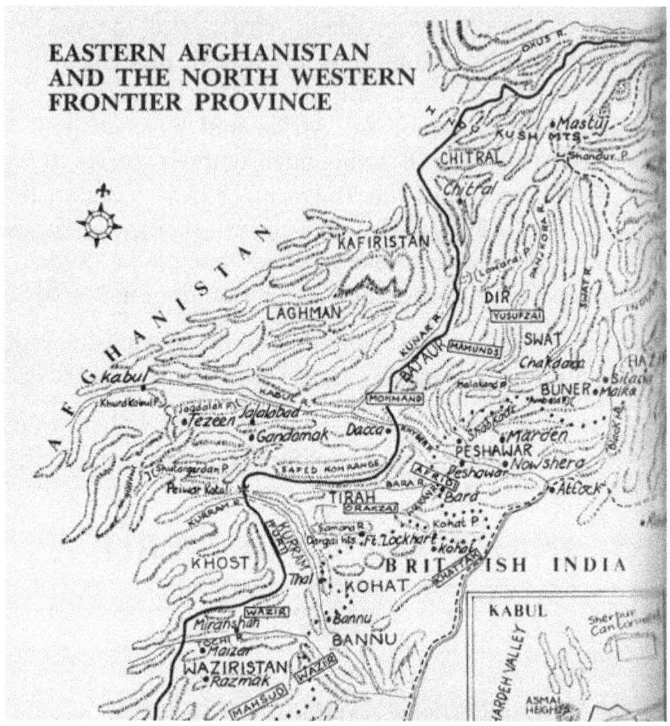

Typical Frontier terrain

(National Army Museum)

North-West Frontier, 1849-1857

The Kohat Pass Afridis, 1850

When the annexation of the Punjab brought the frontier of British India up to the north-western hills, the Indian Government decided to make payments to the Kohat Pass Afridis, in return for the protection of the road through the Kohat Pass. On February 2ND 1850, however, a serious attack was made on a party working on the road near Kohat within British territory. An expedition was organized for the purpose of reinforcing the garrison at Kohat and exacting punishment on the authors of the raid. The village of Akhor was destroyed on the 10TH February. Other villages along the line of advance were also destroyed, while the enemy attacked the flanks and rear of the column as it wound its way through the pass. The 1ST Punjab Cavalry, brushing aside the attacks, pushed on to Kohat. The piquets on the surrounding hills at times were briskly engaged with the enemy. As the 1ST Punjab Infantry moved on to join the Kohat garrison, it suffered several casualties. As a reprisal, they destroyed the village of Basti Khel. As they marched back to Peshawar, the Afridis contested the ground, opposing the force in front, hanging on its flanks, and continuously pressing the rearguard. Some sharp fighting occurred at the Peshawar end of the pass and the enemy was driven off with some difficulty.

Mohmands, 1851-52

In March 1851, several small brushes occurred between the tribesmen and the frontier garrisons. Some of the neighbouring villages on the frontier were destroyed by way of reprisal. During the following year, the raids on British villages grew so frequent and assumed so serious a character that a force was sent out from Peshawar to exact punishment. On 15TH April 1852, a threatening movement was observed on the part of the enemy between Shabkadr and Matta. A troop of forty sabres under Subedar Balwant Singh immediately moved out to cut the tribesmen off from the hills but the latter perceived the manoeuvre in time to make good their escape. Balwant Singh's troop then joined the attack on the rest of the enemy, who numbered 400. On the onslaught, the enemy left several stands of arms on the ground, as he fled to the safety of the hills.

Wazirs, 1852

Trouble arose with the Wazirs directly after the annexation of the Punjab. On the night of December 21ST, 1852, the force comprising of 1ST, 2^{ND,} 4TH Punjab Infantry, 2ND Punjab Cavalry and Punjab police attacked the Wazirs. The surprise was so complete that the enemy was quickly overwhelmed; villages were destroyed and large quantities of cattle and sheep carried off. During these successful operations, a mishap happened to the 4TH Punjab Infantry. Twenty-three men of the regiment were reported missing. It was ascertained afterwards that these men had fallen either out, overcome by sleep and fatigue, or, straggling behind, had missed the road. The Wazirs killed them after they had descended from the heights.

North-West Frontier, 1849-1857

The Black Mountain Expedition, 1852

The commissioner of Peshawar led a punitive expedition from 19TH December 1852 to January 1953, against the Hassanzai clan of the Yuzufzai, to avenge the murder of two British custom officers in the Black Mountain region of the northern end of the Punjab frontier. The tribesmen had refused to surrender the murderers and seized the forts of Chamberi and Shanglai, which belonged to a friendly khan, the Nawab of Amb. The Nawab had tried to bring about a peaceful compliance with the British demands. Attempts were made to induce the Hassanzai to comply with the demands communicated to them. The tribesmen, however, maintained a defiant attitude and were found to be strongly posted in the hills. Accordingly, a force assembled that included a detachment of Corps of Guides and 300 bayonets of 1ST Sikh Infantry, which was unleashed at the tribesmen. The columns started before dawn and by evening had united successfully on the main ridge and occupied Panji Gali. The right column encountered the most opposition. The infantry, covered by the fire of the guns, carried everything before them. In spite of the abatis constructed by the tribesmen in front of their position, a heavy matchlock fire and a series of desperate charges turned the hostile left flank and ensured the success of the whole attack. The centre column found the enemy in strong force halfway up the hill, but by means of turning movements succeeded in gaining the summit and effecting a junction with the left column. The Hassanzai then took up another strong position, but at the advance of the Sikhs, soon evacuated it, and took flight.

Hindustani Fanatics, 1853

The Hindustani Fanatics were the followers of a Mullah (a religious leader) named Ahmad Shah, a native of Bareilly in India. In 1823, establishing himself on the Peshawar border in what was then the Sikh Kingdom; Ahmad Shah proceeded to attract to his side a large following of co-religionists from among the Pathan tribes of the frontier hills. It was not long before he led *Jihad* against the Sikhs. A Sikh force commanded by Prince Sher Singh pursued Ahmad Shah and his fanatics to Balakot at the bottom of Kaghan Valley. In a short sharp engagement, the Sikhs decimated the band of fanatics and Ahmad Shah himself was slain. The remnants of the fanatics escaped to the hills and constructed a fort there, which they called Mandi. In 1852, they seized a small fort at Kotla belonging to the Khan of Amb, who was friendly to the British Government. Accordingly, an attacking force, which included two regiments of Sikh infantry, moved down the left bank of the Indus to Kirpilian on the opposite side of the river to Kotla. On January 6TH 1853, as soon as the Sikhs and the mountain guns attacked Kotla, the defenders, numbering between 200 and 300, took to flight, pursued by the Sikhs. The fanatics were taught a severe lesson, the effect of which lasted until the disturbances of 1863.

North-West Frontier, 1849-1857

Jowakis, November 1853

The Jowakis, who inhabit the country east of the Kohat Pass, began to make serious raids in British held territories in 1851, which increased in daring and frequency. After their exclusion from Peshawar and Kohat had proved futile, an expedition was mounted against them in November 1853. There was some hard fighting, and reinforcements had to be sent more than once to press the attacks on them. When the destruction of the houses in the villages had been carried out, the force withdrew from the valley. Subedar Kor Singh and Sowar Dul Singh of Corps of Guides were awarded the Indian Order of Merit in consideration of their conspicuous gallantry during these operations.

Orakzais, 1855

The attitude of the Orakzais, a Pathan tribe inhabiting the mountains to the northwest of Kohat, became so menacing that a force compiled mostly of Sikh soldiers was despatched for the destruction of the villages of Nasin, Sangar, and Katsah, belonging to the most disaffected of the Orakzais clans. Nasin and Sangar were both situated high up among the hills bordering the Miranzai Valley. Their facilities for defence were so great that the only chance of decisive success lay in simultaneous surprise. Sikhs assaulted the defences at dawn; the enemy, was completely taken by surprise, but contrived to make good his escape, leaving large quantities of cattle in the hands of the Sikhs. The villages of Nasin and Sangar were demolished and the surrounding crops destroyed. As the retirement of the force began, the enemy, following up with some determination, succeeded in overpowering a small party of Sikhs, but was driven back by a savage counter attack.

Sikh Sepoy on the frontier, 1879
(National Army Museum)

SEPOY MUTINY

Sepoy Mutiny, 1857–58

The Sepoys of Bengal Army mutinied at the Meerut cantonment near Delhi on 10TH May 1857. The Mutiny spread to Delhi, Agra, Cawnpore, and Lucknow, starting a year-long insurrection against the British. In the years prior to the mutiny, many factors combined to create a climate of social and political unrest in India. The political expansion of the East India Company, at the expense of native princes and of the Mughal court, aroused Hindus and Muslims alike. The harsh land policies carried out by Governor-General Dalhousie, as well as the rapid introduction of European civilization, threatened traditional India. The last Mughal emperor, the aged Bahadur Shah II, completely controlled by the British East India Company, found it convenient to maintain the fiction of Mughal rule. He was aware that the Mughal dynasty would end with his death. The Indian soldiers were dissatisfied with their pay, as well as with certain changes in regulations, which they interpreted as part of a plot to force them to adopt Christianity. This belief was strengthened when the British furnished the soldiers with cartridges coated with grease made from the fat of cows (sacred to Hindus) and of pigs (anathema to Muslims). They replaced the cartridges when the mistake was realized; but suspicion persisted and in February 1857, there began a series of incidents in which Sepoys refused to use the cartridges. On May 10^{TH,} the Sepoys revolted at Meerut and went on to capture Delhi and proclaim Bahadur Shah II the emperor of all India. 'The Sikhs in the background of their rule in Punjab and egalitarian tradition could hardly be expected to side with Muslim and Hindu princes to regain their kingdoms, nor could religious taboos which affected Hindu and Muslim sentiments, against many of which the Sikh Gurus had led a crusade, in any measure inflame Sikh sentiments. It was on account of all this that the Punjab was not affected by the rebellion, which convulsed the rest of northern India. Punjabi Mussalmans turned a deaf ear to their Hindustani co-religionists' exhortation of Jihad against the pig-eating despoilers of Islam. Punjabi Hindus and, with greater reason, the Sikhs, refused to listen to the belated appeal to save Hindu Dharma from beef eating foreigners who used cow fat to grease their cartridges. The Cis-Satluj chiefs of Patiala, Malerkotla, Kalsia, Nabha, Faridkot and Jind, along with their mercenary forces, rendered full help to the British in suppressing the rebellion. These chiefs owed their existence to the British, who had protected them from the conquests of Maharajah Ranjit Singh. They still remembered with gratitude the support extended to them by the British against Maharaja Ranjit Singh. But for the British protection, Ranjit Singh would surely have sought to annex their kingdoms long ago. This mutiny led the British to recruit for their armed forces heavily among the communities which had been neutral to this rebellion. Especially, Gurkhas, Rajputs of Rajasthan, Punjabi Muslims and Sikhs. Sikhs started enlisting in the British forces and were thus back to the profession of their liking, the military services'. (SikhiWiki, 2009)

Sepoy Mutiny

Delhi, 1857

A rebellious and committed force of 30,000 mutineers defended Delhi, a well-fortified walled city. Five times the size of the assault force, the mutinous force was armed with a greater number and higher calibre of guns and their gunnery was perhaps their strongest point. On 7TH June 1857, a hastily raised force of 4,000 men succeeded in occupying a ridge overlooking Delhi. Known at the time as the 'Army of Retribution', in reality it was far too weak a force to retake the city. Reinforcements gradually arrived from the Punjab, including a siege train of 32 guns and 2,000 men under Brigadier-General John Nicholson. In searing heat, the force held off repeated efforts by the mutineers to take the ridge. By 14TH September, the British had about 9,000 men before Delhi. A third of the force was British while the rest were Sikhs, Punjabis, and Gurkhas. The assault began on 14TH September, when artillery breached the city walls, blew in the Kashmir Gate, and breached the Lahore Gate. The assaulting troops had to make their way down long narrow lanes flanked by flat-topped buildings, from which the Sepoys and their allies maintained a heavy fire. It took a week of vicious street fighting before Delhi was finally taken. The British and their Indian allies then ransacked the city in an orgy of looting and killing. The recapture of Delhi proved the decisive factor in the suppression of the revolt.

Sardar Man Singh, C.I.E.
(Lieutenant E.M. Molyneux.)

Hodson's Horse was the first cavalry regiment to be raised during the Sepoy Mutiny. The first troop of the regiment was raised and commanded by an ex-officer of the Sikh Cavalry, Sardar Man Singh. Their first action was on 14TH July in the Delhi suburb of Sabzi Mandi in which they fought and drove the enemy back into the city. Another engagement in the same area took place on 18TH July. The British finally gained control of Delhi on 19TH September, forcing the rebels out of the city. Hodson's Horse was kept busy once the enemy were out in the open.

When the victory of the British became certain, Emperor Bahadur Shah took refuge at Humayun's Tomb, in an area that was then at the outskirts of Delhi and hid there. 50 Sikh soldiers led by Major William Hodson and Sardar Man Singh surrounded the tomb and compelled his surrender on 20TH September 1857.

Sepoy Mutiny

Allahabad, June 1857

The news of the mutiny in the north caused considerable anxiety at Allahabad, and all British civilians, women, and children were ordered into the Allahabad fort. On the 6TH of June, the 6TH Native Infantry, which was stationed in the cantonments two miles from the fort, unexpectedly mutinied. Incendiary, rapine and murder followed. The mutineers were joined by the entire town rabble and their savagery was terrible and continued for days. As soon as the firing started in the cantonment, Lieutenant Brasyer, with a party of 14TH Ferozepore Sikhs, decided to disarm the guards of the 6TH Native Infantry in the fort. There were three companies of the 6TH Native Infantry, numbering about two hundred men, in charge of the different gates. The Sikhs disarmed all the soldiers of the Native Infantry, made them prisoners, and turned them out of the fort the next day. Lieutenant Brasyer then organized the defence of the fort with four hundred Sikhs, a party of invalid British artillerymen and a small number of volunteer civilians until reinforcements arrived. After the 6TH of June the fort was subjected to a desultory siege, for the place was surrounded by a large force of rebels who remained in possession of the city. The rebels were well armed and had two guns. Brasyer wrote as follows about the Sikhs at this time, "All this time the Seikhs, on whom so much depended, were craving to be led against the enemy outside, or anywhere, rather than be kept idle within the Fortress". A few days later Colonel James Neill arrived with a British battalion and took over command at Allahabad. By this time, the whole countryside had broken out into revolt, so from 12TH June Colonel Neill carried out a series of vigorous sorties against the rebels. The 14TH Ferozepore Sikhs played a prominent part in these operations and won further distinctions. These sorties met with considerable success and the district was soon in a state of submission. On 17TH June, the rebels were defeated and driven out of the city and the British administration was re-established. The situation at Cawnpore was now serious and it was essential to send a force to relieve the British garrison as soon as possible. Transport was immediately collected and an advance column, consisting of Madras Fusiliers and Ferozepore Sikhs, set out for Cawnpore on the 30TH June. On the same day, General Havelock arrived in Allahabad with the 64TH and 84TH Foot and the 78TH Highlanders and set off for Cawnpore a few days later, taking with him his British troops and a detachment of 130 soldiers of Ferozepore Sikhs. By this time, the rebels had captured Cawnpore, so General Havelock decided to drive them out and then march to the relief of Lucknow, where the British were besieged in the Residency. A portion of the Ferozepore Sikhs was left behind in Allahabad, to hold the fort and patrol the surrounding district. Here the Sikhs did excellent work and fought several successful engagements with parties of mutineers in the area. On one occasion a guard of two non-commissioned officers and eight Sikh Sepoys, surrounded by about a thousand rebels at Sahunga, gallantly rescued a wounded British officer and fought their way back through the rebels to the main guard.

Sepoy Mutiny

Allahabad Fort, 1857

The massive, majestic fort built by Emperor Akbar in 1583 A.D stands on the banks of the Yamuna near the confluence. The largest of Akbar's forts, it was matchless in its design and construction and garrisoned by Sikh soldiers. In June 1857, the Sepoys mutinied in Allahabad and were led by Maulvi Liaqat Ali. The city came under their control but the Sikh garrison resolutely defended the fort. Allahabad was a strategic fortress and commanded the eastern approach to the Doab area and its fort contained a very large ammunition magazine. The mutineer's failure to capture Allahabad fort from the Sikhs, with its very large arsenal was the first great strategic failure of the rebels.

Allahabad Fort 1857
(The Illustrated London News)

Cawnpore, 1857

In June, Sepoys under General Wheeler's command in Cawnpore (now Kanpur) mutinied and besieged the European garrison. The Siege of Cawnpore lasted for three weeks, with little water and the garrison suffering constant casualties. On 25TH June, Nana Sahib, a prominent leader in the mutiny, requested surrender of the garrison. General Wheeler had little choice but to accept. Nana Sahib promised safe passage to a secure location. When the British boarded the riverboats, their pilots fled, setting fire to the boats. The rebellious Sepoys then opened fire on the soldiers and civilians. Only one boat with four men escaped. The surviving women and children were led to Bibi-Ghar (the house of the women) in Cawnpore. On 15TH July, three men entered the house, and killed everyone within. The victims were hacked to pieces and thrown down a well. Cawnpore became a war cry for the British soldiers for the rest of the conflict. Nana Sahib disappeared.

Sepoy Mutiny

Cawnpore, June 1857

An advance column, consisting of Madras Fusiliers and Ferozepore Sikhs, set out from Allahabad for Cawnpore on 30TH June. On the same day, General Havelock arrived in Allahabad and set off for Cawnpore taking with him his British troops and the remaining detachment of the 14TH Ferozepore Sikhs. He joined forces with the advanced column on 12TH July and moved on towards Cawnpore in very trying conditions in the hot weather. On the following day, just as the combined force was preparing to camp near the village of Fatehpur, a large party of mutineers advanced from the village to attack them. Although the men were exhausted after a long march under a scorching sun, they utterly routed the enemy in a short, sharp fight. After a much-needed rest on the next day, the force continued the march early on 15TH July. However, it was found that the enemy had re-formed and was holding the village of Aong in strength. General Havelock immediately ordered the attack on the enemy positions. The mutineers were thrown back at the point of the bayonet. The same evening he learnt that a number of women and children had been made prisoner at Cawnpore and they were to be rescued at all costs. Havelock decided to continue the advance immediately, even though his men had had no rest and the column was still twenty-two miles from Cawnpore. On 16TH July, some ten thousand rebels opposed the British advance on the town. The 78TH Highlanders were in the lead and rolled up the enemy's left flank with a brilliant charge. The 64TH and 84TH Foot and 14TH Ferozepore Sikhs then passed through and carried the enemy's position. They captured all the guns on the right as the enemy retreated on their attack. Leaving the guns behind, protected by Ferozepore Sikhs, the British infantry regiments followed up their success and inflicted further losses on the enemy, who eventually lost heart and fled in disorder. General Havelock and his men then camped for the night in the open and entered Cawnpore early on the 17TH July, but were too late to stop the brutal murder of the women and children by the mutineers. On 16TH August, Havelock led his much-depleted force against the mutineers in Bithur. After a long march of eight hours, the weary force made contact with the enemy, who were holding a very strong position around the village. Havelock decided to assault the position immediately. After some hard hand-to-hand fighting, the position was carried and the enemy utterly routed. Ferozepore Sikhs were on the left flank and attacked a large force of the enemy, which was entrenched in the bank of a Nullah, and captured his guns. Owing to casualties and the serious sickness from cholera and other diseases amongst the British troops, Havelock had to remain in Cawnpore for nearly a month awaiting reinforcements. There was very little fighting and the Ferozepore Sikhs were detailed to escort a convoy of sick and wounded to Allahabad. They escorted the wounded safely back, in spite of encountering a number of rebels during the journey, and then returned to Cawnpore.

Sepoy Mutiny

Lucknow, 1857

News of capture of Delhi by rebels reached Lucknow on 12TH May 1857. On receiving the news the local native garrison of 130,000, many of whom were regular Sepoys, mutinied, and besieged the British Residency. The first attempted relief was in September by Generals Havelock and Outram, whose troops reinforced the original garrison. The 14TH Ferozepore Sikhs were at Mirzapore and became part of the British column for the relief of Lucknow. During this course, the battalion fought a series of actions, the most noteworthy being the attack on Little Imambara. It was after this action that the battalion was permitted to wear the red turban as a mark of valour and distinction. The red turban is now the part of the regimental uniform of the entire Sikh Regiment.

Little Imambara

Sikh veteran of Sepoy Mutiny 1857

Sepoy Mutiny

Relief and Defence of Lucknow

On 25TH September, the British advanced from Alam Bagh to Lucknow. General Neill's Brigade was in the lead and the 78TH Highlanders and 14TH Ferozepore Sikhs were detailed as rearguard. They were ordered to hold the bridge at Charbagh until all the troops had passed through, when a large force of rebels attacked them. After three hours fierce fighting, they defeated and dispersed the enemy. As they pushed on, they suddenly encountered some guns, which were holding up General Havelock's advance and rushed at them without ceremony. The 78TH Highlanders and 14TH Ferozepore Sikhs led the advance. General Havelock was determined to reach the Residency quickly and ordered the Highlanders and the Sikhs to immediately advance on the mutineers. The column dashed forward through the narrow streets of flat-roofed, loopholed houses held by the mutineers. They desperately fought their way forward under continuous fire from the enemy and eventually reached the Bailey Guard Gate of the Residency, to the deafening cheers of the garrison. During the day's desperate fighting, many acts of gallantry were performed by the Sikhs. One noteworthy feat of gallantry was that of Sepoy Nihal Singh, who carried General Neill, when mortally wounded in the final charge, to the rear under heavy fire. The rearguard, with a number of sick and wounded, had not been able to reach the Residency and had remained in the Moti Mahal. So on the next day, a detachment of the 5TH Fusiliers and 14TH Ferozepore Sikhs was sent to reinforce them and help them to withdraw to the Residency. Although the Sikhs and Fusiliers fought their way through and drove the enemy back from the buildings and gardens adjacent to the Moti Mahal, the enemy fire from the Kaiserbagh was found to be too heavy to admit the rearguard convoy. Further reinforcements sent forward escorted the rearguard safely to the Residency after dark. Although the rebels had been outwitted, they had not been decisively defeated and still occupied the city in great strength. With the increased number of troops in the Residency, positions had to be enlarged and so for the next few days several sorties were made to improve the position. The 14TH Ferozepore Sikhs were in General Havelock's sector and took part in the sorties along the eastern face of the Residency to clear the enemy from the gardens and houses up to the Chata Manzil. These sorties were entirely successful and improved the defences of the Residency. Lieutenant Cross, of the Ferozepore Sikhs, was wounded in one of these sorties, but otherwise the Regiment suffered very few casualties. On account of the Sikhs' good service, General Havelock promoted each man to a grade higher in rank and all Subedars were granted the Indian Order of Merit. For the next two months, Ferozepore Sikhs were in charge of the Bailey guard, one of the most important positions in the Residency and they held the defences on the right of General Havelock's sector bordering the Pyne Bagh.

Sepoy Mutiny

Relief and Defence of Lucknow (Cont.)

General Outram's force was given no rest by the enemy and it had always to be on the alert. Duties were constant and arduous, while rations were scanty throughout the siege. On one occasion, when the enemy blew a breach in the defences, a detachment of the 14TH Ferozepore Sikhs checked a large force of the enemy who stormed the breach, and gave the garrison time to form and repulse the enemy. At last, on 17TH November, a relieving force under General Sir Colin Campbell, Commander-in-Chief in India, arrived at Lucknow. The situation at Cawnpore, however, had again become critical and General Campbell had to return there as quickly as possible. He decided to evacuate the Residency and return to deal with the rebels at Lucknow later. On the night of 22ND November all the British forces were withdrawn successfully from the Residency together with all the women, children and wounded. The enemy were taken completely by surprise by this operation, which had been carefully planned and boldly executed. General Outram was left with a force of some four thousand men to hold Alam Bagh and contain the enemy at Lucknow. The 14TH Ferozepore Sikhs were included in General Outram's force and held defensive works at Alam Bagh for three months. Duties were very arduous because of the large perimeter to be held, while the enemy kept in constant touch and there were almost daily skirmishes and minor encounters. The enemy delivered a number of attacks, but these were all beaten off with losses to the rebels. On 22ND December, General Outram took the offensive and threw back a large enemy force, which had attempted to sever his communications to Cawnpore. Reporting on this action, Outram wrote: "The gallant way in which, with a 'cheer' the 78TH and 14TH Ferozepore Sikhs, led by their commanders, dashed at a strong position held by the enemy (30,000 men and 6 heavy guns), excited much admiration". (Sikh Cyber Museum, 2003a)

Sketch of Alam Bagh

(Lieutenant C.H. Mecham)

Sepoy Mutiny

Capture of Lucknow, June 1859

At the beginning of March 1858, Sir Colin Campbell, with a large, well-equipped force, joined General Outram at Alam Bagh and started methodical operations against the rebels at Lucknow. The enemy were holding three lines of defences north of the city covering the Kaiserbagh, their citadel. These had been strengthened since the relief of the Residency, houses were now fortified, and roads barricaded. Sir Colin's plan was to send General Outram with his division north of the River Gumti to turn the rebels' position, while his main force attacked the Kaiserbagh from Dilkusha Park. For a few days the 14TH Ferozepore Sikhs, now only three hundred and twenty strong protected the Commander-in-Chief's camp. They were soon in action and took part in the operations to force back the rebels from their first line of defences along the canal. By the 13TH March, the British had reached the Little Imambara, which was held in strength and had to be captured. On 14TH March one hundred men of 14TH Ferozepore Sikhs, under Captain da Costa, with two companies of the 10TH Foot, assaulted breaches in the walls of the Little Imambara, while Captain Brasyer and a hundred more Sikhs assaulted some houses to flank. The Sikhs captured and set fire to the houses on the flank and then, climbing up on to some flat roofs, set out towards the Little Imambara itself. They arrived just as the assault was launched. This diversion enabled the storming troops to advance with unexpected ease. They soon captured the Imambara and the Colours of the 14TH Ferozepore Sikhs were planted over the gateway. The day's objective had been captured, but the Sikhs were eager to follow up their success and Captain Brasyer described the next phase of the battle as follows. "The men were excited and eager to go on. Without orders, my Seikhs like monkeys climbed a wall and opened a large gate, which gave outlet from the smaller Imambara, while I, with other officers, joined them. A rush such as nothing could stop followed. The General (Franks) smiled as he cheered my men, but issued no order. This acquiescence was enough, I knew what he wanted. My Seikhs like greyhounds let loose, passed into the street, deafening cheers encouraged us, while the General and his staff followed in support. We rushed onwards, cleared 40 guns in battery en route, driving all before us. Pickaxe and shovel were next at work, and soon a breach was opened in an outer wall". (Birdwood, 1950) The Sikhs and the 90TH Light Infantry, led by Captains Brasyer and Havelock (son of General Havelock.), rushed forward and fought their way into an enclosure adjoining the Kaiserbagh under terrible fire. Havelock ran back for reinforcements and a party of the 10TH Foot advanced and captured a small bazaar in the rear of the Tara Kothi and mess-house, which were held by some six thousand rebels.

Sepoy Mutiny

Capture of Lucknow, June 1859 (Cont.)

This bold move completely surprised the enemy, who made as though they would rush Brasyer's party and force their way out into the city. However, Havelock, seeing the danger, dashed forward with a party of Sikhs and captured two bastions in the last line of defences, turned the guns on to the rebels and drove them towards the Chatar Manzil. Reinforcements followed up quickly and before long, the whole of Kaiserbagh was in British hands. Meanwhile, Brasyer had dashed into the centre of the palace, climbed on the top, and pushed the Queen's Colour through a gunshot hole in the highest dome, as a signal that the citadel had been captured. The 14TH Ferozepore Sikhs suffered heavy casualties in this battle and Captain da Costa was among those killed. On 16TH March 14TH Ferozepore Sikhs formed part of General Outram's force, which captured the Residency and the iron bridge. Major Brasyer was seriously wounded in these operations, but refused to relinquish command and was carried on a litter at the head of the Battalion for several days. The rebels had been completely defeated in these battles and Lucknow was once again safely in British hands. After the capture of Lucknow the 14TH Ferozepore Sikhs joined the Oudh Field Force and took part in a number of minor encounters in rounding up parties of rebels and pacifying the countryside. During this period, Lieutenant Montague, with the Allahabad detachment, arrived back in the Battalion. Operations ended in June 1859 and the Regiment marched to Ferozepore, its home station. Brasyer wrote; "The remnant of the gallant four hundred marched into Ferozepore on 7TH September, with drums and pipes playing, and colours all tattered and torn, after an arduous campaign of two years and four months, and thirteen years of faithful service under the British Government". (Sikh Cyber Museum, 2003a) For its service in the Sepoy Mutiny the 14TH Ferozepore Sikhs were allowed to bear on its Colours the inscription Lucknow, Defence and Capture. As a special mark of distinction for its outstanding conduct the Governor-General issued orders that, the men of the Regiment of Ferozepore were permitted to wear red Safas (turbans), like those in which they had fought, instead of native infantry caps, a privilege of which the Regiment still avails itself on ceremonial parades. The Staff of one of the Colours was broken by a bullet at the relief of Lucknow and was mended with a plain brass ring. This Staff still carries the Regimental Colour today, although the actual Colour has been renewed on two occasions since that time. Only five British officers served with the 14TH Ferozepore Sikhs during the Mutiny: of these, one was killed and three wounded. The following Sikh officers and men of the Guides Cavalry and Infantry were awarded the Indian Order of Merit during the campaign of 1857: Jemadar Dall Singh, Resaidar Prem Singh, Daffadars Avtar Singh, Isri Singh, Nihal Singh, Kala Singh and Bugler Gurdit Singh.

Sepoy Mutiny

Behar, 1857

The Bengal Military Police Battalion raised in January 1856, by Captain Thomas Rattray consisted of 500 cavalry and 1000 infantry. It is said that Captain Thomas Rattray, who founded the regiment, went through the villages challenging men to wrestle with him. The Sikhs could not resist the offer but the condition was that they had to join up. They were serving in Behar in May 1857, when the Dinapore Brigade mutinied. The Bengal Military Police Battalion was the only battalion loyal to the British between Calcutta and Banares.

The commissioner of Patna asked that the regiment provide a strong guard on Mr Boyle's house at Arrah. Fifty men of the Bengal Military Police Battalion defended the house along with eleven civilians for 5 days at the end of July 1857. The enemy numbered about 2,000 and tried ceaselessly to persuade the Sikhs to defect, at first with offers of a share in the plunder and then with threats of torture if captured. They remained loyal and brave throughout. For this action and for hunting down the mutineers in the province of Behar, the battalion was awarded the Battle Honours 'Behar and Defence of Arrah'. It is the only battalion of the Indian Army to carry these two battle honours. The Battalion became a regular unit of the Bengal Army and in 1874, the famous 45TH Rattray's Sikhs.

On 8TH July 1858, a peace treaty was signed and the rebellion ended. The rebellion saw the end of the British East India Company's rule in India. In August, by the Government of India Act 1858, the company was formally dissolved and its ruling powers over India were transferred to the British Crown.*

Arrah House, 1857
(William Taylor)

*231 Indian Order of Merit medals, for conspicuous gallantry, were awarded to Sikh soldiers during the campaign of 1857.

NORTH-WEST FRONTIER, 1857-1878

The Hindustani Fanatics, 1857

During the Sepoy Mutiny, the only quarter in which trouble arose with any of the border tribes was to the northwest of Rawalpindi, beyond the Indus River. The Hindustani Fanatics, sustained by assistance in men and money from India, were at the bottom of the outbreak. They and the neighbouring clans were held in check by the garrison at Mardan, which was usually garrisoned by the Corps of Guides. At the beginning of the Mutiny, this Corps left to form part of Punjab Movable Column and the 55TH Native Infantry took its place. The latter regiment mutinied in the middle of May, but was attacked and defeated with heavy loss and the remnant scattered in disorganized bodies over the country.

Bozdar, 1857

Bozdars live in the Sulliman Mountains. They were very strict Mohammedans and lived in a perpetual state of feud with their neighbours, in addition to raiding and plundering villages in British territory. After many warnings over six or seven years, a punitive expedition was sent against them in March 1857. The 2ND Punjab Infantry, supported by mountain guns from Punjab Light Field Batteries attacked and carried the enemy's position with the greatest gallantry, not withstanding the enemy's strong resistance. The following Sikh soldiers were awarded the Indian Order of Merit in consideration of their conspicuous gallantry during these operations: - Sepoy Bux Singh and Sepoy Jowahir Singh of 2ND Punjab Infantry.

Kabul Khel Wazirs, 1859

The Kabul Khel, a section of the larger group of the Utmanzai Wazirs, had a long history of crimes culminating in the murder of a British officer. The Maliks of this section refused to deliver up the murderers. A punitive force composed of Guides Infantry supported by 4TH Sikh Infantry was collected in December 1859, to which 100 men of the 32ND Sikh Pioneers were added. The force assembled at Mandani, near Buland Khel, where the Kabul Khel had established an enceinte of strong Sangars to guard the valley. The attacking force drove the tribesmen from all their positions. Next day a foray captured all their winter stores, together with 5,000 sheep, 300 bullocks, and 60 camels, while the Sikh Pioneers accompanied a force in the destruction of fortified towers.

Mahsuds, April 1860

In April 1860, General Chamberlain took the field against the Mahsud Wazir clan. The climax of their iniquities had been their attempt to capture and sack the frontier town of Tank, which belonged to Nawab of the Pawindah tribe. General Chamberlain had asked for the 24TH Sikh Pioneers and 412 of them had joined him. The attacking force also including 4TH Sikh Infantry. As the Sikhs attacked, Mahsuds fled in confusion, the men in the front forcing back the men behind until all became a helpless rabble, straining to gain the safety of the mountains. The result was that about 300 Mahsuds were killed, including six leading Maliks, and many more wounded.

North-West Frontier, 1857-1878

Ambela, 1863

Towards the end of 1863, a force from Peshawar moved out under Brigadier-General Sir Neville Chamberlain, for punitive operations against the Hindustani Fanatics at Malka. When the force was crossing the Ambela Pass, it encountered quite unexpectedly a large lashkars (Army). It became quite clear that the force was opposed by a general combination of tribes from the Indus to the Afghan border. Sir Neville Chamberlain immediately called for reinforcements before proceeding. The 14TH Ferozepore Sikhs were the first to arrive and took part in a series of fierce battles around an important post, Crag Piquet, protecting the British camp on the pass. The tribesmen made many attacks on this piquet and it changed hands several times. At the beginning of November, the Sikhs recaptured this piquet and held it against repeated attacks by large numbers of the tribesmen, while suffering considerable casualties during these engagements. On 18TH November, the tribesmen advanced in great strength and attacked the defences of a camp, held by one hundred and thirty men of the 14TH Ferozepore Sikhs. The tribesmen attacked with great ferocity, but the Sikhs, although completely outnumbered, held out with great determination until reinforcements arrived and the tribesmen were driven back.

The night of 16TH December 1863 was a memorable one for both the 23RD and 32ND Sikh Pioneers. Mr. J. Campbell of the 93RD Highlanders has communicated this interesting account of the Ghazis charge to the Sikh Pioneer's history. 'I happened to be looking when the 200 Ghazis made their splendid charge on the two Muzbee Regiments, and I shall never forget the scene. The Ghazis came down the front of the two regiments, cutting and slashing with their Tulwars, and every one of them was killed. They came out to die and they did die. Thus terminated the first important combined action of the sister regiments, in which they had but gloriously upheld the honour of the Muzbee, their regiments, and the Khalsa and the crown. As in, the days of old in the Khalsa armies the Muzbee were in the front of the fight and bore the first onslaught of the enemy. Pushed back at first by weight of numbers and the suddenness of the attack, they soon rallied, and killed every Hindustani Fanatic of those two hundred, 'not allowing one to escape.' (Macmunn, 1936 p159.)

North-West Frontier, 1857-1878

Sulliman Khels, 1866-67

Jemadar Kishan Singh, 4TH Punjab Cavalry and Daffadar Ujagar Singh, 5TH Punjab Cavalry were awarded the Indian Order of Merit for their conspicuous gallantry in actions against the Sulliman Khel marauders from across the borders of the North West Frontier.

Black Mountain, 1868

The Black Mountain is a mountain range and district on the Hazara border of the North-West Frontier Province. In November 1867, it was decided to establish a body of police in the Agror valley of the Black Mountain range. The police were temporarily located in the village of Oghi, until a fortified post could be built. At daylight on the morning of 30TH July 1968, some 500 tribesmen attacked this body of police, numbering 22 men. The enemy was driven off after fierce hand-to-hand fighting.

Although the local Khan of Amb aided the British Indian forces, it was decided that additional troops would be needed to carry out punitive raid on the offending tribesmen. Troops were called up from the interior of India to reinforce the frontier forces. Some of the troops marched 600 miles in just 29 days to reach the frontier. Two Brigades were formed under Brigadier General Wilde, which included 3RD Sikh Infantry, 20TH Punjabis, 24TH Punjabis, 31ST Punjabis, and 56TH Punjabis. From 3RD to 22ND of October, this force criss-crossed the Black Mountain area and became involved in some hard fought skirmishing and destruction of villages. Eventually it was determined that a force would be permanently stationed in Agror valley, sufficient to meet all attacks, and if possible, to follow up the raiders beyond the British border.

Dewar, 1872-78

On 6TH March 1872, a force was despatched to chastise the Dewaris in the Tochi Valley. The 1ST Sikh Infantry stormed the closed gates of the Dewari village and effected an entry, driving the inhabitants to the north corner of the village, where they made a stand behind some high walled houses. The 1ST and 4TH Sikh Infantry, having obtained entire possession of the left portion of the village set it on fire. The fire, and the determined bearing of the two Sikh regiments, was soon too much for the defenders of the village, and, abandoning their position, they fled towards the plains. As they fled, they found themselves surrounded by the cavalry on the left, the dark coats of the Punjab Infantry in their front, the guns on their right, and behind them the deadly Enfields of the two Sikh regiments. The cavalry was speedily down on them, and sabred many of their numbers, the rest, seeing that all was lost; throwing down their arms ran for the headquarters and surrendered en masse. As the troops charged on, the inhabitants of Hassu Khel and Aipi unconditionally surrendered, whereupon the troops returned to camp, having been under arms for eighteen hours. The 1ST and 4TH Sikh Infantry were especially distinguished during these skirmishes.

North-West Frontier, 1857-78

Jowaki Afridis, 1877-78

In the autumn of 1877, 14TH Ferozepore Sikhs formed part of a column under Brigadier-General Ross and moved into the Jowaki district, for a punitive operation against the Afridis. The Afridis had attacked police posts, plundered and burnt villages and finally burnt a bridge on the Khushalgarh road. As they opposed the advance on the Shergasha Heights, the Sikhs were detailed to assault the enemy. The fighting was, however, not severe and the Afridis withdrew without offering much resistance. The force moved into the Boris valley and destroyed some villages against stout resistance from the tribesmen. It then withdrew to Peshawar in 1878 without incident. Havildar Dharum Singh was awarded the Indian Order of Merit for conspicuous gallantry in action against the Afridis. He was the only soldier to be awarded a gallantry award during these operations.

Utman Khel, 1878

In December 1876, a dastardly attack was made by the Utman Khel tribe on the camp of a number of unarmed coolies employed in the construction of the Swat Canal near Abazai. They surrounded the tents during the night and at a given signal, cut the ropes. Several of the unfortunate men were killed or wounded as they struggled beneath the canvas. The camp was then plundered. Although the necessity for an immediate punitive action was clear, no action was undertaken, owing to the impending outbreak of the Second Afghan War. However, on February 14TH 1878, a force consisting of 280 men of the Guides left Mardan under Captain Wigram Battye and Jemadar Jewand Singh, to exact punishment for the outrage and pecuniary compensation for the relatives of the murdered coolies.

Mian Khan, the organizer of the raid, was located at Sapri; a hill village about five miles northwest of Abazai, and careful precautions were taken to avoid giving him the alarm. The Guides left Mardan and avoiding all villages enroute reached Sapri the following morning, having left their horses near Abazai, and covered the last few miles on foot. The village was rushed at dawn and it was a complete surprise. Mian Khan was killed and retiring with utmost deliberation the Guides reached Abazai, having traversed about forty-five miles in twenty-eight hours. Certain fines and scales of compensation were imposed on the Utman Khel, which were paid within a month, except the shares allotted to a few villages; these, however, submitted on the reappearance of the Guides. In addition to coercing the Utman Khel, the Guides had another little brush with the Ranizais, who had been quiet since 1852, but had lately been committing raids and harbouring outlaws. The Guides surrounded the Ranizais village of Shalkot at dawn on March 14TH 1878 and the unconditional surrender of the tribesmen was received at once. The Guides had seven wounded in this affair, including Jemadar Jaggat Singh, who received the Indian Order of Merit for gallantry in action.

SECOND AFGHAN WAR

Second Afghan War, 1878

The British and the Emir of Afghanistan had agreed upon the boundaries between Afghanistan and India in 1857. In 1877, the Emir Sher Ali, refused to have a British Resident at Kabul, raised an army and signed a treaty with Russia, giving her the guardianship of himself and the right to protect Afghanistan. This was seen as a threat to British India. Britain responded by sending an ultimatum to Shere Ali demanding an explanation of his actions. As no answer was received, the British Indian army invaded Afghanistan on 21ST November 1878. A British force of about 40,000 fighting men, distributed into military columns penetrated Afghanistan at three different points. With British forces occupying much of the country and to prevent a British invasion of the rest of the country, Mohammad Yaqub Khan, Sher Ali's son and successor, signed the Treaty of Gandamak in May 1879. The principle of the Treaty provision required Yakoub Khan to accept a British mission at Kabul. On 3RD September 1879 Afghan troops from the Herati regiments rioted in Kabul, demanding their arrears of pay. The rioters went on to the Bala Hissar fortress, where they stormed the residency, occupied by the British Military Mission under Sir Louis Cavignari and a small escort of Guides Cavalry. After a bitter fight, the Herati troops killed Cavignari and his British and Indian party, thereby rekindling the Second Afghan War.

Bala Hissar Fortress

Second Afghan War

Ali Masjid, 1878

The Afghans were known to be holding a position at Ali Masjid in the Khyber Pass and were supported by the local frontier tribesmen. The British commander, Sir Sam Browne decided to capture the Ali Masjid position by sending 1ST and 2ND Brigades on a wide encircling movement, while 3RD and 4TH Brigades attacked the position from the front. The 14TH Ferozepore Sikhs were the advance guard to the assaulting brigades and set out from Jamrud for the Khyber Pass early on 21^{ST}November. The Regiment arrived some two and a half miles south of Ali Masjid without meeting opposition and the two brigades formed up for the assault, which was due to take place at 1 p.m., when the two encircling brigades were expected to be in position on the flanks. At this time there was no sign of these brigades, but it was decided that the frontal attack should continue according to plan. A company of 14TH Ferozepore Sikhs moved forward with the 27TH Punjabis in support. The assaulting troops made steady progress against strong opposition, and by 5 p.m., the Sikhs were at close grips with the enemy under a very heavy fire. However, there was still no sign of the British turning columns, so Sir Sam Browne decided to break off this attack to avoid unnecessary casualties. The Sikhs, with the Punjabis in support, were in very close contact with the enemy when they were ordered to withdraw. It was a very difficult operation, but the Sikhs, displaying great gallantry and determination, managed to break contact after dark and withdraw. The next morning, 22ND November 1878, the attack was renewed, but it immediately became apparent that the Afghans had withdrawn. The outflanking force was still short of the Khyber and the Afghans made good their retreat largely unimpeded. Eight Sikh soldiers of 14TH Sikhs and 27TH Punjabis were awarded the Indian Order of Merit for gallantry in this action.

Ali Masjid Fort and the Khyber Pass

(James Rattray)

Second Afghan War

Peiwar Kotal, 1878

On 21ST November 1878, Major General Roberts and his Kurram Field Force crossed the Kurrum River upstream from its concentration point at Thal. As Roberts' force moved up the Kurrum valley, the Afghans, 1,800 in number with 12 guns, retreated before them until they reached Peiwar Kotal. They joined the existing garrison, so that 4,000 Afghans with 23 guns held the 4-mile long fortified position centred on Peiwar Kotal. Early on 28TH November 1878 the attacking force moved off to attack Peiwar Kotal. Advancing up a wide slope and halting beneath the Kotal by a steep ridge, up which wound the track to the Afghan position. An account of the fierce fighting relates how:

'Time after time the enemy made determined charges from behind the barricades with which they had obstructed the narrow causeway in front of their position, only to be driven back. But when Roberts ordered a party of 23RD Sikh Pioneers to deliver a counter attack, they, in their turn, were repulsed, losing their leader, Major Anderson. With him fell Havildar Kharak Singh, Lance Naik Jita Singh and Sepoy Ram Singh. A second party of the same regiment, after some hand-to-hand fighting, was likewise compelled to retire, with the loss of one Havildar and three men killed. It seemed as if the two forces might continue facing each other and firing into each other's ranks until the ammunition of one side, or both, ran short'. (Macmunn, 1936 p214.)

The British and Indian troops then attacked along the ridge into the main Afghan positions. Heavy fighting developed as the troops continued to attack, making their way up the northern side of the valley until close to the Peiwar Kotal itself. The mountain battery followed the infantry and opened fire on the Afghan camp and positions. The Afghan troops fled down the valley, pursued by 12TH Bengal Cavalry, while the tribesmen ran for the hills. Havildar Sapuran Singh of Kohat Mountain Battery was awarded the Indian Order of Merit for his conspicuous gallantry at Peiwar Kotal.

Afghan tribesmen at Peiwar Kotal

Second Afghan War

Kabul Residency, 1879

The British Residency was in the Bala Hissar, an ancient fortress located at Kabul, the capital of Afghanistan. On 3RD September 1879, without warning, Afghan soldiers attacked the Residency and were joined by the civilian population. British officers and Indian troops of the Queen's Own Corps of Guides faced countless thousands of Afghan soldiers and civilians. Soon all the British officers were dead. The Guides fought desperately, even charging out of the Residency to bayonet the crews of artillery brought against them. The Afghans set the Residency on fire and the buildings started to collapse. All day the Afghans called upon the Guides to surrender, promising them their lives. The Guides rejected this offer and after 12 hours of fighting the few remaining men commanded by a Sikh Jemadar, Jewand Singh, fixed bayonets and charged out to their deaths. Thirty Sikh soldiers of Guides Cavalry and Infantry sacrificed their lives, and by their deeds they conferred undying honours on the Sikh nation. Over 600 Afghan dead bore witness to the heroic sacrifice of this small force.

The Kabul memorial at Mardan

'The annals of no army and no regiment can show a brighter record of devoted bravery than has been achieved by this small band of Guides. By their deeds they have conferred undying honour not only on the regiment to which they belong but on the whole British Army.'

Sikh officers and men who died in the defence of the Residency at Kabul, on 3RD September 1879:
Jemadar Jewand Singh, Daffadar Hira Singh, Sowars Amar Singh, Wazir Singh, Ratan Singh, Mul Singh, Jiwan Singh, Harnam Singh, Thakur Singh, Deva Singh. Jemadar Mehtab Singh, Havildar Kharak Singh, Havildar Hazara Singh. Sepoys Devi Singh, Jai Singh, Amar Singh, Fatteh Singh, Wariam Singh, Mith Singh, Hira Singh, Chanda Singh, Gurdit Singh, Gaja Singh, Wariam Singh, Nidhan Singh,Tahil Singh, Ranju Singh, Bhagat Singh , Esa Singh, Narain Singh, Hari Singh, Oodam Singh, and Gurdit Singh.

Second Afghan War

Charasia, 1879

The death of the British resident Sir Cavignari, resolved the government in Calcutta for a full invasion of the country, the occupation of Kabul and punitive action against the killers of Cavignari's party. With the occupation of Kabul, the Khyber Pass route would be opened up to establish supply lines with India. On 3RD October 1879, the Kabul Field Force began the final 36-mile march to Kabul. On the evening of 5TH October 1879, General Roberts reached Charasia, a village near the River Logar and encamped. To the north of the camp, by the river, the route to Kabul lay through the Sang I Nawishta defile. On the morning of 6TH October 1879 a force comprising 23RD Sikh Pioneers and 92ND Highlanders with cavalry and 2 guns advanced to the Sang I Nawishta with the task of making sure the route along the Logar River was passable. As the Afghan tribesmen were gathering at his rear, Roberts resolved on immediate attack on the Afghan army, blocking his road to Kabul. During the attack, it was a charge by 23RD Sikh Pioneers, which finally caused the Afghans to break. The brilliant victory of Charasia threw open the road to Kabul, gained over thirteen regular Afghan battalions and a host of tribesmen. The battle at Charasia was a critical one. As on several occasions in the Second Afghan War, the margin between success and disastrous failure was thin. The courage and resource of the Sikh soldiers won the battle against great odds. Eight Sikh soldiers of 23RD Sikh Pioneers were awarded the Indian Order of Merit for gallantry in this action. Lord Roberts, on his march from Kabul to Kandahar in 1880, dispensed with his Sappers and Miners and relied on 23RD Sikh Pioneers as one of the four infantry regiments in the first of his three brigades, to act as engineers when necessary. Such a unit was in no way inferior to other Native infantry and being formed from one of the proudest of the 'Martial Races' would have undoubtedly looked down on other infantry units. The 5TH Punjab Infantry also took a prominent part in the decisive battle of Charasia. At a critical moment, the Punjabis were ordered to attack a key position. The assault was carried out in gallant style by "A" Company under Subedar Budh Singh, who received the Indian Order of Merit for his gallantry in this battle.

An officer of the 23RD Sikh Pioneers at Charasiah

Second Afghan War

Kabul, 1879

General Roberts, after defeating the Afghan Army at Charasia on 6TH October 1879, occupied Kabul. The British and Indian troops then occupied the Sherpur military cantonment north of Kabul, built by their predecessors in 1839 during the occupation of the city in the First Afghan War. They rebuilt the accommodation and finally, in early December 1879, moved into the vast compound. Communications with India were established along the Khyber Pass route, with substantial numbers of troops deployed along its length to keep the mountain tribes at bay.

Roberts restored the Amir, Yakoub Khan, to the Afghan throne. He rounded up the soldiers of the mutinous Afghan Herati regiments, and others reported as having stormed the British residency in the Bala Hissar, killing Cavignari and his Guides escort.

Sherpur, 1879

The British found restoring order to the Kabul region to be a difficult and dangerous task: the Afghan tribes were outraged and the Afghan forces elusive, harassing the marching British columns with long-range sniper fire, cutting telegraph lines and supply lines, and attacking small outposts. Following four days of fierce, protracted fighting around Kabul itself, Roberts took refuge in Sherpur cantonments on 14TH December and dispatched a telegraph requesting reinforcements. Brigadier General Charles Gough was ordered to relieve Roberts as the siege began.

Gatling gun crew on the Sherpur fortifications
(The Illustrated London News)

Second Afghan War

Siege of Sherpur, 1879

Sherpur was a vast rectangular enclave that enclosed a space of some five miles, including the Bimaru Heights to the north. It defended access to the Khyber Pass to the east. Roberts relied on the Khyber Pass route for supplies and communication with the other British Forces in Afghanistan. Roberts spent the first few days of the siege strengthening his defences. Mud towers on the Bimaru heights were connected by an earthwork and gun emplacements were dug. Open gaps in the perimeter were made defensible by the construction of wire entanglements and ditches. Flanking trenches and a blockhouse protected a gorge running through the centre of the Bimaru heights, whilst the northeastern corner, the most vulnerable area of the defences, was buttressed by sandbagging and strengthening an existing fort. An hour before dawn on 23RD December, as the British forces manned their snow-shrouded defences (heavy snowfalls had commenced on 18TH) the Afghans began streaming toward the cantonment in their thousands, their vanguard composed mainly of ghazis (religious zealots). The artillery fired star shell to illuminate the scene and thousands of muzzle-flashes began to ripple along the perimeter as the defenders commenced volley fire. The Afghans attacked all four faces of the perimeter but failed to penetrate the defences. The assault slackened at about 9:30 and petered out altogether by midday. Roberts dispatched a mixed force of infantry, cavalry and guns to sweep the area to the south and east and secure the roads leading to Kohistan and Kabul. Nearby villages and forts were destroyed and straggling fugitive tribesmen were ferreted out of their hiding places and shot without quarter. Charles Gough arrived the following morning, after an epic and dangerous march. Roberts estimated Afghan losses at some 3,000 killed. The British suffered 5 dead and 28 wounded. The power of the tribal coalition was smashed and, for the time being, British forces in the Kabul region could enjoy some respite. (Robson, 1986 p170)

Latabad, 1879 - 23RD Sikh Pioneers

Hundreds of Ghilzais surrounded a small garrison manned by the Sikh Pioneers at Latabad and established a piquet within close range. Subedar Mehtab Singh led forth forty Sikh Pioneers against this piquet with great success. Subedar Mehtab Singh and Havildar Ghulab Singh were awarded the Indian Order of Merit, for their gallantry in this action.

Second Afghan War

Ahmed Khel, 1880

On 19TH April 1880, a column commanded by Lieutenant General Sir Donald Stewart, marching from Kandahar to Kabul to help pacify the area, was attacked by Ghazi and Hazara religious fanatics about 20 miles west of Ghazni. Under their green and black flags, Afghan horsemen swept down on the British flanks, whilst fanatical swordsmen charged the centre. Their initial rush was nearly successful: with a squadron of Bengal Lancers routing into 19TH Punjabis and causing confusion, it looked as if the issue was in the balance. However, 3RD Gurkha Rifles and 2ND Sikhs stood fast and formed a square. The musketry fire of the infantry, particularly of 2ND Sikhs, inflicted heavy casualties on the Afghan tribesmen, who finally turned and fled, pursued by the Lancers; killing all the fugitives they could catch. Having won the battle, the troops then attacked and occupied Ghazni. They also broke up another concentration of tribesmen at Arzu, and then, the area being relatively pacified, returned to Kabul.

Maiwand, 1880

The battle of Maiwand was one of the principal battles of the Second Afghan War. Ayub Khan, a popular Afghan prince and son of Yaqub Khan, claimed the right to rule Kandahar. In order to prevent Ayub capturing Ghazni, the British advanced to Maiwand on 27TH July, and attacked Ayub, who had already seized that place. The Afghans, who numbered 25,000, outflanked and attacked the British. The British were completely routed, and had to thank the apathy of the Afghans for escaping total annihilation. The British were forced to fall back on Kandahar with the loss of over 1000 men.

Kandahar, 1880

After the disastrous defeat at Maiwand, the remnants of battle-wearied army were forced to fall back on Kandahar. Ayub Khan then laid siege to Kandahar, defended by a well-supplied garrison of 5000 men and 13 guns under General Primrose. As soon as news of the defeat and siege reached Kabul, Lieutenant General Stewart ordered General Roberts to form a flying column of one cavalry brigade, three infantry brigades and four mountain batteries. The force comprised 2836 British troops and 7151 Sepoy and Gurkha troops which included 2ND Sikhs, 3RD Sikhs and 15TH Ludhiana Sikhs, 23RD, 24TH Sikh Pioneers and 25TH Punjabis, with its 7000 followers, left for Kandahar on 8TH August. The relief force finally entered Kandahar on 31ST August. After a brief rest, on 1ST September, Roberts sortied out of Kandahar and attacked the Afghan army. Battle commenced at 9.30 am and, after meeting considerable opposition amongst the village and surrounding orchards, the 1ST and 2ND Brigades dislodged the enemy troops after fierce hand-to-hand fighting.

Both brigades then advanced to turn the Afghan position on Pir Paimal and take the rest of the Afghan army in the rear. The Afghans attempted to form a new line, but the British pressed home their advantage with 2ND Gurkha Rifles; 92ND. Highlanders and 23RD Sikh Pioneers storming the Afghan defences in front of

Second Afghan War

Kandahar, 1880 (Cont.)

their camp. Ayub Khan fled, leaving his army to disperse, pursued by the British cavalry.

The Battle of Kandahar ended the Second Anglo-Afghan War. Ayub Khan had been decisively beaten. He had lost the whole of his artillery, his camp, enormous quantities of ammunition and about 1,000 men killed. He became a fugitive along with the small remnants of his battered army. The British appointee Abdur Rahman was thus securely established, under British protection, as Emir of Afghanistan. Having achieved the aims of their invasion of Afghanistan, the British withdrew. Ayub Khan subsequently raised a fresh rebellion against Abdur Rahman, but was swiftly defeated and killed, ending the threat to the new regime. This political settlement was to endure until the Third Anglo-Afghan War in 1919.

The following Sikh soldiers were awarded gallantry awards for their conspicuous gallantry during the Second Afghan War:

Sepoy Kapur Singh
24TH Punjabis

Sepoy Kapur Singh was awarded Indian Order of Merit for conspicuous gallantry in action in Choora Valley on 31ST January 1878.

Naik Dhurm Singh and Naik Soobah Singh
24TH Punjabis

The above soldiers were awarded Indian Order of Merit for their great coolness, under heavy fire of artillery and musketry, in saving the reserve ammunition and entrenching tools from falling into enemy hands.

Havildar Gurdit Singh and Sepoy Asa Singh
27TH Punjabis

The above soldiers were awarded Indian Order of Merit for conspicuous gallantry in action on 21ST November 1878 at Ali Masjid, in advancing to occupy a Sangar close to the enemy's position.

Havildar Dyal Singh
27TH Punjabis

Havildar Dyal Singh was awarded the Indian Order of Merit for conspicuous gallantry in action on 21ST November 1878 at Ali Masjid, in carrying Sepoy Jowahir Singh, when wounded, out of heavy fire.

Subadar Major Jugget and Havildar Natha Singh
29TH Punjabis

The above soldiers were awarded Indian Order of Merit for conspicuous gallantry in action at the assault of the Spin Gawai Kotal on 2ND December 1878.

Second Afghan War

Lance Naik Sher Singh
29TH Punjabis

Lance Naik Sher Singh was awarded the Indian Order of Merit for conspicuous gallantry in the action with the enemy at the capture of the Peiwar Kotal on 2ND December 1878.

Sowar Jhanda Singh
5TH Punjab Cavalry, Frontier Force

Sowar Jhanda Singh was awarded the Indian Order of Merit for conspicuous gallantry in heading the charge of his troop against a force many times its number and under heavy fire, in the fight against the Mangals on 7TH January 1879.

5TH Punjab Cavalry, Frontier Force

The following Sikh officers and men were awarded a collective Indian Order of Merit for their conspicuous gallantry in action at Latabad Pass on 2ND April 1879. Sowar Bussawa Singh, Sowar Natha Singh, K. Daffadar Harsa Singh, Daffadar Kesar Singh, and Daffadar Maiah Singh.

Guides Cavalry, Punjab Frontier Force

The following Sikh officers and men were awarded a collective Indian Order of Merit for their conspicuous gallantry in a cavalry charge against a large body of fanatical Khugiani Ghazis near Fatehbad on 2ND April 1879. Sowar Dewan Singh, Sowar Kardoo Singh, Sowar Prem Singh, Sowar Yakub Singh, Daffadar Jewan Singh, Resaidar Nand Singh.

Subedar Major Gurbax Singh
2ND Sikh Infantry, Punjab Frontier Force

Subadar Major Gurbax Singh was awarded the Indian Order of Merit for conspicuous gallantry in leading and encouraging the men during the advance on the enemy's position, and charging a band of Ghazis while under continuous enemy rifle fire.

Sepoy Ala Singh
2ND Sikh Infantry, Punjab Frontier Force

Sepoy Ala Singh was awarded the Indian Order of Merit for conspicuous gallantry in single handedly attacking several Ghazis and killing two of them, while receiving severe wound in the encounter.

Jemadar Gopal Singh
14TH Bengal Lancers

Jemadar Gopal Singh was awarded the Indian Order of Merit for conspicuous gallantry in action at Churdeh Valley on 11TH December 1879.

Second Afghan War

Sepoy Chattar Singh
23RD Sikh Pioneers

Sepoy Chattar Singh was awarded the Indian Order of Merit for leaping across a wet ditch in the face of some forty of the enemy, and bayoneting several of them on 1ST September 1880.

Sepoy Ganda Singh
23RD Sikh Pioneers

Sepoy Ganda Singh was awarded the Indian Order of Merit for bayoneting two of the enemy, in a charge at their Sangars, in which he was particularly forward, and saving the life of Subadar Dewa Singh, whom these men at attacked on 1ST September 1880.

Subedar Dewa Singh
23RD Sikh Pioneers

Subedar Dewa Singh was awarded the Indian Order of Merit for conspicuous gallantry in action near Kandahar on 1ST September 1879, on which occasion he led the way in charge on one of enemy's Sangars, which he was the first to enter, and in which two guns were captured.

Charasia
23RD Sikh Pioneers

Charasia, situated about six miles from Kabul, was where in October 1879, the Kabul Field Force, advancing to exact retribution for massacre of the British Mission, routed the Afghan field army. The following Sikh officers and men were awarded the Indian Order of Merit in consideration of their conspicuous gallantry during these operations. Sepoy Chanda Singh, Sepoy Jhanda Singh, Sepoy Hardit Singh, Naik Ootum Singh, Jemadar Boor Singh, Havildar Gurdial Singh, Subedar Dewa Singh and Subedar Mehtab Singh.

Maiwand
3RD Sind Horse

The battle of Maiwand was one of the principal battles of the Second Afghan War. The battle ended in defeat for the British Brigade. The following Sikh officers and men were awarded the Indian Order of Merit in consideration of their conspicuous gallantry in keeping off parties of the enemy's cavalry, who were in pursuit, thus saving the lives of many wounded and exhausted men. Sowar Beer Singh, Sowar Lehna Singh, Sowar Soondar Singh, Lance Naik, Bishan Singh, Lance Naik and Jowala Singh.

Sowar Bhagwan Singh
10TH Bengal Lancers

Sowar Bhagwan Singh was awarded Indian Order of Merit for conspicuous gallantry in Afghanistan on 19TH April 1880.

Second Afghan War

Kot Daffadar Hookum Singh
19TH Bengal Lancers

Kot Daffadar Hookum Singh was awarded the Indian Order of Merit for conspicuous gallantry in action at Patkao Shana on 1ST July 1880, in charging single handedly five of the enemy and killing two of them.

Resaidar Jowahir Singh
19TH Bengal Lancers

Resaidar Jowahir Singh was awarded the Indian Order of Merit for conspicuous gallantry in action at Ahmed Khel on 19TH April 1880. On which occasion, at the head of three dismounted men, he dashed through some fifteen or twenty of the enemy, who were resisting their passage, killing two of them with his own hands and receiving a wound in the encounter.

Sowar Gulab Singh
19TH Bengal Lancers

Sowar Gulab Singh was awarded Indian Order of Merit for conspicuous gallantry in action at Ahmed Khel on 19TH April 1880. In dismounting and leading an attack, under a heavy fire, on a number of the enemy who had posted themselves in a ditch, killing more than one of them and setting an excellent example to the other men with him.

Daffadar Naurung Singh
19TH Bengal Lancers

Daffadar Naurung Singh was awarded the Indian Order of Merit for conspicuous gallantry in action at Patkao Shana on 1ST July 1880, on which occasion he led the charge against the enemy and killed several of the enemy himself.

Daffadar Hardit Singh
19TH Bengal Lancers

Daffadar Hardit Singh was awarded the Indian Order of Merit for conspicuous gallantry in action at Ahmed Khel on 19TH April 1880, on which occasion, although severely wounded; he engaged and cut down two of the enemy, who were attacking a fellow cavalryman, Sowar Boota Singh.

Sowar Khushal Singh
19TH Bengal Lancers

Sowar Khushal Singh was awarded the Indian Order of Merit for conspicuous gallantry in action at Ahmed Khel on 19TH April 1880, in rescuing Kot Daffadar Kurram Singh who was severely wounded and nearly overcome in a conflict with two Ghazis.

Second Afghan War

Lance Daffadar Kehar Singh
19TH Bengal Lancers

Lance Daffadar Singh was awarded the Indian Order of Merit for conspicuous gallantry in action at Ahmed Khel on 19TH April 1880, in saving the life of Resaidar Ganda Singh, when the latter was attacked by two of the enemy. Also, on the same occasion, single handedly charging a group of eight or ten Ghazis and killing two of them.

Lance Daffadar Sardar Singh
19TH Bengal Lancers

Lance Daffadar Sardar Singh was awarded the Indian Order of Merit for conspicuous gallantry in action at Ahmed Khel on 19TH April 1880, in charging, with Kot Daffadar Hubboob Singh, a superior number of the enemy who had suddenly attacked the flank of the squadron to which he belonged, killing two of them.

Sowar Ram Singh
19TH Bengal Lancers

Sowar Ram Singh was awarded the Indian Order of Merit for conspicuous gallantry in action at Ahmed Khel on 19TH April 1880, in charging three of the enemy's horsemen who were rushing on Surgeon Murphy, killing one of them and saving that officer's life.

Sowar Uttar Singh
19TH Bengal Lancers

Sowar Uttar Singh was awarded the Indian Order of Merit for conspicuous gallantry in action at Ahmed Khel on 19TH April 1880, on which occasion, although wounded in two places, he charged two Ghazis, killing one of them, and saved the life of Daffadar Narain Singh, whom they had beset.

Sepoy Lal Singh, Sepoy Nand Singh, Sepoy Theraj Singh
45TH Rattray's Sikhs

The above soldiers were awarded the Indian Order of Merit for conspicuous gallantry on 7TH March near Maidan Neck, when on escort duty with a survey party.

Sowar Bootah Singh
1ST Punjab Cavalry, Frontier Force

Sowar Bootah Singh was awarded the Indian Order of Merit for conspicuous gallantry in action at Arzu on 23RD April 1880, in singly engaging and cutting down in hand-to-hand fighting two of the enemy.

Second Afghan War

Daffadar Chait Singh
1ST Punjab Cavalry, Frontier Force

Was awarded the Indian Order of Merit for conspicuous gallantry in action at Patkao Shana on 1ST July 1880, on which occasion he killed three of the enemy, one of them being a deserter, who had gone over to the enemy.

Sowar Jowahir Singh
1ST Punjab Cavalry, Frontier Force

Sowar Jowahir Singh was awarded the Indian Order of Merit for conspicuous gallantry in action at Ahmed Khel on 19TH April 1880, on which occasion he dismounted and attacked two of the enemy who had taken refuge in a Nullah, killing one in hand-to-hand encounter.

Lance Daffadar Gujar Singh
1ST Punjab Cavalry, Frontier Force

Lance Daffadar Gujar Singh was awarded the Indian Order of Merit for conspicuous gallantry on 24TH October 1880, in aiding Resaidar Lahrasaf Khan and Sowar Sawan Singh of the same corps, when attacked by superior numbers of the enemy, several of whom he cut down and killed.

Sowar Kishen Singh
4TH Punjab Cavalry, Frontier Force

Sowar Kishen Singh was awarded the Indian Order of Merit for conspicuous gallantry during the attack made on the Sulaiman Khel village in the Gomal Valley on 5TH January 1879.

Guides Infantry, Punjab Frontier Force

The following Sikh officers and men were awarded the Indian Order of Merit for their conspicuous gallantry in the capture of the Afghan capital Kabul.
Havildar Jowalla Singh, Havildar Jewand Singh, Havildar Utter Singh, and Havildar Wariam Singh.

Sepoy Jai Singh
2ND Sikh Infantry, Punjab Frontier Force

Sepoy Jai Singh was awarded the Indian Order of Merit for conspicuous gallantry in singly attacking several ghazis and killing two of them, while receiving a severe wound in the encounter.

Sepoy Hira Singh and Sepoy Pertab Singh
2ND Sikh Infantry, Punjab Frontier Force

The above Sepoys were awarded the Indian Order of Merit for conspicuous gallantry in exhibiting great coolness and intrepidity under continuous rifle fire from the enemy. They were both severely wounded while prominently leading their platoon during the advance on an Afghan position.

Second Afghan War

Havildar Gurdit Singh
3RD Sikh Infantry, Punjab Frontier Force

Havildar Gurdit Singh was awarded the Indian Order of Merit for conspicuous gallantry in action near Kabul on 14TH December 1879. On which occasion, when a detachment of the regiment was retiring from the Conical Hill near the Alibad Kotal, he ran back under heavy fire and rescued a wounded man, who would otherwise have been killed by the enemy.

Sepoy Punjab Singh
3RD Sikh Infantry, Punjab Frontier Force

Sepoy Punjab Singh was awarded the Indian Order of Merit for conspicuous gallantry in action at the Takht I Shah Hill near Kabul on 12TH December 1879, in proceeding, under heavy fire, to the assistance of an officer, who was severely wounded, remaining with him, and eventually carrying him out of fire.

Naik Sham Singh
3RD Sikh Infantry, Punjab Frontier Force

Naik Sham Singh was awarded the Indian Order of Merit for conspicuous gallantry in action at Mir Karez on 10TH December 1879, on which occasion he was most forward in the attack on the enemy's position and set a brilliant example to the men of the regiment.

Havildar Davi Singh
4TH Sikh Infantry, Punjab Frontier Force

Havildar Davi Singh was awarded the Indian Order of Merit for conspicuous gallantry in action at Gumal on 6TH April 1880, on which occasion, with a detachment of eighteen men, he attacked and drove off a large body of Wazir raiders and saved the village from destruction.

Subedar Budh Singh
5TH Punjab Infantry, Punjab Frontier Force

Subedar Budh Singh was awarded the Indian Order of Merit for conspicuous gallantry in action at Charasia on 6TH October 1880.

5TH Punjab Infantry, Punjab Frontier Force

The following Sikh officers and men were awarded the Indian Order of Merit for their conspicuous gallantry in the capture of the Afghan capital Kabul:
Sepoy Man Singh Naik, Sarwan Singh, Havildar Sham Singh.

Second Afghan War

Sikh soldiers guarding Afghan prisoners, 1880

The Afghan prisoners captured in the advance through the Khurd Khyber are sitting in the centre of the photograph, surrounded by Sikh guards. The 45TH Sikh Regiment was raised in 1856 by Captain Thomas Rattray and was popularly known as Rattray's Sikhs. It had earlier earned glory with its courage and loyalty to the British at the relief of Lucknow during the Sepoy Mutiny of 1857. The Regiment served in the Fourth Infantry Brigade, part of the Peshawar Valley Field Force, during the Second Afghan War. The prisoners were lucky to have survived because in the harsh conditions and terrain of the Afghan Wars no quarter was given to prisoners taken, on both sides.

A group of Afghan soldiers, 1880

NORTH-WEST FRONTIER, 1881-1901

Waziristan, 1881

At the conclusion of Second Afghan War, 14TH Ferozepore Sikhs were detailed to join a column forming at Bannu for a punitive expedition into Waziristan. The Regiment left Ambala by rail for Rawalpindi, arriving on 17TH April. It then marched to Bannu and covered the one hundred and ninety-two miles in eleven days, in very hot weather. The column moved forward into hostile territory on 2ND May and marched to Razmak by the Khaisora valley. At Razmak, the column contacted another column, which had moved out from Tank. The enemy was overcome after stiff resistance and soon submitted to terms. The column was back in Bannu by 22ND May and then returned to Ambala. Subadar-Major Didar Singh, who had been Subadar-major for ten years and had served with the Regiment throughout the Mutiny, died during the expedition.

Black Mountain, 1888

In 1888, the Black Mountain District became the area of military operations. For some years the country in these parts had been in a very unsettled state. A considerable sum in fines was owed by the tribesmen for various offences committed by them, without much prospect of payment. They had also made numerous raids across the British border, particularly in the Agror Valley. To assist the inhabitants of friendly villages in repelling these incursions, a military post was maintained at Aghi, a prominent place in the district. On September 12TH, 1884, a successful skirmish took place between a detachment of 150 Sikhs and the tribesmen, in which the tribesmen received a decided check. But the raids continued at varying intervals, until the matter was brought to a head in 1888 by the murder of two British officers. This incident was the signal for the general gathering of the tribesmen and the despatch of a punitive expedition against the offending clans. The enemy were found in position in northeast of Towara. While the 4TH Punjab Infantry and 34TH Sikh Pioneers cleared the right and left flank of the British advance, the guns opened fire on the enemy's main position. At this moment, a body of fanatical swordsmen, concealed in a masked nulla, running diagonally towards the front, made a desperate attempt to break the British line. Most were shot down, except for thirteen, who were pursued in the jungle and killed by the soldiers of 34TH Sikh Pioneers. Eighty-eight dead were subsequently counted on this spot, among which forty- eight were identified as Hindustani Fanatics. Meanwhile 14TH Sikhs left Jhelum to join the Hazara Field Force, which was formed to carry out punitive operations against the tribes, in the north-west of Abbottabad. There was heavy fighting during the expedition. The 14TH Sikhs formed the advance guard of the column and sustained some casualties in brushing aside resistance by the tribesmen when moving into the area. The regiment camped at Akhund on the crest of the Black Mountain, while small columns moved out and destroyed a number of villages against stiff opposition.

North-West Frontier, 1881-1901

Waziristan, 1894

The operations were necessary owing to the continual attacks by the Wazirs on the Afghan Frontier Delimitation party, on the North West Frontier. The tribesmen suffered heavy casualties from the party's escort. The following Sikh officer and Sowars of 1ST Punjab Cavalry were awarded the Indian Order of Merit for their conspicuous gallantry in the operations against the Wazirs around Wana in January 1894, Daffadar Thakur Singh, Sowar Man Singh, and Sowar Khanda Singh.

Corps of Guides, 1893

On 30TH April 1893, the following announcement appeared in Corps Orders:
"The Commanding Officer having being directed to detail a non-commissioned officer from the Cavalry to form one of the Native Escort for Her Majesty the Queen at the opening of the Imperial Institute in London, selected Daffadar Bahadur Singh, "D" Troop, son of the late Jemadar Jewand Singh, who was killed at Kabul on 3RD September, 1879." (Anon., 1938)

Malakand, 1895

In 1895, a coup d'etat in Chitral cost the life of the ruling chief. The victors attempted to drive out the British representative, which necessitated the dispatch of a 16,000 strong British expedition to reduce the rebels. At the Malakand Pass, on April 3RD, 1895, the invading troops overwhelmed some 12,000 Chitralis, who lost more than 500 men before giving up control of the pass. A dramatic charge by 50 Sabres of Guides Cavalry on 2,000 threatening tribesmen at Khar resulted in the tribesmen fleeing to the safety of the hills. Daffadars Tota Singh and Soba Singh were awarded the Indian Order of Merit for their conspicuous gallantry in this action.

Chitral, 1895

The small British garrison at Chitral fort, consisting of a company of Sikhs and some 300 Kashmir soldiers were besieged for seven weeks and were constantly attacked during March and April but held on until relieved. Captain Townsend, in his report on the siege, wrote: 'The spirit of 14TH Ferozepore Sikhs was our admiration; the longer the siege lasted the more eager they became to teach the enemy a lesson. There could not be finer soldiers than these men of 14TH Sikhs and they were our sheet anchor in the siege'. (Sikh Cyber Museum, 2003b) Younghusband, in his Relief of Chitral, wrote: 'It was the discipline ingrained into these men that saved the garrison. As long as a Sikh was on sentry, while Sikhs were holding a threatened point, Captain Townsend had nothing to fear'. (Younghusband, 1896) In recognition of the gallant and successful defence of the fort at Chitral, His Excellency the Viceroy sanctioned a grant of six months' pay to all ranks. Subedar Gurmukh Singh was appointed to the Order of British India and Jemadar Attar Singh and seven men were awarded the Indian Order of Merit for gallantry.

North-West Frontier, 1881-1901

Relief of Chitral, 1895

The garrison at Chitral Fort held out until the approach of a small force from Gilgit under Colonel Kelly, which caused Chitralis to withdraw. The Chitral relief under General Low, that had approached from the direction of Malakand and the Lowari pass, arrived a week later and took the Afghan commander Sher Afzal prisoner, while commander Umra Khan fled to Afghanistan. Sher Afzal with Amir-ul-Mulk and their leading followers were deported to India on 1ST May and the selection of Shuja-ul-Mulk as Mehtar of Chitral was confirmed.

The 32ND Sikh Pioneers set out from Gilgit to cover 220 miles of very poor road to the relief of Chitral. The importance of the Sikh Pioneer's epic march was never fully recognized, most of the publicity and fame for the relief being lavished on the well-known British regiments. During the relief operations, six Sikh officers and men of 32ND Sikh Pioneers were awarded the Indian Order of Merit.

Chitral Fort 1895

Sikh and British officers of 32ND Sikh Pioneers who marched from Gilgit to relieve Chitral

(National Army Museum)

North-West Frontier, 1881-1901

Koragh, 1895

While 'A' Company of 14TH Ferozepore Sikhs were at Chitral with the political agent, 'B' Company, under Captain Ross, took their place in Mastuj, where they arrived at the beginning of March. A few days later information was received that a Sapper detachment and a party of Kashmir Rifles, en route to Chitral, were about to be attacked near Reshun. Captain Ross immediately set out with his company to support this party. The Sikhs halted the first night at Buni and moved on early the next morning on 8TH of March. Soon the Company entered a narrow defile below the village of Koragh. The defile was about half a mile long and situated where the Mastuj River, a rapid and unfordable torrent, formed a gorge through the mountains. Captain Ross in his hurry, decided to risk entering the defile without first reconnoitring the heights. This decision had disastrous results. As the column was approaching the far end of the defile, the track was found to be blocked and in addition, parties of the enemy were discovered to be holding the hilltops and ridges all round. Since the enemy were in great strength and holding strong positions, it was hopeless to try to attempt to force a way through to Reshun. Captain Ross, therefore, decided to withdraw and sent Lieutenant Jones with ten men to seize the Koragh end of the defile and cover the withdrawal. However, the enemy had already seized this exit and Lieutenant Jones was unable to break out and suffered heavy casualties. The attempt to break out was temporarily abandoned and the whole party took cover in some caves in the riverbank. During the night, two attempts were made to force a way out, but the enemy was on the alert and the Sikhs had to return to the caves. Having rested in the caves during the day, Captain Ross decided that they must break through that night at all costs. The party moved off at 2 a.m. on 10TH March. The enemy was, unfortunately, on the alert and offered strong opposition. Captain Ross was shot dead and many men were killed or wounded. Only Lieutenant Jones, seventeen men and two followers succeeded in fighting their way out on to the plain towards Koragh. Lieutenant Jones halted his party a short way from the defile in order to assist any further survivors in breaking through. In this position, the enemy launched two ferocious charges against the Sikhs, who stubbornly held their ground and drove the tribesmen back time after time. Three more Sikhs were killed in this fighting and of the rest, Lieutenant Jones and nine men were wounded, so the party withdrew slowly to Buni, which was reached at 6 a.m. the next morning. Only Lieutenant Jones and fourteen men survived this disaster.

Lieutenant Jones was awarded the Distinguished Service Order for his leadership. The following fourteen Sikh soldiers, the Indian Order of Merit, for their conspicuous gallantry against the tribesmen: Subedar Sundar Singh, Havildar Bur Singh, Havildar Bhag Singh, Havildar Santokh Singh and Sepoys Jaimal Singh, Ganga Singh, Dyal Singh, Bukan Singh, Dasunda Singh, Jodh Singh, Mal Singh, Sahib Singh, Prem Singh, Sadha Singh, Sant Singh, Thaman Singh, Sham Singh and Mehtab Singh.

North-West Frontier, 1881-1901

Maizar, 1897

A political agent with a military escort of British officers and Indian Sepoys rode out to Maizar, to settle a dispute between the tribal Maliks. As the escort rested under some trees, the tribals suddenly attacked them. Being outnumbered the escort had to make a quick retreat, during which all the British officers were soon wounded. The Sikh officers nobly rose to the occasion. Subedars Naryan Singh and Sundar Singh covered their retreat, in the course of which the latter and ten of his Sepoys sacrificed their lives to enable the remainder to get clear of the village. Ten Sikh officers and men of the Mountain Batteries were awarded the Indian Order of Merit for their conspicuous gallantry in operating their guns to keep the tribesmen at bay. The following Sikh soldiers, who had sacrificed their lives, were awarded the posthumous Indian Order of Merit and their widows granted pensions. Subedar Sundar Singh, Naik Bur Singh, Naik Assa Singh, Lance Naik Kanhaiya Singh, Lance Naik Bela Singh, Sepoy Indar Singh, Bugler Singh, 1ST Regiment Sikh Infantry. Hon. Captain Naryan Singh and Jemadar Shib Singh, 51ST Sikhs. Havildar Ishar Singh and Havildar Bela Singh, 55TH Rifles.

Malakand, 1897

In July 1897, the garrison in Malakand was alerted to a mass attack led by a 'Mad Mullah'. Although there was a fort at Malakand, many of the men were in camps outside the fort. When the alarm sounded the British officers McRae and Taylor ran out with some Sikhs and engaged the attackers in a narrow defile, in which Taylor was killed. This action prevented the enemy from encircling the camp and cutting it off from the fort. The Sikhs held the right of the position against repeated day and night attacks between 26TH and 30TH July. A detachment of the 45TH Rattray's Sikhs clashed with a fanatical tribal horde advancing on the garrison. Outnumbered by swarms of tribesmen, the Sikhs disputed every yard as they retreated to the rest of their regiment. They were required to make a desperate bayonet charge during the storm-laden night of 30TH, which scattered the tribesmen. It was all over by the time reinforcements arrived the next day; the tribesmen had fled back to the hills. Twenty-two Sikh officers and men were awarded the Indian Order of Merit for their conspicuous gallantry in these operations.

Afghan prisoners guarded by Sepoys of the 45TH Rattray's Sikhs
(National Army Museum)

North-West Frontier, 1881-1901

Sargarhi, 1897

On 12TH September 1897, a detachment of 22 men of 36TH Sikhs manned a detached, fortified, signaling post of Sargarhi. The post was surrounded by some 10,000 Afridis and Orakzais who promised the detachment safe conduct if they surrendered. The Sikhs chose to fight instead and repulsed repeated attacks for three days. The tribes set fire to the post, while the brave garrison lay dead or dying with their ammunition exhausted. Next morning the relief column reached the post and the tell tale marks of the epic fight were there for all to see. The tribes later admitted to a figure of 180 dead and many more wounded. This episode, when narrated in the British Parliament, drew from the members a standing ovation in the memory of the defenders of Saragarhi. The story of the heroic deeds of these men was also placed before Queen Victoria. The account was received all over the world with awe and admiration. All the 21 valiant men of this epic battle were awarded the Indian Order of Merit (posthumously). The dependants of the Saragarhi heroes were awarded 50 acres of land and 500 Rupees. Never before or since has a body of troops, that is all of them, won gallantry awards in a single action. It is indeed a singularly unique action in the annals of Indian military history. A tablet was erected in the memory of these brave men. The tablet reads:

"The Government of India have caused this tablet to be erected to the memory of the twenty one non-commissioned officers and men of 36TH Sikh Regiment of the Bengal Infantry whose names are engraved below as a perpetual record of the heroism shown by these gallant soldiers who died at their posts in the Defence of the fort of Saragarhi, on 12TH September 1897, fighting against overwhelming numbers, thus proving their loyalty and devotion to their sovereign, the Queen Empress of India and gloriously maintaining the reputation of the Sikhs for unflinching courage on the field of battle." The Sikh Regiment celebrates 12TH September annually as "Sargarhi Day". The story of this battle of epic dimensions is taught to school children in France and is one of the eight stories of collective bravery published by UNESCO.

Ruins of the signaling post of Sargarhi with Sikh Soldiers on the ramparts

(National Army Museum)

North-West Frontier, 1881-1901

Fort Gulistan, 1897

At the time of the Afridi incursion into the Khyber and Samana ranges, Major Des Voeux was in command of Fort Cavignari at Gulistan. 165 men of 36TH Sikh Regiment occupied the Fort. After the enemy had captured the small post at Saragarhi, and annihilated the gallant Sikh garrison of 21 men, they proceeded to attack Fort Cavignari, which was closely besieged for three days. The attackers had got up to within 20 yards of the walls and had built stone Sangars for cover during the night. It was decided that an attack had to be made on this Sangar. Havildar Kala Singh volunteered to take 16 men to carry it out. At 8 am on 13TH they made the sortie, charging towards the Sangar, but heavy fire wounded several of them and forced the others to stay flat on the ground. Another Havildar, Sunder Singh saw this and without waiting for orders, took 11 men to help them. A concerted effort was made and the Sangar was reached. They drove out the tribesmen capturing three enemy standards in the process, and it is said that the three sections of the tribesmen represented by these standards went off to their homes. Unfortunately, two men had been left behind, wounded. When he realised this, a Sepoy called Bela Singh leapt over the wall and, joined by two of the Sikhs who had just returned from the sortie, brought the wounded men back to safety. Of the 29 men who had taken part in this action, 14 were wounded, three of them fatally. One of these three was Havildar Kala Singh, the original volunteer; died on 15TH September. Gulistan was continuously under attack from about 8000 Pathans. The relieving force reached Gulistan at 1 pm on 14TH September 1897, thus ending the siege. The 36TH Sikhs had been under continuous fire since 9 am on 12TH, a total of 52 hours, suffering 44 men killed or wounded. For their stout-hearted defence of these posts 36TH Sikhs were later awarded the battle-honour 'Samana', a distinction held by no other regiment, British or Indian. Twenty-nine Sikh officers and men were awarded the Indian Order of Merit for their conspicuous gallantry at Ft.Cavagnari.

Pictured here are the survivors of 36TH Sikhs sortie party, with three enemy standards they captured during their attack.

North-West Frontier, 1881-1901

Chakdara Fort, 1897

Chakdara Fort, ten miles away from Malakand, had a garrison of 180 men of 5TH Sikhs and 20 Sowars of 11TH Bengal Lancers. On 26TH July 1897, hordes of Swatis threw themselves at the west side of the fort and were driven back by the garrison. They tried again from the northeast, then the east, then the south. This continued all day and night until 4 am. Later in the morning, a 40-strong party of 11TH Bengal Lancers managed to fight their way into Chakdara. The fighting continued with mass attacks and continuous sniping for three days and nights. Apart from the Sepoys and Sowars in Chakdara itself, there was a detachment of 16 men of 45TH Sikhs, led by Lance-Naik Vir Singh, in a blockhouse tower located on a spur of one of the mountains, 500 yards from the fort. The blockhouse was used as a signalling post so that Chakdara could keep in contact with Malakand using heliograph. The sentries at Malakand received one message on 1ST August; it simply said, "Help us". Luckily, the blockhouse was easily defendable, even when the enemy tried to set fire to it, but it depended on the fort for supplies, and shortage of water was a big problem for 16 men at the height of summer. Towards the end of the 7-day siege, more and more men reinforced the tribesmen so that, whereas the garrison was outnumbered about 8-1 on 26TH, by 1ST August they were outnumbered 50-1. The final and most unnerving part of the siege occurred at daybreak on 2ND August; when a mass attack of between 10,000 and 14,000 tribesmen bore down on the fort in a last ditch effort to overcome the defenders. This battle lasted two desperate hours until the extraction of the tribesmen, mostly with the use of the bayonet.

45TH Sikhs

Siege heroes: Some of the six British officers and 240 Indian troops from 45TH Sikhs who held off 14,000 Pakhtun warriors for six days in 1897 before their fort at Chakdara was relieved by a force accompanied by Winston Churchill.

North-West Frontier, 1881-1901

Shabkadr, 1897

In August 1897, the Mohmand tribe, inspired by the Mullah of Hadda, Najib-ud-din, attacked the village of Shankargarh, some 18 miles north of Peshawar. Most of the villagers had taken refuge in the Shabkadr fort and the Mohmands, who numbered about four to five thousand, made a planned assault on the fort. The fort stood on a mound and had 50 ft. high walls. It was held by a detachment of Border Police, who managed to repel that first attack. The 13TH Bengal Lancers went to the relief of Shabkadr fort and chased the Mohmands back to the hills.

Tseri Kandao, 1897

At Tseri Kandao the Sikhs, numbered by perhaps about 60, were hard pressed against the enemy attacks. However, they commenced to move forward towards the enemy, shouting their war cries. The Sikh muskets and bayonets met the Pathan rush, shooting them down with savage energy. The Pathans were repulsed with terrible slaughter.

Dargai, 1897

There were some 12,000 Afridis on the heights of Dargai in strongly built Sangars, their standards bravely mocking the troops far below. Covered by the divisional artillery and despite heroic efforts, the attackers had to take cover in dead ground. The Gurkhas were the first to attack but were pinned down at the base of the cliffs. The Dorset Regiment followed a couple of hours later and was also pinned down. Then occurred one of the most famous attacks on the Frontier. The Gordon Highlanders and 3RD Sikhs stormed the Dargai Heights. With bayonets glinting in the bright sunlight, they charged across the glacis, past the trapped Gurkhas and Dorsets, and on, up the narrow twisting path, scrambling ever higher towards the muzzle flashes in the Sangars, while all the way, above the shouts and yells, the crash and the rattle of musketry, the pipes screamed their ancient rant with the Sikh cries of "Khalsa! Khalsa! Sat Siri Akal" The Afridis knew it was time to go and everywhere gave way and ran. Soon the Highlanders and the Sikhs crowned the heights and Dargai was won.

Sikhs and Gordon Highlanders assault Dargai Heights
(The Illustrated London News)

North-West Frontier, 1881-1901

The Frontier, 1901

Under the new Viceroy, George Nathaniel Curzon, in 1901 the settled districts of the Frontier separated from the Punjab to form, with the Political Agencies of Malakand, Khyber, Kurram, Tochi, and Wana, and other tribal territory up to the Durand Line, the North-West Frontier Province. This was placed in the charge of a Chief Commissioner who was to be appointed by, and directly responsible to the Government of India, for the administration and political control of the tribal belt. Concurrent with the establishment of the province came new security policy. Curzon summarised the changes as "withdrawal of British forces from advanced positions, employment of tribal forces in defence of tribal territory, concentration of British forces in British territory behind them as a safeguard and a support, improvement of communications in the rear". (Chhabra, 2005) Some of the tribal forces, like the Khyber Rifles, had existed for sometime, and others, like the Kurram, Zhob, North and South Waziristan Militias, Chitral Scouts, came into being, all being placed on a proper military footing under British officers seconded from the Indian Army. Controlled by the Political Agents and formed into wings of 500 lightly armed infantrymen, the Militias were stationed in forts from which smaller garrisons were found for outlying posts. To stiffen up these forces stood the Sikh soldiers on the borders.

First World War, 1914

With the outbreak of war in Europe, India, the Crown Jewel of the British Empire, joined the Allies in battle on 4TH of August 1914. India contributed most volunteers of any of the British imperial holdings that fought in the war. India produced between 900,000 to 1.5 million troops for combat by 1919. Of these troops, the Sikhs, one of the loyal 'martial races' of the British Raj, rallied in enormous numbers for the defence of the British Empire and Europe. At the beginning of the war, Sikh military personnel numbered around 35,000 men of the 161,000 troops of the Indian Army, around 22 percent of the armed forces, yet the Sikhs only made up less than 2 percent of the total Indian population. By the end of the war, 100,000 Sikh volunteers joined the British Armed forces. They went to fight on almost all the fighting fronts. From France, Gallipoli, Salonika, Egypt, Somaliland, East Africa, Aden, Palestine, Syria, Mesopotamia, Persia and the Caucasus.

By the end of the war the Sikhs had won 291 Indian Order of Merits, 27 Military Crosses, 796 Indian Distinguished Service Medals, 13 Croix De Guerre (France), eight Croix De Guerre (Belgium) 12 Medaille Militaire (France) and 15 Crosses of St. George (Russia) and numerous Italian and Serbian Gallantry Awards. They were also awarded 60 Battle Honours to carry on their Regimental Colours.

The British, Distinguished Conduct Medal, is the second highest award for gallantry in action, after the Victoria Cross. Only Seven DCM medals were ever awarded to the Indian soldiers of whom four were awarded to the Sikh gunners of Hong Kong and Singapore Royal Artillery who served with the Imperial Camel Corps in the Western desert and Palestine during the First World War.

THIRD AFGHAN WAR

Sensing post-First World War British fatigue and the frailty of British positions along the Afghan border, Amanullah, the new ruler of Afghanistan, suddenly attacked the British in May 1919 in two thrusts. The British were taken by surprise, and Afghan forces achieved some success in the early days of the war, as Pakhtun tribesmen from both sides of the border joined forces with them. In 1919, the Afghan regular army was a very formidable force and was able to muster some 50,000 men. These men were organised into 21 cavalry and 75 infantry regiments, with about 280 modern artillery pieces, organised into 70 batteries, in support. In addition to this, however, in a boost to the army's strength, the Afghan command could call upon the loyalty of up to 80,000 frontier tribesmen and an indeterminate number of deserters from local militia units under British command. In reality, the Afghan regular army was not ready for war. In meeting this threat, the British could call on a much larger force. The British and Indian Army, not including frontier militia, totalled eight divisions, as well as five independent brigades of infantry and three of cavalry. However, of this force the entire North-West Frontier Province had three infantry divisions and two cavalry brigades, although there was also GHQ India's central reserve of one infantry division and one cavalry brigade. From this, they formed a striking force of two infantry divisions and two cavalry brigades for offensive operations on the Khyber front, with the possibility of using it also in the Tochi and Kurram areas. The troops in India were no longer of the standard that they might otherwise have been at another time. Coming just after the end of a very costly war in Europe, the British will to fight and military-industrial capability to fight another war was very low. The Indian Army had been heavily committed to the First World War and had suffered a large number of casualties. Many of its units still had not returned from overseas, and those that had, had begun a process of demobilisation and as such many regiments had lost almost all their most experienced men. Likewise, the British Army in India had been gutted. Prior to 1914 there had been 61 British regiments serving in India. However, of these all but 10 (two cavalry and eight infantry) had been withdrawn in order to fight in Europe or the Middle East.

Third Afghan War

The conflict began on 3RD May 1919 when Afghan troops crossed the frontier at the western end of the Khyber Pass and captured the town of Bagh. The town was strategically important to the British and Indians as it provided water to Landi Kotal, which was at the time garrisoned by just two companies of troops from the Indian Army. Although initially considered a minor border infraction, this attack was actually part of the wider invasion plan. For whatever reason, the attack was launched ahead of schedule. Amanullah had initially intended to time it to coincide with an uprising being planned in Peshawar for 8TH May. In response to the Afghan attack, the Indian government declared war upon Afghanistan on 6TH May and ordered a general mobilisation of the British and Indian forces. It was decided next that the two companies at Landi Kotal needed to be reinforced, so on 7TH May, 2ND Battalion, Somerset Light Infantry were brought up clandestinely through the Khyber Pass aboard a convoy of 67 Lorries. Meanwhile, a cordon was thrown around Peshawar and demands were made for the population to hand over the uprising's ringleaders. Amid threats that the city's water supply would be cut, the inhabitants complied and by dawn on 8TH May the situation in the city was under control and the threat of an uprising abated. By this stage, more reinforcements were available and the garrison at Landi Kotal grew to Brigade-size. On 9TH May, the British and Indian troops launched an attack on the Afghans, who had seized Bagh the previous week. The attack, however, failed when the brigade commander decided to split his forces and detach almost half his force to protect his flank and as a result was unable to achieve the necessary concentration of force to capture all of his objectives. Two days later on 11TH May a second attack was made on Bagh by the Landi Kotal brigade and this time it proved successful. The rout was total and the tribesman, who were expected to counterattack in support of the Afghan army decided against doing so, instead turning their efforts to looting the battlefield and gathering the arms and ammunition that the retreating Afghan army had left behind. The British decided that it was prudent to continue the advance and the army to pursue the Afghans across the border. On 13TH May, British and Indian troops seized control of the western Khyber and occupied Dacca, however, the British camp was poorly sited for defence, and consequently they came under an intense long-range artillery barrage from Afghan artillery before Amanullah launched an infantry assault on them. This assault was defeated and the British launched a counter-attack the following day, however, they were unable to consolidate their position and as a result, it was not until 17TH May that the area was secured and the Afghans withdrew. Meanwhile, the previous day, British and Indian forces had launched an attack on 'Stonehenge Ridge'. Under cover of a preliminary bombardment to soften up the Afghan defences, men from 11TH Sikh Regiment had launched the initial assault. However, they were forced to stop their attack when they ran out of ammunition at 08.00 hours and although a resupply was effected at 10.30 hours it was not until 14.00 hours that the attack was able to be recommenced.

By this time, the troops were exposed to the heat of the day. Nevertheless, after another barrage was called down, the Sikhs attacked the Afghan line and despite the heat, the attack was carried to the top of the ridge. Upon reaching the escarpment, they found that the Afghans had abandoned the battlefield, leaving behind most of their equipment, artillery and a number of regimental standards. At this time, however, trouble struck in the British rear along their line of communications through the Khyber, where the Khyber Rifles had become disaffected by the situation and began to dessert en masse. As a result, the British decided to disarm the remaining soldiers and disband the regiment in an effort to stop the spread of similar sentiment to other regiments. On 27TH May, the British commander in Quetta attacked and captured the Afghan fortress at Spin Baldak and seized the initiative in the south; however, the situation in the centre of the war zone, around Kurram, remained desperate for the British. The Afghans in this area, under the command of General Nadir Khan, possessed a force of some 14 regiments. Against this, the British at Thal, under Brigadier General Alexander Eustace, possessed only four regiments. To make matters worse, the only troops protecting the upper Tochi Valley were the disaffected North Waziristan Militia. Concerned that they would rise up against him if left to their own devices, Eustace gave the order to abandon the militia outposts, but in doing so precipitated the desertion of the militiamen. This disaffection spread to the South Waziristan Militia in Wana, who turned on their officers and attacked the men who had remained loyal. The survivors, under Major Russell, fought their way out to join a column of the North Zhob Militia, who were on their way to relieve them. Seeing that the situation was deteriorating for the British and seeing an opportunity, Nadir Khan decided to attack the Thal fort. A large Afghan regular force besieged the fort, garrisoned by Sikhs, Gurkha Rifles and a squadron of Indian cavalry. As the Frontier Constabulary had abandoned their posts, the Afghans were able to occupy a tower 500 yards from the fort and from there they were able to set fire to a number of food dumps. These made the situation in the fort dire, as the supply situation had already been low, however, other factors stacked up against the British. Eustace's force was outnumbered, outgunned, and outclassed. He possessed no regular British infantry and his four battalions were all inexperienced Indian units, consisting mainly of young recruits. As a result of this, the British decided to divert the division, which had arrived in Peshawar from Lahore, with the purpose of advancing on Jalalabad and have it move up to Kurram. While part of the division was detached to defend Kohat, a brigade under Brigadier General Reginald Dyer set out to relieve Eustace's force at Thal. Dyer's force consisted of only one British battalion, the London Regiment, the rest were Sikhs, Dogras, Punjabis and Gurkhas and short of rations and possessing no transport, they were forced to march through intense heat to effect the relief.

Third Afghan War

On 1ST June, they ran into a blocking force of tribesman that barred both the northern and southern approaches to Thal. Dyer attacked both ends with his artillery, while sending his infantry against the southern approach. Unable to withstand the attack, the tribesmen withdrew and as a result, the way through to Eustace's garrison was cleared. The next day, 2ND June, at dawn, Dyer's brigade launched an attack on the Afghan regulars that were positioned away to the west of Thal and as this attack went in, Nadir Khan sent out an envoy to deliver a message to the brigade commander. The message told Dyer that Amir Amanullah had ordered Nadir Khan to cease hostilities and Nadir Khan asked Dyer to acknowledge that he would honour the request for an armistice that Amanullah had sent to the Indian government on 31ST May. Unaware that this request had been made, Dyer decided that he would not take any chances and sent the reply: "My guns will give an immediate reply, but your letter will be forwarded to the Divisional Commander". After this Dyer continued his attack and as Nadir Khan's force withdrew from the area, Dyer followed them up with cavalry and armoured cars, while the RAF dispersed the tribesmen that were in the area, which posed a threat of counter attack. On 3RD June, the Afghan camp at Yusef Khel was seized and the armistice was signed. With this a cease-fire came into affect, however, it was not until 8TH August 1919 that the settlement was finally concluded, when the Treaty of Rawalpindi was signed.

The Afghan war ended but this did not improve the situation in Waziristan. A British officer wrote: " At no time in their history had the Mahsuds and Wazirs been so well armed as at this junture, since in additon to their normal armament, considerable quantities of government rifle and ammunition had fallen recently into their hands. To supplement their stocks the tribesmen had received large supplies of ammunition through the agency of anti-British Afghan officials in Khost. These tribesmen have long been remarkable for their courage, activity and hardihood, and when the mountinous and difficult nature of their country is considered, together with the fact that their numbers included about 1,800 army deserters and so highly trained in our tactics and methods of fighting, it will be realized that they constituted a formidable enemy." (General Staff, Army Headquarters, India, 1921)

WAZIRISTAN

During the Third Afghan War, certain tribes of Waziristan made common cause with the Afghans, but at the time, the government of India had not found it convenient to punish them in the manner deserved. The Afghan menace being checked, both the Tochi Wazirs and the Mahsuds were summoned to attend meetings to hear the terms, which the Government intended to impose upon them. In the event of these terms not being accepted, it was proposed to deal first with the Wazirs and later with the Mahsuds. A force of close upon 30,000 men was detailed for any operations, which might become necessary. The offending tribesmen refused to agree to the terms offered them. Consequently, a force named the Derajat Column was assembled at Tank to deal with them.

This was beginning of some of the most difficult and costly operations ever undertaken on the frontier. The morale of the Mahsuds at this time stood at a high level. This was due to their success in several encounters against the British troops during the summer. It was their fervent hope that their actions would compel the British government to discontinue punitive measures against them. That, as in the past, they would succeed in gaining a reduction, if not abrogation of Government's terms, by adopting a threatening attitude. Added to this was their belief that the Great War had reduced the army so greatly in numbers and training that the Mahsuds could defeat any force which could be brought against them.

Jandola Fort, 1919

More than 6,000 Mahsuds and Bhittanis surrounded Jandola fort in the tribal area of South Waziristan, on May 28TH. The tribesmen cut off the fort's water supply, a mile distant from the fort. On the first day of the siege, water was rationed to one water bottle a man a day. The weather was extremely hot and discipline was severely tested by this scarcity of water. On 7TH June a party from the fort rushed out to obtain water, bringing back with them three day's supply. It was during this operation that *Bhishti* (water carrier) Gurdit Singh earned the Indian Order of Merit. He went backwards and forwards continually to carry water. Even after he was wounded, he went out again. On his final trip, his *mashk* (leather water-container) being punctured by bullets in two places, he plugged the holes with his hands, although he was again wounded on his way back. Fortunately, his wounds did not prove fatal and he lived to serve the Battalion for many years.

Waziristan

Spinkai Ghash, 1919

On December 18TH 1919, a military column moved out to take Spinkai Ghash, with the idea of covering the occupation of a camp on Palosina plain, three miles north of Jandola. A Mahsud lashkar about 2,000 strong and about 1,000 Wana Wazirs were on their way to oppose the advance of the column. On 19TH and 20TH, two abortive but costly attempts were made to establish a permanent piquet on Mandanna Hill, which was rushed and captured by the Mahsuds. That evening it was decided to establish a permanent piquet on Black Hill. The units detailed for the task were 82ND Punjabis, 109TH Infantry, and 34TH Sikh Pioneers, supported by some artillery. On 21ST as the units occupied Black Hill unopposed, the Mahsuds rushed the hill from three directions. They drove in the companies of 109TH Infantry and 82ND Punjabis and killed the Company Commander and the Havildar. At this juncture Havildar Maghar Singh took charge and the Sikh Pioneers beat off four attacks and forced the Mahsuds to retire. Havildar Maghar Singh was awarded the well-deserved Indian Order of Merit, the citation reads: "Havildar Maghar Singh was awarded the Indian Order of Merit for conspicuous gallantry and devotion to duty. His company commander having become casualty early in the day, Subedar Maghar Singh although wounded took command and it was due to his fine leadership and example that his company did so well. Although it had suffered heavy casualties, it was one of the last units to withdraw. After withdrawing, although wounded in five places, he helped to reorganize his company and get the wounded under cover."(Duckers, 1999, p.180.)

The Piquets

To secure the Lines of Communication for the advancing force, a system was introduced of establishing permanent piquets at close intervals on the most commanding ground on each side of the route used. These posts were strongly built for all round defence, provided with traverses and protected with thick barbed wire entanglements. Their construction led to the majority of the actions which took place during these operations. The full strength of the Derajat Column had on occasions to be employed to drive the enemy off the ground selected for the various piquets and then to cover and support the working parties whilst the defensive works were being constructed.

Sketch of 45TH Sikhs in Waziristan

Waziristan

Tarakai, December 1919

Two companies of 34TH Sikh Pioneers started constructing the piquet position at Tarakai, building walls and putting up wire, under the protection of 82ND Punjabis. The Pioneers were infantry trained and also performed simple engineering tasks. They had built up a reputation as dour, dogged fighters. They had piled arms fifty yards below the work-site, rolled up their sleeves and started collecting boulders for the Sangar-wall. Only sporadic sniping interrupted the first hour's work. Suddenly there was a heavy burst of rifle fire and a solid mass of several hundred tribesmen emerged from dead ground and dashed towards the piquet, yelling, shooting and brandishing swords and knives. The covering parties lost their nerve and fled. A British officer of 82ND Punjabis tried to shame his men into holding fast and advancing again on top of the hill. 'If you won't follow me,' he shouted, 'I will go alone.' They let him go alone. The Pioneers also ran – but only as far as their piled rifles. Grabbing these, they dashed back to the Sangar, just in time. The walls were only two feet high and there was but one strand of barbed wire stretched across the front, but these were better than nothing. The four British officers in the post, with a Lewis-gun each, were the mainstay of the defence. Charge after charge of the tribesmen was checked by the puny strand of wire. Their onslaught withered away under fire from Lewis guns and the Pioneer's rifles. With ammunition running low, a Jemadar and a seventeen-year old bugler, Sangat Singh, who had no rifle, went down to organize a working party to bring more ammunition from a dump at the bottom of the hill. On their way back, a tribesman in ambush fired at the Jemadar at point blank range, and missed; the Jemadar fired back and missed. Sangat Singh then went for him with a pickaxe and did not miss. He arrived back at the Sangar gleefully carrying his victim's rifle and ammunition. There they found the most savage hand-to-hand fight raging. The post was designed to hold 120 men, and there must have been at least 300 packed into it, hacking and thrusting, slashing and stabbing as a century's hatred between Pathan and Sikh exploded. Then the Regimental Havildar Major roared out with a drill instructor's voice the Sikh war cry. They all took up the war cry and with a concerted effort expelled the Mahsuds from the Sangar. Of the 250 Sikh Pioneers in that action, 189 were either killed or wounded.

The period from 17TH to 28TH December formed the first phase in the operations against the tribesmen. The losses that they had sustained caused the Lashkars to disperse to their homes. Their heavy casualties made them, for a time at least, desist from pursuing the rushing tactics they had used so successfully in their encounters with the Indian troops. During this period, permanent piquets were established at various points in order to complete the defence of the road and give adequate protection to the army conveys.

Waziristan

Ahnai Tangi, December 1919

The Mahsuds were not willing to have roads, posts, and troops in their territory and prepared for a second and more desperate struggle. The fighting continued for about twelve months and the British had to resort to using aircraft on a number of occasions to suppress the tribesmen. There were a number of successes though, notably 5TH Gurkhas' stand during the eight-day battle in January 1920 at Ahnai Tangi, and the efforts of 76TH Punjabis who fought their way through to support them. The Mahsuds took heavy casualties during the fighting at Ahnai Tangi, and it was these casualties that subdued them. The tribesmen owned to 400 dead at the end of this fight. After the heaviest fight in the annals of the Frontier, the road to Mahsud land lay open. The General Officer Commanding Wazir Force paid the following tribute to 76TH Punjabis.

"From December till now 76TH Punjabis have fought splendidly. Whenever they have been ordered to attack they have attacked with great heart and bravery and they have won. General Skeen, the column commander, has told me that whatever task he has asked this regiment to do, they have carried it out splendidly. Undoubtedly this is a second–line battalion, but they have done the best of any regiments here, and on 14TH January they fought with the greatest bravery and fortitude. My hope is that every regiment will do likewise." (Qureshi, 1958, p.255) By the beginning of April, 1920, all major resistance by the Mahsuds had ceased and the Derajat Column was dispersed.

Haidari Kach, 1921

During the fighting at Haidari Kach, Sepoy Ishar Singh won the unique peacetime Victoria Cross. The citation reads: "For most conspicuous bravery and devotion to duty on 10TH April 1921, near Haidari Kach (Waziristan). When the convoy protection troops were attacked, he received a very severe gunshot wound in the chest, and fell beside his Lewis gun. Hand-to-hand fighting having commenced, the British officer, Indian officer, and all the Havildars of his company were either killed or wounded, and the enemy seized his Lewis gun. Calling up two other men, he got up, charged the enemy, recovered the Lewis gun, and, although, bleeding profusely, again got the gun into action. When his Jemadar arrived, he took the gun from Sepoy Ishar Singh, and ordered him to go back and have his wound dressed. Instead of doing, this Sepoy went to the medical officer, and was of great assistance in pointing out where the wounded were, and in carrying water to them. He made innumerable journeys to the river and back for this purpose. On one occasion, when the enemy fire was very heavy, he took the rifle of a wounded man and helped to keep down the fire. On another occasion, he stood in front of the medical officer who was dressing, a wounded man, thus shielding him with his body. It was over three hours before he finally submitted to be evacuated, being then too weak from loss of blood to object. His gallantry and devotion to duty were beyond praise."

Waziristan

Rogha Kot, March 1921

On March 17TH the road protection troops from Wana and Tanai had established communication with the military convoys; the down convoy from Wana had passed through, and the up convoy was about half a mile west of Rogha Kot when it was fired on at close range. By some misunderstanding, an important hill had not been occupied by the troops. The enemy, quick to notice the omission, had promptly seized the hill, held it in strength, and was pouring heavy fire on the convoy. The leading company of 58TH Rifles managed to establish itself on a ridge and a permanent piquet of the regiment, on the far bank of the stream, gave useful support with its Lewis gun. In the meantime, signaller Sepoy Kartar Singh, who had hitherto been unable to open communication with the troops, now very gallantly came out in the open to try to get a message through, but was killed while in the act of sending it. Sepoy Kartar Singh was awarded the Indian Order of Merit, posthumously. The road protection troops had several encounters with the enemy. On 5TH April the tribesmen made an attempt to capture the down convoy and an action ensued in which the escort held the enemy off in a rearguard action, in which four Sepoys were wounded. Subedar Kehar Singh, commanding a platoon on the exposed flank, behaved with conspicuous coolness and gallantry, for which he was awarded the Indian Distinguished Service Medal.

Tora Tizha, April 1921

A piquet of twenty-eight rifles and two Lewis guns, under Havildars Jiwan Singh and Lal Singh of 58TH Rifles, was sent to occupy a hill known as Tora Tizha. Havildar Jiwan Singh's leading platoon suddenly came under heavy and accurate rifle fire, whereby the whole of the accompanying Lewis gun section was wiped out. At the same time, forty of the Wazirs, armed with knives, charged down upon the right flank of the platoon. Supported by the platoon under Havildar Lal Singh, the attack was beaten off and heavy loss inflicted on the assailants. For their conspicuous gallantry, Havildar Jiwan Singh was awarded the Indian Order of Merit, while Havildar Lal Singh received the Indian Distinguished Service Medal.

Waziristan

About 20TH December, Wana force was broken up and the units dispersed to their several garrisons. They were replaced by local levies. Thus ended the Waziristan campaign of unparalleled hard fighting and severity. The enemy fought with determination and courage, which has rarely, if ever, been encountered by the troops in similar operations. The character of the terrain, combined with trying and arduous climatic conditions, presented difficulties before which the most seasoned troops might well have hesitated. The resistance of the enemy was broken and difficulties successfully overcome by a force composed almost entirely of young Punjabi troops.

Waziristan

For a time the Waziristan remained at peace. The countryside was in a more settled and peaceful state than had been the case at any time since the end of the Great War. Mobile training columns from the Garrisons of Razmak, Bannu, Wana, and Mir Ali moved about the country continuously under their own protection. Except for a little sniping with hostile tribesmen, the above operations were entirely peaceful until the arrival of the Faqir of Ipi.

Islam Bibi, 1936

In 1936, a Hindu girl eloped with a young Muslim student. The girl's relatives brought a charge of abduction against the student and the girl's family recovered the girl. In the meantime, the Muslims alleged that she had been converted to Islam, taking the name of Islam Bibi. The decision of the Court at the trial which commenced, was that the girl should be given to the Muslim community. On appeal later, this decision was reversed and the Hindu community was made her custodians.

Faqir of Ipi, November 1936

The Faqir of Ipi took up the issue of Islam Bibi. The quiet Mullah, turned fanatic, led the Duars, a fanatically minded tribe, on Bannu, where the case was to come up again. Action was taken against the tribe, their Lashkar dispersed and their leaders arrested, all save the Faqir, who escaped. The Faqir skilfully intensified his propaganda and managed to unite the tribes of Tori Khel Wazirs, the Mahsuds, and Bhittanis, normally in a state of feud with each other, against the British. A military column sent to Khaisora valley in November 1936, met unusual resistance and the Government decided to build a road from Mir Ali to the Khaisora valley to ensure peace in the disturbed area. By January, the road was completed and Waziristan appeared to be returning to normal, but this did not last long. The Faqir continued his propaganda and gained considerable support from the tribesmen, who feared the construction of the Khaisora road was only a preliminary to the building of more roads and the eventual destruction of tribal independence, by means of making the country accessible to troops. The rising hostility manifested itself in early February 1937, when two British officers were murdered, one in Mahsud and the other in Wazir territory. These outrages were followed by many other hostile acts, which created an alarming situation.

Faqir of Ipi

Waziristan

Tori Khel, December 1936

For the next year trouble and insurrection spread throughout Waziristan, as Wazirs, Mahsuds, Bhittanis and even Afghans from across the border rallied to support the Fakir's cause. By April 1937, four extra brigades had been brought in to reinforce the garrisons at Razmak, Bannu and Wana. At the height of the campaign in 1937; some 60,000 regular and irregular troops were employed by the British in an effort to bring to battle an estimated 4,000 hostile tribesmen. The British attempted to stamp out the insurrection by drawing the lashkars into decisive engagement, but the tribesmen managed to avoid being drawn into battle. Using guerilla tactics of ambush, they inflicted considerable casualties upon the British and Indian troops. In May 1937, two brigades advanced against the heart of hostile activity on the Sham plain, the watershed between the Khaisora and Shaktu valleys, prior to striking at Arsal Kot, a village where the Faqir had a stronghold. As one brigade prepared to advance against the high ground held by 4,000 tribesmen, the Bannu brigade made a daring and hazardous night march up the Iblanke spur to the east. It was pitch dark and the going extremely difficult, but by dawn the troops were in position across the enemy's right flank and rear. The Mountain Battery gunners and machine gunners of the infantry destroyed towers beyond Dakai Kalai, where considerable resistance was experienced. The 2ND Punjabis had to be extricated by the artillery and 11TH Sikhs from a nasty position, in which assistance from the air had to be called in. The Faqir fled to Arsal Kot, which was subjected to constant air bombing. By 14TH both Brigades were back in their stations, having for the time being completely destroyed Faqir's supporters and the Tori Khel accepted Government terms.

Shahur Tangi, April 1937

Shahur Tangi is a narrow gorge winding some three miles through precipitous unclimbable hills, through which runs the Wana-Manzai road. In April 1937, as a convoy entered the Shahur Tangi, a murderous fire was opened on it. Drivers were killed, Lorries splayed all over the road, which was blocked and as officers and men jumped out, they were shot down. The convoy escort, in close combat beat off all the attacks throughout a very long day. They sustained heavy casualties in their magnificent stand, eight killed, and 13 wounded. Not a rifle, bayonet, or round of ammunition fell into the hands of the tribesmen. The tribesmen themselves, under the leadership of a well-known outlaw, Khonia Khan, also suffered severely. An immediate award of the Indian Distinguished Service Medal was made to Company Havildar Major Kehar Singh. The Faqir was never captured but largely Waziristan quietened down and was to remain so for the next eight years. This was just as well, for from 1939 onwards larger and more pressing tasks claimed the attention of the British and Indian armies.

NORTH-WEST FRONTIER, 1923-1947

It would hardly be correct to say that Northwest Frontier Province was at 'peace', since 'peace' as understood in settled or administered Districts has never been applicable to Northwest Frontier Province. Nevertheless the countryside was in a more settled and peaceful state than had been the case at any time since the end of the Great War 1914-1918. Mobile training columns from the garrisons at Razmak, Bannu, and Mir Ali moved about the country continuously under their own protection. Opposition to any of these bodies had not been encountered for years, their camps were seldom even sniped at night, and the tribesmen generally treated both troops and Militia with a considerable degree of respect. Concerning the Regular troops quartered in Waziristan, these did tour of duty for two years, so that in any one year half the garrison of Waziristan was under replacement by fresh troops from India. Regular troops arriving in the Northwest Frontier Province were never allowed to gain the impression that they were in a 'peace station'. Although the phrase 'Semi active service conditions' was being used in official parlance in to Northwest Frontier Province at this time, the troops were trained always to be ready for hostilities at any time. One of the ways by which the Government exercised control over tribes was by means of tribal allowances.

For years, the Sikh soldier had looked to the mountain ranges and high passes of the Northwest; that was where the threat to India lay, out of Central Asia. That region had to be kept stable and secure by watch, ward, and countless expeditions. It was the way the invader had always come, back over the centuries. The Sikhs had wrested Afghan territories to secure the frontier of the Sikh Kingdom. After the fall of the Sikh Kingdom, they had for nigh on a hundred years policed the most sensitive border of the British Empire. The British bestowed the frontier territories upon the Muslims, when they created Pakistan.

11TH Sikh Regiment in action in Waziristan, 1936.

NORTH-EAST FRONTIER

North-East territories of India had been added to India during the British Raj, when British colonial authorities annexed traditionally separate Border States into Indian Territory, to form a buffer between their dominion and external powers. The annexation of the Border States was carried out by the formed regiments of the Indian army. The defence was entrusted to locally raised para military police forces that recruited Sikhs and other Punjabis in considerable numbers. However the Sikhs were not answering so well in Assam as they had done in Burma. The recruiting in their case was stopped for Assam after a few years. As per the North-West Frontier, the Sikh soldier secured and policed the North–East Frontier of British India until 1947 and continues to guard the frontiers of his homeland to this day.

Anglo-Gurkha War, 1814–16,

In 1801, the East India Company occupied the Gorakpur district with which the Gurkhas in Terai became conterminous with the uncertain and ill-defined northern frontier of the British dominions and Nepal. At that time the Gurkhas had conquered Bhutwal, however, the East India Company wrested Bhutwal from them. Thus, the conflicting interest of the Gurkhas and the British sowed the seeds of war. In May 1814, the Gurkhas attacked three British police stations in Bhutwal. In October, Governor-General Lord Hastings declared a war against the Gurkhas. Lord Hastings himself took charge of the war and decided to attack the Gurkhas at four points along the entire line of Satluj to Kosi. To vanquish the Gurkhas was not an easy task for Lord Hastings. It was very difficult for the British soldiers to go through the mountainous region. Major-Generals Marley and John Wood, who were to advance towards Nepal capital, retreated after some unsuccessful attempts. General Gillespie lost his life in Kalanga. Major-General Martindell was defeated at Jaitak. However, all these losses were again retrieved in April 1815, when Colonels Nicholls and Gardener captured Almora in Kumaon and on May 15TH 1815, when General Ochterlony compelled the Gurkha leader Amar Singh Thapa, to surrender the fort of Malaon. Finally, on November 28TH 1815, the Gurkhas signed a treaty of Sagauli. The Nepal Government hesitated to ratify the treaty and the hostilities began again. General Ochterlony advanced towards the Nepal capital and defeated the Gurkhas at Makwanpur on February 28TH 1816. This compelled the Nepal Government to ratify the treaty. As per the treaty, the Nepalese gave up their claims to places in the lowlands along the southern frontier, gave away Garhwal and Kumaon on the west of Nepal to the British, and withdrew from Sikkim. They also agreed to receive a British Resident at Kathmandu. The Nepal Government has ever since remained true to its alliance with the English.[*]

*According to the alliance between Britain and the Sikh Princely state of Patiala, the Patiala state force of Infantry and Cavalry served throughout the Anglo–Gurkha war, alongside the British forces, with great distinction.

North-East Frontier

Sikkim, 1817

During the reign of Tenzing Namgyal, Nepali forces occupied large chunks of Sikkim territory, forcing the Namgyal to flee to Tibet. The Nepali aggression emboldened them to penetrate even into Tibet. This led to Chinese intervention in which Nepal forces were defeated. In China-Nepal treaty, Sikkim lost some of its land to Nepal, but monarchy was restored in the country. Tenzing Namgyal died in Lhasa (Tibet capital) and his son Tsudphud Namgyal was consecrated as Sikkim's Chogyal (King). Following the arrival of the British in India, Sikkim allied with them against their common enemy, Nepal. The defeat of Nepal by the Chinese did little to weaken the Nepalese. They continued to make attacks into neighbouring Sikkim, overrunning most of the region including the Terai. This prompted the British to attack Nepal in 1814. At the conclusion of the war, the Nepalese were confined to their own territory and Anglo – Sikkim's treaty was concluded whereby Sikkim Raja was confirmed in his own dominions. However, ties between Sikkim and the British weakened when the latter began taxation of the Morang region. In 1849 two British doctors, Sir Joseph Dalton Hooker and Dr. Archibald Campbell, the latter being in charge of relations between the British and Sikkim Government, ventured into the mountains of Sikkim unannounced and unauthorised. The Sikkim government detained the doctors, leading to a punitive British expedition against the Himalayan kingdom, after which the districts of Darjeeling and Morang were annexed to British India. The loss of Darjeeling soon became a source of constant jealousy and annoyance to the Sikkim authorities, offering as it did an asylum for escaped slaves. In 1860, the British resolved to occupy Sikkim territory, in order to enforce the restitutions of the persons kidnapped and to ensure a correct attitude on the part of the Sikkim Durbar. After successful operations, a new treaty was concluded by which Sikkim recognized the suzerainty of Great Britain.

A Lepcha man of Sikkim

North-East Frontier

Sikkim (Cont.)

The Maharajah of Sikkim, often protected by Britain in the past, and contrary to his treaty obligation, had resided in Tibet for two years and acquiesced in the invasion of his country. In 1886, 300 hundred Tibetans crossed the frontier and occupied Lingtu in Sikkim, fortifying a position across the trade routes to Tibet from Darjeeling. The Sikkim Expeditionary Force, which included 32ND Sikh Pioneers, was despatched from India to expel the Tibetans. Half a company of the Sikh Pioneers, under Jemadar Nihal Singh, made a reconnaissance and were fired at by Tibetans from a stockade concealed in the jungle. As soon as the main body of Pioneers came up, they stormed the stockade. The Sikh Pioneers, with their bayonets fixed, advanced without firing, to the accompaniment of a fusillade of rifles and muskets, of flying stones and poisoned arrows by the Tibetans. The stockade was soon taken and the Pioneers pursued the now flying enemy for a mile and then pulled up. The Tibetans, with miserable arms, had no real aptitude or heart for battle but came forward again, advancing out of arrogance and bravado. They were defeated and expelled from the country and China recognized Britain's suzerainty over Sikkim by the convention of 1890. Sikkim became a British protectorate and was granted more sovereignty over the next three decades. After India became independent of Britain in 1947, Sikkim became an Indian protectorate. Soon there were rumblings in Sikkim's political rank and file, which demanded the removal of monarchy and the establishment of a democratic setup, which led to wide spread agitation against Sikkim Monarchy. In the process administration completely collapsed in the kingdom and the Kazi (Prime Minister) appealed to the Indian Parliament for a change in Sikkim's status, so that it could become a state of India. At the request of the Prime Minister, the Indian Army took over the city of Gangtok and disarmed the Palace Guards. A referendum was held in which 97.5 percent of the voting people voted to join the Indian Union. A few weeks later, on 16TH May 1975, Sikkim officially became the 22ND state of the Indian Union and the monarchy was abolished.

Maharaja of Sikkim, (1874 - 1914)

North -East Frontier

Assam, 1820

According to tradition, Sikhs came to Assam on an invitation from the Ahom (king) to defend Assamese liberty against the Burmese. King Viswanarayan, sought Maharaja Ranjit Singh's help against the Burmese army. Accordingly, Maharaja Ranjit Singh dispatched 500 Sikh soldiers under the leadership of General Chetan Singh to Assam. The Sikhs fought in a pitched engagement at Hadirachaki and many paid the supreme sacrifice in defence of Assam. After defeating the Burmese, those who survived did not return to the Punjab. They married Assamese women and identified themselves as Assamese Sikhs.

Assam, 1838

After the Burmese invasion of Assam, the British began their campaign against Burma, resulting in the first Anglo-Burma war of 1824-26. During the war, British conquered lower Assam and formally annexed it to British India. The following year they defeated the Burmese in upper Assam, leading to the Treaty of Yandaboo. In March 1828, at the death of King Govinda Chandra, the British annexed the Kachari kingdom under the Doctrine of Lapse. In 1832, they occupied the territories of the Khasi king and increased their influence over the Jaintia ruler. In 1833, upper Assam became a British protectorate under the erstwhile ruler of the kingdom, Purandhar Singh, but in 1838, the region was formally annexed to the British Empire. With the annexation of the Maran/Matak territory in the east in 1839, the annexation of entire Assam was complete. When India got independence, Assam saw the parting of several territories at different times: Arunachal Pradesh was separated in 1948, Nagaland in 1963, Meghalaya in 1977, and eventually Mizoram in 1987.

A family portrait of Assame Sikhs

North-East Frontier

Nagaland, 1838

The Nagas 'the wildest and most turbulent tribes adjacent to the Indian dominions' inhabited the hills that separated Assam from North-West Burma. Although they had maintained friendly relations with the rulers of Assam, their predilection for raiding inspired fear and hatred in all their other neighbours. Naga raids into the Nowgong and Sibsagar districts in the north and Cachar in the south-west commenced soon after the British occupation of the province began. The Angamis were soon found to be the most warlike tribe and most of the subsequent British military activity was directed against them. This went through three distinct phases; between 1832 and 1850 frequent punitive expeditions were launched in an effort to halt raids into British territory; between 1851 and 1865 a policy of non-intervention was adopted; and finally after 1866, a concerted drive towards annexation and control of all Naga territory steadily gained momentum. The less warlike tribes capitulated gladly, looking to the British to protect them from the raids of more aggressive neighbours, but others resisted ferociously. The conflict reached its climax in 1879-80, with the Angamis siege of Kohima and the retaliatory British siege of Konoma, which broke the back of Angamis resistance. After the independence of India in 1947, the area remained a part of the province of Assam. Nationalist activities arose amongst a section of the Nagas, whose Naga National Council demanded a political union of their ancestral and native groups, damaged government and civil infrastructure and attacked government officials and civilians from other states of India. The Union government sent the Indian Army in 1955, to restore order. In 1957, the Government began diplomatic talks with representatives of Naga tribes, and the Naga Hills district of Assam and the Tuensang frontier were united in a single political entity that became a Union territory, directly administered by the Central government with a large degree of autonomy.

Naga Warrior

North -East Frontier

Bhutan

Boundary disputes plagued Bhutanese-British relations. To reconcile their differences, Bhutan sent an emissary to Calcutta in 1787 and the British sent missions to Thimphu in 1815 and 1838. The 1815 mission was inconclusive. The 1838 mission offered a treaty providing for extradition of Bhutanese officials responsible for incursions into Assam, free and unrestricted commerce between India and Bhutan and settlement of Bhutan's debt to the British. In an attempt to protect its independence, Bhutan rejected the British offer. After the British gained control of Lower Assam in 1826, tension between the countries began to rise as Britain exerted its strength. They proceeded in 1841 to annex the formerly Bhutanese controlled Assam Duars (Regions). Early in 1864, Britain sent a peace mission to Bhutan in the wake of the recent conclusion of a civil war there. Bhutan rejected the peace and friendship treaty it offered. Consequently, Britain declared war on Bhutan in November 1864. Bhutan had no regular army and what forces existed were composed of guards armed with matchlocks, bows and arrows, swords, knives and catapults. Some of these guards, carrying shields and wearing chain mail armour, engaged the well-equipped British forces. The Duar War (1864-65) lasted five months and, despite some battlefield victories by Bhutanese forces, resulted in Bhutan's defeat, loss of part of its sovereign territory and forced cession of formerly occupied territories. Under the terms of the Treaty of Sinchula, signed on November 11TH, 1865, Bhutan ceded territories in the Assam Duars and Bengal Duars, as well as the eighty-three-square-kilometre territory of Dewangiri in southeastern Bhutan. In the 1870s and 1880s, renewed competition among regional rivals resulted in the ascendancy of Ugyen Wangchuck, the ponlop of Tongsa. The British government promptly recognized Ugyen Wangchuck and, under British influence, a monarchy was set up in 1907. Three years later, a treaty was signed whereby the British agreed not to interfere in Bhutanese internal affairs and Bhutan allowed Britain to direct its foreign affairs. This role was assumed by independent India after 1947. Two years later, a formal Indo-Bhutanese accord returned the areas of Bhutan annexed by the British, formalized the annual subsidies the country received and defined India's responsibilities in defence and foreign relations.

Fort Dalimkote, Duar war print 1865

North -East Frontier

Manipur, 1891

The first relations of the British with Manipur date from 1762, when the raja solicited British aid to repel a Burmese invasion of his country. The British repelled the Burmese and little communication between the two countries took place until 1824, on the outbreak of the first Burmese War. The Raja invoked British assistance again and the Burmese were finally expelled from both the Assam and the Manipur valleys. The Raja of Manipur, Chandra Kirti Singh, died in 1886 and was succeeded by his eldest son, Sur Chandra Singh. In 1890 another brother, the Senapati (Commander-in-Chief) Tikendrajit Singh, dethroned the Raja. In March 1891, the chief commissioner of Assam (Quinton) marched to Manipur with 400 Sepoys, in order to settle the question of succession. His purpose was to recognize the new ruler and to remove the Senapati. An attempt was made to arrest the Senapati, but after some sharp fighting, Senapati escaped and the Manipuris then attacked the British residency with an overwhelming force. Quinton was compelled to ask for a parley and accompanied by Colonel Skeen, Grimwood, Cossins and Lieutenant Simpson, unarmed, went to the fort to negotiate. They were all treacherously murdered and when the news arrived, the outnumbered Sepoys retreated to Cachar. The murder of the British officials led to a military expedition, in which the regent, Senapati, was captured. After a formal trial, the Senapati and one of the generals of the rebellion were hanged and the regent was transported to the Andaman Islands. But it was decided to preserve the existence of the state and a child of the ruling family, named Chura Chand, of the age of five, was nominated raja. Meanwhile the administration was conducted under British supervision. In May 1907, the government of the state was handed over to Chura Chand. Thereafter, the region saw two kings only - Maharaja Chura Chand Singh (1891-1941) and Maharaja Budhachandra Singh (1941-1949). Manipur merged into independent India in 1949.

The start of the Manipur expedition from Shillong, Assam frontier in 1891

North-East Frontier

Tibet

In May 1841, the 5,000 strong Dogra army in service of the Sikh Kingdom, advanced eastwards in three divisions. Overcoming all the Tibetan and Chinese opposition it set up base at Taklakot in September 1841, after traversing a distance of 450 miles from the Indian frontier. With the onset of severe winter and the lack of provisions, they were overcome by a Sino-Tibetan force on 12TH December 1841. The Tibetans and their Chinese allies then invaded Ladakh but were defeated at the Battle of Chushul. The boundary between Ladakh and Tibet was finally settled by the Treaty of Chushul. At the fall of the Sikh Kingdom, when Britain sold Kashmir to Gulab Singh, they informed the Chinese of their suzerainty over Kashmir and suggested that the Sino-Sikh treaty be amended. The Sino-Sikh treaty was consequently redrafted in August 1846, as desired by the British. Tibet was a vital geographic location; it had served as a springboard for the invasion of Nepal and a threat as a base for attacking India. In 1793 a Chinese army of over 70,000 men had crossed the Himalaya Mountains from Tibet into Nepal on the Indian side, via the Kirong Pass and had dealt a crushing defeat on the Nepalese near their capital. With this understanding the British knew Tibet could be used as a penetrable frontier to attack India and so it could not allow Tibet to be acquired by any hostile power. If Britain's great rival Russia was allowed to establish herself in the rich valley of Lhasa or exert influence in the region, then it would have far-reaching political effects all along the British eastern frontier for over a thousand miles, in the north from Ladakh to Kashmir and in the south from Nepal to Assam. This could have also possibly led to a combination of Himalayan states siding with Russia against British India. It could prove militarily costly for Britain, who would have to go to enormous lengths to ensure that the eastern frontier was fortified and that the standing army would have to be substantially increased.

Sketch of Jingals in action

North-East Frontier

During "The Great Game", a period of rivalry between Russia and Britain, the British desired a representative in Lhasa to monitor and offset Russian influence. At the beginning of the twentieth century the British and Russian Empires were competing for supremacy in Central Asia. To forestall the Russians, in 1904, a British expedition led by Colonel Francis Younghusband was sent to Lhasa to force a trading agreement and to prevent Tibetans from establishing a relationship with the Russians.

"Further west the Great Game was becoming inhibited by the terrible consequences of a false step. The grey and khaki pawns, if they were not jostling each other, could not move of any significance without endangering world peace. Only in Tibet, where neither side's pieces were yet committed might an adroit stroke thwart the adversary's plans before he could put them into effect." (Fleming, 1961 p30.)

Guru, March 1904

Younghusband's mission was expanded into a full scale military force consisting of 23RD and 32ND Sikh Pioneers and 8TH Gurkhas with sixty-five Mounted Infantry, formed from the above regiments. Soon the Mounted infantry was to be raised to one hundred strong, with ten more men from 23RD Pioneers and sixteen from 32ND under the command of Jemadar Prem Singh. Three more Sikh officers were sent for from India i.e. Subedar Sangat Singh, Jemadar Hazara Singh and Jemadar Thakur Singh. By early December, it was poised at the Jelap La Pass, the 14,000 foot entrance into Tibet the "roof of the world". To the hazards of travel over some of the roughest and highest terrain in the world, was added sub-zero winter cold. Conditions were frightful. Rifle-bolts froze into the breaches and subalterns kept the Maxims' bolts warm in their own beds. The troops' clothing, though lavish by the standards of those days, offered no real protection and was, in addition, too bulky to allow free movement for firing. Yet, although scouts kept reporting that they had sighted large Tibetan forces in the hills, Younghusband was not attacked. It was not until the two opposing forces reached the tiny village of Guru on March 31ST, 1904, that they came into direct conflict. Two thousand Tibetan troops were waiting there, blocking the caravan trail, which the British had to follow if they were to get to Gyantse. On March 31ST, 1904, the British reached the Tibetan fortifications. The Tibetan general galloped up and told them to withdraw. Younghusband replied giving them 15 minutes to clear the way. A quarter of an hour passed and nothing happened. Then, slowly the troops advanced until they were covering the Tibetans at point-blank range. Another company of Sikhs was brought up and formed into a line. Younghusband ordered the Sikhs to disarm the Tibetans. As the two forces wrestled with each other, the situation began to turn ugly. Then the Tibetan general, who in a sudden impulse of anger at seeing his orderly being disarmed, drew his pistol and blew off the jaw of the Sikh Sepoy who was taking the arms.

Guru (Cont.)

Fighting broke out instantly. Volley after volley of British bullets crashed into the solid mass of Tibetans. There were certainly 1,500 Tibetans and had they not been fired on promptly, they would have rushed on and easily cut up the 150 Sikh Sepoys confronting them. On the outbreak of the firing, the Tibetans in the Sangars on the hill began throwing stones and firing on the Sikhs and 2ND Mounted Infantry, and then the fight became general. Suddenly Tibetans turned and fled for the village of Guru with the Sikhs, with the two companies of Mounted Infantry in hot pursuit. Guru village was rushed and cleared and as they retreated along the Gyantse road, they were pursued for twelve miles and thoroughly dispersed. After the fight, two companies of 32ND Pioneers and 2ND Mounted Infantry held Guru Village. The total Tibetan loss was 620 killed and wounded, besides the ones taken prisoners.

Red Idol, April 1904

The advance on Gyantse was resumed on 2ND April, but this was not effected without some opposition, for the Tibetans, about 2,000 strong, were found to be occupying a series of ridges above a deep gorge, the Zamdong (the Red Idol). They held a very strong position among some loose boulders on the right, two miles beyond the gully, which the Gurkhas had ascended to make their flank attack. The rocks extended from the bluff cliff to the path, which skirted the stream. No one could ask for better cover; it was most difficult to distinguish the drab-coated Tibetans who lay concealed there. To attack the strong position General Macdonald sent Captain Bethune with one company of 32ND Pioneers, placing Lieutenant Cook with his Maxim on a mound at 500 yards to cover Bethune's advance. Bethune led a frontal attack. The Tibetans fired wildly until the Sikhs with fixed bayonets were within fifty yards of them and then fled up the valley. Not a single man of 32ND was hit during the attack, though one Sepoy was wounded in the pursuit by a bullet in the hand, from a man who lay concealed behind a rock within a few yards of him. While 32ND were dislodging the Tibetans from the path and the rocks above it, the Mounted Infantry galloped through them to reconnoitre ahead and cut off the fugitives in the valley. They also came through the enemy's fire at very close quarters without a casualty. On emerging from the gorge, the Mounted Infantry discovered that the ridge the Tibetans had held was shaped like the letter S, so that by doubling back along an almost parallel valley they were able to intercept the enemy, whom the Gurkhas had driven down the cliffs. The unfortunate Tibetans were now hemmed in between two fires and hardly a man of them escaped. Finally, the Sikhs dashed through the gorge digging the enemy out of caves and from behind boulders. The honour of the day was an award of the Indian Order of Merit to Sepoy Sahib Singh, who had entered a cave and bayoneted all the occupants in it.

North-East Frontier

Karola, May 1904

On May 3RD, Colonel Brander left Gyantse with his column of 400 rifles. The column comprised of three companies of 32ND Pioneers, under Captains Bethune and Cullen and Lieutenant Hodgson; one company of 8TH Gurkhas with two 7-pounder guns; the Maxim detachment of the Norfolks, and forty-five of 1ST Mounted Infantry, under Captain Ottley. The column marched up the pass and encamped about two miles from where the Tibetans had built their wall. A reconnaissance that afternoon estimated the enemy at 2,000, and they were holding the strongest position on the road to Lhasa. They had built a wall the whole length of a narrow spur and up the hill on the other side of the stream, and in addition held detached Sangars high up the steep hills. Their flanks rested on very high and nearly precipitous rocks. The fire from the wall was very heavy and the advance of Cullen's and Bethune's companies was checked. Then compelled by some fatal impulse, Bethune with half a company, left the cover of the riverbed and rushed out into the open, within forty yards of the main wall, exposed to a withering fire from three sides. Bethune fell, shot through the head. It was a gallant, reckless charge against uncounted odds. The frontal and flanking attacks had failed. Bethune and seventeen men were killed. The guns had made no impression on their wall and a large reinforcement of at least 500 men coming up to join the enemy. The situation was critical. When the front attack had failed, fifteen men of 32ND were sent up the hill. The party, led by Subedar Wasant Singh, scaled the 'almost perpendicular face of the 1,500-foot southern scarp'. Subedar Wasant Singh's gallant section poured down deadly rifle fire on the Sangar. Twice the Tibetans rushed out, and, coming under a heavy Maxim fire, bolted back again. The third time they fled in a mass while the Maxims mowed down about thirty. The capture of the Sangars was a signal for a general stampede. From the position they had won the Sikhs could enfilade the main wall itself. The Tibetans on the wall turned and fled in three huge bodies down the valley. Thus, the fifteen Sikhs on the right saved the situation and Subedar Wasawa Singh and Sepoy Bhagwan Singh were awarded the Indian Order of Merit for their conspicuous gallantry. Directly the flight began, 1ST Mounted Infantry poured into the valley and harassed the flying masses, riding on their flanks and pursuing them for ten miles to within sight of the Yamdok Tso. It showed extraordinary courage on the part of this little band of Sikhs and Gurkhas. They did not hesitate to hurl themselves on the flanks of the enormous body of men, like terriers on the heels of a flock of cattle, though they had had experience of their stubborn resistance the whole day long. They rode through the bodies of their fallen comrades. Not a man drew rein. The Tibetans were caught in a trap. The hills that sloped down to the valley afforded them little cover. Their fate was only a question of time and ammunition. The mounted infantry returned at night with only three casualties, having killed over 300 men. The sortie to the Karo la was one of the most brilliant episodes of the campaign.

North-East Frontier

Gyantse (Chang Lo) May 1904

The expedition reached Gyantse on 11TH April. General Macdonald, bearing in mind the difficulty of procuring supplies for the whole force, announced his intention of returning to Chumbi with the larger portion of the escort, leaving a sufficient guard with the mission. The guard left behind consisted of four companies of 32ND Pioneers, under Colonel Brander; four companies of 8TH Gurkhas, under Major Row; 1ST Mounted Infantry, under Captain Ottley; and the machine-gun section of the Norfolks, under Lieutenant Hadow. The next morning the post was attacked at dawn. It appears that the Shigatze forces, about 1,000 strong, on hearing that very few troops were guarding the mission, determined to make an attack on the post. The attack was sudden and simultaneous. A Gurkha sentry had just time to fire off his rifle before the Tibetans rushed to the walls and had their muskets through the loopholes. The enemy did not for the moment attempt to scale, but contented themselves with firing into the post through the loopholes they had taken. This delay proved fatal to their plans, for it gave the small garrison time to rise and arm. The brunt of the Tibetan fire was directed on the courtyard of the house, where the tents of the members of the mission were pitched. The Sikhs, emerging from their tents with bandolier and rifle, in extraordinary costumes, were directed towards the loopholes. Some were sent on the roof of the mission-house, whence they could enfilade the attackers. Elsewhere various junior officers had taken command. Captain Luke took charge of the Gurkhas on the south and west fronts. Lieutenant Franklin, the medical officer of 8TH Gurkhas, rallied Gurkhas and Pioneers to the loopholes on the east and north. Lieutenant Lynch, the treasure-chest officer, who had a guard of about twenty Gurkhas, took his men to the main gate to the south. There were at this time in hospital about a dozen Sikhs, who had been badly burnt in a lamentable gunpowder explosion a few days previously. These men, bandaged and crippled as they were, rose from their couches, made their painful way to the tops of the houses and fired into the enemy below. A few of the enemy got inside the defences and were immediately shot down. The fire was so heavy and so well directed that it was not more than ten minutes from the time the first shot was fired to the time the enemy began to withdraw. They were pursued almost to the very walls of the fort. Indeed, but for the fringe of houses and narrow streets at the base of the jong, they would have gone on. The Tibetans, however, turned as soon as they reached the shelter of walls. It would have been madness to attack five or six hundred determined men in a maze of alleys and passages, with only a weak company. Major Murray accordingly made his way back to the post, picking up a dozen prisoners en route. The enemy in the jong began to fire into the camp and it was realized that the jong entirely dominated the post; that walls and stockades, protection enough against a direct assault from the plain, were no protection against bullets dropped from a height.

North-East Frontier

Gurkha Post, May 1904

On 18TH May, the enemy occupied a building 500 yards away from the post and as the fire from the Lhasa Martinis was disconcerting, it was decided to storm the building next morning. The two companies of 8TH Gurkhas under Major Murray, with an explosion party of Sikh Pioneers under Lieutenant Gurdon, were detailed to the storming, with two companies of 32ND in reserve. Silently they slipped out of the Post at 3.30 a.m. and were not detected until close under the walls of the building. The defenders then woke up to hurl stones and fire heavily, while the jong also joined in. As an entrance could not be forced, the Gurkhas lay down to wait till the Sikhs had done their share; a roar and a column of smoke soon followed; after which a period of dead silence ensued and even the jong ceased firing. Then the Gurkhas, with kukri and bayonet, did their bit and those Tibetans who had not escaped met their fate. From the garrison of about sixty, forty were killed; twenty threw themselves from the walls, of whom the reserve Sikhs accounted for half. The Post was put into a state of defence and garrisoned by fifty Gurkhas. The Gurkhas were to spend and anxious time, threatened by night attack and fired at from the jong. The inconvenience of the investment was instanced that very day, when a party of eight Mounted Infantry, bringing in the mails, were ambushed close to the river.

Captain Ottley galloped out with his mounted infantry and was only just in time to save a party of his men, who were coming up from Kangma with the letter-bags. These Sikhs - eight in number - were riding along the edge of the river, when they were met by a fusillade from a number of the enemy, concealed amongst sedges on the opposite bank. Before the Sikhs could take cover, one man was killed, three wounded and seven out of the eight horses shot down. The remaining men showed rare courage. They carried their wounded comrades under cover of a ditch, untied and brought to the same place the letter-bags, and then lay down and returned the fire of the enemy. The Tibetans, however, were beginning to creep round, and the ammunition of the Sikhs was running low, when Captain Ottley dashed up to the rescue. Without waiting to consider how many of the enemy might be hiding in the sedge, Ottley took his twenty men splashing through the river. Nearly 300 Tibetans bolted out in all directions, like rabbits from a cover. The mounted infantry, shooting and smiting, chased them to the very edge of the plain. On reaching hilly ground the enemy, who must have lost about fifty of their number, began to turn, having doubtless realized that they were running before a handful of men. At the same time shots were fired from villages, previously thought unoccupied, on Ottley's left, and a body of matchlock men were seen running up to reinforce from a large village on the Lhasa road. Under these conditions, it would have been madness to continue the fight and Ottley cleverly and skilfully withdrew without having lost a single man.

North-East Frontier

Gurkha Post, May 1904(Cont.)

It now appeared that the Tibetans were drawing a cordon in the rear of the Post across the communications. 32ND accordingly moved out against the villages of Kaha, Chilra, and Tagu. The first two were empty and were set fire to, but the other two were obstinately held. Suddenly fire was opened from the upper windows of the two houses. All the doors were found blocked with bricks and stones. Two Sikhs were killed and, for the moment, it seemed as if they would lose heavily. But Lieutenant Gurdon, with half a dozen men, rushed up with a box of explosives. The first attempt to blow a breach failed, matches having got wet wading the river, but the next attempt in which Lieutenant Gurdon and Havildar Wasawa Singh laid the charge was successful, though Wasawa Singh was shot through the head. Many of the garrison jumped from the walls, only to fall into the hands of another company of Sikhs and the whole garrison was killed or captured. A posthumous Indian Order of Merit was bestowed on Wasawa Singh, his widow receiving the special pension attached thereto, and the same to Sepoy Prem Singh.

Preparations were now made for taking the remaining village. This was protected by a high loopholed embankment, which sheltered about five or six hundred of the enemy. The Pioneers had just extended and were advancing, when someone who happened to be looking at the jong through his glasses suddenly uttered a loud exclamation. Turning round, they saw a dense stream of men, several thousands in number, forming up at the base of the rock, evidently with the intention of rushing the mission post whilst the majority of the garrison and the guns were engaged elsewhere. Colonel Brander immediately gave the order for the whole force to retire into the post at the double. The withdrawal was effected before the Tibetans made their contemplated rush, but all felt that it was rather a narrow shave. Troops were to have gone out again the next day to clear the village that had been left untaken, but the mounted infantry, reconnoitring in the morning, reported that the enemy had fled and that the lines of communication were again clear. On the succeeding day, a large convoy and reinforcements under Major Peterson, 32ND Pioneers, came safely through. The additional troops included a section of 7TH (British) Mountain Battery, under Captain Easton; one and a half companies of Sappers and Miners, under Captain Shepherd and Lieutenant Garstin; and another company of 32ND Pioneers. Major Peterson reported that his convoy had come under heavy fire from the village and monastery of Naini. Accordingly, on 24TH, a column marched out to Naini. But the monastery and the group of buildings outside it were found deserted. The walls were far too heavy and strong to be destroyed by a small force, which had to return before nightfall, but Captain Shepherd blew up the four towers at the corners and a portion of the hall in which the Buddhas were enthroned.

North-East Frontier

Kangma, June 1904

On 5TH June, Colonel Younghusband went through to Kangma and was to go on next morning to Kalatso. There was not sufficient room in the post to admit the extra Mounted Infantry being put inside and they were, therefore, picketed outside in the open, together with the Yak Corps and their escort of about twenty men of 1ST Battalion 2ND Gurkhas. About 4 a.m. next day, the Mounted Infantry saddled up and were waiting to start with Colonel Younghusband for Kalatso. Most of the men, at the invitation of their comrades, the two companies of 23RD Sikh Pioneers garrisoning Kangma, were inside the post having some warm tea. Subadar Sangat Singh and Jemadar Prem Singh and about six or eight men were with the ponies. Most of the yaks and over half the Gurkha escort were well on their way to Kalatso. The rest were just ready to go, when Jemadar Prem Singh, of the Mounted Infantry, walked about 200 yards up the hill. He espied about 1,000 Tibetans get up out of a Nullah, where they had concealed themselves, and make straight for the post. The Jemadar ran back and gave the alarm. Subadar Sangat Singh, thinking of his ponies, collected the five or six Sikh and Gurkha Mounted Infantry men, who were lying down practically in the open, prepared to defend their ponies, and well they did it, else the lot would have been killed, wounded or cut loose. The attack was so sudden that although the Subadar and his party shot down numbers of the enemy and checked them, some had got amongst the ponies and were killing them, cutting them loose, or trying to ride them away. Some Tibetans had even mounted, without loosing the picketing rope, but were unused to the slippery English saddles, and the ponies, resenting this rude treatment, bucked them off again. Just then, the Mounted Infantry men inside the post, hearing the commotion outside, rushed out with fixed bayonets and drove the Tibetans out of the pony lines, untied the ponies and took them all inside the post, still covered by the Subadar and his party. The garrison of two companies of 23RD had commenced rifle fire on the Tibetans, who were compelled to retire, leaving numbers of dead behind. Immediately the Tibetans showed signs of going, Captain Pearson sallied out of the post with one company of 23RD, led by their fine old Subadar, Jiwan Singh, an old Afghan war veteran. Moreover, the Mounted Infantry, turning out sharp, caused the wavering Tibetans to turn and flee. They did not know that so large a body of Mounted Infantry was in the post and had tarried just too long; they were caught by the mounted men, who, led by their own native officers, rode through them, using their rifles from horseback, and chased them down the Gyantse road, and up the Ealung road. The attack had completely failed and the Tibetans had sense enough never to attempt another on posts in the lines of communication, which, though weakly held, were proved capable of withstanding their assaults.

North-East Frontier

Palla, 1904

On their advance, the reduction of the village of Palla was decided on. In it was a strong, imposing building known as the Palace. The Tibetans had been seen fortifying it, but hitherto occupation of it had been out the question. At early dawn on 29TH, a force sallied forth, consisting of the four guns of the column, one maxim, two companies of Sikh Pioneers and one of Gurkhas, with two sapper storming parties. The first explosion gave access to the outer works, but the garrison was on the upper tier, with all the ladders removed. The firing of another charge frightened the garrison into one strong house, which the Sikhs now rushed, killing its defenders. Meantime the main body of the assaulting column, after extraordinary effort, took the Palace. Palla was now put into a state of defence and garrisoned with one company, 32ND Pioneers under Subedar Sher Singh. The fight at Palla was the last affair of any importance in which the garrison was engaged, pending the arrival of the relieving force. The Tibetans had received such a shock that in future they confined themselves practically to the defensive, with five half-hearted night attacks, which were never anywhere near being pushed home.

Lhasa, September 1904

On 26TH June, Lieutenant Colonel Brander led a small portion of his force with his guns to assist the attack on Naini monastery, where the Tibetans were reported to be barring the way. This force got into position close on the spurs above Naini and opened fire with its guns. The monastery was then captured with ease by the main column, which then marched into Gyantse without further incident. The force then proceeded to seize forts and high points in the vicinity, and generally engaging any Tibetans they encountered. On 6TH July, the force proceeded to attack Gyantse itself. The Pioneers furnished explosion parties, but a feeble attempt at resistance was experienced. The town and jong being carried easily once the breaches had been made. The force then started for Lhasa some 2,000 strong. By now the attitude of the Tibetans had changed. The British must be got rid of, and finally on 7TH September a treaty was signed, amid considerable ceremony. On 23RD, the force, which had been reduced to 180 Mounted Infantry and 1,450 rifles, marched out for India. It was a march almost as arduous as the advance and carried out for the most part in two columns. It is related that as the column marched away, several Tibetan magnates and Lamas rode after it to offer thanks for the orderly behaviour of troops and the magnanimous treatment of the city.

North -East Frontier

The Sikh Pioneers

The two Sikh Pioneer regiments that played a prominent role in the Tibet Mission, were veterans of frontier warfare but unusual in that they fought with a pick-axe in one hand and a rifle in the other, having been raised to take on a dual role, combining the duties of a pioneer regiment with that of fighting infantry. The present mission was the third 'show' in which 23RD and 32ND had been together during the last nine years. In Chitral and Waziristan, they fought side by side. It is no exaggeration to say that these regiments had been on active service for three years out of five, since they were raised in 1857. The original draft of 32ND, it will be remembered, was the unarmed volunteer corps of Mazbi Sikhs, who offered themselves as an escort to the convoy from Lahore to Delhi during the Sepoy Mutiny. The Mazbis were the most lawless and refractory folk in the Punjab, and had long been the despair of the Government. On arrival at Delhi, they were employed in the trenches, rushing in to fill up the places of the killed and wounded as fast as they fell. A detachment of them carried out and laid the powder-bags to blow in the Kashmir Gate, which led to the fall of the city. The whole detachment of nineteen men were killed or wounded. A hundred and fifty-seven of them were killed during the siege. With this brilliant opening it is no wonder that they had been on active service almost continually since. A frontier campaign would be incomplete without 32ND or 23RD. It was 32ND who made a great name for themselves in 1895 at the lifting of the siege of Chitral, when they forced a path through five feet of snow over the Shandur Pass, to bring the guns through. The 23RD Pioneers were also raised from the Mazbi Sikhs in the same year of the Mutiny, 1857. The history of the two regiments is very similar. The 23RD distinguished themselves in China, Abyssinia, Afghanistan and numerous frontier campaigns. They had distinguished themselves in recent frontier operations against the Utman Khel, the Afridis, the Wazirs, and the Mahsuds. One of the most brilliant exploits was when, with the Gordon Highlanders under Major (now Sir George) White, they captured the Afghan guns at Kandahar. Both these regiments had been employed on every kind of military duty as Pioneers, Engineers, Infantry soldiers, artillerymen, and now they had added one more branch of the service to their long list of experiences and had proved themselves as good mounted infantrymen as they were Pioneers.

Today the men of the two regiments meet again as members of the same corps on the Lingmathang Plain. Naturally, the most cordial relations exist between the men, and one can hear the veterans discussing old campaigns as they sit round their pinewood fires in the evenings.

North-East Frontier

The Mounted Infantry

It was the first occasion that the Native Mounted Infantry in the Indian Army, had been employed on active service on or beyond the Indian frontier in Asia. Ever since the employment of mounted Infantry in the Indian army, it had been a sore point with the three Sikh Pioneer regiments that the regulations did not permit them to send some of their men to be trained at the mounted infantry schools, like all other native infantry regiments. A proposal was made to the military authorities that the Pioneers, like other regiments, should go in for a course of mounted infantry training. The reply caused much amusement at the time. The suggestion was not adopted, but orders were issued that 'every available opportunity should be taken of teaching the Pioneers to ride in carts.' It was fortunate for 23RD and 32ND Sikh Pioneers that General Macdonald was of a different opinion. General Macdonald wanted mounted infantry on the spot when he advanced into the Chumbi Valley in December 1903. As he then had only three regiments in the Tibet Mission Force viz., 23RD and 32ND Sikh Pioneers and 8TH Gurkhas, he made up his mind to form some mounted infantry out of those three regiments, whether the men were trained or not. The corps was raised at Gnatong in December, and though many of the men had not ridden before, after two months' training they cut a very respectable figure in the saddle.

"The Mounted Infantry – a jolly, swashbuckling crew who regarded themselves as a *corps d'elite* – were to prove invaluable in reconnaissance and demoralising pursuit." (Fleming, 1961 p158)

Subedar Sangat Singh, First Mounted Infantry

North-East Frontier

The following Sikh soldiers were awarded gallantry awards for their conspicuous gallantry during the Tibetan campaign:

Subedar Wasawa Singh (Posthumous)
32ND Sikh Pioneers

On 18TH May1904, the Tibetans occupied a building at Lhasa, from where the fire from Martinis was most disconcerting. It was decided to storm that building. A party of Sikh Pioneers under Subedar Wasawa Singh was detailed for the storming. As an entrance could not be forced, the Sikh Pioneers blew open the gates and slaughtered the garrison. The Pioneers then moved out against the Tibetans at the village garrisons of Karola, Chilra, and Tagu. They captured the first two garrisons, but the third garrison was obstinately held. As Havildar Wasawa Singh laid a successful charge to blow a breach, he was shot through the head. The Pioneers in their fury stormed through the breach and killed all the Tibetans in the garrison. A posthumous Indian Order of Merit was bestowed on gallant Wasawa Singh; this was a Bar to the Indian Order of Merit he was awarded for the relief of Chitral Fort in 1895.

Sepoy Prem Singh
32ND Sikh Pioneers

Sepoy Prem Singh was awarded the Indian Order of Merit for his conspicuous gallantry in the attack and destruction of the Tibetan garrisons at Tagu and Karola in 1904. This was a Bar to the Indian Order of Merit he was awarded for the relief of Chitral Fort in 1895. The 32ND Sikh Pioneers set out from Gilgit to cover 220 miles of very poor road to Chitral. The importance of the Sikh Pioneer's epic march was never fully recognized, most of the publicity and fame for the relief being lavished on the well-known British regiments like 60TH Rifles and Gordon Highlanders.

Sepoy Sahib Singh
32ND Sikh Pioneers

In January 1904, the invading force in Tibet commenced their hard marching from Phari to Gyantse. A highly disciplined and equipped force of the Sikh Pioneers proceeded towards Tibetan camp at Changra and was ordered to disarm the men in the camp. During the disarming of the armed men, a Tibetan general drew his pistol and blew off the jaw of the Sikh Sepoy, who was taking their arms. That started the conflagration. The Sikhs charged and pursued the Tibetans to the village of Guru, where the Tibetans were either killed or taken prisoners at the point of the bayonet. The total Tibetan loss was 620 killed and 222 taken prisoners. Then the Sikhs advanced against the gorge of the Red Idol, where the Tibetans were entrenched behind the boulders and hiding in the caves. The Sikhs charged and captured the Tibetans at the gorge of the Red Idol. Sepoy Sahib Singh was awarded the Indian Order of Merit for conspicuous gallantry at Red Idol; he had entered the caves alone and bayoneted the occupants.

North -East Frontier

Havildar Labh Singh
32ND Sikh Pioneers

In January 1904, the invading force in Tibet commenced their hard marching from Phari to Gyantse. A highly disciplined and equipped force of the Sikh Pioneers proceeded towards Tibetan camp at Changra and was ordered to disarm the men around. During the disarming of the armed men, a Tibetan general drew his pistol and blew off the jaw of the Sikh Sepoy who was taking their arms. That started the conflagration. The Tibetans were pursued to the village of Guru, which was taken at the point of the bayonet. The total Tibetan loss was 620 killed and 222 taken prisoners. Havildar Labh Singh was awarded the Indian Order of Merit for his conspicuous gallantry and leadership.

Subedar Wasant Singh
32ND Sikh Pioneers

On 7TH May, the attacking force had covered forty-five miles to Karola in three marches, much of it on foot and in single file. A tremendous exertion walking let alone climbing. The Tibetans had built their wall about a mile and half beyond the pass and put up a series of Sangars in front of and above the wall at both ends, both flanks of the wall were unapproachable, and the only method of attack was in front. The attack was launched with two companies of 32ND Pioneers and half a company of Gurkhas. They were to ascend the cliff against Sangars high up the hillside. Both the Sikhs and the Gurkhas were pinned down by the Tibetans' fire and could not make any headway. There was a deadlock, and no means could be found to drive the enemy from the advanced defences which they were holding so gallantly. There seemed little chance of doing anything more until nightfall. It was an anxious moment. A party of a dozen men led by Subadar Wasant Singh scaled the almost perpendicular face of the 1,500-foot southern scarp. Subadar Wasant Singh's gallant section poured down deadly rifle fire on the Sangar. The defenders lost their nerve and bolted! And the Pioneers carried the position. It was a notable victory; the Tibetans numbered 3,000 and lost 270 killed and many taken prisoners. Subadar Wasant Singh was awarded the Indian Order of Merit for conspicuous gallantry in a unique action, having been fought 16,500 feet above the sea level.

Sepoy Bhagwan Singh
32ND Sikh Pioneers

Sepoy Bhagwan Singh accompanied Subedar Wasant Singh in scaling the 1,500-foot escarpment and was most forward in carrying the Tibetan position. He was awarded the Indian Order of Merit for his conspicuous gallantry in a unique action, having been fought 16,500 feet above the sea level. This was a Bar to the Indian Order of Merit he was awarded for the relief of Chitral Fort in 1895.

North-East Frontier

Naik Jhanda Singh
32ND Sikh Pioneers

Naik Jhanda Singh was awarded the Indian Order of Merit for his conspicuous gallantry in the attack and destruction of the Tibetan garrisons at Tagu and Karola.

Subedar Kesar Singh and Sepoy Sahib Singh
32ND Sikh Pioneers

Subedar Kesar Singh and Sepoy Sahib Singh were awarded the Indian Order of Merit for their conspicuous gallantry at Palla Manor. The Tibetans heavily reinforced a complex of buildings that made Palla Manor. On 28TH May, the Sikhs and the Gurkhas took the buildings, one by one at the point of the bayonet. The occupants to their everlasting credit, fought magnificently. They lost four hundred of their numbers, killed or wounded. Another hundred and fifty were taken prisoners.

23RD Sikh Pioneers

The 32ND Sikh Pioneers took a prominent part in the Tibetan campaign. However, 23RD Sikh pioneers were involved in the original advance to Gyantse and then proceeded to work as far as Kangma, next post below Chumbi, which they garrisoned. A wing of the regiment formed part of the reinforcing column, which reached Chumbi in June 1904. After severe fighting at Chumbi, they took part in the advance on Lhasa.

Sepoy Tilok Singh, Sepoy Jowala Singh, and Sepoy Rolla Singh
23RD Sikh Pioneers

Sepoy Tilok Singh, Sepoy Jowala Singh, and Sepoy Rolla Singh were awarded the Indian Order of Merit for their conspicuous gallantry in the severe fighting at Chumbi.

Sikh Mounted Infantry at Karo La Pass

North-East Frontier

The Sikh Pioneers

At the conclusion of Tibetan adventure, the Sikh pioneers set of for India without any sort of ceremony, but shouting out their "Fateh" (Victory) cry.

Mounted Sikh Infantry soldiers break the ice on the Saddle of the Tang La.

(Lieutenant F.M. Bailey)

Tibetan prisoners being brought into the British camp by Mounted Sikh Infantry.

(Life Magazine, 1904)

BURMA

The British began conquering Burma in 1824. By 1886, Britain had incorporated it into British India. Burma was administered as a province of British India until 1937, when it became a separate, self-governing colony, independent of the Indian administration. During World War II, the Japanese succeeded in expelling the British from most of Burma. The British counter-attacked using primarily troops of the Indian Army and by July 1945, they had defeated the Japanese and retaken the country. Burma became independent from the United Kingdom on 4TH January 1948.

First Anglo-Burmese War, 1826

Burma, located on the edge of British India, was a thorn in the side of the British East India Company. The King of Ava increasingly became expansionist and aggressive towards the British-held territories. In 1766, the Burmese had seized Tenasserim from Siam. 1784 saw the incorporation of Arakan into the kingdom of Ava and 1813 saw the conquering of Manipur, which lay near the Surma Valley. This expansion and advance towards the Indian border made an Anglo-Burmese War inevitable. The final straw came in September 1823, when the Burmese seized the Shalpuri Island near Chittagong, which was owned by the East India Company. The declaration of war came on 24TH February 1824. It was a hard fought battle. Artillery had to be manhandled through the jungle, soldiers were falling thick and fast due to disease and each town was heavily defended. However, the Burmese army were slowly pushed back up the Irrawaddy Valley. By February 1826, the Anglo-Indian army had advanced three hundred miles to the town of Yandaboo. The advance on the capital began on 9TH February 1826 and was reached just two weeks later. The King of Ava sued for peace and signed a treaty by which he agreed to pay the expenses of the war and forego a considerable part of his territory. Thus closed the first Burmese war, resulting in the loss to the Burman monarch of all the territories which his ancestors had taken from the Siamese, and of Arakan, which had been conquered by his father and his exclusion from all interest in Assam, Cachar, and Manipur, where his predecessors had been paramount.

Type of Burma Military Police in 1886

Burma

Second Anglo-Burmese War, 1852

In 1852, the Viceroy of India, Lord Dalhousie, dispatched Commodore Lambert to Burma to deal with a number of minor issues related to the previous treaty. The Burmese immediately made concessions, including the removal of a governor whom the British had made their Casus belli. Lambert eventually provoked a naval confrontation in extremely questionable circumstances and thus started the Second Anglo-Burmese War in 1852. The force detailed for the invasion was taken partly from Bengal and partly from Madras. One of the Native Infantry regiments refused to go on board ship, though they expressed their willingness to march wherever they were ordered. It was then discovered that, by the terms of their enlistment, they were not liable to service overseas, and the orders for them to proceed were consequently at once cancelled. Shortly afterwards the following regiments of Sikhs, of their own accord, came forward and informed their officers of their willingness to proceed to Burma should reinforcements be required: - 3RD and 4TH Sikh Local Infantry and the regiments of Ferozepur and Ludhiana (14TH and 15TH Sikhs.) On 21ST May 1852 a General Order was published expressing the satisfaction of the Governor-General at this exemplary conduct and later on, when reinforcements were required, the Regiment of Ludhiana Sikhs and 4TH Sikh Local Infantry were employed in Burma.

The general situation in August 1852 was that the British controlled the whole of the streams of the Irrawaddy River from Prome to the sea. The Burmese had shown no sign of any intention to submit, nor was there the slightest ground for believing that any such overtures would be made. As soon as the reinforcements arrived, which included 4TH Sikh Light Infantry and the Regiment of Ludhiana, the troops advanced up the Irrawaddy and arrived off Prome on 9TH October and were immediately fired on by the Burmese. The attacking force met resistance which was estimated to be about 4,000 strong and dispersed it. They went on to capture the town and storm the Pagoda, to find that the enemy had abandoned it during the night. General Godwin's force, which included 4TH Sikh Infantry, successfully relieved the garrison at Pegu, which had been hard pressed from 5TH December. On receiving the dispatches informing him of the occupation of Prome and Pegu, the Governor General felt the time had come to declare the annexation of Pegu. The letter to the King, after the annexation of Pegu, warned him that if he attempted to interfere with the British occupation of that province, the British Government would continue hostilities until the entire kingdom of Burma was subjugated.

Burma

Operations against Decoits

It is now necessary to turn to the operations against the bands of marauders, which were the only enemy left in the neighbourhood of Prome after the Burmese army had disappeared at the beginning of the conflict. Parties of these freebooters sprung up in all directions and were in some cases, owing to their numbers and resolution, dangerous opponents. The Bassein district, which was overrun by Decoits, was successfully cleared by the commissioner, Captain Fytche, with 4TH Sikh Light Infantry and a small local force which he raised for this purpose, but a dacoit named Myat Tun, who commanded a large following, gave a considerable amount of trouble before he was subdued.

Third Anglo-Burmese War, 1885

In February 1853, King Pagan was dethroned by a revolt against his oppressive rule and the leader of the revolt, Mindon, was crowned as his successor. While not provoking British military action, King Mindon initially refused to accept the British occupation of Pegu, but he accepted a British envoy at his court in 1855. In 1862, the province of 'British Burma' was created and in 1867, a treaty was agreed at Mandalay, which established normal diplomatic relations between Britain and Burma. Upon Mindon's death in 1878, his son Thibaw succeeded him. Thibaw's rule caused some internal unrest; the British Resident was withdrawn in 1879, but Thibaw encouraged diplomatic contacts with France and Italy. Finally, Burmese interference with British trade and the imposition of a huge fine upon the Bombay-Burma Trading Corporation, prompted the Viceroy, Lord Dufferin, to issue and ultimatum, demanding protection of British subjects and interests. On 7TH November, Thibaw instructed his subjects to drive the British into the sea and two days later his rejection of the ultimatum was received in Rangoon. Consequently, the British assembled three brigades intent on the removal of Thibaw. The British advanced at such speed that the Burmese had little chance to organise; they pushed up the Irrawaddy, engaging and neutralising Burmese shore-batteries and on 17TH November dispersed a Burmese force at Minha. On 26TH November, Thibaw offered to surrender and ordered his army to lay down its arms. On 28TH November, Mandalay was occupied and with Thibaw in custody, the war was over in less than a fortnight. The British went on to conquer the remainder of the country, which resulted in total annexation of Burma.

The elements of the Burmese army, which had been permitted to disperse with their arms, became guerillas or bands of dacoit bandits. The problems they caused were so serious that reinforcements had to be sent from India and much arduous service was experienced amid the jungles as successive operations were mounted against the dacoits.

Burma

The Chin

The Chin comprised of a number of warlike tribes who frequently made slave raids and headhunting forays against their neighbours. 'Numerous abortive expeditions were launched against the Chin from Manipur and Burma prior to British annexation of these countries. Conquest of Upper Burma finally gave the British access to Chin's mountainous homeland at the end of 1880's, and subsequent expeditions mounted in 1889-90 and 1892-3 eventually brought them to heel. They were progressively disarmed after 1893, and the Chin Hills became a province of British Burma in 1895'. (Heath, 1999 p17)

Chin Hills, 1889

Owing to constant raids made by various Chin tribes on the plains of Burma, two columns were sent into the Chin Hills under the supreme command of Brigadier General Faunc. A post was established at Tokhlaing, afterwards called Fort White, from which various columns operated all through the winter months, with the result that the Chins were severely punished and over 200 Burmese captives were recovered. British losses in the expedition amounted to thirty-six killed and fifty-four wounded.

Chin-Lushai, 1889

The renewal of Chin and Lushai raids on the British territories, prompted the British on the Chin-Lushai expedition of 1889. The expedition involved 7,400 men in three columns, one operating from Chittagong against the Lushais, the other two from Burma against the Chins. The British defeated the raiders and went on to annex all Naga territory west of the Dikhu River to the British Empire. Several further British expeditions between 1889 and 1895 ended with the complete subjugation of the Lushai Hills.

Yadwin, 1891

In January 1891, the Chins made a serious raid on Yadwin post from Panchaung, and it was evident that severe measures were necessary for the punishment of the tribe. Captain Hastings was consequently ordered to proceed from Myingyan to effect the release of captives and chastise the Chins. He arrived in Yadwin on 4TH February, and succeeded in severely punishing all the villages implicated in the attack, and in reducing the whole Yaw district to subjection.

Burma

Kachin Hills, 1895

The Kachin Hills form a mountainous district of Upper Burma, inhabited by the Kachin people. To deter their raiding, numerous small actions were necessary and two larger expeditions. British occupation of Bhamo from December 1885 initiated trouble with the Kachins, but the main hostilities were Kachin attacks on a police column and settlements in December 1892. An expedition was put in hand immediately and the rising had been crushed by March 1893. From 1895 a definitive northern border was established. The British taking responsibility for the Kachin tribes on their side, those to the north were told they would be unmolested provided that they did not raid into British territory. However, continued unrest necessitated the dispatch of two small columns in December 1895, which quickly suppressed the trouble. It remained necessary to keep a strong police presence in the area as a guard against possible trouble.

Kachin Hills, 1896

The continued unrest of the Kachins from beyond the administrative border rendered punitive measures necessary. They had remained unpunished since the attack on Myitkyina in December 1892. Two columns were sent up, one of 250 rifles from Myitkyina, the other of 200 rifles from Mogaung, marching in December 1895. The resistance was insignificant and the operations were completely successful. A strong force of military police was stationed at Myitkyina, with several outposts in the Kachin hills.

Kachin Hills, 1898

The last operations in the Kachin Hills were connected with the ejection of an armed force of Chinese-Shans from the Bhamo district. In March 1898 the Sawbwas of Mongwan and Mongna sent an armed force to establish posts at Sadon, Seingmye, and Manipat in the Bhamo district on the British side of the provisional boundary. At the same time, they endeavoured to persuade the Kachins to build stockades and to refrain from paying their accustomed tribute to the British. The British consequently decided to send a party of Military Police to eject this force and to destroy their stockades. As the Chinese had refused to retire, the stockade was attacked and captured. The next day the column proceeded to Seimgye and Maipat and destroyed the stockades there. On destroying all the stockades between the Kulong and Chapak Khas, and promising to refrain from further attempts to coerce the Kachins, the prisoners captured were eventually released.

Burma

Burma Military Police

Upper Burma was formally annexed on 1ST of January 1886, and the work of restoring the country to order and introducing settled government commenced. This was a more serious task than the overthrow of the Burmese government and the experience of the occupied years. This was in part due to the character of the country, which was one vast military obstacle, and in part to the disorganization, which had been steadily growing during the six years of King Thibaw's reign. It was recognized that troops alone could not suffice for the work of pacification. The difficulties in Burma could only be overcome by the creation of an efficient Military Police. In 1886, the Government of India sanctioned the raising of the Military Police to facilitate the withdrawal of the main part of the regular forces in Burma. The military police battalions were organized like regular army regiments and their duties were entirely military. The Military Police at the end of 1888 included 3,937 Sikhs.

The organization of the Military Police and the establishment of Military Police posts, in place of posts held by troops, contributed greatly towards the progress of pacification. As soon as the pacification of any district was sufficiently advanced, the military posts were withdrawn and Military Police posts established. Between these protective Military Police posts, the Civil Police, consisting of the locally recruited Burmese, held intermediate posts. To enable long marches and prompt pursuits to be made, each battalion had a mounted detachment, often of Sikhs, whose duties included standing watch over the frontiers and the regions that had not been brought under formal British control. During 1887-88, great progress was made in the pacification of Upper Burma. The result was, however, not effected without much toil and hardship. The story of the year is a record of endless marches by day and night, through dense jungle where the path could hardly be traced, along paths so thick in mud that the soles of men’s boots were torn off as they marched, over sandy tracts devoid of water, over hills where there were no paths at all. Rarely was there the chance of an engagement to cheer the troops; stockades were found empty, villages deserted, camps evacuated, and yet everywhere there was the probability of sudden ambush from every clump of trees or line of rocks, or at any turn of the road.

During the First World War, the Burma Military Police Battalions were milked dry for volunteers to serve in various regiments in Egypt, Persia and Mesopotamia. The ‘Indian Order of Merit’, was awarded to the following Sikh soldiers of the Burma Military Police during the First World War:

Lance Naik Kahan Singh, in 1917, during an attack on Turkish trenches in Mesopotamia, he was given an immediate award of the Indian Order of Merit.

Jemadar Mit Singh was awarded the Indian Order of Merit, for conspicuous gallantry in Egypt in 1918.

Sepoy Jai Singh was awarded the Indian Order of Merit, for conspicuous gallantry in Egypt in 1918.

Burma

During the Second World War, British possession of Burma was a rich prize for the Japanese, partly for its oil, rice and rubber, partly as a stepping-stone westward into India, partly as a buffer against the Chinese in the north. Within a week of their initial attacks across Southeast Asia on 8TH December 1941, the Japanese had reached Burma, and after air raids on the Burmese capital, Rangoon, they began invading from Siam early in 1942. The Indian, British and Burmese troops were forced to commence a long withdrawal. At one point, thanks to the premature demolition of a bridge across the Sittang River, half 17TH Indian Division found itself marooned on the wrong side of the river. Most of the men managed to reach safety, but all their equipment was lost. By 9TH March, the Japanese had captured Rangoon. In April, they crushed the Chinese, in May they pushed the Allied British and Indian forces back into India. By the end of 1942, the Japanese had consolidated their position in Burma. One of the most difficult places on earth to fight in with its thick jungles, Razorback Mountains, steep wild valleys, and a plethora of debilitating and deadly tropical diseases. Recapturing the country would take the Allies' 14TH Army, known with bitterly realistic humour as the 'Forgotten Army', three years of desperate fighting. Late in 1942, a preliminary Allied offensive was launched from India into the Arakan peninsula in north-west Burma. The 14TH Indian Division was among the forces that advanced into the Arakan and down the Mayu range of hills between the Kalapanzin River and the Arakan coast. But in spite of attacks against the Japanese early in 1943, the offensive ended in failure. At the start of the dry season in early 1944, 14TH Army launched a second offensive into Arakan. The Indian Air Force supported this offensive, with No 6 Squadron among those in the thick of the action against Japanese 'Oscar' fighters. The Indian contingent of ground troops included 5TH and 25TH Indian Divisions. In the Mayu hills, 5TH tried and failed to capture Hill 551, a vital strongpoint which commanded a section of the Maungdaw-Buthidaung road between two tunnels. The 25TH Indian Division accomplished the task in capturing the strong Japanese fortifications. Almost simultaneously with the start of the second Allied offensive into Arakan, the Japanese launched an offensive of their own. A diversionary thrust in Arakan, codenamed Ha-Go, drew attention away from the main U-Go offensive westward by 80,000 Japanese troops into the north-eastern Indian province of Assam. The hill settlements of Imphal and Kohima lay in their path, and were to prove their obstacles. By February 1944, the 2,000 defenders of Kohima were besieged and those at Imphal surrounded. But General Sir William Slim's 14TH Army resisted countless Japanese attacks, often in the grimmest of hand-to-hand fighting. Kohima was besieged for 64 days of intense fighting, with the Japanese occupying all the heights but one around the town.

Burma

The famous Battle of the Tennis Court saw Allied and Japanese soldiers exchanging grenade and small arms fire from positions separated only by the width of the District Commissioner's tennis court. Most of the medical staff were Indians, working in appalling conditions – at one point they had to launch a raid on the Japanese stores to secure medical supplies. The siege was initially relieved on 19TH April. In May, 7TH Indian Division arrived as reinforcements and it was Indians and Gurkhas who succeeded in taking the strategically essential high point of Church Knoll from the Japanese. The town of Imphal possessed important airfields, and for three months, the Japanese held the Imphal-Kohima road while they tried to over-run Imphal. On 30TH March, the siege began, a few days before 17TH Indian Division reached the plain surrounding Imphal after a fighting withdrawal that had lasted three weeks. The 17TH was soon in action, fighting the Japanese south-west of Imphal. The 5TH Indian Division met the first Japanese attacks, and it was 23RD Indian Division that experienced some of the worst fighting in May. However, counter-attacks began to turn into solid advances. On 22ND June, 5TH Indian Division met the British 2ND Division on the Kohima-Imphal road, which was reopened to end the siege. Air supply had kept both sets of defenders in the game. By June, the Japanese U-Go offensive had come to a halt. Around 12,000 Indian casualties had been sustained, out of a total of almost 18,000 allied killed, wounded, and missing. Of nearly 100,000 Japanese soldiers who took part in the U-Go offensive, only about 20,000 recrossed the River Chindwin unscathed. Some 30,000 had been killed in battle, and another 23,000 were wounded or fell victim to disease. The rest of the year was spent chasing the Japanese back through the jungles of Burma. In December 1944, 14TH Army launched its third and decisive Arakan offensive. The Indian 25TH Division, in January 1945, secured the key port of Akyab. On 14TH of that month, 19TH Indian Division crossed the Irrawaddy north of Mandalay, and a month later, 20TH Indian Division got across south of the city. The 51ST Brigade of 25TH Indian Division took Kangaw. Mandalay itself fell on 19TH March to 19TH Indian Division. On 1ST May, Indian paratroops landed to the south of Rangoon; the following day saw unopposed amphibious attacks into the city. By 3RD May, the Burmese capital - along with most of the country - was back in Allied hands. On 4TH January 1948, Burma became independent, and unlike other former British colonies, it left the Commonwealth.

The annals of Sikh history are replete with examples of gallantry on the battlefield. The following pages preserve forever the memory of the Sikh soldiers, who won gallantry awards, during the re-conquest of Burma.

Burma

Naik (Later Jemadar) Nand Singh VC

The Japanese had taken Burma and were poised for the invasion of India. 1ST Battalion, 11TH Sikh Regiment became part of 7TH Indian Division formed for the re-conquest of Burma and the destruction of the Japanese forces. The Japanese would not surrender; and had to be killed one by one. On the night of March 11TH/12TH, 1944, a Japanese platoon about 40 strong, with medium and light machine-guns and a grenade discharger, infiltrated into the battalion's position covering the main Maungdaw-Buthidaung road. They occupied a dominating position where they dug foxholes and trenches on the precipitous sides of the hill, threatening to hold up the main advance. A platoon was ordered to capture the position at all costs. Naik Nand Singh, a section commander, led his men on a narrow path up to the top of a very steep knife-edged ridge. This necessitated proceeding in single file under heavy machine-gun and rifle fire. Shouting the famous Sikh battle cry "Sat Siri Akal". Nand Singh led the attack. Although wounded in the thigh, he rushed ahead of his section and captured the first enemy trench. He then crawled forward alone under heavy fire. Although wounded again in the face and shoulder by a grenade that burst one yard in front of him, he took the second trench at the point of his bayonet. Shortly afterwards, when all his section had been either killed or wounded, Naik Nand Singh dragged himself out of the trench and captured a third trench, killing all the occupants with his bayonet. Due to the capture of these three trenches, the remainder of the platoon were able to seize the top of the hill and deal with the remaining Japanese. During these operations, Nand Singh personally killed seven of the enemy.

Owing to his determination, outstanding spirit, and magnificent courage, the dominating position was won back from the enemy and he was awarded the Victoria Cross.

In the 1947 conflict over Kashmir, Nand Singh was mortally wounded while leading a bayonet attack on the enemy. For his supreme sacrifice in this action, Nand Singh was awarded MVC (Mahavir Chakra), the second highest military award for valour in India. Nand Singh is the only Indian soldier to have been awarded both the VC and MVC.

Born at Bahadurhur Village, Patiala State, Punjab, India, in 1914.
Killed at Uri, Kashmir, 12TH December 1947, aged 33.

Burma

Havildar (Later Major) Parkash Singh VC

In Burma on January 6TH, 1943, near the Japanese-occupied village of Donbaik, the enemy hurled a salvo of grenades at the leading armoured troop carrier. Havildar Parkash Singh's superior officer, Captain Bert Causey, was immediately wounded. Parkash took command while Causey retired. He saw that further forward two other carriers were bogged down and under heavy fire from the advancing Japanese. With his Bren gunner wounded, he drove forward with one hand, firing the Bren with the other. He charged into the ranks of the astonished Japanese, scattering them and continued into their fixed positions causing such consternation that they fled. He then returned to pick up the stranded men. Despite a hail of fire from a fresh Japanese attack, all eight men embarked and crouched, shaking, on the floor with rifle and machine-gun fire hammering against the casing all the way back to the British/Indian lines.

On January 19TH, the carriers were ordered to advance along the beach and draw the enemy's fire. They were greeted by a burst of anti-tank gunfire against the lightly armoured carriers. Several were wrecked, including Causey's, whose driver had both legs shot off. Dragging his terrified driver out of a trench, Parkash guided his carrier down to the beach again, through a hail of small and large calibre gunfire. He discovered that Causey and his driver were too badly injured to be moved. Ignoring Causey's pleas to retreat and save himself, Parkash rigged up a makeshift tow-chain, exposing himself to enemy fire as he scuttled between the two vehicles. Causey was too weak from his wounds to put his vehicle in neutral and Parkash vaulted from one vehicle to the other to free the jammed lever. One of the more hair-raising tows in vehicular history then took place; over rough ground with anti-tank rounds ripping through the hulls of both carriers. For the last hundred yards, in a gesture of admirable bravado, Parkash sat on top of his vehicle, a splendid, be-turbaned figure with arms folded, impassively ignoring the Japanese bullets whistling around his ears. As they came into their own lines one observer said presciently "There's a fellow winning a VC".

In 1947, Parkash Singh was transferred to the Sikh Regiment, retiring with the rank of Major in 1968.

Born at Sharikar, Lyallpur District, Punjab, India, 31ST March 1913.
Died in London, 23RD March 1991 aged 78.

Burma

Lieutenant Karamjeet Singh Judge VC

In Burma on 18TH March 1945, Lieutenant Karamjeet Singh Judge was ordered to capture the Cotton Mill area on the outskirts of Myingyan.
Up to the last moment Lieut. Karamjeet Singh Judge dominated the entire battlefield by his numerous and successive acts of superb gallantry. Although cover around the tanks was non-existent, Lieutenant Karamjeet Singh Judge remained with the tanks, regardless not only of heavy small-arms fire directed at him but also of extremely heavy shelling directed at the tanks. Lieut. Karamjeet Singh Judge succeeded in recalling the tanks and personally indicated the bunkers for the tanks to deal with, thus allowing the infantry to advance. In every case, Lieutenant Karamjeet Singh Judge personally led the infantry charges against the bunkers and was invariably the first to arrive. In this way, this brilliant and courageous officer eliminated ten bunkers. On one occasion, as he was going into attack, two Japanese with fixed bayonets suddenly rushed at him from a small Nullah at a distance of only ten yards. He killed both. About fifteen minutes before the battle finished, a last nest of three bunkers was located in a position that was difficult for the tanks to approach. An enemy light machine-gun was firing from one of them and holding the advance of the infantry. Undaunted and at great personal risk, Lieutenant Karamjeet Singh Judge directed one tank to within 20 yards of the bunkers, and then threw a smoke grenade as a marker. After some minutes firing from the tank, he asked the commander to cease firing whilst he went in with a few men to mop up. He then went forward and got within 10 yards of the bunker, when the machine-gun opened fire again, mortally wounding him in the chest. By this time, however, the remaining men of the section were able to storm this strong point and so complete the long and arduous task. During this battle, Lieutenant Karamjeet Singh Judge was an example of cool and calculated bravery. In three previous and similar actions, this young officer had already proved himself an outstanding leader of matchless courage. In his last action, Lieut. Karamjeet Singh Judge gave a superb demonstration of inspiring leadership and outstanding courage.

Born at Kapurthala, Kapurthala State, Punjab, India, and 25TH May 1923.
Killed in action at Myingyan, Burma, 18TH March 1945 aged 22.

Burma

Naik (Later Subedar Major) Gian Singh VC

In Burma, on March 2ND 1945, the Japanese were holding a strong position astride the Kamye-Myingyan road. As all water supply points were within the enemy's position, it was vital that he should be dislodged. The attack on the first objective was successful and one platoon was ordered to attack a village to the right. This platoon's attack, with the aid of tanks, advanced very slowly under very heavy enemy fire. Naik Gian Singh was in command of the leading section. The enemy was well concealed along the cacti hedges but Naik Gian Singh soon observed enemy foxholes some 20 yards ahead. Ordering his light machine-gunner to cover him, he rushed the enemy foxholes alone, firing his Tommy gun. He was met by a hail of fire and wounded in the arm. In spite of this, he continued his advance alone, hurling grenades. He killed several Japanese including four in one of the enemy main weapon pits. By this time, a troop of British tanks moved in support and came under fire from a cleverly concealed enemy anti-tank gun. Naik Gian Singh quickly saw the threat to the tanks, and ignoring the danger to himself and in spite of his wounds, he again rushed forward, capturing the gun and killing the crew single-handed. His section followed him, and he then led them down a lane of cacti hedges, clearing all enemy positions, which were being firmly held. Some 20 enemy bodies were found in this area, the majority of which fell to Naik Gian Singh and his section. After this action, Naik Gian Singh was ordered to the Regimental First-Aid Post but, in spite of his wounds, requested permission to lead his section until the whole action had been completed. This was granted. There is no doubt that many casualties to Naik Gian Singh's platoon were prevented by his acts of supreme gallantry, they enabled the whole operation to be carried out successfully with severe losses to the enemy. Although wounded, the magnificent gallantry, devotion to duty and leadership of Gian Singh throughout this action could not have been surpassed.

At the division of the Indian Army in 1947, Gian Singh was posted to The Sikh Regiment. During the Indo-China War of 1962, Subedar Major Gian Singh was again decorated, on this occasion with the Indian MC.

Born at Shahbazpur Village, Jullunder District, Punjab, India, 5TH October 1920. Died in peaceful retirement at Jullunder, 6TH October 1996 aged 76.

Burma

Lieutenant Avtar Singh
The Sikh Regiment

"On 2ND March 1945, Lieutenant Avtar Singh was detailed as Field Operations Officer with the leading company of 4TH Battalion, the Sikh Regiment, during the operations which led to the capture of Meiktilla in Burma. The enemy had mined the town very thoroughly and numerous snipers were active. An enemy gun opened fire as they neared the railway crossing and knocked out one Sherman tank. Lieutenant Avtar Singh brought down a concentration of fire, which temporarily neutralized the gun. When later the gun opened fire again, in spite of the heavy sniping, Light Machine Gun and Maxi Machine Gun fire and bursting mines, Lieutenant Avtar Singh climbed up into an adjoining house and brought down another concentration of fire on the area where the gun flash was seen. This enabled the Tank Squadron Commander who was near him, to move to a position from which the gun could be engaged directly with fire from the Tank's 75mm gun, and the enemy gun was finally silenced. By his initiative, disregard of personal danger, appreciation of the urgency of the situation and accurate shooting, he definitely aided the "Cleaning up" operation and materially speeded up the conclusion of the battle of Meiktilla."

Lieutenant Avtar Singh was recommended for the Military Cross. This was approved and details were published in the London Gazette of 13TH July 1945.

Subedar Bishan Singh
The Sikh Regiment

"Subedar Bishan Singh has been present with the Battalion throughout the Burma campaign from 1942 to 1945, and he has at all times displayed outstanding leadership and gallantry. He has been in the forefront of some of the fiercest fighting seen by the Battalion and has been wounded no less than four different occasions, when leading his men against the Japanese. In June 1944, he displayed exceptional courage and devotion to duty, when operating behind the enemy lines north of Kanglatongbi. On one occasion during these operations, over seventy Japanese, launched a fanatical attack against his platoon, and overran his leading section. Subedar Bishan Singh was wounded early in the action, but refused to be evacuated and remained with his platoon. There is no doubt that his great courage and leadership so inspired his men that they successfully beat off superior Japanese Forces in some fierce close-in fighting. Again, at Pagn in February 1945, he displayed outstanding bravery and leadership on two occasions against superior numbers of Japanese. It was due again to his leadership and bravery that considerable losses were inflicted on the enemy. Finally, in the closing stages of the war, he displayed courage beyond the call of duty in several attacks in the fighting in the Sittang bend, where he was seriously wounded for the fourth time leading his men against strong Japanese positions to relieve the troops encircled at Nyaungkashe. It was partly due to this officer's leadership and determination that the operation was successfully accomplished," He was strongly recommended for and awarded the Military Cross.

Burma

Jemadar Bhag Singh
The Sikh Regiment

"On the night of 3RD and 5TH July, Jemadar Bhag Singh was in command of an isolated platoon in the village of Satthagyen in Burma, some three miles away from the Battalions position. The total strength of the platoon numbered 22 men. At about 21.00 hours, approximately 150 Japanese heavily attacked the platoon. The telephone line was cut and owing to the heavy rain, the wireless ceased to function and all communication with the Battalion was lost, so that no defensive fire could be given from supporting arms. A determined enemy under cover of heavy Mortar, Grenade Discharger and Automatic fire, heavily attacked the platoon throughout the night. Jemadar Bhag Singh moved continuously from trench to trench cheering and encouraging his men and by his inspired leadership, the platoon succeeded in beating off all enemy attacks. On the morning of 4TH July, an attack was launched to relieve the platoon, but it was not until 10.00 hours that the contact was established. When relieved the platoon had less than five rounds of ammunition per man and 29 enemy bodies were found on the wire surrounding the position. The inability of the enemy to take the village largely contributed to holding off the offensive. Again, at Abya on the night of 6TH and 7TH July Jemadar Bhag Singh was commanding his platoon in an attack on a very strongly fortified Japanese position and was severely wounded in the arm. Despite his wounds, he continued to lead his platoon with the greatest gallantry and resolution. After the attack, owing to the shortage of Viceroy's commissioned officers, Jemadar Bhag Singh refused to be evacuated. In the five days hard, bitter fighting the conduct of Jemadar Bhag Singh was beyond praise. His gallantry and tenacity were an inspiration to all ranks of the Battalion and he richly deserved the award of the Military Cross."

Jemadar Didar Singh
Burma Regiment

"In Kohima area in Burma on 28TH May 1944, Jemadar Didar Singh led his platoon in a counter–attack on a position recently captured by the enemy and succeeded in capturing his objective, destroying two Light Machine Gun Posts and two other Automatic Gun Posts, inflicting several casualties on the enemy. He showed great coolness and clever leadership, being responsible for leading the Company to the objective through thick jungle. On all Operations he has shown courage and initiative, and is very strongly recommended for the Military Cross." Jemadar Didar Singh was awarded the Military Cross on 15TH October 1944.

Burma

Subedar Gurcharan Singh, MC and Bar
The Sikh Regiment

"On 21ST May 1945, Subedar Gurcharan Singh was commanding the right forward Platoon of the Company in Burma. He was ordered to capture the village of Kabaing, which was held by a strong party of the Japanese. The assaulting troops had to cross 500 yards of open country, which included a wide Chaung with precipitous sides and deep running water, and during this phase, the Platoon came under very heavy small arms fire. The men were tired after a long gruelling march. Subedar Gurcharan Singh personally led his leading section to the assault; he dashed at the first Light Machine Gun post and bayoneted two of the enemy. With great dash, courage and determination he continued to lead the assault on to each succeeding enemy post. His Platoon killed thirty-nine of the enemy with bayonet and grenade with small loss to themselves. It was largely due to the inspired leadership of Subedar Gurcharan Singh that the Company achieved such overwhelming success; sixty-seven of the enemy was killed and much valuable equipment captured." Subedar Gurcharan Singh was awarded the Military Cross on 20TH June 1945.

Subedar Jogindar Singh
The Sikh Regiment

"At Pagan, Burma, in 1945, Subedar Jogindar Singh was 2ND I/C of the 'B' company which with tank support was attacking an enemy position. A party of the enemy about 150 strong slipped behind the company cutting them off from their base. The company was pinned down to the ground by very heavy fire in open country and was in a critical position. The Company Commander was seriously wounded. Subedar Jogindar Singh took command of the Company and under heavy machine gun fire, with complete disregard for his own personal safety, rapidly reorganized his company, moving from one Platoon to another encouraging his men. He then moved to the tanks, which had been singled out a special target by the enemy and coolly directed their fire on the enemy concentrations and strong points. Only due to his great gallantry, coolness and initiative a very critical situation was converted to an overwhelming victory. Thereafter, having inflicted heavy casualties on the enemy, he successfully withdrew his Company together with all the wounded back to the Battalion position. He was slightly wounded during this engagement but refused attention at that time until the time of evacuation. On the night of 18/19TH February, his company was heavily attacked. Subedar Jogindar Singh again showed great coolness, initiative, and gallantry, moving from position to position under very heavy Grenade Discharger and Medium Machine Gun fire, he located the enemy concentrations and assembly areas, and directed mortar fire onto these concentrations. He was instrumental in beating off this attack with heavy losses to the enemy. He has shown a devotion to duty of a higher order than that normally expected of a VCO". Subedar Jogindar Singh was awarded an immediate Military Cross on 25TH May 1945.

Burma

Subedar Gulcharan Singh
The Sikh Regiment

"On 20TH February 1944, in Burma, Subedar Gulcharan Singh commanded No 10 Platoon, which had been ordered to carry out an attack on an enemy position. At 1330 hours, his platoon had reached their rendezvous in the Nullah. Shortly afterwards two of his men were wounded by enemy Mortar fire (one fatally) and the Platoon came under Light Machine Gun fire from the hill feature. Disregarding these mishaps, Subedar Gulcharan Singh carried on, and led his platoon forward immediately below the feature called Sikh Hill. The success of the attack very largely depended on keeping in close to the tanks, and strictly adhering to the timetable arranged. When the covering fire ceased the attacking Platoon was within 50 yards of the enemy's positions. Showers of Grenades and Light Machine Gun fire some 20 yards from the enemy halted Subedar Gulcharan Singh's forward section, three men having been wounded and one killed. Covered by a few Mortar bombs from the rear and Grenades from the leading section, he now attacked from the right. This attack was also checked when three men were wounded. A third attack was then made on the left, again being halted after one man had been killed, and one wounded. So far the Platoon had suffered two men killed and seven wounded. Subedar Gulcharan Singh's platoon was now in a semi circle about 15 yards from the enemy, who was in a strong entrenched position. Headquarters had now reinforced the platoon with three sections, two of which were covering the right flank. A general attack was then made, during which some of the enemy left their trenches and ran away. Other Japanese stuck it out; Jemadar Gulcharan Singh personally shot one and bayoneted another. The remainder were bombed out. He now took a patrol forward to search the Southern and Western slopes of Sikh Hill. He moved two parties along two parallel spurs. About 30 yards from the main position he saw a party of 7 Japanese in a Nullah between the two spurs and immediately attacked. Three were killed from bursts by a Light Machine Gun and as the other four were trying to escape, Jemadar Gulcharan Singh ordered the rest of his patrol on the other side to get forward. This they did, sighting the Japs and killing them all with rifle and Light Machine Gun fire. From the moment that the orders for the attack were issued until the last Japanese was killed, Jemadar Gulcharan Singh was an inspiration to his men and to the whole Company. He displayed outstanding tactical ability, remaining cool and level headed throughout the action. He was with his leading men during the whole attack, cheering and leading them on. He proved himself to be a leader in every sense of the word." Jemadar Gulcharan Singh was strongly recommended for and awarded the Military Cross on 22ND February 1944.

Burma

Lieutenant Pritam Singh
The Sikh Regiment

"Lieutenant Pritam Singh has shown gallantry and leadership of a very high order while in command of the Mortar Platoon during recent operations in Burma. During a prolonged enemy attack throughout the whole of a night in May, his cool courage and example inspired his men to maintain their Mortars in action in spite of Artillery, Mortar, Grenade and Medium Machine Gun fire at very close range, both on the Mortar position and Observation Point. Although the enemy was threatening the mortar position on several occasions, the mortar Platoon fired continuously throughout the action and assisted in no small way in repulsing the enemy with great loss. Lieutenant Pritam Singh has carried out difficult patrols behind the enemy lines with great courage and determination. He has on several occasions set an example to the men by his complete disregard for his own safety and his determination to support rifle companies under all conditions and at any cost. Lieutenant Pritam Singh gave a fine example of this on 30TH May when the enemy commenced shelling his Observation Post while covering an attack near the village of Modhung. He continued to direct the fire of his Mortars in spite of shells falling all around him. He brought down such accurate and effective concentrations on the enemy that the leading Platoon was able to get on to its first objective with little loss. He stayed at his Observation Post directing fire of his Mortars until he was badly wounded and became too weak to observe fire." He was strongly recommended for and awarded the Military Cross on 6TH October 1944.

Subedar Ishar Singh IDSM
The Sikh Regiment

"Subedar Ishar Singh has shown gallantry and devotion to duty of the highest order. His steadfastness and leadership have maintained the morale, determination, and fighting spirit of his men throughout a long and arduous campaign in Burma. On numerous occasions under fire, Subedar Ishar Singh set an example to his company; an example which has always been an inspiration to his men. He has been wounded in four different actions and each time refused to go back to have his wounds dressed until the end of the action; and when all other casualties had been evacuated to safety. On one occasion during a Japanese attack on his Company Subedar Ishar Singh crawled round under heavy fire to each Platoon to give them encouragement. While at another time when his Company was severely shelled and mortared prior to an attack, he so encouraged his men that they moved forward and captured the objective according to plan, inspite of a number of casualties in the forming up area. Subedar Ishar Singh has displayed great courage and shown that he is fearless in action." Subedar Ishar Singh was strongly recommended for and awarded the Military Cross on 5TH April 1945.

Burma

Subedar Naranjan Singh
The Sikh Regiment

"Subedar Naranjan Singh has shown himself to be an outstanding Platoon Commander during all the Burma Campaigns from 1942 to 1945, having seen a great deal of heavy fighting. In particular, on 3RD of May 1945, he was detailed to contact and destroy an enemy party of 40 in the village of Mondaing in Burma. To reach this village entailed a march of four miles over very open country in daylight. With great skill and leadership, he led his men to Mondaing where he made contact with the enemy, killing a Japanese officer and three men without loss to his Platoon. In addition, he captured and destroyed an enemy truck with much ammunition. On the night of 10TH May, Subedar Naranjan Singh was in command of an ambush party, which while returning to the Battalion area came on to the 'B' Echelon transport of a large enemy force attacking the Battalion position. Without hesitation, he led his Platoon to attack and inflicted great number of casualties on the enemy and damage to his transport. He continued to harass the enemy from the rear until the Japanese force stopped its attacks and retreated from the front of the Battalion position. He had been slightly wounded during the last two months but on both occasions refused evacuation. The leadership and skill of Subedar Naranjan Singh has throughout been of the highest order and he has in great measure contributed to the successes obtained by his Company." He was strongly recommended for and awarded the Military Cross on 19TH July 1946.

Lieutenant Ujagar Singh
The Sikh Regiment

"At Aronyaung, Mayo Peninsula in Burma on the night of 20TH April, Lieutenant Ujagar Singh was Second–in–Command of the Company holding a high ridge on the right of the Battalion's position. At about 2000 hours Lieutenant Ujagar Singh, who was in a position at the foot of the ridge, received an urgent message from his Company Commander to come to his assistance on the ridge top. By the time Lieutenant Ujagar Singh with his Platoon had reached the top, the Japanese had attacked, the Company Commander and two men were missing, and the rest of the men were out of the trenches and disorganised. Lieutenant Ujagar Singh at once got all his men back in their trenches, and going from position to position encouraged his men to such good effect that they held on to their hill in spite of being attacked twice more in the night, and heavily mortared and grenaded the next morning". For his leadership and stout resistance Lieutenant Ujagar Singh was strongly recommended for and awarded the Military Cross on 16TH December 1943.

Burma

Subedar Gurbachan Singh
The Sikh Regiment

"On 6TH July 1945 at Atya in Burma, Subedar Gurbachan Singh was the senior officer of 'A' Company, which was detailed to attack a strongly fortified Japanese position, situated in an isolated Pagoda in the centre of flooded paddy fields. The attack was across 300 yards of open, flooded paddy fields often waist deep in water and swept by shell and Machine Gun fire. The Company Commander was seriously wounded and the Company Officer Lieut. Jogindar Singh was killed while moving forward to take over command of the Company. Subedar Gurbachan Singh at once took command and endeavoured to lead two Platoons round in a flank attack under the covering fire of the leading Platoon, which was already pinned to the ground by the enemy fire. Heavy casualties were suffered and to save further loss of life the Company was ordered to withdraw. With complete disregard for his own safety, Subedar Gurbachan Singh moved from section to section-passing orders, cheering, and encouraging his men. It took Subedar Gurbachan Singh twenty four hours to extricate his Company, together with all their wounded, arms and ammunition and throughout this time he was always to be seen where the fire was hottest and the situation most critical. With gallantry, resolution and complete disregard for his own safety Subedar Gurbachan Singh was an inspiration to all ranks and entirely responsible for the successful extrication of his Company from an untenable position." Subedar Gurbachan Singh was awarded an immediate Military Cross.

Subedar Mohinder Singh
Sikh Light Infantry

"On 18TH March 1945, Subedar Mohinder Singh was Second-in-Command of 'B' Company, Sikh Light Infantry. The Company was ordered to capture the village of Kandaingbauk in Meiktilla area of Central Burma. Within the first five minutes of the advance, the Company Commander was killed and all the Platoon Commanders wounded. Subedar Mohinder Singh was severely wounded in the leg. Despite his wound, he took command of the Company and continued the advance, until the Company was pinned down, by accurate Medium Machine Gun, Light Machine Gun, and Mortar fire. Subedar Mohinder Singh re-organised the Company under fire and withdrew them to a more favourable position. He was the last man to withdraw and refused to have his wound dressed until all his men had been treated. The Company had suffered heavy casualties; 25 killed and 53 wounded, including all officers and Platoon Havildars, yet this young officer, though in considerable pain, showed his powers of leadership and command and extricated his Company skilfully. When his wound had been dressed, he asked permission to attack again. Throughout the action Subedar Mohinder Singh displayed outstanding instigative drive and courage in the best traditions of the Sikhs." Subedar Mohinder Singh was awarded the Military Cross on the 2ND March 1945.

Burma

Subedar Bachan Singh
The Sikh Regiment

"At Skanemtkyi in Burma on 6TH May 1945, Subedar Bachan Singh was the senior officer of the advance guard companies, who spotted a party of fifteen Japanese bathing in the Pani Chaung by Kaemgngegy. They were immediately attacked, some were killed, and the remainder chased across the Nullah into the village. Once reaching the village the Platoon came under very heavy rifle and Medium Machine Gun fire. The Japanese held the village in great strength and the attackers suffered a number of casualties. Subedar Bachan Singh realised that, owing to the close proximity of several wounded men to the enemy trenches, any further advance would be impossible until these men had been evacuated. With complete disregard for his own safety, he therefore led three men forward in an endeavour to silence the enemy trench, which was preventing the collection of the wounded. Under heavy fire, this party crawled forward to within ten yards of the enemy trench, where it was stopped by a six-foot bamboo fence. They endeavoured to throw grenades over this fence into the enemy trench but became an easy target for the enemy and the three men were rapidly killed, leaving Subedar Bachan Singh as the sole survivor. He crawled back, collected another section and again endeavoured to close in with the enemy strong point from another direction, but the party was again stopped from closing in with the enemy by another bamboo fence and further casualties were suffered. Subedar Bachan Singh, realizing that further attacks on this strong point would only result in further casualties, ordered two men to give covering fire while he crawled forward and dragged six wounded men back into the cover of a nearby trench. Then under cover of Mortar fire he led a third and successful attack, which succeeded in capturing the village and liquidating the enemy. The gallantry, tenacity and complete disregard for his own safety of Subedar Bachan Singh were an inspiration to the whole Company and resulted in nearly 30 of the enemy killed and many more wounded, and a large amount of equipment being captured and destroyed. The enemy was approximately a 100 strong and after their first surprise fought with dogged courage. The courage, self sacrifice, and devotion to duty of Subedar Bachan Singh was of the highest order and far succeeded the call of duty." Subedar Bachan Singh was awarded an immediate Military Cross on 6TH May 1945.

Burma

Lieutenant Baldev Singh
1STt Patiala Infantry

"On the night of 18TH April 1944, a superior enemy force took up a position close to the Company. On the morning of 19TH April, Lieutenant Baldev Singh was ordered to keep this enemy force occupied, in order to prevent it digging in before the arrival of the main force. Lieutenant Baldev Singh organised constant "Jitter" parties around the enemy position, himself leading one of these parties. He successfully prevented the enemy digging more than one foot in ten hours. This greatly assisted the main force in capturing the position and saved many casualties. Subsequently on 28TH April, he led a party of twenty strong on a special mission lasting four days. This party operated at a radius of ten miles from the main base, behind the strong enemy position at Sanjing. In carrying out this mission, Lieutenant Baldev Singh's party was for seventy-two hours on the main Japanese line of control, during which time he laid three successful ambushes against superior enemy forces. As a result of these ambushes, 29 of the enemy were killed; three of them by Lieutenant Baldev Singh, and in addition much valuable information was obtained. His casualties were one man wounded. The success of this mission was due to the personal gallantry and leadership of Lieutenant Baldev Singh. Lieutenant Baldev Singh's determination, devotion to duty and disregard for personal safety has been noticeable in previous operations to which he had taken part." Lieutenant Baldev Singh was strongly recommended for and awarded the Military Cross on 15TH August 1944.

Subedar Ajmer Singh
1ST Patiala Infantry

"On 24TH July 1944, Subedar Ajmer Singh was commanding the forward platoon, when his Company was ordered to capture Ralph Hill, a prominent feature covering the enemy line of control on Tamu road in Burma. His forward Sections were held up by heavy enemy fire. His Platoon was now in a position overlooked by the enemy. There was no other approach to the enemy's position. Subedar Ajmer Singh at once went forward, encouraging his men and with complete disregard for his own safety, he personally led his Platoon up the steep slopes of the hill with great determination and dash, completely annihilating the enemy platoon. Subedar Ajmer Singh's brilliant leadership and bravery enabled his men to kill 17 of the enemy and capture all their arms and equipment. On 27TH July 1944, he led a very successful fighting patrol at Lockhao River, killing many Japanese who wanted to escape that way. And from 27TH July to 31ST July, when the Company had succeeded in establishing themselves in the rear of the enemy's position, he successfully led many small Jittering parties the whole day, to stop the enemy from strengthening their positions before the final attack. Throughout the bitter fighting at Sakpao and subsequent operations, Subedar Ajmer Singh set a magnificent example and was an inspiration to all ranks of the Battalion." Subedar Ajmer Singh was strongly recommended for and awarded the Military Cross on 12TH October 1944."

Burma

Jemadar Amir Singh
1ST Patiala Infantry

"On 19TH April 1944, a strong enemy force occupied a position between Jemadar Amir Singh's Company and the Imphal-Ukhrul road in Burma. Jemadar Amir Singh was therefore given the task of harassing this enemy force, in order to prevent him from digging in before the arrival of the rest of the Battalion. Jemadar Amir Singh led a section, which operated on the enemy's flank and continuously harassed the enemy to great effect. When he was due to be relieved he again volunteered to lead another section, as he considered that his knowledge of the area would be of great assistance. He was eventually recalled for further operations. During the whole of the period he successfully kept the enemy occupied and inflicted a number of casualties on them. Later in the same day, Jemadar Amir Singh was commanding a leading Platoon in an attack on a hill feature covering the main enemy position. Under heavy enemy fire, he led his Platoon with such dash and determination that the enemy was forced to beat a hasty retreat. Subsequently another Platoon passed through his position; he then repulsed the enemy counter attack on the flank of the other Platoon, inflicting heavy casualties. Again, on 29TH April he commanded a party of 20 which was sent out, with the task of conducting Guerrilla operations on the enemy in the Samshak area. His party operated continuously for 18 hours on the Japanese line of control and laid several successful ambushes, with the result that at least 12 Japanese were killed and valuable identifications obtained, without any loss to his party. Throughout these operations Jemadar Amir Singh led his Platoon with skill and determination". Jemadar Amir Singh was strongly recommended for and awarded the Military Cross on 16TH August 1944.

Jemadar Rakha Singh
1ST Patiala Infantry

"On 19TH April 1944, during an attack on Sakpao in Burma, Jemadar Rakha Singh's Platoon was ordered to capture a steep hill overlooking Sakpao. The enemy had established himself on this hill but Jemadar Rakha Singh, by skilful use of the ground, completely surprised the enemy and carried the position at the point of the bayonet, making the enemy withdraw hurriedly and in disorder. Later when his Company Commander was killed and he was severely wounded, with great determination and disregard for his own safety, he took over the command of the company, reorganized his defences and met a second counter attack successfully. He refused to be evacuated and remained in command until the arrival of the Company Commander. He showed leadership, determination and gallantry under fire of the highest order". Jemadar Rakha Singh was awarded the Military Cross on 21ST May 1944.

Burma

Jemadar Sarwan Singh
1ST Patiala Infantry

"During the advance on enemy positions in the Chamol area in Burma, on 34TH July 1944, Jemadar Sarwan Singh was commander of the forward Platoon and established himself on the bound, after pushing back a small enemy party to a hill beyond. Another Platoon, ordered to leapfrog through, had not yet arrived, when Jemadar Sarwan Singh saw two enemy platoons advancing towards the targeted position. Realizing that the enemy position would become very strong on arrival of the reinforcements, Jemadar Sarwan Singh at once, without waiting for orders, led a charge on the advancing enemy. When his forward section was held up by heavy Light Machine Gun fire from the front and a bunker position on his right, he put his 2 inch Mortar and reserve section to neutralize the right position. Without hesitation, shouting at the top of his voice" Patiala Will Not Be Held Up By The Japanese", and with complete disregard for his own safety, personally led the forward sections into uphill charges. After a stiff fight, in which many enemy soldiers were killed, he succeeded in capturing both enemy positions before the arrival of his reinforcements. The enemy soon put up a counter attack on their lost positions. Again, quite regardless of his own safety, he moved between his three sections, first to ensure that fire was held until the enemy were within forty yards and later to exhort the men under his command during the actual attack. The enemy was forced to retreat in disorder, abandoning four of their dead comrades on the field. From the noise in the Nullah nearby it appeared that considerable damage was done to the enemy. By his very fine personal example and leadership, under almost intolerable weather conditions, he captured the position, which if allowed to be reinforced would have resulted in a major operation and many casualties. Earlier, when in occupation of a defensive position near Chamsol, he exhibited remarkable qualities of leadership and personal gallantry in beating off all enemy attacks. Although wounded during the four attacks, he refused to be evacuated until ordered by his Company Commander the next morning. On 25TH July 1944, when his Company was boxing-in the enemy position in Chamsol area, he again proved himself most resourceful in preventing all his efforts to escape. Jemadar Sarwan Singh's dash throughout these operations has been of a very high order, he showed most outstanding power of leadership under most difficult conditions, while his personal bravery and relentless determination to close with the enemy can seldom have been surpassed." Jemadar Sarwan Singh was strongly recommended for and awarded the Military Cross on 12TH October 1944.

Burma

Subedar Darbara Singh
1ST Patiala Infantry

"On 25TH July 1944, at Ralph Hill, after the capture of the enemy position, a platoon under the command of Subedar Darbara Singh was sent to clear a road to 1ST Seaforths Highlander's position, about two miles away. His scouts saw an enemy party in position in their front, covering a gun withdrawal, which was escorted by one company. Subedar Darbara Singh, who was moving with the leading section, at once led the charge, without waiting for the rest of the platoon to come up. He succeeded in capturing the position, after killing all seven Japanese occupants. He then advanced further and with his whole platoon captured a feature overlooking the road. He again inflicted heavy casualties on the enemy's main party, including two gun mules. Later, when the enemy counter attacked in superior force to regain the feature, he repulsed the attack with heavy losses to the enemy, with the result that the enemy had to leave all gun ammunition and vital parts of the gun on the spot. Subedar Darbara Singh's dauntless courage, self sacrifice, and bold leadership were of a very high order and were responsible for the loss of a gun and heavy casualties to the enemy." Subedar Darbara Singh was strongly recommended for and awarded the Military Cross on 16TH November 1944.

Subedar Chaiju Singh
1ST Punjab Regiment

Officers and men of 1ST Punjab Regiment in Burma, in their race for Rangoon, performed many daring and gallant deeds. On May 16TH, Subedar Chaiju Singh's fighting patrol contacted a party of thirty Japanese, dug in on a small feature. Despite his numerical inferiority, the Subedar led a direct attack against the Japanese machine-gun post and personally killed a Japanese officer in close combat, while his patrol accounted for ten others; the remaining Japanese took to their heels. Subedar Chaiju Singh was awarded the Military Cross for his conspicuous gallantry and leadership.

Subedar Gurbachan Singh
1ST Punjab Regiment

"During the Second Arakan Campaign in Burma, 1ST Punjab Regiment had commenced its epic struggle to clear the Ngakyedauk Pass of the enemy. Various tactical positions were occupied on the western slopes of the Mayu Range. On February 10TH, while advancing to its objective, which was held up by the Japanese in a strongly entrenched position, the Commanding Officer was killed almost immediately. Subedar Gurbachan Singh carried on and silenced the post by courageously crawling forward and throwing grenades at the post. As no further progress could be made the company, with its dead and wounded, withdrew on the following morning. The commanding officer and five other ranks were killed and Jemadar Lall Singh and seven other ranks wounded." For his gallant conduct and leadership, Subedar Gurbachan Singh was awarded the Military Cross.

Burma

Sepoy Sewa Singh
1ST Punjab Regiment

"On May 16TH 1945, 'A' company, on its dash for Rangoon, had to mop up many Japanese companies on the way and their advance was held up by heavy automatic fire from concealed positions. Subadar Sewa Singh took a reconnaissance patrol forward through dense jungle, directed artillery fire on the Japanese bunker holding up the advance and personally led a small party which drove the Japanese from their positions, killing three of them." For his gallantry and leadership, Subedar Sewa Singh was awarded the Military Cross.

Subedar Sukhmandar Singh
1ST Punjab Regiment

"On 12TH February 1944, Subedar Sukhmandar Singh was commanding No.8 Platoon of 'A' Company on Cresta Run in the Naguebaik Pass in Burma. He was ordered by his Company Commander to take point 1070 with his platoon. After a stiff climb, the platoon reached its objective and started to dig in, but before much progress had been made, it was attacked from the North end of the feature. This was beaten off successfully and the Japanese party driven off the feature, with the loss of four apparently wounded men. Twice parties of about 15 to 20 Japanese again attacked the platoon, both of which were successfully driven off. In the second attack, a Bren gun jammed at a critical moment and Subedar Sukhmandar Singh personally held the enemy off with a Tommy gun until the stoppage was rectified. The platoon held the feature for another 24 hours, when a Company of another regiment relieved it. Subedar Sukhmandar Singh, a Sikh, was commanding a platoon of young Jat Sepoys inexperienced in war and the fact that his platoon put up such a stout-hearted defence reflects the greatest credit on this officer. In addition he displayed personal courage, determination and leadership of a very high order." Subedar Sukhmandar Singh was awarded the Military Cross 22ND June 1944.

Captain Budh Singh, MC and Bar
1ST Punjab Regiment

"During the night of 12TH/15TH March 1943, at Hitzwe in Burma, Captain Budh Singh's Company was attacked six times by strong determined Japanese forces. All the attacks were driven off with heavy losses to the enemy. Captain Budh Singh throughout the night was an inspiration to his men and it was largely due to his magnificent example that the attacks were so successfully defeated. At dawn on 14TH March, a force of approx. 300 Japanese attacked a platoon of Captain Budh Singh's Company holding a hill guarding Battalion Headquarters. Captain Budh Singh went with reinforcements to his platoon and took charge of the situation. The attack was driven off, leaving 73 dead Japanese around the position. Captain Budh Singh on both these occasions displayed courage and leadership of a very high order." For his valiant leadership, Captain Budh Singh was awarded a bar to his Military Cross on 4TH March 1943.

Burma

Captain Budh Singh
1ST Punjab Regiment

"On the Donbaik front in Burma, the 'D' company, 1ST Punjab Regiment had advanced with great gallantry on the right. As it reached the start-line, it found the two companies of the Enniskillen Fusiliers were not quite up on the start-line. Not wishing to lose the effect of the artillery barrage, the company, under the command of Captain Budh Singh, advanced over the open and bullet-swept country and captured its objective. At that moment both its flanks lay open, owing to the Japanese–occupied position on its left and the momentarily absence of the Enniskillen Fusiliers on the right. Terrific fire on the front and flanks took a heavy toll on the attackers. Captain Budh Singh realized that all that he could do now was to withdraw across the open to his original position. This he did with cool courage, collecting as many of the wounded men as he could on his way back. The company strength was reduced to forty-four through casualties including Jemadar Surjan Singh and Havildar Major Indar Singh." For his gallantry during this engagement, Captain Budh Singh was awarded the Military Cross on 4TH March 1943.

Subedar Sarjit Singh
1ST Punjab Regiment

"Subedar Sarjit Singh came up with the Battalion to the Burma front in 1942 and had fought with it throughout. He was second in command of the Mortar Section. Early in March 1943, when the enemy at Hitzwe attacked the Battalion Headquarters position most violently, most of his men were casualties. With only two other men, he manned both the three inch mortars and kept on engaging the enemy with Medium Machine Gun fire for about one hour, until enough men were raised to attack and drive the enemy away. He proved himself a perfect example of a gallant leader of men. Owing to Subedar Sarjit Singh's steadiness, courage and power of leadership, he was given accelerated promotion and given command of the only Sikh Company of the Battalion, soon to be followed by the position of senior V.C.O. in the Company. As the other two platoons of the Company were composed of very young and raw men, all the difficult tasks in the Company's role were invariably given to Subedar Sarjit Singh. His patrol actions during the Ngakyedauk and Sialamum operations contributed largely to the success of the forthcoming Battalion Operations. The constant outstanding work done by Subedar Sarjit Singh throughout the war and the cool headedness and gallantry that he had shown on all occasions had earned him respect from all ranks of the Battalion." Subedar Sarjit Singh was strongly recommended for and awarded the Military Cross on 19TH March 1945.

Burma

Subedar Munsha Singh
1ST Punjab Regiment

"Subedar Munsha Singh, had been commanding the Sikh platoon in 'A' Company throughout the Burma campaign. He was wounded during the fighting in the Litan area of Arakan and Imphal front. He first distinguished himself in the operations in the Ngakyedauk pass when his platoon led the successful attack on Pt.1070. Next day, in the attack on Sugar Loaf, he led the final assault, which cleared the feature of Japanese soldiers. In this attack, he displayed great qualities of determination and leadership and personally led the bayonet charge, which drove the enemy from his positions. Again fighting in the Litan area, he and his platoon were conspicuous for their excellent work. He was severely wounded leading a counter attack on a strongly held Japanese position. Subedar Munsha Singh had always displayed military qualities of a very high order. A natural leader, his courage and determination were outstanding and an example to all ranks of his Company." Subedar Munsha Singh was strongly recommended for and awarded the Military Cross on 12TH March 1944.

Subedar Kartar Singh
2N Punjab Regiment

"On 23RD November 1945, during an attack in Ngemplak area of Sourabaya in Burma, two sections of the leading platoon of Subedar Kartar Singh's company, of which he was second in command, were pinned down to the ground by enemy automatic fire from two strong concrete bunkers. Subedar Kartar Singh dashed forward from Company Headquarters, under very heavy fire, to take charge of the situation. He then, at very great risk to himself, carried out a personal reconnaissance before leading the third section of the platoon in an outflanking movement, which culminated in a magnificent charge onto the enemy position. While leading this extremely gallant charge, Subedar Kartar Singh fell, severely wounded in the stomach. From where he lay, he continued to shout words of encouragement to his men until they had over-run the position. He refused to be evacuated until he was certain the platoon could continue its advance without him. Subedar Kartar Singh's outstanding leadership and utter disregard for his own safety were superb examples of courage and devotion to duty and inspiration to all." Subedar Kartar Singh was awarded an immediate Military Cross on 23RD November 1945.

Burma

Major Bhag Singh
2ND Punjab Regiment

"On 16TH September 1944, at the commencement of the operation against the Japanese rear guard at Tongzang in Burma, Major Bhag Singh was sent with his Company to cut the Imphal-Tiddim road in the area of Tutee. Owing to the necessity for speed, he had no opportunity to recce the route nor was information available as to enemy dispositions in that area. By skilful navigation, mostly at night, over three miles and a 4,000 foot descent and climb, Major Bhag Singh led his Company through thick jungle over an untracked Nullah crossing to the appointed position. There he positioned his men on the escape route of approximately 100 enemies, whom he had located on the heights dominating the crossing of the Manipur River. The following night the enemy, forced to withdraw, ran into the Company position and finding their way blocked prepared to attack it. Their determined attack was repulsed and the enemy left behind twelve dead, including two officers and much material. A Japanese Sergeant Major was captured, who gave information of vital importance about their future operations. Throughout this and the following night, Major Bhag Singh and his men held on to their position and carried out aggressive patrolling, often under considerable fire and heavy sniping from numerous enemy in the vicinity. The aim of this skilful and difficult operation was to separate two portions of the enemy rear guard, and finally to force the withdrawal of some 200 disorganised Japanese soldiers, which was successfully carried out." Major Bhag Singh was strongly recommended for and awarded the Military Cross on 16TH December 1944.

Subedar Mangal Singh
1ST Punjab Regiment

"Subedar Mangal Singh was ordered to attack and capture a feature, the approach to which was over a very narrow knife-edge, covered the whole way by enemy Medium Machine Guns. Subedar Mangal Singh successfully captured the enemy's forward post, destroyed a Medium Machine Gun, and a section of seven enemies. Soon afterwards another pocket of the enemy was spotted, about 30 yards away and Subedar Mangal Singh charged at them with his two sections, but unfortunately came under a shower of grenades from two previously undiscovered enemy positions, and half the force became casualties, including himself. He successfully brought all his casualties back and to reach the seriously wounded, he had to creep right forward. While doing so, another grenade blew most of his right toe off, as he carried the wounded man back to his trenches and continued to command his platoon until relieved later. Subedar Mangal Singh, during this action and throughout the previous campaign, had shown the finest example of gallantry, daring, and leadership and had earned the praise of all ranks." Subedar Jaswant Singh was strongly recommended for and awarded the Military Cross on 25TH February 1944.

Burma

Major Harbans Singh Virk
12TH Frontier Force Regiment

"On 8TH March 1945, Major Virk was in command of "C" Company and with Royal Deccan Horse in support, was ordered to attack and capture the village of Sadaung, in Burma, which was known to contain a strong force of the enemy with 75mm guns, Medium Machine guns and Mortars. He went in from the North at 1315 hours, and inspite of heavy enemy fire, secured a firm base well inside the village. At 1430 hours, however, his company was held up by heavy mortar fire from South of the village, and very accurate Medium Machine Gun fire from the front and a pagoda to the left flank. Discharger Grenades were also being showered in to his position. Nothing daunted this gallant officer, filled with determination to exterminate the enemy, he left the platoon in what cover was available, and extricated his other two platoons, with the objective of putting in an attack from the Eastern Flank. The country here was very boggy and two tanks at once sank into the mud, but relying on swift and decisive action to achieve success, he ordered the tanks away to high ground on the left to give covering fire and formed his men for the attack. At 1600 hrs, he rose and with a great shout to his men, dashed into the centre of the enemy position, which was quickly over run. He then led his men in a further magnificent charge, to clear the southern portion of the village, and finally reported at 1700 hrs that the enemy was beaten and running. The tanks then came into their own and demoralized the running Japanese. The enemy killed by Major Virk and his company on this afternoon, amounted to over one hundred and the booty included two 75mm guns, five Medium Machine Guns, two 81mm Mortars and quantities of small arms and equipment, at the cost of comparatively light casualties to the Company. This victory was solely due to the high courage and initiative of this lion-hearted officer. Throughout the action, under extremely heavy fire, he was ubiquitous, climbing on to the tanks to give orders under hails of bullets. He so inspired his men with his indomitable spirit, that when he gave the order for the charge, they followed him with the utmost dash and the battle was won. This officer had shown the highest qualities of courage and leadership throughout the present operations, and had led and inspired his men on to victory on several previous occasions. It was the faith in their leader, inspired and bred from previous actions that gave the great impetus to the company to achieve what they did on this day. His personal count of dead Japanese had been considerable." Major Harbans Singh Virk was awarded an immediate Military Cross followed by the DSO on 27TH May 1945.

Burma

Jemadar Phaga Singh
12TH Frontier Force Regiment

"On 2ND March 1945, Jemadar Phaga Singh was a Platoon Commander in 'A' Company, which was part of an attacking force ordered to capture and clear the area of Meiktilla town in Burma. The attack was supported by a troop of tanks. Shortly after crossing the starting line, Jemadar Phaga Singh's platoon came under very heavy automatic, mortar, grenade and rifle fire, and was pinned to the ground, suffering casualties. The whole area was a mass of bunkers and foxholes, and infested with cunningly concealed snipers. Without hesitation, Jemadar Phaga Singh ran forward to his leading Sections, pinpointed the opposition in front of each, and then rushed back to the tanks, giving them instructions, led them up to positions from which they could bring fire to bear on the enemy. Throughout the action he was under heavy fire, and his complete disregard for his own life, and the devotion with which he calmly directed the fire of the tanks, thus enabling his men to advance and mop up, was beyond praise, and an inspiration not only to his own men, but to the tank crews in addition. He was greatly to the fore in the evacuation of his casualties. His indomitable courage and determination to exterminate every Japanese soldier, throughout eight gruelling hours of stiff hand-to-hand fighting was worthy of the highest standards of the Indian Army, and his personal count of enemy dead was considerable. As part of the same operations, Jemadar Phaga Singh's platoon was ordered to form part of Road Block on the Mandalay Road. On the morning of 14TH March, the enemy attacked the position, but was driven off with heavy casualties. Thereafter supported by armoured cars, Jemadar Phaga Singh's platoon was ordered to go forward and capture a Japanese gun that had been located the previous day. On hearing the advance, the enemy opened up with concentrated fire and made determined attempts to destroy the armoured cars with magnetic mines. In this, they were frustrated, but the cars were forced to withdraw to a safer distance. Jemadar Phaga Singh then went in to the attack, and under his inspiring leadership, the Frontiersmen overran the enemy position, killing 20 Japanese in hand-to-hand fighting and completely routing the enemy force, considerably superior in numbers to their own. In the two actions detailed above Jemadar Phaga Singh showed the highest qualities of courage and true leadership, and the great success achieved against determined enemy are due to the outstanding qualities of a great leader in the Field." Jemadar Phaga Singh was awarded an immediate Military Cross at the conclusion of the above fighting.

Burma

Jemadar Udham Singh
12TH Frontier Force Regiment

"On 10TH March 1945, Jemadar Udham Singh was the platoon commander of No.3 Platoon, 'A' Company, detailed to attack and clear up an enemy position astride the road Meiktila-Mahlaing in Burma. A troop of tanks was operating in support of his platoon. The platoon deployed and went into action with the tanks on the left of the road and at once came up against fanatical Japanese resistance. The country here was broken, and covered with thick scrub, and a network of defences and foxholes, which proved more than usually difficult to locate. Jemadar Udham Singh, however, resolved to deal harshly with the enemy, and led his section in with great dash and vigour. He led his men, in this close and difficult country, in an exemplary manner, without thought of personal danger, being always to the fore and quick to expose himself whenever it became necessary to direct the fire of the tanks. He took his platoon into action at 25 strong and after magnificent fighting on the part of all, he had only 12 men left, the remainder either being killed or wounded. The troop of tanks then went off, leaving his small force to carry on without them and surrounded by snipers on all sides. This situation, however, merely goaded this gallant leader to redouble his efforts, rallying his men he went forward again, clearing up trench after trench, and inflicting great slaughter amongst the enemy. It was not until 1400 hours that a fresh company, supported by tanks, could be sent forward to relieve him on the ground to carry on the fight. Jemadar Udham Singh had killed many Japanese, both with grenades and Sten gun, and it was his gallantry and inspiring leadership that spurred on the remnants of his gallant band of men to fight with frenzy, until finally ordered to withdraw and reorganize. Jemadar Udham Singh's conduct in the evacuation of all his casualties under heavy fire, both small arms and artillery, was of the highest order, and his bravery and inspiring leadership was an example to all members of the Battalion." Jemadar Udham Singh was awarded an immediate Military Cross on 10TH March 1945.

Sketch of a Sikh soldier in Burma

Burma

Jemadar Narain Singh
12TH Frontier Force Regiment

"On 10TH April 1945, Jemadar Narain Singh was a platoon commander of 'B' Company, when the Battalion was ordered to attack and consolidate the Frontier Force lines area of the main Pyawbwe-Meiktila road in Burma, as there was a strong enemy presence there. The 'B' Company had to advance across 1,000 yards of bullet-swept, open country. Jemadar Narain Singh was in the vanguard of the advance, which was an inspiration to the remainder of the Battalion, who were privileged to witness his determined progress. Jemadar Narain Singh kept the platoon under perfect control, inspite of casualties from the enemy's Light Machine Guns. On arrival, it was found that contrary to reports, the Frontier Force lines area was very strongly held by the enemy. The attack went in on a two Company front, with 'B' Company on the right. Jemadar Narain Singh's platoon at once came under heavy mortar and automatic fire and the platoon suffered casualties. Holding his ground, however, Jemadar Narain Singh arranged, at great personal risk to himself, the evacuation of his wounded and then personally directed the artillery fire, preliminary to his further advance. He then led his platoon forward, but the enemy once again replied with everything he had and the attacking platoon suffered more casualties. Time was precious, however, and without further ado, Jemadar Narain Singh led the charge, and rushed in at their head to capture the first objective. Inspired by his leadership his men fought magnificently and the area was soon under control. There remained the wooded area, around the church and up to the railway line to be captured. Again, 'B' Company was on the right, and Jemadar Narain Singh urgently requested that his platoon lead the attack. His request was granted and the men went in at the head of the tanks. The enemy fought back bravely and tenaciously, as the platoon cleared the whole area yard-by-yard. Throughout this day, Jemadar Narain Singh led his men with utmost gallantry. His fierce cries of 'Sat Siri Akal', and the encouragement he gave his men, going from section to section and personally directing the attack, were an inspiration to all, and his imperturbability under the heaviest fire was beyond praise. On this day, Jemadar Narain Singh personally killed six Japs and his platoon added another 133 to a very substantial Battalion total. Within the Company he earned for himself the name of 'Sher' (Lion)." Jemadar Narain Singh was awarded an immediate Military Cross on the 10TH April 1945.

Burma

Subedar Kartar Singh
12TH Frontier Force Regiment

"Throughout the period from May to August 1944, Subedar Kartar Singh was employed as senior Viceroy's Commissioned Officer in the Sikh Company of the Battalion in Burma. In this capacity, he was also the Company's Second in Command. During this period, the Company took part in many engagements against the Japanese and Subedar Kartar Singh was with the Company on each of these actions. When in action, he conducted himself in every respect within the highest traditions of the Indian Army. Subedar Kartar Singh was always at the head of his Company, shouting words of encouragement and inspiration to the men. His utter fearlessness and complete disregard for personal danger was an invaluable steadying influence upon the men of the Sikh Company, a large proportion of which were young and without experience of war. His personality and vitality were most pronounced in battle and he proved to be as steadfast and courageous in adversity as in success. He was a dashing leader in close hand-to–hand fighting. During periods of rest, Subedar Kartar Singh's knowledge and control of the men of his Company was of great value to the Company Commander in his work of reorganisation and rehabilitation. Subedar Kartar Singh was an excellent administrator and under his charge, the internal administration of the Company, so essential to success in operations, worked with great smoothness. He constantly displayed gallantry, leadership, and initiative of a very high order and was at all times an example to the Company, of offensive spirit and desire to close in with and destroy the enemy. He was a fine officer, with a fine influence in the area of a difficult command." Subedar Kartar Singh was awarded an immediate Military Cross in August 1944.

Jemadar Ujagar Singh
14TH Punjab Regiment

"On 14TH October 1944, Jemadar Ujagar Singh, was in command of a fighting patrol of 25 men, which had arrived on the Mamgheng ridge in the Chin Hills in Burma. Early in the morning, the patrol encountered an enemy force of over 500 armed with 31 Light Machine Guns and Mortars. The battle which ensued, lasted for over three hours, and many casualties were inflicted upon the enemy. During these operations Jemadar Ujagar Singh commanded his patrol with marked ability and courage and though opposed by overwhelming odds kept up the battle until casualties and lack of ammunition compelled him to disengage." Jemadar Ujagar Singh was strongly recommended for and awarded the Military Cross on 28TH February 1945.

Burma

Subedar Karam Singh
12TH Frontier Force Regiment

"Subedar Karam Singh had commanded a Machine Gun platoon for eighteen months in the forward area of the Arakan front in Burma. During this period, he had shown outstanding qualities of leadership and devotion to duty. On 9TH October 1944, in the area south of Maunder, one his sections was preparing to take up a position on the Sausage feature, when it came under concentrated artillery fire from a Japanese 75mm gun. One of his Sepoys was badly wounded and Subedar Karam Singh, regardless of his personal safety, ran out into the open and brought him back into a trench. In the afternoon of the same day, one of his Sections was giving supporting fire on to Point 305 feature, and shortly after opening fire; its guns came under direct fire from an enemy 75mm gun, but encouraged by Jemadar Karam Singh's presence and coolness under fire, the Section maintained its concentrated fire. The platoon thus neutralized the enemy's small arms fire and enabled the operation to be carried out successfully with few casualties. For a further month, until its withdrawal in November, Subedar Karam Singh commanded his Platoon with great courage, under constant enemy shellfire. He was at all times an inspiration and example to his men and was responsible for the many successful attacks carried out by his Platoon against the enemy." Subedar Karam Singh was awarded the Military Cross on 26TH December 1944.

Jemadar Santa Singh
13TH Frontier Force Rifles

"On 6TH April 1945, 'A' Company was in position on the summit of a high, steep feature, East of Taungup Road in Burma. The summit was divided into two knolls of equal height, separated from each other by a bare narrow ridge about a hundred yards long and five yards wide. The sides of the ridge were almost precipitous. The enemy, about thirty to forty strong, with medium Machine Gun and two Light Machine Guns, were dug in on the Eastern Knoll. Jemadar Santa Singh led his platoon along the ridge, with supporting fire from tanks and Medium Machine Guns on the South and North flanks respectively. When supporting fire ceased he led his platoon straight in on the enemy positions. Although wounded in the first rush he charged on, inflicting heavy casualties on the enemy with his Sten gun. The attack and subsequent consolidation were successful, the enemy Medium Machine Gun was captured and heavy casualties inflicted on the enemy, sixteen bodies being recovered, including that of an officer. With this attack, the enemy resistance on Point 370, which had been the scene of bitter fighting for two days, ceased. Throughout, the great personal courage and skill shown by Jemadar Santa Singh, allied to his complete disregard for personal risk, was an inspiration to his platoon, which under his command nothing would have stopped, and a vital factor in the complete capture of the feature." Jemadar Santa Singh was awarded an immediate Military Cross.

Burma

Major Kehar Singh Rai
12TH Frontier Force Regiment

"On 8TH July 1944, a Japanese force of some 500 strong, supported by Artillery, Mortars, and Medium Machine Guns, attacked positions in the village of Chepu in Burma, held by a Battalion of 12TH Frontier Force Regiment. The Japanese managed to occupy the North and higher end of a hill feature overlooking the village, thus dominating the positions below with Medium Machine Guns. The troops in the lower positions were very exposed, but it was essential to the success of the operations that these positions should continue to be held. Major Kehar Singh Rai was ordered to take his company forward into these positions to reinforce the Company already there. On arrival in the positions, Major Rai found that both the Company Commander and the Company Officer of this Company had been killed and that the Company had suffered heavy casualties. He at once rallied the men and reorganized the defence of the area. Later in the afternoon, two platoons of another Company were despatched to strengthen Major Rai's position. The Company Commander was seriously wounded immediately after arrival in the position. Major Rai at once took command of these men and personally led them to their positions, despite heavy fire from Medium Machine Guns. Throughout the many attacks made upon his position by the Japanese during the day and despite heavy Mortar, Artillery, and Medium Machine Gun fire, Major Rai remained completely unperturbed and was always in complete control of the situation. His personal gallantry and determination in the hand-to-hand fighting, which accompanied these attacks, was a great source of inspiration and encouragement to his men. Major Rai displayed complete contempt for personal safety at all times and was always in the thick of the fight, encouraging his men by both word and deed to even greater efforts. Major Rai's sustained offensive spirit and refusal at any time to permit the initiative to remain in the hands of the attacking Japanese largely contributed to the success of the defence of that day, and the infliction of very heavy casualties upon the Japanese." Major Kehar Singh Rai was strongly recommended for and awarded the Military Cross on 7TH August 1944.

Burma

Major Amrik Singh
12TH Frontier Force Regiment

"During the period Major Amrik Singh was in command he proved himself to be a brave and skilful commander. He fought and led his Company with great distinction at Meiktilla in Burma. On the second day of the attack on the town, and although wounded himself in the shoulder, he refused to be evacuated, and by evening had cleared the enemy from the whole of the built-up area from North to South. In the process, his Company suffered heavy casualties, but his determination to defeat the enemy, and his fine personal example, inspired his men to win through bitter and difficult hand-to-hand fighting. A few days later, he organised a most successful roadblock on the Mandalay Road, when his Company killed 40 Japanese and captured several guns. Again, on the Meiktilla–Mahlaing road he led his Company in to attack and capture the high ground against numerically superior enemy forces over most difficult and broken country, thickly entrenched and bunkered. In two days fighting the infantry with the Tanks in support, and despite their own heavy casualties, they killed over 200 of the enemy. Major Amrik Singh distinguished himself again at Kandaung and at the battle of Pyawbwe, numerous Japanese being killed and much equipment captured on both occasions. Finally, it was Major Amrik Singh and his Company, which after a day and night of tough, close quarter fighting, secured the bridgehead over the Pegu River, thus enabling the Division to continue its advance southwards. This gallant and capable officer was an inspiration and example to his men throughout these operations, and showed a high standard of personal skill and bravery. Despite very heavy casualties amongst his command, he maintained a magnificent fighting spirit in his Company. The Company bears the proud record of never having failed to win all objectives given to them. No praise can be high enough for the way Major Amrik Singh led and commanded his Company throughout these operations." Major Amrik Singh was strongly recommended for and awarded the Military Cross on 15TH May 1945.

Frontier Force Regiment

Burma

Subedar Gurbux Singh
14TH Punjab Regiment

"Subedar Gurbux Singh was second in command of 'A' Company, when the Company carried out an attack on the enemy position on the Windwin feature 5648, on 15TH January 1944. Early in the action the Company Commander, with two platoons, carried out an encircling attack on the enemy and was seriously wounded. On receiving the information, Subedar Gurbux Singh went forward from the covering platoon and on arrival he found that with the Company Commander, the Leading Platoon Commander was also wounded and the Platoon Havildar killed. He reorganized these two platoons, under heavy grenade fire, and pressed home the attack. This was carried out with great dash, largely through Subedar Gurbux Singh's leadership, and the position was taken. On 17TH January 1944, the Company was attacked from the rear by approximately one platoon of the enemy. The attack lasted for two hours and was repulsed. Subedar Gurbux Singh again showed great coolness in the control of his Company. During these actions Subedar Gurbux Singh showed personal courage and leadership powers of high order." Subedar Gurbux Singh was awarded and an immediate Military Cross on 19TH January 1944.

Jemadar Kesar Singh
15TH Punjab Regiment

"On 11TH May at Seitpudaung in Burma, Jemadar Kesar Singh was in command of a fighting Patrol and came under heavy fire from Japanese automatic fire. Four of the platoon were wounded immediately, including Jemadar Kesar Singh. Ignoring his own wounds Jemadar Kesar Singh fought back and by skilful disposition, extricated his platoon, taking his casualties to Paddaukon Village. The Japanese again attacked and attempted to surround him, but Jemadar Kesar Singh again fought back and skilfully extricated his platoon again. He made repeated contact with the enemy and finding all routes blocked by superior numbers of the enemy, took up a defensive position for the night. By ignoring his own wounds and by his cheerfulness and personal example, the Jemadar so heartened the wounded that they too made light of their wounds. On the third day Jemadar Kesar Singh, although in pain, so inspired his platoon that they continued in excellent fighting spirit, fought their way back to their Company line and brought in all their wounded and identifications of enemy killed. The platoon had been out for 56 hours, surrounded by enemy and, though short of food, had covered many miles in thick jungle and fought with conspicuous success, inflicting many casualties on the enemy. It was Jemadar Kesar Singh's high standard of military skill and leadership, his complete disregard for personal safety, his steadiness, determination, and example that inspired his men to such heights of endurance." Jemadar Kesar Singh was awarded an immediate Military Cross.

Burma

Lieutenant Sucha Singh
15TH Punjab Regiment

"Lieutenant Sucha Singh was commanding "D" Company, 15TH Punjab Regiment during the Kama Bridgehead operations near Prome in Burma. On 27TH May 1945, the Company was ordered to move its position to the right in order to close up with the next Company and block a possible escape route of the Japanese in the Bridgehead. Owing to late receipt of the orders, only two platoons of the Company had reached the new position and were not dug in when the Japanese put in their first attack. This was repulsed with heavy loss to the enemy. The third platoon came up before dusk and the defensive position was dug, but not wired, as none could be brought up. A further attack by the Japanese was also beaten off. During the night, altogether seven attacks were put in by the Japanese on this position, which proved that it lay across an important Japanese escape route. Twice during these attacks, the direction of which was from three sides, the Japs penetrated the position but were driven out by grenades and the bayonet. Throughout the engagement, Lieutenant Sucha Singh directed the defence with utmost coolness and determination, encouraging the Company with cheering remarks. During one attack, he killed a Japanese soldier who was creeping up unnoticed along a covered approach. His communication throughout the night was only by a 48 set to the next Company, and his N.C.O.'s set did not work. Nevertheless, he passed all orders through his set with complete coolness and caused most accurate artillery defensive fire to be brought down in front of his position. The Company counted forty-eight dead Japanese bodies' around the position the next morning and the Company had suffered four killed and seven wounded. The leadership of Lieutenant Sucha Singh throughout the whole engagement was of the highest order and contributed very largely to the successful defence of the position and the blocking of one important Jap escape route. In view of the fact that the officer was a subaltern commanding a Company for the first time in action, his performance is considered especially outstanding." Lieutenant Sucha Singh was awarded an immediate Military Cross.

Captain Piara Singh
16TH Punjab Regiment

"On 9TH April, 1944, at Wilugyaung in Burma, Captain Piara Singh was sent to the aid the recovery of three Patrols that were cut off by the enemy. After seven days without food and most of his ammunition exhausted, Captain Piara Singh returned through the enemy lines with these Patrols. On 21ST April 1944, at Khomwei a superior Japanese force attacked his position. He drove them back and chased them some two miles across the plain, inflicting severe casualties on them. On 27TH April, at Laukai, where identification of the enemy was required, he captured two Japanese soldiers, as a result of a skilful ambush. The leadership, high standard of courage and devotion to duty shown by this officer was an example of the highest degree to all his men." Captain Piara Singh was strongly recommended for and awarded the Military Cross on 1ST August 1944.

Burma

Subedar Hari Singh
15TH Punjab Regiment

"During the period 16TH November 1944 to 15TH February 1945, Subedar Hari Singh, a Platoon Commander of "A" Company, showed initiative and personal courage of the highest order on several occasions. On 25TH January at the Ngapyin Bridgehead, in Burma, "A" Company was sent out to investigate the result of an air strike, which had been made about 200 yards outside the Brigade perimeter. Subedar Hari Singh's platoon was leading and had completed its first bound. Subedar Hari Singh was between the two leading sections and had signalled his right hand section Bren gun to move forward slightly. As the Bren gun section moved forward the enemy opened fire and the No 1of the Bren gun was killed. At the same time, fire was opened on the Subedar from his right and front. With great coolness, Hari Singh ordered his Platoon Havildar to man the right hand Bren gun and engage the enemy's Light Machine Guns. Four enemies were killed but the Light Machine Guns were not silenced. Simultaneously a party of about 20 Japanese charged the Platoon position and was engaged by the left hand section, 7 enemies being killed. The Platoon was then ordered to withdraw and Subedar Hari Singh carried out the withdrawal with exceptional ability. Under cover of 2-inch Mortar and Light Machine Gun fire, he withdrew the Platoon group by group without suffering further casualties and bringing back his dead. On several previous occasions, Subedar Hari Singh's Platoon had withstood the worst of strong enemy attacks during the establishment of the Bridgeheads. The excellent control and personal example displayed by Subedar Hari Singh enabled the Platoon to inflict many casualties on the enemy, with little loss to the platoon. At all times Subedar Hari Singh had been an outstanding example to his fellow Viceroy's Commissioned Officers." Subedar Hari Singh was strongly recommended for and awarded the Military Cross on 25TH June 1945.

Major Mohinder Singh
Indian Artillery

"During May, June and July 1944, Major Mohinder Singh commanded his Battery with conspicuous success throughout the operations on the Assam-Burma borders. His technical efficiency, disregard for his own safety under fire and personal encouragement to his subordinates were responsible for the success of such artillery support, asked for by the Infantry at Kohima, Kidena and Ukhrul. During the arduous march to Ukhrul his initiative, energy and the example he set to the men, played a major part in the surmounting by his Battery of obstacles of the utmost severity. Throughout these operations Major Mohinder Singh on all occasions displayed the highest qualities of leadership, devotion to duty and courage, setting thereby an example, which was an inspiration to all with whom he came in contact." Major Mohinder Singh, Singh was strongly recommended for and awarded the Military Cross on 5TH April 1945.

Burma

Jemadar Kapur Singh
15TH Punjab Regiment

"During 16TH November to 15TH February 1945, Jemadar Kapur Singh was an outstanding example to his fellow Viceroy Commissioned Officers for his courage and initiative. On several occasions his Platoon was heavily attacked by the enemy and in particular on the night of 22ND and 23RD January 1945 in the Ngapyin Bridgehead. Attacks started at 1230 hours and immediately his Platoon suffered casualties. One section was completely disabled, having 4 men killed and 2 wounded, leaving a dangerous gap. With a composite section drawn from his Platoon Headquarters and remaining two sections, he continued to deny the ground to the enemy until he was reinforced. The attacks continued throughout the night and Jemadar Kapur Singh, under heavy fire, moved amongst his section posts, exhorting his men with complete disregard for his own safety. In an action a few days later Jemadar Kapur Singh was wounded, while leading his Platoon. Throughout the operations Jemadar Kapur Singh set a high example of courage and determination." Jemadar Kapur Singh was awarded the Military Cross on 28TH August 1945.

Subedar Gurdas Singh
16TH Punjab Regiment

"At the Imphal Area in Burma, on 28TH May 1944, Subedar Gurdas Singh was second in command of his company. The Japanese shelled the Battalion position for some three hours, particularly concentrating on his company's position. The fire was extremely accurate and came mainly from 105 mm guns. These shells in many cases pierced the head cover of the bunkers and the company suffered heavy casualties. Subedar Gurdas Singh moved from bunker to bunker while the shells were exploding. He bandaged up the wounded in bunkers and encouraged the remainder to stand firm. While moving from bunker to bunker, he was wounded by a bursting shell. Unable to move he refused to leave the company position until the Company Commander ordered his stretcher-bearers to carry him out. The fearless example displayed by Subedar Gurdas Singh inspired the whole company with the resolution to hold on at all costs, and undoubtedly contributed to the firmness with which his company beat off subsequent Japanese attacks." Subedar Gurdas Singh was awarded the Military Cross on 3RD July 1944.

Burma

Subedar Narinjan Singh
16TH Punjab Regiment

"Shortly after dark on 27TH July 1944, "A" Company, after a long and arduous flank march of fourteen hours through thick jungle, reached the road Palel-Taku, in Burma, four miles in front of advanced positions occupied by the Battalion. The Company had been ordered to lay an ambush astride the road in this area. The road at this point was completely overlooked by Hill 87, which a patrol of Subedar Narinjan Singh's platoon reported to be occupied by the enemy in great strength. Subedar Narinjan Singh was ordered to attack the hill and drive off the enemy. The ground, over which the attack was to be made, and the exact positions and the strength of the enemy were unknown. Despite this and all the other difficulties inherent in a night attack over un-reconnoitred ground, Subedar Narinjan Singh resolutely led his platoon towards the enemy position. When advancing some distance, the platoon came under fire from automatic rifles. Making an accurate and rapid appreciation of the situation, Subedar Narinjan Singh ordered his platoon to attack. He led the attack to capture the position at the point of the bayonet, driving out the enemy, who fled, leaving a quantity of automatic weapons, rifles and other equipment. By his resolution, courage and skilful handling of his platoon Subedar Narinjan Singh was responsible for capturing, under very difficult conditions, a feature which was essential for the further advance of the Brigade. Subedar Narinjan Singh had constantly shown great personal courage and outstanding leadership, and was an inspiration to his Company throughout the operation." Subedar Narinjan Singh was awarded the Military Cross on 11TH August 1944.

Jemadar Gurbachan Singh
Indian Armoured Corps

"During the attack of Pyawbwe in Burma, on 10TH April 1945, Jemadar Gurbachan Singh was commanding a troop of tanks leading the attack. With superlative dash and vigour, and in order to give the maximum support to the attacking infantry, he led his troops unscathed through a heavily mined area, onto the enemy position, where he found himself almost on top of two enemy Light Machine Gun posts. Disdaining to reverse his tank, and leaning far out of his turret, he succeeded in throwing grenades into and destroying both positions. He then engaged and destroyed a 70 mm gun, a 37 mm gun, and a Light Machine Gun position, and forced a 75 mm gun to be pulled out of action, which was later found abandoned. The alert, fearless and dashing leadership of Jemadar Gurbachan Singh was commented on by all ranks taking part in the attack and was of great assistance in the capture of the position, which caused the enemy to withdraw that night." Jemadar Gurbachan Singh was strongly recommended for and awarded the Military Cross on 24TH May 1945.

Burma

Subedar Sham Singh
16TH Punjab Regiment

"On 1ST April 1944, when his Company was in a position southwest of Buthidaung in Burma, Subedar Sham Singh was in command of a recce patrol, which was ambushed and encircled by jungle set on fire by the enemy. Subedar Sham Singh kept complete control of his patrol and fought his way out of the ambush, wiping out an enemy Light Machine Gun and killing at least four of the enemy. In this action, the Patrol lost one man killed. Subedar Sham Singh having withdrawn his Patrol went back, recovered the body, searched the Japanese position, and reported the area clear. In this action, Subedar Sham Singh was wounded but refused to leave his Company. On the following day, Subedar Sham Singh led another patrol against the enemy. After a personal recce of a route used by the enemy, he set up an ambush in which 25 Japanese were killed and injuries were inflicted on the ones fleeing the ambush. Again, on 3RD April Subedar Sham Singh lead a patrol of two sections to the South of Comma position, where they encountered the enemy in superior strength. With great dash and gallantry, the Subedar personally lead his Patrol in a charge. In the ensuing, hand-to-hand fighting, six of the enemy were killed with the bayonet, ten by rifle fire, and at least fifteen more badly wounded, with the loss of only two killed to the patrol. Then Subedar Sham Singh skilfully extricated his patrol under heavy Mortar and Light Machine Gun fire, bringing back an enemy body and enemy weapons for identification. He was the last to withdraw after ensuring that his own dead were recovered. In all these actions, the Platoon's casualties were extremely light. The success obtained by the patrols in these actions was entirely due to the cool-headedness, clear planning, and complete disregard for his own safety of Subedar Sham Singh, who throughout by his leadership, example, and determination to close with the enemy was an inspiration to his men." Subedar Sham Singh was awarded an immediate Military Cross.

Jemadar Pritam Singh
Indian Armoured Corps

"Jemadar Pritam Singh fought in all the actions in which "A" Squadron had been engaged, from the period between crossing the Irrawaddy until the capture of Pegu in Burma. Throughout this campaign, he commanded his tank with extreme competence and effect, and his conduct was deserving of very high praise. He had twice been wounded, and once burnt, when his tank was destroyed by an enemy action on 28TH April 1945. He always showed tremendous keenness to close with the enemy, and fought his tank with an efficiency and relish for action, which called for the highest praise. His conduct throughout was a constant source of inspiration to the men under his command, and the object of confidence and admiration of his Squadron Commander." Jemadar Pritam Singh was awarded the Military Cross on 5TH November 1945.

Burma

Jemadar Lal Singh MC and Bar
Indian Armoured Corps

"At Singu in Burma on 11TH February 1945, Jemadar Lal Singh was Commander of one of the leading tanks, which came under heavy and accurate automatic and close range anti tank gunfire. His tank received multiple hits and the petrol tank began to leak. In spite of the grave risk of fire, Jemadar Lall Singh remained in action, returning the fire of the guns and making calm and accurate reports to his troop leader. Later while still engaging the gun, which had not yet been silenced, his tank was again penetrated frontally. Jemadar Lall Singh, unperturbed, reported the position of the flash, which he could now see and with the help of other tanks silenced it. Although his tank had received 13 direct hits of which 3 penetrated, he kept his tank in action until assaulting troops reached the objective. He only then halted, when all his petrol had expired. His skill, dogged determination, and splendid courage were an inspiration to the remainder of the Squadron." Jemadar Lal Singh was strongly recommended for and awarded the Military Cross on 24TH April 1945.

Jemadar Lal Singh, MC
Indian Armoured Corps

"At Pozut in Burma, on 25TH April 1945, Jemadar Lall Singh encountered a party of Japanese in strongly defended positions. As he was unable to depress the guns of his tank sufficiently to fire at the enemy, he threw grenades from the turret of his tank. The enemy returned fire and wounded him in the shoulder. Undeterred, he dismounted from his tank and by throwing more grenades, killed four of the enemy. Unable to dislodge the remainder, he returned to the Squadron Commander to report the situation and although suffering from his wound, led a section of attached Infantry back to the position where, under his leadership, the remaining enemy were destroyed. Jemadar Lall Singh set a very high example of gallantry and his leadership and disregard for his personal safety was an inspiration to all ranks." For outstanding services and continuous gallantry in action, Jemadar Lall Singh was awarded an immediate Bar to his Military Cross.

Jemadar Sarwan Singh
Burma Regiment

"On the night of 11TH and 12TH May 1946, Jemadar Sarwan Singh, The Burma Regiment, was in command of a platoon, which was in action against a desperate gang of Decoits at Butt Erfly Bend, near Maurin, in the Delta. The fire of the Dacoits was accurate and caused the death of two Sepoys, which in turn caused the troops to hold back. However, Jemadar Sarwan Singh rallied his men and retrieved the situation with a gallant charge, which resulted in the rout of the dacoits, of whom a number were killed, wounded, and captured." Jemadar Sarwan Singh was awarded the Military Cross on 26TH August 1946.

Burma

Risaldar Waryam Singh
Indian Armoured Corps

"On 16TH May 1944 Lieutenant Bishop's troop, of which Risaldar Waryam Singh was the senior Tank Commander, was in support of a Company of 2ND Punjab Regiment, carrying out an attack on the enemy position at Kanglatongbi in Burma. Early on in the action, Lieutenant Bishop was killed and Risaldar Waryam Singh took over the command of the troop. He showed great power of leadership and displayed outstanding dash and initiative. At one time he went forward with one tank ahead of the infantry, clearing up small parties of enemy and was ordered to withdraw. Later he received orders to go forward with one tank and rescue the crew of the ditched tank. The tank was extremely difficult to locate and this operation took an hour to accomplish. During which time he showed great skill and initiative and by his fine example of coolness and imperturbability on the wireless, reassured the trapped crew until he was able to come alongside the tank and take the crew aboard. After this, Risaldar Waryam Singh commanded his troop until the Squadron finally came out of the action at the end of June. Again, on 7TH June, the Squadron was in support of 2ND West Yorkshire Regiment. Risaldar Waryam Singh's troop, with one Platoon of the Yorkshires, was detailed as right flank protection. Here a considerable amount of enemy opposition was encountered, including a 75mm gun. Throughout this action, Risaldar Waryam Singh gave the utmost support to the Infantry and personally knocked out the enemy gun. He maintained his troop in action for 7 hours, showing great coolness and resourcefulness during the whole of the action." Risaldar Waryam Singh was strongly recommended for and awarded the Military Cross on 5TH April 1945.

Jemadar Kartar Singh
Indian Artillery

"From 7TH to 10TH February 1944, between Kreingyaug and east of Ngakyedauk Pass in Burma, during repeated attacks on the gun position, Jemadar Kartar Singh showed great initiative and complete disregard for his own safety. His cheerfulness and calmness under fire served as an inspiring example to all ranks serving under him. He continually moved about from post to post, directing and encouraging the defence, exposing himself thereby to Light Machine Gun fire and grenades at short range." Jemadar Kartar Singh was awarded an immediate Military Cross on 10TH February 1944.

Burma

Risaldar Hazara Singh
Indian Armoured Corps

"At Chaukggyin in Burma on 26TH November 1944, Risaldar Hazara Singh was in command of a troop of tanks leading the advance. The enemy permitted the troop and its escorting infantry platoon to advance right up to his positions before opening heavy automatic and grenade fire on the Infantry, and Mortars and Artillery fire on the tanks. The tanks quickly neutralized the enemy fire, then switched accurate fire on to the other enemy positions, enabling the infantry platoon to assault the forward enemy posts. Throughout the action, which lasted some two hours, Risaldar Hazara Singh displayed great coolness, skill and initiative in engaging enemy positions, maintaining contact with his Infantry platoon and in sending back clear and accurate information by wireless. He withdrew only on orders from the Infantry Brigade Commander. The success of this action, during which considerable casualties were inflicted on the enemy, was very largely due to the skill, leadership and courage of Risaldar Hazara Singh." Risaldar Hazara Singh was strongly recommended for and awarded the Military Cross on 22ND March 1945.

Major Uttam Singh Sidhu
Indian Medical Service

"Major Uttam Singh was Officer Commanding 4TH Bearer Company during the fighting beyond Tiddim, in Burma. Throughout this period he was responsible for their devoted and arduous work in extremely difficult country. In an attack on 16TH December 1943, in particular, his leadership and example were outstanding. Often under heavy fire, he organised his men forward of the Regiment Aid Post and evacuated casualties from behind the heaviest fighting. He was later second-in-command of 37TH Field Ambulance and in the absence of his Commanding Officer, an officiating A.D.M.S. had been thrust upon him. During the withdrawal of the Division, the heavy responsibility not only of collecting casualties from delaying actions but of safely conveying them some 160 miles to Imphal, the casualties and sick gradually mounting to 1000. He carried out this unexpected and difficult task with great initiative and determination. When they came under enemy shellfire, his fine example of courage, devotion to duty and disregard for his own safety inspired confidence in both wounded and medical personnel and was largely responsible for their safe conduct. His behaviour was worthy of the highest traditions of the Indian Army." Major Uttam Singh was strongly recommended for and awarded the Military Cross on 1ST August 1945.

Burma

Jemadar Babu Singh
Indian Artillery

"On 18TH May 1945, at Zalon, a few miles north of Prome in Burma, Jemadar Babu Singh was the artillery observation officer in an isolated position near the bank of the Irrawaddy. At 0445 hours the Company was heavily attacked and the Company Commander was badly wounded, and later died. Jemadar Babu Singh took command, moved boldly about encouraging all ranks, and for a time himself engaged the enemy with a Bren gun. Later, on getting in touch with his guns, he brought down most effective fire on the enemy. At 0900 hours, as all communications failed and the ammunition was running low, Jemadar Babu Singh volunteered to try to get out for help, in spite of the obvious great risk involved in getting through the enemy ring. But before going far he had attracted the attention of one of our light aircraft. Jemadar Babu Singh recognized it as a plane being used for artillery observation and by improvising various signals, made the pilot understand something of the situation. Shortly after the Jemadar got through a message by wireless for help. At 1015 hours, the Royal Air Force began to attack the enemy position and then attacked the Company itself with bombs and machine guns, causing several casualties. With complete disregard for his own safety, Jemadar Babu Singh at once left his trench, and stood up waving and firing Very Lights in an attempt to show the aircraft that they were friendly. At 1530 hours boats arrived, to take away casualties and he helped the success of their evacuation, effectively neutralizing the enemy near the riverbank. During the night, the Company was subjected to grenade and gunfire, which caused several casualties. Before dawn, the enemy again opened up with automatics. Once again, Jemadar Babu Singh neutralized the enemy threat. Early on 19TH May, after assisting in the making of a fire plan to cover the withdrawal, Jemadar Babu Singh executed the withdrawal most skilfully without further trouble. Throughout, Jemadar Babu Singh displayed exceptional initiative doing much more than his normal duty. His example of courage and coolness was magnificent and inspired many. His skill in directing the fire of his guns and in so doing, successfully covering the Company's final withdrawal, earned the praise of all ranks." Jemadar Babu Singh was awarded an immediate Military Cross.

Sikh soldiers operating heavy artillery during Second World War
(J.S. Khurmi)

Burma

Lieutenant Mehar Singh Jawanda
Indian Artillery

"At Sirurukhong in Burma on 14TH June 1944, Lieutenant Mehar Singh was Forward Observation Officer with a Company which was attacking the village. Owing to the conformation of the ground and to the number of buildings in the village, observation was very limited; clear fields of view of over thirty yards were rarely available. Lieutenant Mehar Singh accompanied the leading platoon of the company in the initial assault onto the forward edge of the village. Immediately entering the village the platoon was held up by heavy rifle and Light Machine Gun fire to their front. From the platoon's position, Lieutenant Mehar Singh was unable to pin point accurately the position of the Japanese. Accordingly, he crawled forward until, from a distance of thirty yards, he was able to see the enemy weapon pits. Giving his fire orders from behind a very shallow bund, he brought down fire from the Mountain Battery onto these positions and eliminated them. The platoon advanced and Lieutenant Mehar Singh accompanied it, moving with the leading section. He was constantly on the alert for targets, and once sighted, engaged them without hesitation and with great accuracy. Lieutenant Mehar Singh displayed complete contempt for personal safety and on several occasions carried out reconnaissance of his targets from forty or fifty yards distance, under persistent and heavy, light and medium machine gun fire. His personal bravery and keenness were exceptional and throughout this action, he displayed initiative and dash of a high order in engaging surprise targets. The successes of the attacks were in a large measure due to the excellent control of the Mountain Battery by Lieutenant Mehar Singh." Lieutenant Mehar Singh was awarded the Military Cross on 12TH August 1944.

Jemadar Budh Singh
Indian Artillery

"On 7TH July 1944, at Chepu in Burma, 3RD Mountain Battery was across the lines of withdrawal of a large party of Japanese, who attacked desperately all day in an effort to breakthrough. Jemadar Budh Singh, with about twenty men of his battery, took over a sector of the position just below a ridge whence the main strength of the enemy attacks developed. When a party on his flank was driven back, Jemadar Budh Singh's party held their ground and continued successfully to engage the enemy at a range of a few yards, though their flank was temporarily left open. Jemadar Budh Singh acted with conspicuous gallantry and his determination to hold his ground and to beat the enemy off was an inspiration to his men. Although wounded, he continued to carry out his duties and set a fine example of leadership and courage." Jemadar Budh Singh was awarded an immediate Military Cross.

Burma

Risaldar Banta Singh
Royal Indian Army Service Corps

"In Letmauk Area in Burma from 20TH to 28TH March, Risaldar Banta Singh was commanding a party of 58 AT Company, detached from its parent unit and under command of 2ND Infantry Brigade. The later operations of this Brigade lay through trackless and dense bamboo jungle and culminated in their being surrounded by the enemy and forced to remain in a defended locality for over three weeks until extricated. The terrain embraced by this defended area was most unsuitable for any pack animals and ponies in particular. The area was repeatedly attacked, jittered and subjected to harassing fire by the Japanese. In spite of all these adverse conditions and the fact that he spoke no English and the West Africans knew no Urdu, Risaldar Banta Singh displayed outstanding qualities of initiative, leadership, calmness, and devotion to duty. Throughout he cheerfully rendered the maximum assistance to his Brigade, and all officers who had contact with him, had nothing but the highest praise for his actions, which were an example and inspiration to British, Indians and Africans. His animal management during this most arduous and trying period was of such high order that casualties to men and animals were remarkably slight. The behaviour and example of Risaldar Banta Singh throughout were those of a highly courageous and devoted soldier." Risaldar Banta Singh was strongly recommended for and awarded the Military Cross on 17TH January 1946.

Subedar Sukh Singh
Indian Artillery

"As senior Subedar of the Regiment, Subedar Sukh Singh was specially attached to Scindia Battery. His tact and powers of leadership were most striking. But more than this, his complete coolness under shellfire and courageous example, which steadied the soldiers exposed to fire for the first time, were admired by every man in the Battery and transcended all considerations of different castes. Notably at Kyigon in Burma on March 15TH, he assisted in evacuating casualties to the Regimental Aid Post, when a gun pit received a direct hit from a shell, and shells continued to fall on the troop position. Again, he displayed courage of the highest order when at Meiktilla Dropping Zone. A serious ammunition fire had broken out; ignoring the danger from exploding mortar bombs, he personally led a party of his own men in an attempt to drag valuable stores and ammunition to safety. A parachute ignited a mortar bomb close to him and he was severely wounded in the leg, but continued to encourage the only organised party, until he fainted from his wound. His courage and leadership on this occasion were beyond praise." Subedar Sukh Singh was strongly recommended for and awarded the Military Cross on 16TH November 1945.

Burma

Jemadar Nand Singh
Indian Engineers

"In Arakan, Burma, whilst engaged on operations for the capture of the Westraji Tunnel on the Maungdaw-Buthidaung road on 26th March 1944, Jemadar Nand Singh was in charge of his section, erecting S.B.G. Bridge over a bridge, which had been demolished by the enemy. The work was carried out under fire from enemy snipers. He organised the whole of this task, which was not finished until the following morning. During the night, there were Japanese in close proximity and the Section was sniped and mortared. As soon as the bridge was finished, this enabled tanks to get up to the mouth of the Tunnel and to clear the enemy. Later in the operations in the Eastern Tunnel, with some of his section, he lifted enemy mines laid on the road near the Tunnel and carried out a reconnaissance into the enemy territory. During the whole period, his keenness, in the danger from enemy action, set a high example to his men, which inspired them with confidence, and by his leadership enabled them to carry out their duties in a highly efficient manner." Jemadar Nand Singh was strongly recommended for and awarded the Military Cross on 26TH October 1944.

Military Cross and Bar

In the Burma theatre, the following Indian officers were awarded a Bar to their Military Cross; that is, they won the MC again:

Subedar Gurcharan Singh
11TH Sikh Regiment

Lieutenant Budh Singh
1STPunjab Regiment

Jemadar Lall Singh
Indian Armoured Corps

The 1ST Patiala Regiment performed prodigal feats against the Japanese in Burma.
Field Marshal Slim had this to say about the Patialas: "I want it conveyed to 1ST Patiala that if I were to pick one unit for any special task, it would be 1ST Patiala. I am sanctioning a special one month's leave to the whole unit at Shillong." (Shorey, 2005)

The Burma campaign was the longest campaign fought by the British in the Second World War. It began in December 1941, for the British, with disaster, retreat, and irreversible loss of face in front of the subject population. It ended, in August 1945, in triumph with the total defeat of the occupying Japanese army. Japan suffered her greatest defeat on land in her history and the chief instrument of that defeat was the Indian Army, with the Sikh soldier in the vanguard of all the battles.

CHINA

First Anglo-Chinese War, 1842

Until the 18TH century, opium use in China had consisted mostly of medicinal purposes. By the early 1800s, however, millions of Chinese had become addicted to opium and the illegal drug thrived through black market trade. The main purveyors of opium were the British, though merchants from the United States and other European countries also participated in the trade. One chest of opium contained around 135 pounds of the substance, and the importation of chests grew from 5,000 in 1821 to 35,000 in 1837. Captain Charles Elliot, the British chief superintendent of trade in Canton, put pressure on the Chinese government to legalize the opium trade. Meanwhile, the fatality rate amongst the population caused the Emperor of China to appoint an official to oversee the drug use. Commissioner Lin Zexu had battled the problem of drug use in the provinces of Hubei and Hunan, and now attempted to eliminate opium use. He blockaded the foreign community, stopped trade, ordered Chinese servants to leave, arrested a leading foreign dealer, and demanded that the merchants surrender their inventory of opium. After 47 days, Captain Elliot handed over 20,283 chests to Lin, who destroyed them. In an 1839 letter to Queen Victoria, Lin made the assumption that the British government was not involved in the opium trade, and pointed out that it would be in the best interests of both nations to stop the trade. The letter never reached England. The situation escalated until the British declared war on China in November 1839. The Chinese were technologically no match for the British, and the military was poorly trained for such a showdown. In August 1842, the Treaty of Nanjing officially ended the brutal war. The treaty, among other things, handed Hong Kong over to the British, opened new ports including Shanghai, and granted Britain to be the "most favoured nation".

Second Anglo-Chinese War, 1860

The Chinese government were anxious about British opium trading activity in their country and forced the British to remain within Hong Kong. An incident in 1856, when the Chinese authorities seized 'Arrow', a ship flying the British flag, and arrested its Chinese crew for piracy, caused the British to send an expedition under Lord Elgin. In 1858, the British seized Canton and followed up by an unsuccessful naval attack on the Taku Forts, situated at the mouth of the Pei-ho River. The Chinese refusal to comply with the Treaty of Tientsin caused the escalation of the war and in 1860, a British attacking force gathered in Hong Kong under Lieutenant General Sir J. Hope Grant. There were 4 infantry brigades of British and Indian troops that included 15TH Ludhiana Sikhs, 23RD Sikh Pioneers, 20TH Punjab Regiment and 27TH Punjab Infantry. The cavalry brigade included Probyn's Horse and Fane's Horse. Both regiments were raised during the Sepoy mutiny from the disbanded soldiers of the Khalsa armies of the Sikh Kingdom. In all, there was 11,000 British and Indian troops, plus 6,000 French troops. 1ST Sikh Cavalry (Probyn's Horse) consisted of 446 men and Fane's Horse 352 men.

China

Second Anglo-Chinese War, 1860 (Cont.)

The British expedition landed at Odin Bay on 1ST August. They fought actions on 3RD, 12TH and 14TH August around Sinho. Probyn's Horse armed with the lance for the first time was up against Tartar cavalry armed with bows and arrows. Probyn's casualties at this stage were two officers, two sergeants and two rank and file wounded. Sowar Muttah Singh was wounded in the chest and later died. The Chinese forces encountered during this campaign were, with the exception of the troops holding Taku Forts, composed almost entirely of Tartar cavalry, mounted on small hardy horses. They were very fast and capable of great endurance. The Tartar horsemen were nearly all Mongols of fine appearance, especially enrolled for the service of their clansman the Emperor. A combined British and French force of infantry carried out the attack on Taku Forts. Inside the leading fort a bloody hand-to-hand encounter ensued, and of the Chinese garrison of 500 strong, only 100 succeeded in escaping, many indeed jumped from the walls, but to be impaled on the stakes outside. The fate of the fort had not been lost on the defenders of the succeeding fort and almost before the assaulting troops had reached the walls, flags of truce were put up. The allies took 2,000 prisoners, besides taking possession of several brass and iron guns. This completed the capture of the famous Taku Forts that had defied a strong Naval Contingent the year before, as the Southern Forts surrendered next day to a small force of 2ND Division that included 23RD Sikh Pioneers. The advance to Peking, 100 miles from the Taku Forts, resumed on 8TH September. During the advance, Probyn's Horse played a major role. Chinese cavalry hovered in large masses on their entire left flank, so that Sir J. Michel was unable to perform the flank movement that had been intended, until 1ST Sikh Cavalry (Probyn's) had, by a brilliant charge, discomfited the Tartar Horse. This enabled the Allies to advance and drive the enemy back for some miles. Another action at Pa-li-Chiao, which involved a cavalry charge, drove the enemy back to within six miles of Peking. During the advance on Peking, the first opposition was met at Chan Chai Wan. Sir Hope Grant in his journal relates: "Sir John Mitchell encountered such heavy masses on his left that he had difficulty in holding his position, and was attacked by a large body of Tartar Cavalry. Probyn, who had only 100 of his regiment with him at the time, was ordered to charge to the front, which he did in most gallant style, riding in amongst them with such vigour and determination that they could not withstand his attack and fled in utter consternation. The Sikhs advanced in a steady line carrying everything before them, and taking several gun. The whole of the position was now captured and it was found the enemy had evacuated Chan Chai Wan. Advancing through it with the Sikhs, about a mile on the other side, we came to a large Chinese camp in which we took several guns." (Grant, 1875)

China

Second Anglo-Chinese War, 1860 (Cont.)

The Xianfeng Emperor then dispatched ministers for peace talks, but relations broke down completely when a British diplomatic envoy, Harry Parkes, was arrested during negotiations on 18TH September. He and his small entourage were imprisoned and interrogated (some were murdered). The Anglo-French force clashed with Sengge Rinchen's Mongolian cavalry on 18TH September near Zhangjiawan, before proceeding toward the outskirts of Peking for a decisive battle in Tongzhou District of Peking. On 21ST September, at the Battle of Palikao, Sengge Rinchen's 10,000 troops, including elite Mongolian cavalry, were completely annihilated after several doomed frontal charges against the concentrated firepower of the Anglo-French forces, which entered Peking on 6TH October.

With the Qing army devastated, Emperor Xianfeng fled the capital, leaving his brother, Prince Gong, to be in charge of negotiations. Xianfeng first fled to the Chengde Summer Palace and then to Rehe Province. Anglo-French troops in Peking began looting the Summer Palace and Old Summer Palace immediately (as it was full of valuable artwork). After Parkes and the surviving diplomatic prisoners were freed, Lord Elgin ordered the Summer Palaces destroyed, starting on 18TH October. Peking was not occupied; the Anglo-French army remained outside the city. The destruction of the Forbidden City was discussed, as proposed by Lord Elgin, to discourage the Chinese from using kidnapping as a bargaining tool, and to exact revenge on the mistreatment of their prisoners. Elgin's decision was motivated by the torture and murder of almost twenty western prisoners, including two British envoys and a journalist for The Times. The Russian envoy Count Ignatiev and the French diplomat Baron Gros settled on the burning of the Summer Palaces instead, since it was "least objectionable" and would not jeopardise the treaty signing. After emperor Xianfeng and his entourage had fled Peking, the emperor’s brother, Prince Yixin, ratified the Treaty of Tianjin in the Convention of Peking on 18TH October 1860, ending the Second Chinese War.

Regiment of Ludhiana Sikhs in China 1860

China

Boxer Rebellion, 1900

In 1900, the Boxers, a xenophobic movement in China, carried out a series of attacks on foreign missionaries, merchants, and property. The Chinese government did little to remedy the situation and in June 1900 issued an edict, which amounted to support for the Boxers. The foreign legations in the Imperial capital Peking were besieged and held out for three months, despite having a small garrison. An international relief force composed of around 16,000 men, was organised by seven nations, to rescue the legations. The only cavalry that was of any use was that from the Indian army; the Japanese had only a cavalry regiment, so poor in quality that only 60 horses out of 400 reached Peking! All the work was carried out by the Indian troops, which also included 34TH Sikh Pioneers and 14TH Ferozepore Sikhs; the Sikhs also bulked out the cavalry regiments. On 14TH August, British-Indian regiments entered Peking by the water gate at the Tatar City Wall, and the central gates were flung open to receive the rescuing British troops. The siege was over after 55 days. Over 200 people had been killed and wounded in the legations; in the country itself 30,000 Christian Chinese were killed by the Boxers. Two weeks after, a siege victory parade was held, marching through the city. Later some of the Boxers who had been captured were beheaded in public. The Ch, I Nien, hall of annual prayers, was at the Temple of Heaven, where the Chinese Emperor would pray for a good harvest. After the siege, Sikh Infantry posed here with their British officers. Lance Naik Lehna Singh and Naik Dial Singh were awarded the Indian Order of Merit for their conspicuous gallantry during the operations.

China

Hong Kong

In 1839, Lin Zexu was appointed by the emperor, as a special commissioner to Guangzhou to stop the drug trade. He and his troops used force to impel the foreign factories to surrender their stocks of opium. This act was the stepping-stone to the First Opium War, when the Chinese and the British could not comply with one another's demands. As a result of the war and the Chinese' fear of British military threats, Hong Kong was awarded to the British under the Convention of Chuen Pi in January 1841. On January 26TH 1841, the British flag was raised at Possession Point on Hong Kong Island, and British occupation began. A few months later, officials were selling plots of land and the colonization of Hong Kong took flight. Hong Kong inaugurated Sir Henry Pottinger as its first governor in August 1841. Pottinger dedicated his time to building up Hong Kong's future, as he realized its potential. He inspired long-term building projects and awarded land grants. In order to make peace with the Chinese, he sent his troops to the Chang Jiang (Yangtzi River) and threatened to attack Nanjing (Nanking). In August 1842, the Chinese yielded and the two governments signed the Treaty of Nanjing, which officially gave Hong Kong to the British. With that, Hong Kong carried on to progress as a port under British influences and became one of the greatest port cities the world has ever seen. With the involvement of the British, Hong Kong prospered. Hostilities between the British and the Chinese continued to heighten, leading to the Second Opium War. Subsequently, other foreign nationals of Russia, France, Germany, and Japan, realized the importance of having easy access to trade with China and began to secure ports all along the Chinese coastline. Several treaties were signed between the different nationals. Later, the British took possession of the New Territories, which became a part of the overall territory of Hong Kong.

Hong Kong, Fragrant Harbour

China

Hong Kong Police, 1862

For several decades Hong Kong was a 'rough-and-tumble' port with a 'wild west' attitude to law and order. Consequently many members of the Police force were equally rough individuals. After his appointment as Superintendent of Police in 1862, William Quinn, who had served in the Bombay police force, decided to recruit police officers direct from India. However, he was not impressed with the work of the police officers recruited from Bombay, and began recruiting Sikhs from the Punjab instead. The Sikhs, with their generally strong physique and presence, were effective in the opinion of the British, in intimidating the Chinese Secret Societies and deterring the activities of the other 'Eastern criminal classes'. They built up a healthy respect among the population, with their strong-armed policing and military capabilities. Their performance proved more satisfactory and the Force continued recruiting them over the years. In deference to their customs and religious beliefs, the Hong Kong Police Force allowed them to retain their turbans and exempted them from wearing police caps. With more Sikh police officers recruited into the Force, many high-ranking British police officers were sent to India from time to time to learn their language. This arrangement continued until just before the Second World War. Just prior to the British capitulation to the Japanese during the Second World War, commissioner Pennefather-Evans issued instructions to members of the Force to assist the Japanese invaders in maintaining law and order in the event of a Japanese occupation of Hong Kong. The Force was urged to serve under the Japanese so as to protect local residents from harsh and unfair treatment by the Japanese and their Chinese collaborators. To this end, some members of the Force had no choice but to work for the enemy. After the Japanese surrender, doubts about the willingness of Hong Kong people to accept Indian officers who had worked, and often abused their authority, under the Japanese administration forced authorities to wind down the Sikh contingent. However, some individual Sikh police officers with impeccable service records were retained until the early 1960s.

Sikh Policemen of Hong Kong Police

China

Hong Kong Police

Chinese pirate being escorted by Sikh police officers to his execution October 1887

Sikh Police officers of Hong Kong Police

1903

1930

China

Hong Kong Police

Constable Inder Singh Brar

Constable Inder Singh Brar was born in the village of Khai, Punjab, India on June 15TH, 1910. He was recruited from the village of humble peasant background, along with his older brother Sunder Singh Brar who served with the Police Force in Shanghai and Hong Kong and his younger brother Zora Singh Brar who served with the British Army in Burma. Inder Singh joined the Hong Kong Police Force on September 2ND, 1932. He was taught how to read and write Punjabi at the Hong Kong Police Training School. Police rules, regulations, and training were then conducted in the Punjabi language. All Sikh recruits were required to keep the Sikh identity as a condition of service, and were dismissed on the spot and sent back to India if the recruit shaved, cut his hair, and did not wear the turban. If a Sikh recruit did not have the discipline to live with the requirements of his faith, his discipline and loyalty to the Crown was under question. Inder Singh learned the Cantonese Chinese colloquial on his own, interacting with the Chinese public, and married Lau Wai Ying (Karam Kaur) at the Sikh Temple, Hong Kong, on May 14TH, 1944.

During his service in the Police Force, he was awarded 1939/45 Star, Pacific Star, British War Medal, and Defence Medal for War Services, St. John's Ambulance Association First Aid Certificate and Colonial Police Long Service and Good Conduct Medal.

Inder Singh retired from Police service on May 11TH, 1952.

The late Inder Singh and Karam Kaur Brar have four adult children, seven grandchildren, and two great-grandchildren, all living in Calgary, Alberta, Canada.*

*By kind courtesy of the descendants of Inder Singh Brar

China

Hong Kong & Singapore, Royal Garrison Artillery

The Hong Kong and Singapore Royal Garrison Artillery was one of the largest colonial units of the British Empire. It garrisoned the two colonies that gave the regiment its name and operated outposts dotted across the Indian Ocean for more than a century. A Royal Artillery company was based in Hong Kong for the first time in 1842. To spare the British gunners the enervating labour of moving guns and ammunition, native auxiliaries were recruited from Madras and they arrived in Hong Kong in 1847. The formation of a second Lascar Company was sanctioned in 1881, and it was suggested the new company be made entirely of Sikhs. Colonial authorities favoured the use of the burly warriors of the Punjab over all other Indians for military and police formations. A local Sikh police officer was given the task of returning to India to raise the new company, which arrived in the colony in 1881. Two double companies of Lascars were formed in an 1891 reorganisation, each composed of a company of Sikhs and a company of Punjabi Muslims in equal numbers. Each of the four Companies was to be commanded by a Subedar and assisted by a Jemadar. The Sikh Companies were: No. 1 Company - Subedar Iqbal Singh and Jemadar Teja Singh; No. 3 Company – Subedar Labh Singh and Jemadar Bhoop Singh. This was an important change, because it was now recognised that these units were no longer just Gun Lascars. They were now capable of operating batteries themselves, not just as assistants to European Gunners.

The year 1891 also saw the formation in Singapore of a local artillery company made up of Sikhs and Punjabi Muslims. By 1892, Indian gunners operated the Artillery Companies in Hong Kong, Singapore and Mauritius. In 1898, the Hong Kong and Singapore Batteries were grouped as the Hong Kong – Singapore Battalion. Three companies of the Hong Kong and Singapore Royal Garrison Artillery (HKSRGA) were based in Hong Kong and single companies in Singapore and Mauritius. Imperial policing became the regiment's regular duties. There was a great deal of anti foreign feeling in China, due largely to the occupation of certain parts of its territories by foreigners, which led to the Boxer Rebellion. In June 1900, the German Minister in China was murdered in Peking and the foreign legations besieged. The HKSRGA Companies armed with Maxim and Mountain guns, helped to defend the besieged international settlement at Tientsin and took part in the subsequent march on Peking. The mountain gunners blasted their support when the Russian and French troops stormed the Chinese capital. In 1903-4 the British, under Colonel Francis Younghusband, sent an expeditionary force of 10,000 soldiers into Tibet. The aim was to prevent encroachment by the Russian Empire and ensure that Tibet remained as a secure buffer state for Britain's own Indian Empire. A short but confused war ensued in which the Mountain Gunners held a "world record" for setting up an assault at 17,200 feet in the Himalayan Mountains.

China

Hong Kong & Singapore, Royal Garrison Artillery

With the outbreak of the First World War in 1914 the Hong Kong and Singapore Battalion, Royal Garrison Artillery, was employed on coastal defence duties at Hong Kong, Singapore and Mauritius. In 1915 No. 1 Battery composed of big brawny Sikhs, two hundred and forty strong, was formed into a 6-gun Mountain Battery and equipped with 10-pounder guns. They embarked for Egypt, where they served with the Imperial Service Cavalry Brigade. After a tour of duty in the Suez Canal defences, the Battery took part in the western desert campaign. In early 1916, the Battery was stationed at Abassia, where it was re-equipped with camel instead of mule transport and then attached to the Imperial Camel Corps. It then saw service in Palestine where it took part in the battles of Maghdada and Rafah. In January 1917, it was again re-equipped, this time exchanging its 10-pounder mountain guns for 2.75-inch guns. The Battery then took part in the three battles of Gaza, the action at Nebi Samil, the capture of Jerusalem and the attacks on Amman. With the limited range of its guns, the Battery had to fight from a position well forward in both attack and defence. Its personnel were highly regarded for their bravery in action and professionalism. The Distinguished Conduct Medal is the second highest award for gallantry in action, after the Victoria Cross. Only Seven DCM medals were ever awarded to the Indian soldiers of whom the following four were awarded to the Sikh gunners for their conspicuous gallantry in the Desert and Palestine Campaign: Havildar Fatteh Singh (26TH April 1917); Havildar Kishen Singh (3RD September 1918); Havildar Chajja Singh (1ST May 1918); and Havildar Rur Singh (21ST October 1918).

Sikh Gunners of the Hong Kong and Singapore (Mountain) Battery
In the Desert Campaign of the First Word War

China

Hong Kong & Singapore, Royal Garrison Artillery

In the early 1930's HKSRGA comprised a mountain battery and three heavy batteries in Hong Kong and a single heavy battery in Singapore. Three new heavy batteries were formed in 1938, with one each allotted to Hong Kong, Singapore and Penang in Malaya. The formation of the Anti Aircraft Battery, for the first time, started in September 1938 when the Sikhs from 2ND Mountain Battery were attached to 7TH Anti Aircraft Battery. The Record of Service of the Battery records this period in these words, "This marks the beginning of the period when the Sikhs proved that they could deal with any peacetime crises and that no form of equipment could daunt them. On 8TH December 1938, they formed two anti aircraft sections. It is heartening to see their adaptability."(Rollo, 1991 p116) HKSRGA gun crews fought in the first battles on the mainland when the Japanese attacked Hong Kong on 8TH December 1941. The gunners were soon overwhelmed by the much more numerous and experienced Japanese artillery. Gun crews fired over open sights at attacking Japanese infantry in often-vain attempts to save their guns. Just seven men survived when a section was overrun on Tytam Hill. HKSRGA survivors who had lost their guns were formed into infantry units. The men were untrained in the infantry tactics and most of them were killed or captured by the Japanese. Sections of the regiment cut off and surrounded in different parts of the island fought to the end. HKSRGA sustained heavy losses in the battle for Hong Kong and virtually all of the survivors taken prisoner.

HKSRGA unit were among the first troops to engage the Japanese forces that attacked the string of British airfields defending northern Malaya. The gunners at Khota Bharu and Alo Star valiantly struggled to protect the airstrips against repeated air strikes by Japanese bombers and fighters. With most British aircraft lost or out of action, the RAF began to abandon the airfields. Repeatedly the RAF and the infantry guarding the airfields retreated without warning, leaving the gunners virtually alone to defend the airfields. Nonetheless, the gunners fought hopeless rearguard actions, and inflicted a rising toll on the attacking Japanese, as they retreated to Singapore. During the long withdrawal, the gunners shot down 51 planes and claimed another 30 probable kills. They accounted for most of the 72 planes reported shot down by the British forces during the campaign. Fourteen of the regiment's guns had been destroyed or lost and dozens of its men killed, wounded, or posted as missing by the time Malaya was abandoned. All the surviving HKSRGA guns were deployed to face the coming invasion of Singapore Island.

China

Stonecutters Island

The Emperor of China ceded Stonecutters Island to Britain through the Convention of Peking in 1860. The island was initially used for quarrying by the British, hence the English name for the island. A British Royal Navy signals base was previously established on the island. In the post World War II years the island became host to British Army units including 415 Maritime Unit RCT and the Ammunition Sub-Depot RAOC. Explosive storage became more important, following the Hong Kong riots in 1967. The Hong Kong Mines Division elected to have all commercial explosives stored on Stonecutters Island, prior to being issued to the various blasting sites in the colony. British Army soldiers oversaw all commercial explosive issues post 1968, until the colony was transferred to China in 1997. Sikh Soldiers policed the island; the choice was obvious because of their martial reputation. The Army Department Police (ADP), as they were known, saw continuous service on the island during the British era. Field hockey was the game they loved and they were often seen playing bare-footed on the Padang. During 1982-1984, the ADP boasted two Indian national hockey players. It was common to see their blue pagris (turbans) drying in the sun outside their barracks. There was also a commercial interest on the island; Jardine/Du Pont erected an explosive factory on the island to cater for the ever-growing need for commercial blasting explosives. The island factory manufactured several tonnes of water gel and other commercial explosives per week. Limited stocks of PRC, British and other commercial explosives were stored in the island's Victorian explosive storage tunnels. During the 70s and 80s, the island was also the FOB (forward operating base) of a Royal Navy Hovercraft unit, deployed to assist the Hong Kong government with anti illegal immigration operations.

The Army Department Police, Stonecutters Island
(Colin Atchison Public Gallery)

China

Shanghai

Shanghai International Settlement was created in 1854 to serve the British, French and American foreign concessions in Shanghai, China. The Shanghai International Settlement always remained Chinese sovereign territory. The Shanghai Municipal Police brought order to the bustling activity of the International Settlement. Dating back to 1854, the Shanghai Municipal Police had grown from a small complement of Britons, recruited from the Hong Kong police, into a large ethnically diverse force. The Sikh Branch, recruited in 1884 from officers who had retired or left from Sikh military detachments in China, reached about 800 men. They were very effective in keeping the generally lawless elements of the population under effective control and in the prevention of rioting and mob violence within the International Settlement. In 1927, the cause for alarm stemmed from the threat that the Chinese Nationalists would seize Shanghai and endanger the foreign residents there. The Mounted section of the Sikh Police was mobilized to patrol the limits of the International Settlement. Shanghai was once again threatened in early 1932 after hostilities broke out between the Chinese and the Japanese. The fighting became so intense that the Sikh Mounted Contingent and the American 4TH Marines manned the barricades of the International Settlement. In 1937, the situation developed into a series of potentially explosive crises and once again Sikh reinforcements were rushed in to support 4TH Marines.

The Shanghai Municipal Police was disbanded in 1943, when the settlement was retroceded to Chinese control. In the decades that followed the founding of the People's Republic of China, the country's Sikh population virtually slowly disappeared.

'Sikh is the figure above all others who today represents the treaty port period in Shanghai's popular memory. They formed a surrogate military reserve for the Shanghai Municipal Council. Tall and imposing, Sikh added a touch of imperial authenticity to the squatter settlement.' (Bickers, 2003 p84)

Shanghai 1927

In 1927, the outbreak of conflict between nationalists and communists in China created international concern about the safety of the large European population in Shanghai. Together with Japan, the United States, France and Italy, Britain dispatched a substantial force from both Britain and India. Regular Indian regiments* that contained Sikh companies were rushed to Shanghai to safeguard the International Settlement. After 1928, this force was reduced gradually but Indian troops did not finally leave Shanghai until 1939.

*4 Battalion, 1ST Punjab Regiment
3 Battalion, 14TH Punjab Regiment

China

Shanghai

Sikh Branch, ***Shanghai Municipal Police***
(Shanghai Daily)

Sikh mounted contingent of the Shanghai Municipal Police

China

Auxiliary Military Police Battalion

(By Mr. David A. Kaufman)

One of the most novel and interesting organizations in China under the supervision of the Provost Marshal is the Auxiliary Military Police Battalion. The Battalion was formed in Shanghai on 1ST November 1945. The organization at that time was composed principally of Sikhs under the supervision of British citizens who were former members of the International Settlement Police Force. The novelty is based on the fact that its ranks are filled by former members of the Russian Imperial Army, the Shanghai Municipal Police, the French Foreign Legion and various other nationalities, which represent the colonial expansion of Europe in the Orient. They are men who held high ranks and positions in Czarist Russia, who rode with the legions of the Czar in his domain, representing officers and men of all ranks. The Sikhs, with their colourful turbans and black beards, lend dignity to an otherwise drab occasion and in their mind's eyes, the past glory of China glistens. This Battalion is used to supplement American troops who are engaged in protecting United States property. The outfit is clothed in U.S. Army uniforms, using a Geneva insigne on the left sleeve and the name of the AMP on the shoulder. The system of the rank is the same as the Army and the insigne is worn on the right sleeve. The men carry themselves with pride and it has been instilled in them that they represent in their own way the integrity and responsibility that the United States Army has placed in them.
Auxiliary Military Police Battalion deactivated in 1949.

Auxiliary Military Police Battalion

The above very rare picture by kind permission of Mr. David Kaufman, editor of the "The Trading Post"

China

Tsingtao, 1914

Tsingtao was the most important German possession in China. At the end of the nineteenth century, Germany had gained control of part of the Shandong peninsula, and founded a port at Tsingtao. The port then became the headquarters of the German Far East Squadron. At the start of the First World War, that squadron was under the command of Admiral Graf von Spee. His squadron inflicted an early defeat on the British at the battle of Coronel (1ST November 1914), before being destroyed at the battle of the Falkland Islands on 8TH December 1914. The Germans had a 4,000 strong garrison in Tsingtao. This may have been enough to deter an early British attack, but at the end of August 1914, Japan joined the war on the Allied side, hoping to gain control of the German empire in the Far East. The attack on Tsingtao began on 18TH September 1914 when 23,000 Japanese troops landed above the city and began to prepare for a formal siege, digging siege parallels that slowly approached the city. At the same time, a Japanese fleet prepared to bombard the port. A small force of British troops joined the Japanese. 2ND Battalion South Wales Borderers, 36TH Sikh Regiment, personnel of Royal Army Medical Corps and Army Service Corps (1,500 strong) as well as a squadron of British warships. Tsingtao came under bombardment from land and sea while the siege works approached the city. The final assault came on the night of 6TH and 7TH November. The allies fought their way into the main line of defence, capturing most of the important strong points. The Japanese suffered 1,800 casualties, the Germans around 700 and the British only 70. Many of the Japanese casualties came when a mine sank a cruiser. The next morning (7TH November) the German garrison surrendered. The Japanese would go on to capture Germany's island possessions in the Pacific.

The 36TH Sikhs, under the command of Lieutenant Colonel Sullivan had disembarked at Lao- Shan- Bay, and were stationed as part of the Garrison of Tianjin and took part in the Siege of Tsingtao. On night of 4TH November 36TH Sikhs lost two Sepoys killed and two officers wounded during heavy artillery fire directed on the Sikh trenches.

The following Sikh officers and men were mentioned in the despatch of Brigadier General N.W. Barnardiston on 13TH November, 1914: Subadar Gurmukh Singh, I.O.M.; Jemadar Sundar Singh; Jemadar Jaimal Singh; Havildar Massa Singh; Lance Naik Bhagat Singh; Lance- Naik Harman Singh; Lance Naik Hari Singh; Sepoy Fakir Singh; Sepoy Ram Singh; and Sepoy Bant Singh.

At the end of the war, 36TH Sikhs was warded the Battle Honour 'Tsingtao', becoming the only Indian battalion to gain the distinction.

MALAY STATES

English traders had been present in Malay waters since 17TH century, but it was not until the mid 18TH century that the British East India Company, based in India, developed a serious interest in Malayan affairs. The growth of the China trade in British ships increased the Company's desire for bases in the region. Various islands were used for this purpose, but the first permanent acquisition was Penang, leased from the Sultan of Kedah in 1786. This was followed soon after by the leasing of a block of territory on the mainland opposite Penang (known as Province Wellesley). In 1795, during the Napoleonic Wars, the British occupied Dutch Malacca to forestall possible French interest in the area. When Malacca was handed back to the Dutch in 1815, the British governor, Stamford Raffles, looked for an alternative base, and in 1819 he acquired Singapore from the Sultan of Johore. The twin bases of Penang and Singapore, together with the decline of the Netherlands as a naval power, made Britain the dominant force in Malayan affairs. British influence was increased by Malayan fears of Siamese expansionism, to which Britain made a useful counterweight. During 19TH century the Malay Sultans became loyal allies of the British Empire. In 1824, British hegemony in Malaya was formalised by the Anglo-Dutch Treaty, the decisive event in the formation of modern Malaysia. The Dutch evacuated Malacca and renounced all interest in Malaya, while the British recognised Dutch rule over the rest of the East Indies. In 1826 Penang, Malacca, Singapore and Labuan were united as the Straits Settlements. The Straits Settlements were initially administered under the East India Company in Calcutta, India, before Penang, and later Singapore became the administrative centre of the crown colony, until 1867, when they were transferred to the Colonial Office in London. During the late 19TH century, many Malay states decided to obtain British help in settling their internal conflicts. The commercial importance of tin mining in the Malay states to merchants in the Straits Settlements led to British government intervention in the tin-producing states in the Malay Peninsula. The wealth of Perak's tin mines made political stability there a priority for British investors, and Perak was thus the first Malay state to agree to the supervision of a British resident. British gunboat diplomacy was employed to bring about a peaceful resolution to civil disturbances caused by Chinese and Malay gangsters employed in a political tussle between Ngah Ibrahim and Raja Muda Abdullah. The Pangkor Treaty of 1874 paved the way for the expansion of British influence in Malaya. They concluded treaties with some Malay states, installing "residents" who advised the Sultans and soon became the effective rulers of their states. Johore alone resisted, holding out until 1914. By the turn of 20TH century, the states of Pahang, Selangor, Perak and Negeri Sembilan, known together as the Federated Malay States, were under the de facto control of the British, leaving only Johore independent.

Malay States

In 1909 the weakened Thai kingdom was compelled to cede Kedah, Kelantan, Perlis and Terengganu to the British. (Thailand retained the Sultanate of Patani, leaving a Muslim minority in the south, which has been a source of much trouble for successive Thai governments.) Sultan Abu Bakar of Johore and Queen Victoria were personal acquaintances and recognised each other as equals. It was not until 1914 that Sultan Abu Bakar's successor, Sultan Ibrahim accepted a British adviser. The four previous Thai states and Johore were known as the Unfederated Malay States. By 1910 the pattern of British rule in the Malay lands was established. The Straits Settlements were a Crown Colony, ruled by a governor under the supervision of the Colonial Office in London. Their population was about half Chinese, but all residents, regardless of race, were British subjects. The first four states to accept British residents, Perak, Selangor, Negeri Sembilan and Pahang, were termed the Federated Malay States: while technically independent, they were placed under a Resident-General in 1895, making them British colonies in all but name. The Unfederated Malay States (Johore, Kedah, Kelantan, Perlis and Terengganu) had a slightly larger degree of independence, although they were unable to resist the wishes of their British Residents for long. Johore, as Britain's closest ally in Malay affairs, had the privilege of a written constitution, which gave the Sultan the right to appoint his own Cabinet, but he was generally careful to consult the British first. The outbreak of war in the Pacific in December 1941 found the British in Malaya completely unprepared. During the 1930s, anticipating the rising threat of Japanese naval power, they had built a great naval base at Singapore, but never anticipated an invasion of Malaya from the north. Because of the demands of the war in Europe, there was virtually no British air capacity in the Far East. The Japanese were thus able to attack from their bases in French Indo-China with impunity and, despite stubborn resistance from British, Australian and Indian forces; they overran Malaya in two months. Singapore, with no landward defences, no air covers and no water supply was forced to surrender in February 1942, doing irreparable damage to British prestige. British North Borneo and Brunei were also occupied. After the Japanese defeat and reoccupation, Malaya gained its Independence on 31ST August 1957. Malaysia formally came into being on 16TH September 1963, consisting of Malaya, Sabah, Sarawak and Singapore. Singapore was separated from the rest of Malaysia on August 9TH 1965, and became a sovereign, democratic and independent nation.

STRAITS SETTLEMENTS

The Straits Settlements was a group of territories established in 1826 as part of the territories controlled by the British East India Company. The Straits Settlements came under direct British control as a crown colony on 1ST April 1867. The Settlements consisted of the individual settlements of Malacca, Penang (also known as Prince of Wales Island) and Singapore, as well as (from 1907) Labuan, off the coast of Borneo. With the exception of Singapore, these territories now form part of Malaysia.

Malacca

Malacca rose from a humble fishing village to become a major centre of the spice trade, forming a vital link between the East and the West. In 1511, the first of many foreign invasions of Malacca took place when the Portuguese arrived. The Portuguese were determined to control the East-West trade; so Malacca retained its importance as a trade centre until 1641, when the Portuguese surrendered Malacca to the Dutch. The Dutch, who had a stronger foothold over the Indonesian archipelago, swung the trade centre over to Sumatra. In the meantime, Malacca's trade also declined due to the silting of its port. In 1795, Malacca was given to the British, to prevent it from falling to the hands of the French when the Netherlands was captured during the French Revolution.

Malacca Police Force

Following the assimilation of Malacca into the British Empire, a modern police organisation was formed on 25TH March 1807. Most of the officers were of British origin. Later, this organisation was developed in the Straits Settlements and other Malay states, particularly the Federated Malay States. At that time, independent police forces were established for each respective state. The Sikh contingent in the Malacca Police Force was formed on 1ST April 1883. It was made up of one Sergeant, two Corporals, and 22 Constables. In 1886, another seven Constables were added to the Sikh Contingent. By 1891, the strength of all ranks was 38 but it was still insufficient for the duties required of them. Their duties also included escorting prisoners and lunatics when removed to Singapore. Only after World War II was a central police organization formed, known as the Civil Affairs Police Force. After the anarchy of Japanese occupation, a British colonial official, H. B. Longworthy, led the police organization and stabilized all the police forces. During the British colonial period that followed, Malacca, however, became the focal point in the struggle for independence. So when Malaya gained its independence, it was only fitting that the Declaration of Independence was proclaimed in Malacca, where it all began.

Straits Settlements

Penang

Originally part of the Malay sultanate of Kedah, Penang was ceded to the British East India Company in 1786, by the Sultan of Kedah in exchange for military protection from Siamese and Burmese armies, who were threatening Kedah. On 11TH August 1786, Captain Francis Light, known as the founder of Penang, hoisted the Union Jack, thereby taking formal possession of Penang. Penang was the first British possession in the Malay States and Southeast Asia. The location of the island attracted the British East India Company to use the island as a natural harbour and anchorage for their trading ships, and as a naval base to counter growing French ambitions in the region. In 1887, the Sikh Contingent of Penang police had two Sergeants, two Corporals, and 60 Constables. Apart from their police work, they also performed Guard and Escort duty. They were quartered in Fort Cornwallis, where they had their own Gurdwara Sahib (temple). They were regarded as a valuable para-military reserve force.

Penang suffered devastating aerial bombardments during World War II and finally fell to invading Japanese forces on 17TH December 1941. The British withdrew to Singapore after declaring George Town an open city. During the Japanese occupation of Penang from December 1941 to September 1945, the Gurdwara Sahib became a sanctuary for many families who had to abandon their homes due to the bombing of George Town, first by the Japanese and later by the Allied Forces.

The British returned at the end of the war and in 1946 Penang was reorganized into the Malayan Union, before becoming in 1948 a state of the Federation of Malaya, which gained independence in 1957, and subsequently became part of Malaysia in 1963.

A Native Village in Penang

SINGAPORE

Singapore

In 1818, Sir Thomas Stamford Raffles was appointed as the Lieutenant Governor of the British colony at Bencoolen. He was determined that Great Britain should replace the Netherlands as the dominant power in the Malay archipelago, since the trade route between China and British India, which had become vitally important with the institution of the opium trade with China, passed through the archipelago. The Dutch had been stifling British trade in the region by prohibiting the British from operating in Dutch-controlled ports or by subjecting them to a high tariff. Raffles hoped to challenge the Dutch by establishing a new port along the Straits of Malacca, the main ship passageway for the India-China trade. Raffles arrived in Singapore on 29TH January 1819 and soon recognized the island as a natural choice for the new port. He found a small Malay settlement, with a population of a few hundreds, at the mouth of the Singapore River, headed by Temenggong Abdu'r Rahman. The island was nominally ruled by the Sultan of Johore, Tengku Rahman, who was controlled by the Dutch. However, the Sultanate was weakened by factional division. Raffles offered to recognize Hussein as the rightful Sultan of Johore and provide him with a yearly payment; in return Hussein would grant the British the right to establish a trading post on Singapore. A formal treaty was signed on 6TH February 1819 and modern Singapore was born. The modern history of Singapore began in 1819 when Raffles established a British port on the island. Under British colonial rule, it grew in importance as a centre for both the India-China trade and the entrecote trade in Southeast Asia, rapidly becoming a major port city.

Singapore 1880

Singapore

Singapore

On 7TH June 1823, Raffles signed a second treaty with the Sultan of Temenggong, which extended British possession to most of the island and brought the island under British law, with the provision that it would take into account Malay customs, traditions and religion. In 1824, Singapore was ceded in perpetuity to the East India Company by the Sultan. The status of Singapore as a British possession was cemented by the Anglo-Dutch Treaty of 1824, which carved up the Malay Archipelago between the two colonial powers with the area north of the Straits of Malacca, including Singapore, falling under Britain's sphere of influence. In 1826, Singapore was grouped together with Penang and Malacca to form the Straits Settlements, administrated by the British East India Company. In 1830, the Straits Settlements became a residency, or subdivision, of the Presidency of Bengal in British India. Despite Singapore's growing importance, the administration governing the island was understaffed, ineffectual and was unconcerned with the welfare of the populace. Administrators were usually posted from India and were unfamiliar with local culture and languages. While the population had quadrupled during 1830 to 1867, the size of the civil service in Singapore had remained unchanged. Most people had no access to public health services and diseases such as cholera and smallpox caused severe health problems, especially in overcrowded working-class areas. As a result of the administration's ineffectiveness and the predominantly male, transient, and uneducated nature of the population, the society was lawless and chaotic. In 1850 there were only twelve police officers in the city of nearly 60,000 people. Prostitution, gambling, and drug abuse (particularly of opium) were widespread. Chinese criminal secret societies (analogous to modern-day triads) were extremely powerful, and some had tens of thousands of members. Turf wars between rival societies occasionally led to hundreds of deaths and attempts to suppress them had limited success.

Singapore Police

The success of the Sikhs as police officers and Sepoys in Malaya, led the British to bring some down to Singapore. The first batch from Patiala, Ludhiana and Ferozepore, from the Punjab in India was brought to Singapore in the late 1870s and formed the first Sikh Police Contingent stationed at Sepoy Lines, later known as Pearl's Hill, overlooking Chinatown. Sikh police officers were also recruited by the Tanjong Pagar Dock Company to form the Tanjong Pagar Dock Police Force. In March 1881, Assistant Superintendent Stevens, recruited 54 Sikh police officers for Singapore. In August 1881, more Sikhs arrived from the Punjab and the strength totalled 100 men. By the end of 1883, the strength was 207 men and by 1898, it increased to 300 men. The Sikh Contingent was well trained and armed and under some circumstances had to use brutal means to restore order.

Singapore

Singapore Mutiny, 1915

Singapore was not much affected by World War I (1914–18), as the conflict did not spread to Southeast Asia. The only significant event during the war was a 1915 mutiny by the Muslim Sepoys of 5TH Light Infantry, garrisoned in Singapore. After hearing rumours that they were to be sent off to fight fellow Muslims of the Ottoman Empire, the soldiers revolted, killing their officers and several British civilians. The Singapore Sikh Police Contingent, the Sikh Mountain Battery of the Malay States Guides and a detachment of 36TH Sikhs, stood with the British and participated in operations, to a large extent, in overcoming the Mutiny and capturing the mutineers. More than 200 Sepoys were tried by court-martial and 47 were executed, 64 were transported for life, and 73 were given terms of imprisonment ranging from seven to 20 years. The public executions by firing squad took place at Outram Prison, witnessed by an estimated 15,000 people.

Fall of Singapore, 1942

On 7TH December 1941, Japan attacked Pearl Harbour and the Pacific War began in earnest. One of Japan's objectives was to capture Southeast Asia and secure the rich supply of natural resources, to feed its military and industrial needs. Singapore, the main Allied base in the region, was an obvious military target. The British military commanders in Singapore had believed that the Japanese attack would come by sea from the south, since the dense Malayan jungle in the north would serve as a natural barrier against invasion. Although the British had drawn up a plan for dealing with an attack on northern Malaya, preparations were never completed. On 8TH December 1941, Japanese forces landed at Kota Bharu in northern Malaya. They advanced swiftly southward through the Malay Peninsula, crushing or bypassing Allied resistance and were poised to attack Singapore. The causeway linking Johore and Singapore was blown up by the Allied forces in an effort to stop the Japanese army. However, they managed to cross the Straits of Johore in inflatable boats days after. Several heroic fights by the Allied forces and Sikh soldiers against the advancing Japanese, took place during this period. However, with most of the defences shattered and supplies exhausted, Lieutenant-General Arthur Percival surrendered the Allied forces in Singapore to General Tomoyuki Yamashita of the Imperial Japanese Army on Chinese New Year. After the British capitulation, Indian soldiers were separated from their European officers, though not from their Indian officers and Viceroys of India's Commissioned Officers.

Singapore

The fall of Singapore to the Japanese Army, on February 15TH 1942, is considered one of the greatest defeats in the history of the British Army and probably Britain's worst defeat in World War II. Singapore, an island at the southern end of the Malay Peninsula, was considered a vital part of the British Empire and supposedly impregnable as a fortress. The British saw it as the "Gibraltar in the Far East". Improvements to Singapore as a British military base had only been completed at great cost in 1938. Singapore epitomized what the British Empire was all about – a strategically vital military base that protected Britain's other Commonwealth possessions in the Far East. Once the Japanese expanded throughout the region after Pearl Harbour (December 1941), many in Britain felt that Singapore would become an obvious target for the Japanese. However, the British military command in Singapore was confident that the power they could call on there would make any Japanese attack useless. British troops stationed in Singapore were also told that the Japanese troops were poor fighters; all right against soldiers in China who were poor fighters themselves, but of little use against the might of the British Army. The Japanese onslaught through the Malay Peninsula took everybody by surprise. Speed was of the essence for the Japanese, never allowing the British forces time to re-group. This was the first time British forces had come up against a full-scale attack by the Japanese. Any thoughts of the Japanese fighting a conventional form of war were soon shattered. The British had confidently predicted that the Japanese would attack from the sea. This explained why all the defences on Singapore pointed out to sea. It was inconceivable to British military planners that the island could be attacked any other way – least of all, through the jungle and mangrove swamps of the Malay Peninsula. But this was exactly the route the Japanese took. By December 9th 1941, the RAF had lost nearly all of its front line airplanes after the Japanese had attacked RAF fields in Singapore. Any hope of aerial support for the army was destroyed, before the attack on Singapore had actually begun. Britain's naval presence at Singapore was strong. A squadron of warships was stationed there, lead by the modern battleship "Prince of Wales" and the battle cruiser "Repulse". On December 8TH 1941, both put out to sea and headed north up the Malay coast to where the Japanese were landing. On December 10TH both ships were sunk by repeated attacks from Japanese torpedo bombers. The RAF could offer the ships no protection, as their planes had already been destroyed by the Japanese. Only the army could stop the Japanese advance on Singapore. Lieutenant General Arthur Percival led the army in the area. He had 90,000 men there – British, Indian and Australian troops. The Japanese advanced with 65,000 men lead by General Tomoyuki Yamashita. Many of the Japanese troops had fought in the Manchurian/Chinese campaign and were battle-hardened. Many of Percival's 90,000 men had never seen combat. On February 8TH 1942, the Japanese attacked across the Johor Strait. Many Allied soldiers were simply too far away to influence the outcome of the battle.

Singapore

On February 8TH, 23,000 Japanese soldiers attacked Singapore. They advanced with speed and ferocity. At the Alexandra Military Hospital, Japanese soldiers murdered the patients they found there. Percival kept many men away from the Japanese attack, fearing that more Japanese would attack along the 70-mile coastline. He has been condemned for failing to back up those troops caught up directly with the fighting although, it is now generally accepted that this would not have changed the outcome, but may only have prolonged the fighting. The Japanese took 100,000 men prisoner in Singapore. Many had just arrived and had not fired a bullet in anger. The fall of Singapore was a humiliation for the British government. The Japanese had been portrayed as useless soldiers, only capable of fighting the militarily inferior Chinese. This assessment clearly rested uncomfortably with how the British Army had done in the peninsula.

The following Sikh soldiers were awarded gallantry awards for their conspicuous gallantry in Singapore:

Subedar Jaswant Singh
1ST Punjab Regiment

"On the morning of 11TH February 1942 in the action on Reformatory Road on Singapore Island where the Battalion held the forward position of the Brigade, Subedar Jaswant Singh took over command of the Company after the Company Commander was severely wounded. The company was being subjected to heavy shelling; continuous mortar and Light Machine Gun fire, sustaining heavy casualties to its forward platoons. Subedar Jaswant Singh immediately commenced to rally the Company, got up reinforcements, reorganized the position, and had casualties removed. His gallant action in face of the enemy re-established confidence and enabled the Company to hold on to the Right Forward position of the Battalion until later in the afternoon, when other plans were evolved. Again in the operations, which succeeded this action, as second - in - Command of the Company, Subedar Jaswant Singh continually encouraged and heightened the morale of his Company by his gallant behaviour and disregard of personal danger." Subedar Jaswant Singh was strongly recommended for and awarded the Military Cross on 19TH December 1942.

Captain Pritam Singh
16TH Punjab Regiment

Captain Pritam Singh was wounded in 1942 during World War II in the battle of Singapore, and taken prisoner by them Japanese. He escaped from the notorious Nee Soon Prisoner of War Camp and made his way through Malaya, Thailand, Burma, reaching India after over six months of life-threatening experiences. In so doing he travelled thousands of kilometres through enemy territory on foot, boat and train. Captain Pritam Singh was awarded the coveted Military Cross for exemplary couragee and resolve. Pritam Singh later served in the Army of Independent India and retired with the rank of Brigadier.

Singapore

Jemadar Amar Singh
Hong Kong and Singapore Artillery

"At police Barracks, Mount Pleasant, on 13TH February 1942 Jemadar Amar Singh was in command of a 40 mm gun. This particular position was subjected to persistent and repeated bombing and machine gun attacks by low flying aircraft throughout the day. Jemadar Amar Singh fought with his gun in the coolest possible manner, never failing to engage a suitable target and bringing down at least one enemy aircraft and certainly damaging others. This action was an inspiration to neighbouring units and was an outstanding feature of day's fighting." For his outstanding courage and tenacity, Jemadar Amar Singh was awarded the Military Cross in 1942.

All the surviving Hong Kong & Singapore, Royal Garrison Artillery guns were deployed to face the coming invasion of Singapore Island. There was no sign of the British infantry that had been positioned nearby, so the gunners destroyed their guns and fought as infantry, suffering heavy losses. The survivors were either butchered or taken prisoner by the Japanese. The end of the war and the rush to end British rule of the Indian subcontinent raised questions about the HKSRGA future. India and Pakistan were unlikely to countenance the recruiting of their citizens to uphold British imperialism in Asia. And with that, a proud regiment passed into history.

Lieutenant Colonel Gurbaksh Singh
Jind Infantry

"Throughout the operations in Malaya, this officer commanded a battalion, which was responsible for the ground defence of two main aerodromes in Singapore. These areas were regularly and heavily bombed, and later dive-bombed and machine-gunned. Lieutenant Colonel Gurbaksh Singh was most successful in avoiding heavy casualties in his unit by skill and resource in the dispositions of his command. He maintained a very high standard of morale and efficiency, for which his own gallant bearing under fire and his determined personality were responsible. In the later stages of the fighting when the forward troops withdrew in the Tengah area, leaving the flanks of the aerodrome unprotected, the battalion defended their position on 10TH and 11TH February with commendable tenacity, inflicting heavy casualties on the enemy. The battalion eventually withdrew in good order, having suffered considerable loss, after an action of which an Indian State Force Unit should be very proud. Subsequently Lieutenant Colonel Gurbaksh Singh took a prominent part in the defence of the outskirts of Singapore, where he again displayed a high degree of courage and leadership under continuous shelling and mortar machine gun fire." Lieutenant Colonel Gurbaksh Singh was awarded the DSO on 13TH December 1945.*

*Lieutenant Colonel Gurbaksh Singh was also awarded 'Order of the British Empire'

Singapore

Indian National Army

The Indian National Army (INA) or Azad Hind Fauj was an armed force formed by Indian nationalists in 1942, in Southeast Asia during World War II. The aim of the army was to overthrow the British Raj in colonial India, with Japanese assistance. The I.N.A. was initially formed in 1942, immediately after the fall of Singapore under the leadership of Captain Mohan Singh of 14TH Punjab Regiment. In December 1942, Captain Mohan Singh ordered the Indian National Army to disband after severe disagreement with the Japanese. Mohan Singh was subsequently arrested by the Japanese and exiled to Palau Ubin, an island off Singapore. The majority of the Indian National Army soldiers returned to the status of Prisoner of war again. The I.N.A. was revived under the leadership of Subhas Chandra Bose in 1943 and proclaimed the army of Bose's Arzi Hukumat-e-Azad Hind (The Provisional Government of Free India). This second I.N.A fought ineffectively along with the Imperial Japanese Army against the British and Commonwealth forces in the campaigns in Burma. The end of the war saw a large number of the I.N.A. troops repatriated to India, where some faced trial for treason and became a galvanising point of the Indian Independence movement.

Sikh Prisoners

Some of the Sikh prisoners, who had fought bravely against the Japanese and had refused to join the I.N.A., were summarily executed by the Japanese. Hundreds were sent ahead to labour for the Japanese across the Pacific theatre. More Sikhs were transported to New Guinea than anywhere else. Most were shipped in mid-1943 to Wewak or New Britain and dispersed from there. Others came from Banjermasin via Batavia to Surabaya and to Biak, others continuing to Hollandia. Some went from Singapore to Palau and on to Hollandia. It seems that perhaps 10,000 Indians were sent to New Guinea, New Britain and Bougainville, with smaller parties in the Admiralties, Timor and New Ireland. A small party was sent to Los Negros in the Admiralty Islands, where they were used as labourers. When the Admiralties were seized by the US 1ST Cavalry Division in March 1944, the 69 Sikh prisoners there became the first substantial group of prisoners taken at Singapore to be liberated. Throughout the final year of the war in the Pacific, Australian troops in several parts of the South-West Pacific Area encountered hundreds more survivors of parties of men of the Indian Army, who had been captured by the Japanese and sent to labour in distant parts of their empire. Throughout captivity they had retained what the Indian Army referred to as their martial spirit. Indeed, manifestations of the survival of their soldierly character were evident at the moment they reported to Australian patrols and in the camps administered by Australian formations. It would seem that many Indian soldiers captured at Singapore maintained a loyalty unimpaired even in the darkness of captivity under the Japanese.

Singapore

Sikh Prisoners

These sets of photographs were found amongst Japanese records when the Allied troops entered Singapore after the Second World War. Some are visibly Sikh soldiers who were used as target practice and eventually bayoneted to death.

Singapore

Sikh Police Contingent, 1930
(Karam Singh, 2009, p.214)

Jemadar Jwala Singh, 1945

Jemadar Jwala Singh retired in 1945, after serving 26 years in the Sikh Police Contingent. (Karam Singh 2009, p213)

Singapore

Chief Inspector Santa Singh

Chief Inspector Santa Singh had been awarded the King's Police Medal for Gallantry in 1920. He had taken command of the Singapore Police Contingent during the harrowing Japanese occupation of Singapore.

Assistant Commissioner Gurdial Singh

Sardar Gurdial joined the Sikh Contingent in 1939 and retired as Assistant Commissioner in 1969.

Singapore

Singapore Police

Assistant Commissioner Kuldip Singh Sandhu

Assistant Commissioner Kuldip Singh Sandhu is currently the highest-ranking Sikh police officer in the Singapore Police Force. Assistant Commissioner Kuldip Sing Sandhu was born in the historical town of Malacca in South Malaysia. He obtained a degree from the University of Malaya in Kuala Lumpur, Malaysia. After graduation, he applied to join the Singapore Police Force, and entered the Police Academy in 1978. In the words of Kuldip Singh: "The Police Force accorded me enriching experiences and good training and I was exposed to the many facets of policing. I have notably served as the Commander of Airport Police, Director of Logistics and Director of Police Custody. I am currently the Director of Service Development and the Inspectorate, and concurrently the Quality Service Manager of the organisation. Such experiences as a Sikh and as a simple small town boy were truly God sent and I will always be eternally grateful to my parents for their guidance's and blessings. Policing is never tough if it is from your heart and more importantly, our Sikh principles are in perfect tangent with the police values of courage, loyalty, integrity, and fairness. There has never been any conflict and I feel that as a Sikh I am already imbued with the necessary authority and internalised values to do a good policing job. I guess this has been the secret to my progression in work. I am married with two charming daughters and, of course, we spend quite a bit of our holidays in Malaysia." (personal communication, 14 July 2011)

Singapore

Singapore Police

SWO Amar Singh

On 11TH February 2011, the Military Police Command welcomed SWO Amar Singh as its Commanding Officer (CO) as he took over command of the Military Police Training School (MPTS) from MAJ Kenny Loh.

SWO Amar Singh is the second Warrant Officer to assume the position of CO after SWO Lee Sung Cheng assumed command as CO Specialist and Warrant Officer Advanced School on 31ST January 2011. The move to appoint Warrant Officers as COs is part of the Army's effort to empower the Warrant Officer and Specialist (WOSPEC) Corps in line with the new Enhanced Warrant Officers Scheme.

Highlighting the benefit that a Warrant Officer can bring to the job of CO, SWO Amar Singh summed it all up in one word – 'experience'. "What I think Warrant Officers can bring to the job of CO is our years of experience. I have been in the Army for 34 years now, so I am able to suss out potential problems when it comes to training. Whenever I encounter a problem, I can look back to the past when similar problems were encountered and use that experience to resolve issues," explained SWO Amar Singh.

As the new CO, SWO Amar Singh's approach to running MPTS is based on two key principles. "Firstly, I believe in maintaining physical fitness. Secondly, I want to be friendly, firm, fair, and flexible as a CO. Having faith in your commanders, colleagues, and subordinates is important." he said.

As one of the first two Warrant Officers in the position of CO, SWO Amar Singh is grateful for the opportunity and hopeful that his assumption of command will serve as an encouragement to the rest of the WOSPEC Corps. "I am very honoured that my years of service have been recognised through my appointment as CO MPTS. I really hope that other WOSPECs will follow suit and achieve higher levels of command." (Punjabis.sg. 2012)

Singapore

Singapore Armed Forces

'A.H. Dickinson (Inspector-General of Police of the Straits Settlements), in a written order instructed the Police Officers on 11TH February 1942, that they were not to resist the enemy force of arms. Their sole duty was the maintenance of internal order, and in the event of the fall of Singapore, the civil population would be best served by placing their organisation at the disposal of the Japanese Commander if he wished to make use of it'. (Karam Singh, 2009 p227) On 15TH February 1942, the British surrendered unconditionally to the Japanese army in Singapore. 'In the early stages of the Japanese occupation, a programme was initiated by the British for the people of Singapore to facilitate the Japanese administration, in British hopes that the Japanese would treat them humanely. However, as time went on the Japanese treatment became harsh and even brutal in some cases. (Karam Singh, 2009, p.232) To safeguard their livelihood, the majority of the Sikh police officers retained their employment during the Japanese occupation. The Sikh Police Contingent continued to function and some policemen were sent to Changi Prison to guard the British internees. After the Japanese surrender, senior British police officers who had been made internees during the Japanese occupation in Changi Prison recommended to the British that the Sikh Police Contingent be disbanded. 'They emphasised that they would not work as Police Officers anymore if the British continued to employ Sikh Police Contingent men. The British authorities had to accede to their requests, as they needed their services of re-building the police force in Singapore after the British return. Consequently, the Sikh Police Contingent was disbanded at the end of 1945. However, individual Sikhs were continually recruited in the Singapore police'. (Karam Singh, 2009, p.279) The end of the war and the rush to end British rule of the Indian subcontinent raised questions about the future of the Sikh police officers in Singapore. India was unlikely to countenance the recruiting of their citizens to uphold British imperialism in Asia. The Sikh police officers became the pioneering Sikh immigrants into Singapore. Their descendants, the Singaporean Sikhs, continue to maintain the Sikh martial tradition in the Armed Forces of Singapore.

Decades after the war saw the rise of anti-colonial and nationalist sentiments. The British, on their part, were prepared to gradually increase self-governance for Singapore and Malaya. On 1ST April 1946, the Straits Settlements was dissolved and Singapore became a separate Crown Colony with a civil administration headed by a Governor. In August 1958, the State of Singapore Act was passed in the United Kingdom Parliament providing for the establishment of the State of Singapore. Elections for the new Legislative Assembly were held in May 1959. Lee Kuan Yew, a young Cambridge-educated lawyer, became the first Prime Minister of Singapore. British troops remained in Singapore following its independence, but in 1968, London announced its decision to withdraw the forces by 1971 and Singapore set out to build its military, called the Singapore Armed Forces.

Singapore

A glimpse of Singaporean Sikhs that are carrying on the martial traditions of their ancestors in the Singapore Armed Forces:

Brigadier-General Ravinder Singh

Chief of Army
Singapore Armed Forces

Brigadier-General Ravinder Singh, a Sikh, was appointed as the chief of the Singapore Army on March 25TH 2011. Brigadier-General Ravinder Singh joined the Singapore Armed Forces (SAF) in December 1982. He was awarded the SAF Overseas Training Award (Academic) in 1983 with which he attained a Bachelor of Arts (First Class Honours) in Engineering Science at the University of Oxford (UK) in 1986. He subsequently attained a Master of Arts (Engineering Science) from the University of Oxford in 1992. In 1995, he was awarded the SAF Postgraduate Scholarship and obtained a Master of Science in Management from the Massachusetts Institute of Technology (USA) in 1996. Brigadier-General Singh earned his commission from the Officer Cadet School at SAFTI Military Institute as a Signals officer in December 1986. In 1991, he was deployed to UNIKOM as a member of the Singapore observer team and in 1995; he attended the US Army Command and General Staff College at Fort Leavenworth. BG Singh's distinguished military career has seen him hold key appointments in the Singapore Army, SAF, as well as the Ministry of Defence. These include Head System Development Group, Commander 2 Singapore Infantry Brigade, Commander 6 Division, Chief of Staff-Joint Staff, Deputy Secretary (Technology), and at present, Chief of Army. BG Singh's illustrious list of awards is testament to the outstanding contributions he has made to the SAF. He received, among others, the SAF Long Service Award (25 years) in 2008, Public Administration Medal (Silver Military) in 2005, and the United Nations Medal and SAF Overseas Service Medal – both in 1992. BG Singh is married to Kohila and they have two sons.

Singapore

Singapore Armed Forces

Brigadier Sarbjit Singh

Commander, Air Power Generation Command

Brigadier Sarbjit Singh assumed command of Air Power Generation Command (APGC) on 17TH April 2009.

Brigadier Sarbjit Singh joined the Republic of Singapore Air Force on 17TH January 1983, attained his pilot wings in 1985, and went on to serve as an operational pilot on the F-5 and F-16 aircraft. He progressed on to become a Pilot Attack Instructor and an Officer Commanding, before attending the Air Command & Staff College in Maxwell AFB, Montgomery, Alabama, in 1996. On his return, he took over command of 144 Squadron in Paya Lebar Air Base and thereafter became a Branch Head in Ops Planning Group, in Air Operations Department. In 2002, he attended the Air War College in the USA, and returned in 2004 to assume the appointment of Deputy Head Air Operations (Ops Planning) in Air Operations Department. Subsequently, he assumed the appointment of Deputy Commander Tengah Airbase before becoming the first Commander of UAV Command when it was stood-up in February 2007.

Brigadier Sarbjit Singh graduated with a BSc (Political Science) degree from Auburn University Montgomery, Alabama, USA. He was awarded Summa Cum Laude honours for his academic achievements.

Brigadier Sarbjit Singh has been awarded the Singapore Armed Forces Good Service Medal (5 years), Singapore Armed Forces Long Service and Good Conduct Medal (12 years), Singapore Armed Forces Long Service and Good Conduct Medal (22 years), and The Long Service Medal (Military). In 2008, he was awarded The Public Administration Medal (Bronze) (Military).

Brigadier Sarbjit Singh and his wife, Bhupinder Kaur, have two daughters, Namjot Kaur and Anand Kaur, and a son, Mohkam Singh.

Singapore

Singapore Armed Forces

Colonel Mancharan Singh Gill

The late Colonel Mancharan Singh Gill was born in Muar, Malaya on June 28TH, 1934. He graduated from University of Singapore in 1956 with a degree in Physics, and thereafter commissioned in the Singapore Volunteer Corps in early 1961. During the Konfrontasi (Indonesia–Malaysia confrontation), he saw active service in South Johore and Sabah. In August 1957 after Independence, then defence minister, Goh Keng Swee, tasked a young Captain Mancharan Singh Gill, with the responsibility of building up the Singapore Artillery. Mancharan Singh Gill served the Singapore Armed Forces with great distinction and held several key commands including:

- Chief of Artillery 1969 – 1971 and 1973 – 1976
- Director Singapore Armed Forces Training Institute 1971 – 1973
- Assistant Chief of General Staff (Logistics)
- Assistant Chief of General Staff (Training)
- Commander Singapore 3RD Division 1979 – 1982
- Deputy Chief of General Staff 1982 – 1986

During his military career, Colonel Mancharan Singh Gill received numerous public awards inclusive of the Public Administration Medal (Silver) (Military) and Public Administration Medal (Gold) (Military) in 1971 and 1982 respectively. He retired from active military service in August 1986, but continued to serve as the President of the Singapore Armed Forces Veteran's League. Colonel Mancharan Singh Gill passed away peacefully on 20TH June 2008.

Singapore

Singapore Armed Forces

Colonel Mancharan Singh Gill and Minister Dr. Goh Keng Swee escorting HRH Queen Elizabeth and HRH Prince Philip on their visit to Singapore in 1972

Colonel Mancharan Singh Gill delivering his farewell speech at Khatib Camp on August 1986

Singapore

Singapore Armed Forces

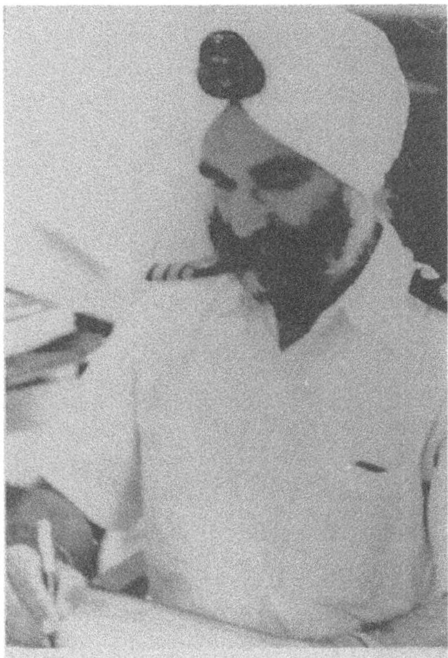

Lieutenant Colonel Jaswant Singh Gill

Lieutenant Colonel Jaswant Singh in his own words: "On 15TH May 1923, I was born in Moga, Punjab, into a poor farming family. One of my uncles was educated in English and had obtained a clerical job in Singapore at Police Headquarters. When I was 6 years old, I was packed off to Singapore and my uncle was instructed by the family elders to arrange to give me a good education. I was educated up to a Senior Cambridge and London Chamber of Commerce General Certificate at Raffles Institution. In 1941, I joined the Government General Clerical Service as a Clerk/Stenographer. In 1948, I obtained a transfer to the Ministry of Education as a Trainee Teacher. During the day I taught in school and also attended Teachers Training College. During the Evening, I joined the Royal Naval Volunteer Reserve and was trained by the Royal Navy to be a Naval Officer. I qualified as a teacher and also did my Post Graduate Teachers Course and was appointed Principal of Dunearn Secondary Vocational School in 1965. By 1966, I had passed various Naval Exams and had risen to the rank of Commander. After doing some active naval service against the Indonesians, I was mobilized by the Singapore Ministry of Defence in 1966, as Singapore's First Chief of Naval Staff with HQ at Blakang Mati. In 1968, I was appointed Head, Training Department and General Staff Division. In 1971, I was appointed Commander Tengah Air Base. In 1971, I was appointed Commander, Changi Air Base, which was Britain's largest Air Base in the Far East. I retired from Government Service in 1973".

(communicated to Singapore Khalsa Association in January 2012)

Singapore

Singapore Armed Forces

Lieutenant Colonel Jaswant Singh Gill (Cont.)

The honours-roll in the office of the Chief of Navy starts with a picture of LTC (Ret.) Jaswant Singh Gill. On 28TH December 2006, Gill caught up with the Chief of Navy, Ronnie Tay, four decades after handing over the helm of the Navy in 1968. He shared with CNV his memories on the beginning of the Navy and the challenges that he faced then. The period after 1945 was the period in which many Asian countries, who were colonies, were seeking Independence from the west. Gill was also fired up with this feeling of Independence and felt that we, as Singaporeans, should train to prepare ourselves for our Independence. While teaching and undergoing the Teacher's Training Course during the day, Gill trained with the Royal Naval Volunteers Reserves (RNVR) during the evenings to become a Naval Officer. He rose through the ranks from being a sailor to Commander in the RNVR, where the Navy comprised mainly of volunteers totalling about 1,000 men only. The call allowed Gill to touch base personally with the Navy family. Upon hearing personally the advancement the Navy had made over the years, Gill was filled with pride. CNV remarked the current achievements are built on the firm foundations made by the pioneers of the Navy. Despite having retired forty years earlier from the Navy, Gill still feels strongly for the Navy and enjoys reading the Navy News. Since leaving the Navy, he has been actively engaged. He taught for 10 years at United World College and went into business after his retirement at 60 years. On 29TH December 2006, he was also recognised for his contributions to the Sikh community at Singapore Khalsa Association's 75TH Anniversary celebrations.

Singapore

Singapore Armed Forces

Colonel Sukhvinder Singh Chopra

Colonel Sukhvinder Singh Chopra joined the Lee Kuan Yew School of Public Policy as Director Administration in January 2007 and is responsible for the overall administration of the School and its Research Centres. In this capacity, he is in charge of several key areas, which include Human Resources, Finance, and Corporate Services. Sukhvinder also shares responsibility for the overall strategic management and growth of the School and its Research Centres. Sukhvinder joined LKY School after nearly three decades of distinguished service in the Singapore Armed Forces (SAF), Republic of Singapore Navy (RSN). He is an experienced operational leader, mentor, and coach for individuals and teams. During his tenure in the SAF-RSN, Sukhvinder held senior leadership appointments, which included the command of a squadron of the largest modern ships in the Navy and command of the Naval Officers' Advanced School, where he was responsible for training and developing Naval Officers to hold intermediate to command-level appointments. He was the first Senior Officer in the SAF-RSN to be appointed to lead a Task Group for operations in the Gulf to assist rebuild Iraq. For his sterling contributions in service, Sukhvinder is the recipient of Singapore's Public Administration Award. Sukhvinder graduated from the University of Tasmania, Australia with a Masters Degree in Business Administration. He has a Post Graduate Diploma in Change Management, Leading, and Sustaining Change awarded by Singapore's Civil Service College. He successfully completed an Executive Programme in International Management that was jointly awarded by the Stanford Graduate School of Business and the National University of Singapore's Business School. In 2008, he achieved a Post Graduate Certificate in Coaching by Lancaster University, United Kingdom, testimony of his belief in people development and continuous learning.

Singapore

Singapore Armed Forces

Marine Col. Sukhvinder Singh Chopra

By Dharmesh Thakkar

As the turbaned commander deftly maneuvered the modern warship RSS *Endurance* into the small channel to berth at Green Gate last February, Indian naval officers felt pride and admiration. For Lieutenant Colonel Sukhvinder Singh Chopra is commanding officer of the Singapore Navy warship, the first Indian to hold this position. RSS *Endurance* was a part of the recently concluded International Fleet Review.

The vessel had berthed to unload humanitarian and relief aid donated by the Singapore public for Gujarat earthquake victims. The relief included $ 20,000 of medical supplies and 17 tonnes of rice, clothing and bedding.

"It was an honour to participate in the International Fleet Review. The Indian Navy conducted the mammoth and impressive feat in a professional manner right down to the minute details," said Lieutenant Colonel Chopra, all praise for Mumbai's hospitality and warmth.

Born and bread in Singapore to immigrant Indians, Lieutenant Colonel Chopra commands the Singapore Navy's newest and largest ship, "Singapore offered me all the opportunities to achieve my goals. Hard work and dedication are rewarded in disciplined Singapore," he said.

Another Indian in the Singapore Navy is Lieutenant Commander Dinesh Singh, on a two-year tenure as midshipman instructor for training cadets and junior officers in navigation. The multi-purpose RSS *Endurance* to meet Singapore's transportation and training needs is designed indigenously. "We have utilized innovative maritime technology to build a ship that is optimized to meet our requirements and operated by a small crew," said Lieutenant Colonel Chopra.

The ship has 197 personal on board, including 65 crew members, 87 midshipmen, seven foreign officers and training instructors. The midshipmen are on board to undergo the midshipman sea training on navigation, communications, weapons, fire fighting and damage control. Lieutenant Colonel Chopra said the Singapore Navy invited foreign officers to interact with midshipmen to build rapport and strengthen defence relations with other navies. The seven foreign officers include nationals of Brunei, China, India, Indonesia, South Korea, Thailand and United Kingdom.

Singapore

Singapore Armed Forces

Colonel Sukhmohinder Singh

Colonel Sukhmohinder Singh is currently the Head of the Singapore Armed Forces Centre for Leadership Development. He is a Commando Officer by vocation. He served the Commando formation as a Platoon Commander, Quartermaster, Officer commanding, and Officer commanding of the Commando Training Wing. He was also the Head of Operations of the Commando Formation, where he planned and facilitated the execution of Peace Support Operations overseas. He was appointed Commanding Officer 3RD Singapore Infantry Regiment, where the Battalion emerged as the Best Infantry and Best Combat Unit. He was appointed as Aide De-Camp to the President in 1994 and served until 1999. He went on to command the 10th Singapore Infantry Brigade. In 2000, he moved on to command the Army Officers' Advanced School while he was on the Graduate Diploma programmed on Organizational Learning by the Institute of Public Administration and Management, Civil Service College. He has also made it a critical feature of leader development for all leaders to be skilled in coaching and facilitating learning, by designing an enduring system for training and operationalisation across the Singapore Armed Forces. Colonel Sukh assumed the appointment as Head SCLD in Jan 2003. He was instrumental in setting up the Centre and growing it from a 12 man team to a 28 man team. As Head of SCLD, he was responsible for formulating the strategies and implementation plans for Leadership Development in the Singapore Armed Forces. He was nominated to be the organizing Chairman for the Organizational Learning Conference in Feb 2006, where he led a team comprising of members from 9 public sectors. Colonel Sukh is a certified Executive Coach by Lancaster University. He is also a certified trainer for Myers-Briggs Type Indicator assessment and Fundamental Interpersonal Relations Orientation-Behavior assessment. He has currently developed the Leadership Development Master Plan for 2015, as the next lap for the Singapore Armed Forces. Colonel Sukhmohinder Singh retires on 31ST December 2011, after serving 31 years in the Singapore Armed Forces.

Singapore

Singapore Armed Forces

SINGAPORE PUBLIC SECTOR

HUMAN CAPITAL CONFERENCE 2008

Leadership Development in the Singapore Armed Forces

By Colonel Sukhmohinder Singh, Head, SAF Centre of Leadership

Development, SAFTI Military Institute, Singapore Armed Forces

Colonel Sukhmohinder Singh will share the Singapore Armed Force's journey since 2000 in researching, designing and operationalising systematic leadership development. In the light of the evolved operational environment since 9/11, where the Singapore Armed Forces, like many other militaries, is expected to operate in an expanded spectrum of operations, the development of leaders has taken on an equally expanded approach and with increased emphasis. The operational environment is described as being volatile, uncertain, complex and ambiguous. With this comes the need to develop more values based, dynamic and adaptive leaders capable of making ethically correct and effective decisions consistent with the mission, purpose and values of the Singapore Armed Forces. The presentation will provide insights into the background leading to the formalisation of the Singapore Armed Force's behavioral leadership development framework. It will showcase how content systematization is balanced with process systematizations a formula for achieving an enduring outcome in the Singapore Armed Force's efforts at developing leaders. Finally, some of the key Singapore Armed Force's leadership development initiatives that have already been implemented in the Singapore Armed Forces will be shared. Colonel Sukhmohinder is a Commando Officer by vocation. He has served in these for 32 years in numerous command appointments up to the Brigade level, as Head of Operations in the Commando Formation and as Commander of the SAF Advanced Schools. He is a graduate of the Singapore Armed Forces and US Ranger Schools, US Pathfinder and Special Forces Qualification course. He graduated at the top of his class in the Singapore Command and Staff College. He is currently the Head of the SAF Centre of Leadership Development. In the last 5 years, he was tasked to strategize and implement an enhanced leadership training and development effort among the Singapore Armed Force's officers and warrant officers in the transformation towards 3RD Generation Singapore Armed Forces. Colonel Sukhmohinder holds a BA (History and Political Science) from the National University of Singapore. He also has a Graduate Diploma in Organizational Learning.

THE FEDERATED MALAY STATES

The protectorate of the Federated Malay States was established after the four Rulers of Selangor, Perak, Negeri Sembilan and Pahang agreed to a federation and centralized administration in 1895. The Treaty of Federation was drawn up and signed on 1ST of July, 1896. By this treaty and the previous acceptance of the British Residents System in Selangor (1875), Perak (1874), Negeri Sembilan (1873) and Pahang (1888); the Federated Malay States were officially turned into a nominally independent protectorate of Great Britain.

Perak

By the 1860s, the District of Larut in the State of Perak was a rich tin mining area under the control of Ibrahim Ngah bin Jaafar, the Mantri of Larut. The Chinese workers in these mines were from two different clans. The rivalry between these two clans resulted in the Larut Wars. The wars were fought over the control of mining areas, which involved different Hakka clans. The Hai San miners were mainly Hakka men from Cheng Sheng. The first two battles (1861 and 1865) were between the Cheng Sheng Hakka of the Hai San and the Hui Chew Hakka of the Ghee Hin. The last two (1872 and 1873) were between the Cheng Sheng Hakka of the Hai San and the Sin Neng Hakka of the Ghee Hin. The quarrelling Malay chiefs, who had taken sides in the Larut Wars, were alarmed at the disorder created by the Chinese miners and secret societies. In July 1873, Ngah Ibrahim the Mantri of Larut appointed Captain T.C.S. Speedy (the Superintendent of Police, Penang) to recruit a force of Sepoys from India to deal with the Chinese miners. Captain Speedy recruited a force of 110 Sepoys (Sikhs and Pathans) armed with Krupp guns for the Mantri's service. This small force stationed in Taiping served as Military Police. It was styled the Perak Armed Police. The Straits Settlement Penang Chinese, seeing their investments destroyed in the Larut Wars, sought intervention from the British. Over 40,000 Chinese from the Go-Kuan and Si-Kuan were engaged in the fratricidal war involving the Perak royal family. In August 1873, Archibald Edward Harbord Anson, the last Lieutenant Governor of Penang, sought to bring about a ceasefire between the two parties and convened a meeting at the beginning of the month. The two sides agreed to keep the peace, pending British arbitration, with Ngah Ibrahim taking responsibility for the Hai San and Abdullah taking responsibility for the Ghee Hin. Abdullah completely failed in his task in ensuring that Ghee Hin kept the peace, so that the British were prompted to back Ngah Ibrahim and the Hai San. The incoming governor, Sir Andrew Clarke's main objective was to mediate peace between the two Chinese factions and settle their differences, so that tin production could resume and threats to the internal security of British-held Penang would cease.

Federated Malay States

Perak Police

It was also at this time that Sir Andrew Clarke, the Straits Settlements governor, saw an opportunity to settle the question of succession to the throne in Perak and to make use of that as a means to further British interests in the Malay Peninsula, by getting the sultan to accept a British Resident. The British intervention in the affairs of the Malay States resulted in the Treaty of Pangkor. In 1874, on 20TH January, Clarke convened a meeting aboard the H. M. S. Pluto, anchored off Pangkor Island. Documents signed aboard the ship on 20TH January 1874, settled the Chinese dispute, cleared the Sultan's succession, and paved the way for the acceptance of British Residency. On 2ND November 1875, Mr. J. W. W. Birch, the first British Resident of Perak, and his orderly Sepoy Ishar Singh were murdered at Pasir Salak. Ishar Singh was probably the first Sikh to die on duty in Malaya. Captain Speedy was appointed to administer Larut as assistant to the new British Resident. The British recognised Abdullah as Sultan and installed him on the throne of Perak in preference to his rival, Sultan Ismail. In 1877, Captain Speedy resigned his commission and left Malaya. Early in 1879, Lieutenant Walker joined the Perak Armed Police as Acting Commissioner and formed a good opinion of the Sikh Police. In 1883, Walker was sent to India to engage about two hundred and fifty Sepoys for Perak Armed Police. He went to the Punjab to interview and recruit men from the well-known Sikh Regiments, 14TH Sikhs, 15TH Sikhs, and 45TH Sikhs. Many of those selected had seen active service on the North West Frontier of India. Thus in 1884 there were about 650 Sikhs in Perak Police. About 100 were stationed at Taiping and the rest distributed in the various police stations from Parit Buntar in the North to Telok in the South. In 1888, it became 1STPerak Sikhs under Captain Walker. The Pahang rebellion took place in the years 1892 – 1894. Captain Walker was in charge of the operations against the rebels and sought Sikh Police from every state and Singapore to quell the rebellion. On June 28TH the chief stronghold of the rebels at Kuala Tembling was stormed. Captain Walker led the attack on the stockade. This was the first battle in which the Sikh Police earned name and fame. The Sikh Police force was to grow from a strength of about 100 strong in the year 1873, to a force of 900 strong in 1896. With the Federation of the Malay States in 1896, the police force of Perak was to give up its own name and become a contingent of the Federated Malay States Police Force.

Federated Malay States

Selangor Police

In 19TH century, the economy in Selangor boomed due to the exploitation of huge tin reserves and the growing importance of Rubber. This attracted a large influx of Chinese migrant labourers. Chinese secret societies, allied with Selangor Chiefs, fought for the control of the tin mines. Sultan Abdul Samad ruled Selangor at that time. The Sultan had appointed Tengku Kudin (Zai'u'd-in), a prince from Kedah who had married the Sultan's daughter, as a Viceroy of Selangor. Following the disputed recognition of Abdul Samad as Sultan in 1860, Malay chiefs gradually became polarized into two camps; generally the lower-river versus the upper-river chiefs. The main issue concerned the lucrative collection of duties on tin exports. Raja Mahdi, the dispossessed son of the previous ruler in Klang seized and held the prosperous town of Klang for two years, with tacit approval of dissident upper-river chiefs. When the Sultan granted favours to his son-in-law Zia-ud-din, he further alienated the dissident chiefs and intermittent fighting commenced. At this point Chinese tin miners in the Selangor and Klang valleys began feuding over control of the mines. The miners predominantly belonged to the Ghee Hin and Hai San secret societies, which increasingly sought allies among the Malay chiefs. Thus, by 1870 the Chinese had joined opposing sides in the civil war: the Ghee Hin had joined Raja Mahdi's forces, and the Hai San had sided with Zia-ud-din. Meanwhile, the British Straits Settlements was becoming increasingly dependent on the economy of Selangor. Selangor through 19TH and 20TH centuries was one of the world's major tin producers. Since Selangor's security affected tin trade, the British felt it needed to have a say in Selangor politics. They saw Tengku Kudin as a ticket to reach out to Selangor's royal court. Therefore, the Straits Settlements led by Andrew Clarke implicitly supported Tengku Kudin. With British aid, and his Chinese allies, Tengku Kudin reversed several years of setbacks, defeated Mahdi, and his supporters. When the HMS. Rinaldo had shelled his enemies out of Kuala Selangor, the Viceroy Tengku Kudin garrisoned the place with 100 Sikhs and some 30 to 40 of his Kedah followers. The officer of the Sikhs was a European named Pennefather. In November 1873, however, pirates near Kuala Langat, Selangor, attacked a ship from Penang. The sultan expressed concern over Selangor's security and requested assistance from Sir Andrew Clarke. This led to the appointment of a British Resident in Selangor in 1874. The first resident was J. G. Davidson, a lawyer from Singapore. He was Tengku Kudin's friend. The war ended in 1874 and was won over by Tengku Kudin and Raja Ismail while Raja Mahadi stepped down. In the 1880s, in the State of Selangor, Captain H.C. Syers had a force of about 530 Military Police, known as the Selangor Sikhs. With the Federation of the Malay States in 1896, the police force of Selangor was to give up its own name and become a contingent of the Federated Malay States Police Force.

Federated Malay States

Negeri Sembilan Police

The new Governor of the Straits Settlements, Sir Andrew Clarke, arrived in November 1873 and within a year, took all the States of Negeri Sembilan under British Protection. Sungei Ujong was the first of the Negeri Sembilan states to come under British Protection. Other Negeri Sembilan states that asked for British officers were Jelebu in 1883, Rembau in 1887 and by 1895, the whole of Negeri Sembilan became British protected territory. The number of states within Negri Sembilan has fluctuated throughout history. The former states included Naming in Malacca, Kelang in Selangor and Segamat in Johore. The British had started to recruit Sikh police for Negeri Sembilan in 1874, when Captain P.J. Murray took Sikh police officers from Straits Settlements to Negeri Sembilan to form its first police force. One contingent served the Sungei Ujong and Jelebu Districts, while a second contingent looked after the other districts.

Pahang, 1888

Sultan Ahmad Muadzam Shah, otherwise known as Wan Ahmad, became the undisputed ruler of Pahang after defeating his brother Tun Mutahir, following the death of their father, Bendahara Tun Ah in 1857. Sultan Ahmad Muadzam Shah was a single-minded ruler and was opposed to British influence in his State. The British on the other hand were keen to have some measure of control over the government of Pahang with a view of safeguarding their commercial interests, which they feared were in jeopardy by indiscriminate concessions, often ill defined and overlapping, given by the Sultan to various people. Their interest in gaining political control of the State was further heightened by rumours of Pahang's great mineral wealth. Unwilling as the Sultan was, in 1887 through the urging of a British official Hugh Clifford and persuasion of the Sultan of Johore, who two years earlier had signed a similar treaty, Sultan Ahmad Muadzam Shah finally relented and agreed to sign an Anglo-Pahang Treaty. Under the treaty, Hugh Clifford became a British Agent in Pahang with consular status. This was the beginning of the British intervention in the State. In the following year (1888) the murder of a Chinese named Jo Hui (Go Cui), who was allegedly a British subject provided a first class opportunity for Clement Smith, the Governor of the Straits-Settlements, to seize upon the incident to extract a sort of recapitulation letter from the Sultan. In this letter dated 24TH August 1888, the Sultan acknowledged responsibility for the murder, requested the British Government to send a British officer to assist him "in matters relating to the Government of Pahang on a similar system to that existing in other Malay States under British protection". In return, the Sultan asked for the British guarantee to him and his successors, all their privileges and powers, and also an undertaking not to interfere with Malay custom and Islamic religion. In October 1888, J. P. Rodger was appointed the first British Resident to Pahang.

Federated Malay States

Pahang (Cont.)

When J. P. Rodger left Singapore for Pahang on 18TH October 1888, he took with him a force of 25 Sikh police officers from Selangor, which was augmented by 25 Sikhs from the Singapore Police Contingent. He then asked Superintendent Syers, the head of Selangor police force, to set up a police force in Pahang. Syers soon realised that the existing force was insufficient and obtained 50 more Sikh police officers, recruited and trained in Singapore. They were armed with snider rifles and were sent to Pahang under Surain Singh, who had served for many years in Straits Settlements Police. At the beginning of 1890, Pahang police consisted of 104 Sikhs and 142 Malays. At the end of 1890 a further 50 Sikhs were recruited for the Pahang police.

Dato Bahman

During 1888-95, the British consolidated their control over Pahang and started developing roads and railways. These measurers heightened discontent amongst the local chiefs. The development of roads and railways decreased their income, as it meant rivers upon which they could levy tolls, were used less for transport. They could not levy tolls on the new roads and railways as these were built and owned by the British administration. Dato Bahaman was one such chief; he defied British demands to stop levying taxes on boats passing along the Semantan River. Under pressure from the British, the Sultan deprived Dato Bahaman of his chieftainship in December 1891. Dato Bahaman fled into the jungle with a force of about 200 men and began his rebellion against the authorities.

Semantan River

On December 15TH 1891, 15 Sikhs and 6 Malay police officers went up the Semantan River and arrested three of Dato Bahman's followers for minor charges. In retaliation, Brahman and his followers ambushed the little force in which two police officers were wounded and three Sikh police officers captured and killed. The remaining police officers managed to make their way back to Temerloh. Dato Bahman's followers soon increased to 500/600 and with such following, he attacked Temerloh and went on to fortify points along the Semantan River. Meanwhile 60 Sikh police officers, along with a force of 200 men led by Tengku Mahmud and accompanied by the Resident, took the field and destroyed Bahaman's fortifications.

Sungei Duri. 1892

In 1892, rebels led by the Panglima Muda of Jumpol murdered two European employees of the Pahang Exploration Company, Stewart and Harris at Sungei Duri and then moved on to attack Pekan. A detachment of Sikhs from Singapore and the steamships HMS Hyacinth, Plover and Rattler were sent and most of the rebels were arrested.

Federated Malay States

Budu

On 18TH May 1892 Captain Walker, left Raub for Budu with 107 Perak Sikhs including 13 gunners with 7 Pounder guns. The rebel chief, Mat Kilau held the stronghold in force and refused any peaceful negotiations. As the Sikhs attacked the stronghold, Mat Kilau and his followers fled into the jungle, where they joined forces with Dato Bahman and his followers. The stronghold and the villages evacuated by the rebels were burned. Friendly Malays then held Budu, recalling the real inhabitants of the place, who were frightened away by the rebels.

Sungei Jumpul

In June 1892, 45 Sikhs entered Sungei Jumpul area in pursuit of the rebel Panglima Muda, whose group had killed two British officials at Sungei Duri. The Sikhs attacked the rebels, killing four and arresting forty-three. The Jumpul outbreak was finally quelled in October 1892, when a Malay force despatched by the Sultan killed Panglima Muda.

Kuala Tembling, 1894

On 18TH May 1892, Mat Kilau and Dato Bahaman were compelled to flee to Kelantan and Terengganu. In June 1892, they crossed the border from Terengganu into Pahang and attacked the stockade at Kuala Tembling, which was manned by 11 Sikh police officers. During the attack, five Sikh police officers were killed and the rest managed to escape. During their flight, Ram Singh and Kishen Singh fought heroically against some of the rebels. Kishen Singh died fighting while Ram Singh suffered more than thirty wounds and yet managed to reach Pulau Tawar and raise the alarm. Panglima Garang Yusoh, a pro-British chief, collected his men and attacked the rebels, killing one of the rebel leaders and seven of his men, compelling the rest to abandon Kuala Tembling. The other rebels managed to get away and constructed stockades on the right and left banks of the river at Jeram Ampi. Ram Singh was awarded the Imperial Service Medal for his bravery and courage. The Sikhs retook the fort and later overran the rebels' stronghold at Jeram Ampai, forcing Mat Kilau and Dato Bahaman to flee north. During the attack on Jeram Ampai, four Sikhs were killed and four wounded.

The British had deployed 200 Sikh police officers from Singapore, Perak, and Selangor for the anti-insurgency operations in Pahang and for the pursuit of the rebels into Terengganu and Kelantan. Private Ishar Singh was killed and Privates Kharak Singh and Teja Singh were wounded during the attack on the rebels' fort in Pahang. By late 1895, the insurgency in Pahang was practically over.

With the Federation of the Malay States in 1896, the police force of Pahang was to give up its own name and become a contingent of the Federated Malay States Police Force.

UNFEDERATED MALAY STATES

The Unfederated Malay States consisted of the states of Johore, Kedah, Kelantan, Perlis, and Terengganu. Johore accepted a treaty of protection with the United Kingdom in 1885, and eventually succumbed to British pressure to accept a resident "Advisor" in 1904. Unlike the other Malay states under British protection, Johore remained outside of the Federated Malay States (formed in 1895). Under the Bangkok Treaty of 1909, Siam transferred its rights over the northern Malay states (Kelantan, Terengganu, Kedah, and Perlis) to the United Kingdom. These states then became British Protected States. The Sultans of the Unfederated Malay States exercised complete control over their states. Under the advice of British, they set up police forces in their own states. They exclusively recruited Sikhs in their forces as the Sikh's reputation as the 'Motor Muscle' of imperial policing preceded them.

Kedah

In the 17TH Century, Kedah was attacked by the Portuguese, who had already conquered Malacca, and by the Acehnese from Sumatra, who saw Kedah as a threat to their own spice production. In the hope that the British would help protect what remained of Kedah from Siam, the Sultan handed over Penang to the British in the late 18TH century. Nevertheless, in the early 19TH century Kedah once again came under Siamese control, and remained a vassal state, until early 20TH century, when Siam passed control of Kedah to the British. In 1883, Sultan Abdul Hamid Halim Shah, employed Sikhs police officers for service in Kedah, who were directly recruited from the Punjab. When the Siamese Government returned the territories of Perlis and Setol to Kedah, these Sikhs provided the security on that occasion. Kedah became one of the first Unfederated Malay States to employ Sikh police officers. By 1905 there were 145 Sikhs of all ranks in the Kedah police force and in 1909, 154. The Sikh contingent was armed with Gruy's rifles, which had been discarded by the French army. The rifle was 4 feet 3 inches long and proved too long for use by the Malay detachment who then continued with the Snider Carbines. Most of the Sikhs were stationed at Alor Star, Kulim, and Kuala Mudah. The ones who did not perform police duties, were in reserve for para military duties; they also provided guards at various important buildings. The most famous officer of the Kedah Police Force was Subedar Bhall Singh of Kulim. Upon the retirement of Mr. B.E. Mitchel, commander of Police Kedah, Subedar Bhall Singh took charge of the Police force in Kulim. In addition to his duties as police officer, Subedar Bhall Singh, was also appointed Paymaster for all districts. He retired on pension after long service in 1912. He was later made Justice of Peace. During the Second World War, Kedah was the first part of Malaya to be conquered by the Japanese. After the war Kedah returned to British rule, until it became part of the Federation of Malay in 1948 and together with other states attained independence on August 31ST, 1957. On September 16TH, 1963, Kedah became one of the component states of Malaysia.

Unfederated Malay States

Perlis

Perlis was originally part of Kedah, though it variously fell under Siamese and Acehnese sovereignty. After the Siamese conquered Kedah in 1821, the Sultan of Kedah made unsuccessful attempts to regain his territory by force until 1842, when he agreed to accept Siamese terms. The Siamese reinstalled the Sultan, but made Perlis into a separate vassal principality with its own Raja. As with Kedah, power was transferred from Siam to the British under the 1909 Anglo-Siamese treaty and a British resident was installed at Arua. Government of Perlis also established a Sikh police force. 'The Sikh police were also jail warders, because it was more convenient, in the interest of discipline and equitable promotion, to combine the two'. A formal treaty, between Britain and Perlis, was not signed until 1930. During the Japanese occupation in the Second World War, Perlis was 'returned' to Thailand (Siam). After the war, it reverted to British rule until it became part of Malayan Union and then the Federation of Malay in 1948 and together with other states attained independence on August 31ST, 1957. On September 16TH, 1963, Perlis became one of the component states of Malaysia

Kelantan

Sultan Muhammad II leveraged on his loose alliance with Thailand to form the modern Kelantan state in 1835. The death of Sultan Muhammad II triggered a civil war among claimants to the throne. Tuan Long Mansur triumphed over his uncles and cousins and assumed the throne in 1891. To consolidate his position, he established a police force comprising mainly of Sikhs recruited from Singapore. Following the death of Tuan Long Mansur, Tuan Long Senik Sultan Muhammad became the ruler in 1900. In view of continuing challenges to his rule in Kelantan, Sultan Senik started strengthening the Sikh police force. The strength of the Kelantan Police Force at the beginning of 1905 totalled 327, of which 106 were Sikhs. The Sikh portion of the police, formerly known as the Kelantan Military Police, constituted the states standing army and operated as a para- military force. Under the terms of the Anglo-Thailand Treaty of 1909, the Thais relinquished their claims over Kelantan to Great Britain and Kelantan thus became one of the Unfederated Malay States with a British Adviser. The number of Sikh police officers increased in 1915 and barracks built for them at Kota Bharu, the capital of Kelantan. Kelantan was the first place in Malaya to be occupied by the Japanese, who invaded on December 8TH, 1941. During the Japanese occupation, Kelantan again came under control of Siam, but after the defeat of Japan in August 1945, Kelantan reverted to British rule. Kelantan became part of the Federation of Malaya on February 1ST, 1948 and together with other states attained independence on August 31ST, 1957. On September 16TH, 1963, Kelantan became one of the component states of Malaysia.

Unfederated Malay States

Johore

The history of modern Johore began with Dato' Temenggong Daing Ibrahim, the son of Temenggong Abdul Rahman, who was a descendant of Sultan Abdul Jalil IV of Johore. In 1855, under the terms of a treaty between the British in Singapore and Sultan Ali of Johore, the control of Johore was formally ceded to Dato' Temenggong Daing Ibrahim. The Temenggong was succeeded by his son, Dato' Temenggong Abu Bakar who later took the title Seri Maharaja Johore. Temenggong Abu Bakar continued his father's efforts in cultivating friendly relations with the British. In 1866, he was formally crowned Sultan of Johore. He gave Johore its constitution and developed an efficient system of administration. The moving of the seat of government from Teluk Belanga to Tanjung Puteri (renamed Johore Bahru) in 1841 led to the rapid development of the town as government offices, police stations, mosques, and courthouses were built. His successor, Sultan Ibrahim, continued to maintain close relations with the British and in 1910, requested for the services of a British advisor to counsel him on matters of state. Under the advice of the British advisor, he set up a police force in his own state and the Sikh police officers formed a significant part of the Johore police force, which also garrisoned the towns of Kluang and Muar. They also provided the Sultan’s personal Guard. Under the able administration of Sultan Ibrahim and his successors, Johore continued to thrive and prosper. In 1941, the peninsula fell under Japanese occupation. After the defeat of Japan Johor joined the Federation of Malaya in 1948 and together with other states attained independence on August 31ST, 1957. On September 16TH, 1963, Johore became one of the component states of Malaysia.

Johore State Police

(Police Museum Kuala Lumpur)

MALAY STATES GUIDES

The need for the Malay States to assist effectively in the defence of Singapore, as well as to deal with bushfire wars in the Peninsula, clearly demanded a force under a purely military command and separation for the ordinary police and this was effected in 1896. Walker, (its first commandant), raised a new force, the Malay States Guides, from the Sikh forces of the four states of Perak, Selangor, Negri Semblan and Pahang. Subedar Major Bhola Singh commanded the Malay States Guides detachment, which represented the Federated Malay States at the Jubilee Celebrations of Queen Victoria in London. The detachment was made up of all Sikhs. The Guides had been more or less on continuous service within the States since 1856. During the First World War, the battery and the infantry joined the Aden Defence Force from October 1915 onwards. The Battery had 3 Indian Officers, 54 gunners, 50 drivers and 5 followers, and the infantry numbered 788 all ranks. They were almost continuously in contact with the Turks, with frequent engagements and a great deal of marching under a very hot sun for five years. The following Sikhs of the Malay States Guides were awarded the Indian Order of Merit for their exceptional gallantry while fighting the Turks in Aden. Havildar Kehar Singh, Jemadar Gurdit Singh, Naik Sawan Singh, and Sepoy Sarwan Singh.

5TH Light Infantry (mainly made up of Indian Muslims) mutinied on 5TH February 1915 in Singapore. The mutiny was suppressed by the Sikh police contingent of Singapore and small detachments of 36TH Sikh Regiment and The Malay States Guides. The Guides Battery and Infantry were disbanded in late 1919. On Armistice Day, the Regimental colours of the disbanded Malay States Guides were taken in a ceremonial procession to be permanently placed at the All Saints Church, Taiping.

Malay States Guides sharp shooters at Bisley, England, in 1910
(W.A. Graham)

Malay States Guides

Subedar Major Gurdit Singh

This photograph shows the Subedar Major Gurdit Singh, who was previously the personal escort of the Commissioner of the Federated Malay States Police Force. Subedar Major Gurdit Singh was also a member of the Malay States Guides. For distinguished service during the Second Afghan War, Lord Wolsley presented him with the sword of honour.

Sowar Buta Singh

The photograph shows Sowar Buta Singh of the Malay States Guides in Taiping 1919, after war service in Aden. That same year the Guides were disbanded and the members recruited into the Federated Malay States Police Force.

BORNEO

North Borneo, 1882

North Borneo is located on the northeastern end of the island of Borneo. It is now the state of Sabah, East Malaysia. In 1878, Alfred Dent formed a British syndicate and persuaded the Sultan of Sulu to cede parts of North Borneo to the syndicate. Later the British North Borneo Company was formed which took over the concession granted to the syndicate. The British North Borneo Company applied for and received a charter from Queen Victoria in 1881. The conditions laid down were that the company must remain British and that the religion and customs of the native inhabitants must be respected. Because of possible complications with foreign powers, a British Protectorate was declared over the northern part of Borneo in 1888, which included Sarawak, Brunei and the state of North Borneo. The Crown took over external affairs, while the Chartered Company remained in control of internal administration of their territory, except that the Governor, chosen by the directors of the company sitting in London to represent them in Borneo, was to have the approval of the Colonial Secretary. Hence North Borneo was a British protectorate under the sovereign British North Borneo Company from 1882-1946, and subsequently a crown colony of the United Kingdom from 1946-1963.

One of the earliest problems for the owners of North Borneo had been to maintain peace amongst the various tribes and security for the company officers. The British North Borneo Chartered Company officials soon found that owning 30,000 square miles of territory was only one aspect of the story. Keeping it and deriving beneficial income was another. Thus when W. B. Pryer became the Resident of Sandakan, one of his first tasks was to establish law and order. In order to do this, he had to have a police force. Since the local natives considered the British as transgressors in their land, hostility towards the authority of the British North Borneo Chartered Company was natural. His first contingent of police was, therefore, made up of Sikhs. They were eagerly sought for recruitment in the British Army because of their proven loyalty and bravery. Furthermore, their stature alone must have been quite frightening to some of the natives.

Datu Paduka Mat Salleh was a prominent warrior in a series of uprising against the British, 1894 -1900

Borneo

British North Borneo Police, 1882

The Police force in North Borneo, established in 1882 by the North Borneo Chartered Company, recruited some "majestic Sikhs" from Perak with the help of the British Resident of Perak, Sir Hugh Low. Inspector De Fontain became the police commandant in 1883. The police force numbered just 300 men, mainly Sikhs. This was the entire strength of the police force of the territory. In May 1884 when 'amok' (from the Malay meaning "mad with uncontrollable rage") at Kawang occurred, Jemadar Asa Singh, Sergeant Major Narain Singh and Private Gendah Singh were the first fatal casualties among the Sikh police. The force is now an integral part of Royal Malaysian Police.

Cross of Valour The medal issued to those serving in the North Borneo Armed Constabulary, for gallantry during a number of small police actions between 1884 and 1915. These involved the pursuit of bandits and rebels, largely via rivers meandering through mangrove swamps and the across jungle clad hills, in tropical rainstorms, with ambushes and much sweat and toil by British Company officers, with Sikh police, and Dyak guides. Owen Rutter, describing the attack on Mat Sallah's Ranau fort near Tambunan on 13TH December 1897, during which Mr Jones and 4 Sikhs were killed and 9 wounded, gives an example of the circumstances resulting in these awards. "Throughout the action the Indian police behaved splendidly, even after the severe handling they had received, and were anxious to make a second attempt. During the action, Sergeant Natha Singh, although seriously wounded, succeeded after two attempts in picking up Mr Jones's body and carrying it back to a place of safety, after which he returned to the attack. For this gallant action in face of a point-blank fire he was given a commission and the Company's Cross for Valour". (Rutter, 1922) A few years earlier Jemadar Assa Singh was posthumously awarded the Cross-for Valour.

British North Borneo Police (Sikhs and Malays)
(The Illustrated London News)

Borneo

Sarawak

Sarawak is one of two Malaysian states on the island of Borneo. It is the largest state in Malaysia and is situated on the north-west of the island. In 1839, Sarawak, then a dependency of the Brunei sultanate, was in rebellion against the central power. Looking for commercial ventures with his well-armed schooner, a young British adventurer by the name of James Brooke arrived on the scene. He soon found himself involved in the local disputes. The young Brooke assisted the Sultan's representative to bring peace to the area. For his services, the Sultan made him the Rajah of Sarawak in 1841. James Brooke tried to expand his territory; strived to pacify the many warring tribes and to stamp out the practices of head hunting and piracy. In 1857, the Chinese uprising started in the gold mining town of Bau, which is about 20 miles from the town of Kuching. Sir James Brooke fled to Singapore, where he took refuge with the Governor of the Straits Settlements. He subsequently recruited Sikh officers for the Sarawak Police Force in Singapore. The first batch of Sikhs arrived in Kuching, led by Dewa Singh Akhara. These Sikhs played an important role in bringing peace, law, and order to the area. The Sikhs recruited later joined the Sarawak Police forces stationed at Miri and Bua. The Government also employed them as prison wardens. The Sarawak Shell Company also employed them as security personnel at Miri. The Sarawak Rangers were a para-military force founded in 1862 and were highly skilled in jungle warfare and general police duties, being equipped with various western rifles, cannons and native weaponry. They were based in a number of forts constructed at strategic locations in towns and at river mouths. Aside from protecting Sarawak's borders, they were used to fight any rebels and were engaged in a number of campaigns during their history. By 1907, there were 66 Sikhs in the Sarawak Rangers. The Sarawak Rangers were mobilized for the Second World War, in which they attempted to defend Sarawak from Japanese invasion in 1942. After the abdication of Charles Vyner Brooke in 1946, the Sarawak Rangers became a colonial unit under direct British control and saw action in both the Malayan Emergency and the Borneo Confrontation. In 1963, after the formation of Malaysia, the Sarawak Rangers became part of the Royal Ranger Regiment.

Sikh Police, Sarawak Police Force, Kuching, 1939.
(Sarawak Royal Police Head quarters)

MALAYA

Kota Bahru

The British-owned peninsula of Malaya was a prize target for the Japanese when they launched their unheralded lightning strikes across the Far East. The war in Malaya began with the Japanese landings at Kota Bahru, on Malaya's northeastern coast. The Japanese objective was to seize the three airfields in the vicinity of Kota Bahru. The defence of Kota Bahru was assigned to 8TH Indian Brigade of 9TH Division. This comprised four Indian infantry battalions. The Japanese landed 56TH Infantry Regiment, which were three battalions strong. The landings were costly to the Japanese. Japanese casualties were heavy at around 30%. However, they managed to secure a beachhead. Despite attempting a counterattack with their reserve, the British were unable to dislodge the Japanese beachhead. However, at Singora and Patani, the Japanese 5TH Division came ashore unopposed.

Singapore, December 1941

In a co-ordinated attack, 17 Japanese Navy bombers, flying from Saigon, attacked Singapore's Keppel Harbour Docks, Naval base, and air bases at Tenngah and Seletar. Incongruously Singapore's streetlights stayed ablaze throughout the bombing and the air raid sirens were silent. Within two hours of the Singapore raid, orders were given to intern all Japanese civilians in Malaya and Singapore, and to arrest all Japanese vessels in Singapore harbour.

Air Raids, December 1941

During the day, Japanese aircraft attacked British airfields at Ator Star, Sungei Patani, Butterworth, and Penang Island on Malay's northwest, and Kuala Terengganu, and Kuantan on the east coast.

Kota Bahru airfield, December 1941

Advancing Japanese, now backed by freshly landed tanks, hurled back the Indian defenders, and swung south to capture Kota Bahru Township. Indian units sustained fearful casualties in vain attempts to hurl back the Japanese thrusts. Malaya Command issued orders for the retreat to Kuala Krai and the secret withdrawal of the defeated Kota Bahru force to Kuala Lipis.

Kroh, December 1941

Japanese launched a heavy attack on 3RD Battalion, 16TH Punjab Regiment and eighty five Japanese dive-bombers directed massive air raids on Penang, inflicting 2,000 casualties on the islands civilian population.

Thailand, December 1941

Betong, Southern Thailand, driving south, down the Patani-Kroh road, a detachment of the Japanese 5TH Division wiped out Indian troops and rushed north across the frontier to Betong.

Malaya

Jitra, December 1941

The Battle of Jitra was the first major engagement fought between the invading Japanese and British forces in Malaya. The actual battle was fought from 11TH – 12TH December 1941. On 11TH December, 1ST Battalion, 14TH Punjab Regiment at Changlun was directed to occupy an intermediate position before Asun. Now came catastrophe. As the Punjabis were assembling to occupy their new position, a Japanese mechanized force, headed by medium tanks, broke through the rearguard, caught the anti-tank guns limbering up, destroyed them, smashed through, and swarmed right through the battalion. By evening, 14TH Punjab Regiment had ceased to exist as a fighting formation. The 16TH Punjab Regiment with Major Brown's Sikhs withdrew and took part in the confused fighting at Anak Bukit and formed part of the rear guard at Simpang Ampat.

Kampar, December 1941

The Kampar position was one of the strongest in Malaya. The 28TH Brigade held the hill, when the Japanese attacked on 31ST December. There, in a four day battle, the Japanese suffered heavy casualties and the Sikhs carried out bayonet charges through machine-gun and mortar fire. By January 2ND though, the Indian 11TH Infantry Division was out flanked, cut off from the road to Singapore and so they withdrew to some prepared positions at Trolak, five miles north of the Slim River.

"Leading the Sikh company against the Japanese occupied trenches Graham and his gallant Sikhs, the first and second lines at bayonet point, and through shouts of "Sat Sri Akal", they struggled against heavy Japanese gunfire. In the final charge, Graham had only 30 Sikhs left and a Japanese hand grenade blew away both his legs below the knees, as the small group reached the crest. Even then, Graham and his Sikhs continued to fight until all the Japanese survivors ran off to safety. The Battle of Kampar had proved that the gallant Sikh soldiers were superior, man to man, to the Japanese; A Havildar at the 1/8TH Punjab headquarters said, on hearing Captain Graham's death – " Mera dil tut gia. Aisa Bahadur admi khabi nahin honge" (This very brave act has never been fully told). So, due credit has never been given to these men, who fought so bravely. The Sikh soldiers, with shouts of Sat Sri Akal, charged up the rear slope of Thompson Ridge. They stormed the Japanese lines with their bayonets bristling in the sunlight, their eyes aglow with the fury of battle. The noise of the guns was deafening and then suddenly firing stopped. The Japanese were licking their wounds, their dead lying in trenches and some of them throwing away their arms in a desperate bid to escape, others being bayoneted before they could turn. Once on the objective, the Sikhs continued the slaughter, firing on groups attempting to cover. The bogey of the super Japanese samurai warrior had been laid bare."*

*Extract taken from an article: *Saluting the Unsung Heroes - Battle of Kampar* by Daljit Singh, posted on *www.sikhnet.com* on October 26TH, 2010.

Malaya

Jemadar Wir Singh
8TH Punjab Regiment

"Jemadar Wir Singh displayed very high qualities of leadership until severely wounded at Kampar in Malaya in 1942. Throughout the earlier battles, he showed great courage. In the successful counter-attack by his Company at Kampar, he was the sole officer surviving, both British officers being killed early in the engagement. His handling of the Company was exemplary. By the end of fighting at Kampar his Company had lost 75 percent, killed and wounded. Jemadar Wir Singh was largely responsible for the high morale of the survivors." Jemadar Wir Singh was strongly recommended for and awarded the Military Cross.

Slim River

After the defeat of Jitra, 11TH Indian Division continued its withdrawal to the south of Malaya, pursued by the Japanese vanguard. The British High Command in Singapore planned to restore a defensive line on the Slim River, north of Kuala Lumpur. But the Indian infantry, exhausted by a 250 kms long retreat, was unable to prepare solid defensive positions before the Japanese attack. On 7TH January, 1942, Japanese light tanks attacked first. Some were destroyed by mines or grenades in close combat, but others broke through the Indian lines. Japanese infantry that followed the tanks, overwhelmed Indian positions by bayonet charges. On the evening, the bridge on the Slim River was captured by the Japanese. By 9TH January, the British situation was extreme and General Wavell (Commanding) decided to withdraw the entire British Army to north Johore, leaving Kuala Lumpur free for occupation, which the Japanese did on 13TH January.

The Muar, January 1942

The Battle of Muar was the last major battle of the Malayan campaign. It took place from 14TH January to 22ND January 1942, around Gemensah Bridge and on the Muar River. Allied soldiers, under the command of Major General Gordon Bennett, inflicted severe losses on Japanese forces. By late afternoon the Japanese, who had already made the crossing higher up, stormed into Muar Town and captured the garrison headquarters, killing all the officers. By nightfall of 16TH January, Muar Town and the harbour had fallen into Japanese hands. The remnants of the garrison retreated down the coast several miles, as far as Parit Jawa. Japanese ambushes were soon deployed to repel any Allied counter-attacks.

Niyor, January1942

The action at Niyor, 1942, was the last engagement fought in Malaya. Thereafter the retreating troops destroyed the causeway connecting the peninsula to Singapore Island. The battle for Singapore began.

Malaya

In 1948, the government declared a state of emergency throughout the country, following the murder of three British planters in Perak by armed members of the Malayan Communist Party (MCP). This marked the start of a 12-year war against the communists. During WWII, the communist-led Malayan People's Anti-Japanese Army had spearheaded local resistance against the Japanese. By the end of the war, the MPAJA had emerged as a formidable political organization. For a while, before the return of the British, units of the MPAJA gained control of some small towns. In the months leading up to the declaration of Emergency, there were many violent incidents perpetrated by the MCP, which sought political change. MCP-infiltrated trade unions agitated for improvements in salaries and working conditions and organized industrial action. In Response, the British arrested trade union and MCP leaders. This set the stage for armed conflict between the MCP and the British. It is estimated that following the declaration of Emergency, some 7,000 to 10,000 MCP supporters, mainly Chinese, went into the jungle to fight the British. The insurgents targeted rubber estates and tin mines, hoping to damage the economy and defeat the government. On Sept 8TH, 1955, the Government of the Federation of Malaya offered amnesty to the communists. The failure of the Baling talks with the MCP and its leaders, including Chin Peng, led to the amnesty offer being withdrawn by Tunku Abdul Rahman in February 1956. With Merdeka declared on August 31ST, 1957, the insurrection lost its rationale and momentum as a war against the British colonialists. On July 31ST, 1960, the Malayan government declared the state of Emergency over. During the conflict, security forces killed 6,710 communists and captured 1,287. A total of 2,702 guerrillas surrendered during the Emergency, and 500 at the end. A total of 1,345 Malayan troops and police were killed, as well as 519 Commonwealth soldiers. Some 2,478 civilians were killed, and another 810 reported missing.

Malaysia

Malaysia is a Federal parliamentary democracy with a constitutional monarch. Malaya gained Independence on August 31ST, 1957. In 1963 Malaya, Sabah, Sarawak, and Singapore formed Malaysia. Singapore became an independent country in 1965. Malaysia's multi-racial society contains many ethnic groups. Malays comprise a majority. About a quarter of the population is ethnic Chinese. Malaysians of Indian descent comprise about 7 percent of the population and include Sikhs. Malaysian Sikhs form a vibrant minority within the country.

MALAYSIAN ARMED FORCES

Malaysian Sikh Soldiers

(With Colonel Baldev Singh Johl)

This segment records the contributions of Sikhs, who form a tiny minority of the population of Malaysia, but are found in leading roles in all walks of life in Malaysia. Valiant Sikhs played a great part in the history of the Malaysian Armed Forces. The origins of the Malaysian Armed Forces started on 1ST March, 1933. It was the formation of 1ST Battalion Malay Regiment army under British rule. It was predominantly an ethnic Malay unit, which took part in the Malaya Campaign during World War II - 1941-1945, (the Japanese Occupation of Malaya). Sikhs soldiers were present during the campaign but they were under the British, the colonial master. The early Sikhs that joined the Malaysian Armed Forces (then Malayan Army) can be traced to the early 1950s, when Sir Gerald Templer's twelve selected local cadets were sent to the Royal Military Academy, Sandhurst, United Kingdom for officer training. The first Sikh officer selected was Lakhbir Singh Gill, who formed part of the famous Templer's twelve. From then on there was a gradual recruitment of Sikhs into the Malaysian Armed Forces to this day. Sikhs were part of units and establishments in which they held key appointments and partook in missions/assignments to defeat threats to the country or accomplish set missions.

Campaign Coverage

This segment/campaign covers the period after the Japanese Occupation until today.

- The fight against the Malayan Communist Party (MCP) during the First Emergency (1948 to 1960) and the Second Emergency (1968 to 1989) when the communist threat was eventually eradicated. During this period, the government counter measures included Security and Development (KESBAN), a methodology that synergized the efforts of security forces with other government agencies to eliminate the MCP. Civic action groups included Sikh medical officers, engineers and infantry officers and men whose efforts greatly paved the way for the 'Hearts and Minds' battle to be won.
- The period of Confrontation (1962 to 1965) during which Indonesia opposed the formation of Malaysia* (1963) and launched an offensive to oppose the formation, that was eventually subdued.
- Episodes in United Nations sponsored operations that the MAF participated in.
- Other operations in support of the Malaysian government during public disorder and national disasters.

*Malaysia – the union of Malaya, Singapore, the states of Sabah and Sarawak (East Malaysia) on 16TH September 1963. Singapore subsequently pulled out of this union in 1965 for political reasons.

Malaysian Armed Forces

Enlisted Sikhs served with distinction, humility, and compassion. Their sacrifices were justly rewarded in some cases but many went unnoticed and unrewarded. True to the traditions of their forefathers, MAF Sikhs served unconditionally – giving their best and expecting nothing in return. Only four Sikh officers are on record, to have earned some form of award for gallantry.

Brigadier General Rajbans Singh Gill

Brigadier General Rajbans Singh Gill joined the Army in February 1953. He was trained at Eaton Hall, UK in May 1953 and was commissioned on 5TH September 1953. He was posted to 1ST Federation Regiment. He was awarded ***'Mention in Despatch'*** * on 19TH June, 1959, while serving with the UN in Congo. He commanded 3RD Royal Ranger Regiment May 1970 to January 1971. He was promoted to Brigadier General on 1ST December 1979 (the first Sikh to attain the general rank) and commanded Rejang Area Security Command (RASCOM), a brigade group organization, from January 1980 to February 1981. RASCOM was tasked to eliminate the communist threat (Malayan Communist Party) in the Rejang area of Sarawak. He served as the Chief of Staff General Branch, Army Corps HQ from March 1981 to December 1982 and commanded 10TH Brigade in 1983 to 1985.

Brigadier General Baljit Singh

Brigadier General Baljit Singh joined the Army on 2ND February 1953. He first trained at Eaton Hall, UK from 29TH August 1953 to 17TH December 1953 and later at RMA Sandhurst from 10TH March 1954 to 27TH July 1955. He was commissioned on 28th July 1955 and was posted to 1ST Federation Regiment. He served with the Malayan Special Force Congo Group (UN) from November 1961 to August 1962. He was awarded ***'Mention in Despatch'*** for actions in the Congo. He later commanded 1ST Royal Ranger Regiment from April 1971 to January 1973. He served as Defence Attaché to the Republic of Cambodia from January 1975 to January 1976 and New Zealand from October 1976 to December 1977. He later commanded RASCOM from January 1978 to December 1979. He was later the Commandant of the Malaysian Army Combat Training Centre from 1ST January 1981 to 31ST December 1981. He was promoted to Brigadier General on 1ST January 1982 (the second Sikh officer to be promoted to the rank in the Malaysian Army) and commanded 1ST Malaysian Infantry Brigade from January 1982 to December 1983. He also commanded 10th Malaysian Infantry Brigade from January 1984 to October 1985. He later was the Commandant of the Malaysian Armed Forces Defence College from November 1985 to April 1986. He retired in January 1988 leaving behind the legacy of his command and leadership.

*Mention in Despatch (KPK). This is an honour/award given to serving members of the MAF who have shown courage and bravery while executing their tasks.

Malaysian Armed Forces

Brigadier General Ranjit Singh Ramday

Brigadier General Ranjit Singh Ramday was trained at the Royal Military College, Kuala Lumpur and was commissioned on 31ST October 1974. He was posted to 3RD Royal Ranger Regiment. Having served in various appointments in the early years, he volunteered to join 8TH Royal Ranger Regiment, the newly formed Malaysian Parachute Infantry Battalion. He served in the regiment as a company commander, second-in-command and finally commanded the regiment from June 1996 until June 1999. He also served with the UN HQ (MONUC) in the Democratic Republic of the Congo from May 2004 to June 2005. He was a Directing Staff at the Malaysian Armed Forces Staff College from January 2000 to January 2003 and later at the Malaysian Armed Forces Defence College from July 2007 to February 2011. On 28TH February 2011, he was posted to the Army Training Command as Chief of Staff and was promoted to Brigadier General (the third Sikh officer to be promoted to the rank in the Malaysian Army). He is currently the Director of Training Management at Army Training Command.

Brigadier General Dato Ranjit Singh Gill

Brigadier General Ranjit Singh Gill joined the RMC in February 1968 and commissioned as a Pilot Officer in September 1968. He got his "Wings" in January 1970. He was an active helicopter pilot supporting ground missions against the Malayan Communist Party in the border regions with Indonesia and Thailand. He rose to become a Pilot Examiner and a Category 'A' Instructor. He had a short stint as a Fixed Wing Pilot flying the Twin-Engine Cessna 402B Transport Aircraft. He commanded the training base at Kluang, Johor from 1992 to 1995 and later the operational base at Subang, Selangor in 1996 and 1997. He served as the Chief of Staff in No. 2 Air Division in Subang and shortly after set up and commanded the Air Force's Safety, Standards, and Readiness (SSR) Department, which carried out examinations of all pilots and cabin crew. This included the examination and assessment of the Operational Readiness Inspections (ORI) of all RMAF units. Ranjit had the distinction of being the first Sikh General in the Air Force and the third in the Malaysian Armed Forces (MAF) after Brigadier General Rajbans Singh and Brigadier General Baljit Singh. He was also involved in the conduct of two LIMA Air shows, Malaysia's premier air, and maritime shows in Langkawi in 1999 and 2001. Before his retirement in 2003, he was bestowed with the title of 'Dato' * by His Royal Highness, The Sultan of Pahang, the first Sikh in the Malaysian Armed Forces to be granted such an award.

* 'Dato' is the highest state title conferred by the Ruler on the most deserving recipients who have contributed greatly to the nation or state.

Malaysian Armed Forces

Colonel Harchan Singh

Colonel Harchan Singh was trained at Eaton Hall, UK from 24TH April 1953 to 22ND August 1953 and at the RMA Sandhurst from 9TH September 1953. He was Commissioned on 3RD March 1955 and posted to 1ST Federation Regiment. He served with the Malayan Special Force Congo (UN) from September 1961 to December 1962. He was awarded the ***'Mention in Despatch'*** in September 1965. He commanded 2ND, 4TH, 5TH, and 9TH Royal Ranger Regiments at various times. He was appointed as Defence Attaché to Vietnam from December 1976 to January 1979. He retired in April 1985 leaving behind the legacy of his command and leadership.

Lieutenant Colonel Baldev Singh Johl

Lieutenant Colonel Baldev Singh Johl was trained at the Royal Military College, Kuala Lumpur from April 1969 to April 1971. He was posted into the Royal Ranger Regiment and held several appointments in the various units he served in. In 1974, as the unit Intelligence Officer of 7TH Royal Ranger Regiment, his analysis led to an ambush operation that resulted in the elimination of 5 communist terrorist (CT) of the MCP within a day of execution. In 1977, in a similar ambush operation, a subunit of his company eliminated 2 CTs in the Malaysia/Thailand border region. He commanded 6TH Royal Ranger Regiment from 1991 to December 1993, during which time the regiment was involved in a humanitarian effort to rescue the victims of a massive Highland Tower collapse. Later in 1999, while serving with the UN Military Observer group in East Timor, he intervened in a militia raid on refugees, escaping into the UN HQ in Dili. On the night of 10TH September 1999, a militia group was in hot pursuit of refugees escaping into the UN HQ. Colonel Baldev stepped out to halt the militia raid. His timely intervention brought the militia raid to a stop. While negotiating, the militia leader threatened him with two grenades and advised Colonel Baldev to withdraw and go home. The pause in action enabled the refugee group of women and children, to scramble hurriedly through the wire obstacles, into the safety of the UN compound.

Malaysian Armed Forces

Major Lakhbir Singh Gill

Major Lakhbir Singh Gill was one of the twelve potential officers selected personally by General Sir Gerald Templer, the High Commissioner for the Federation of Malaya, in July 1952, to attend officer training at the RMA Sandhurst. The basis for his selection, as platoon commander, was to form the first multi-racial battalion (1st Federation Regiment) for Malaya. It was part of the effort to unite the Malayan people in the fight against the MCP and to prepare for Malaya's independence. Major Lakhbir was trained from 10TH September 1953 and was commissioned on 3RD February 1955. He was posted to 1ST Federation Regiment. He held various appointments in the army and was a model officer for young Sikhs in the army.

Major Jagdeesh Singh Gill

Major Jagdeesh Singh Gill was a graduate of the Royal Military College, Kuala Lumpur and was commissioned to 3RD Royal Ranger Regiment in 1968. Operation RADAK was an operation planned to search and destroy an insurgent group of the MCP, operating in the Kulim area of Kedah. On 15TH May 1971 at about 1720 hrs 2ND Lieutenant Jagdeesh Singh Gill, commander of No 9 Platoon, contacted three Communist Terrorists (CTs) that were part of the unit's objective. Jagdeesh launched an immediate assault on the group and succeeded in killing 2 CTs. The third was killed by another group from the regiment, which eliminated 7 CTs in the operation. In recognition of his gallant act, 2ND Lieutenant Jagdeesh Singh Gill was awarded the ***'Mention in Despatch'.***

Captain Hardev Gurdial Singh

Captain Hardev Gurdial Singh was commissioned from the Royal Military College, Kuala Lumpur on 25TH February 1968. Having served at various appointment and units, Captain Hardev was posted to 6TH Malaysian Infantry Brigade in May 1973 as the Brigade Intelligence Officer (G 3 Intelligence). On 10TH April 1975, during Operation SEDAR in the Gubir area of Kedah, while leading a military convoy in the operation area, the convoy was ambushed by Communist Terrorists (CTs). Captain Hardev put up stiff resistance during the ambush but was killed. He left behind a legacy of true grit and a 'man of action'. Subsequent operations caused great destruction on the CT group and its withdrawal from its firm bases.

Malaysian Armed Forces

Captain Mukhtiar Singh

Captain Mukhtiar Singh had the unique distinction of serving in the Police and the Army. Born in India he migrated to Malaya in the late 1950s, and joined the Home Guards and Special Constables unit under the police. As an Acting Inspector in 1958 (during the First Emergency), Mukhtiar was instrumental in the elimination of the MCP threat in Selangor. He worked under extreme conditions: patrols were dangerous as many of the constables were untrained and did not have proper equipment for jungle warfare but his perseverance and through true grit, he led his unit in turning the tables on the MCP groups. He had several close encounters; this included one with the notorious group that had killed the OCPD and an inspector earlier in 1953. But Mukhtiar's aggressive actions put the insurgent group under severe pressure and by the end of 1959; the threat in Selangor was eradicated. Mukhtiar was recognized for his role in a special parade held to mark the end of the communist threat in the state. He was also awarded the ***Colonial Police Medal for Gallantry in Action*** by Her Highness Queen Elizabeth 11 and the ***Selangor Meritorious Service Medal*** awarded by His Highness, The Sultan of Selangor. When the Emergency ended in 1960, the Home Guards and Special Constables were disbanded, and Mukhtiar joined the Territorial Army (TA) and rose to the rank of Captain. He served as an instructor for 16 years in the TA army until his retirement.

Mukhtiar and his 'Killer' Jungle squad

Malaysian Armed Forces

Colonel Dara Singh with Lord Louis Mountbatten

In 1939, when 4,000 Chinese from Malaya volunteered for service in China, Dara Singh went along with them. "I was the only Indian in the party, but then I knew Chinese". As a Chinese speaking Sikh, called Dara Ah-Leng, in the Kuomintang army, he had some hard times proving he was as good as his Chinese comrades. However, he succeeded and rose from Sergeant to Colonel in two years and then was personally promoted to Brigadier-General by Chiang Kai Shek in 1943. Later he served with the American forces in Burma and worked closely with General Joseph W. Stillwell, who was commanding Chinese troops against the Japanese. Here he was the General's aide, bodyguard, and interpreter, making good use of the language skills he had nurtured in Malaya and China. He spoke fluent Hokkien and six other Chinese dialects, Malay, English, Hindi, Tamil, Punjabi, and Burmese. Working with General Stillwell then provided the opportunity to work with Lord Louis Mountbatten, the World War II Allied Chief of Combined Operations, and South East Asia. It was during this period that he rescued Lord Louis from a jeep crash. He had been struck in the eye with bamboo while driving and lost control of the vehicle. Prompt first aid from Dara and then a fast trip to a field hospital with him saved Mountbatten's sight, something acknowledged publicly by Lord Louis at a reception in Malaysia in 1967. When he finally returned to Taiping after the war, the Chinese gave him a hero's welcome and for one year, everything was given free to him and his family as a thank you for what he had done. Free food, accommodation, clothes and more, everything was free! Appointed as Protector of Aborigines (Orang Asli) he made friends with them and their children by handing out used tennis balls no longer required by the clubs. When he left the post he was crowned by the Aborigines "Tata (grandfather) of all Aborigines". He turned down the post of Ambassador to an African country, offered by the Prime Minister Tun Abdul Razak, preferring to stay in Malaysia and live a simple life, working hard, without any form of pension, to ensure his children were educated.

Malaysian Armed Forces

Superintendent Gurcharan Singh

Assistant Superintendent of Police Gurcharan Singh was dubbed "the Lion of Malaya". Gurcharan Singh was born in 1914 and was a police officer in Malaya when World War II broke out. He organised a resistance group and started printing counter propaganda pamphlets to help keep up the morale of brutalised people. His propaganda pamphlets signed *'Singa'* spread the truth about the war situation as he heard it on the Allied radio broadcasts. He extolled the virtue of resisting the Japanese. His counter-propaganda helped to lift sagging morale and there were people reading his posters wherever they appeared, sometimes in the most outrageous places, much to the fury of the Japanese. His one-man show was a truly astounding feat of defiance against a ruthless enemy. A high price was put on his head. Torture compelled one of his agents to reveal his whereabouts. He was captured but eventually escaped. After the war, he was promoted to Inspector and in June 1957 was appointed as Personal Security Officer to Tunku Abdul Rahman who became Malaya's first Prime Minister. Gurcharan died on 6TH March 1965 in a road accident. (Khoo, 1982)

Commissioner Santokh Singh

Sardar Santokh Singh became the first Malayan Police Officer to undergo the F.B.I. course in Washington, United States of America. In 1965 he became the first Asian Officer serving in the Malayan Police Force to qualify as a barrister in law. In 1966, he was promoted Assistant Commissioner of Police, the youngest in the country. In 1973, he became the fist Sikh to be appointed Deputy Director of the C.I.D. in Malaysia. In 1974, having the rank of Assistant Commissioner of Police he assumed duties as the Chief Police Officer for the state of Selangor, the first Sikh to do so!

Malaysian Armed Forces

Wing Commander Jaswant Singh
Royal Malaysian Air Force Pioneer.

Jaswant Singh was born in Kuala Lumpur, where he lived all his life. His father, Hajura Singh, had been brought to Malaya at a tender age around the turn of the century by his own father – they were yeoman Puneas from Jalaldiwal village (near Raekot) in Sangrur district – and in the 1920s he supported his young family with his earnings from humble employment in the Audit department of the colonial administration.

The young Jaswant, the eldest of three siblings, was educated at the Victoria Institution, the capital's premier day school, but the war years meant that his tertiary education would be limited to cycling forty miles most days to buy and sell coconuts and pineapples to occupying Japanese troops. With his Senior Cambridge results received after the war, he joined the newly revived British civil service. In 1951 the RAF advertised for volunteers for an auxiliary air force to train local Malayans to empower themselves for national defence. Jaswant, then merely contemplating flying as a hobby, applied along with half a dozen other Sikh friends and was accepted as a cadet officer. Thus began an 18-year flying career that would see him become the first local pilot of the Malayan Auxiliary Air Force, and a pioneer member of the Royal Malayan Air Force. Early training was in Tiger Moths, Chipmunks and Harvards and by the time he earned his wings in April 1955 he had done 470 hours, including bombing, gunnery, interceptions and drops, in single- and twin-engine aircraft. He clocked the magic 500 two months later as the only local pilot in the fly past on the 2ND anniversary of the coronation of Elizabeth II.

During the communist insurgency, all through the mid-1950s to mid-60s, Jaswant flew relief and supply missions to police and military jungle forts, often putting down his Single Pioneer on postage-stamp sized grass landing strips, earning mention in dispatches for distinguished service in difficult and dangerous conditions, which saw some of his brave friends perish. In 1965, Squadron Leader Jaswant became the first commander of the now Royal Malaysian Air Force's Labuan base off Borneo, where he also served as senior RMAF officer for the newly incorporated states of East Malaysia.

With British RAF personnel still holding top positions in the RMAF, Jaswant returned to the peninsula in 1966, and now as Wing Commander, becoming Deputy Commandant of the main air force base in Kuala Lumpur, ending there, in December 1969, his air force career, at the same place where it all began.

CHRISTMAS ISLAND

Christmas Island Police, 1899

Christmas Island was annexed by Great Britain in 1888; and was governed under the jurisdiction of the colony of Singapore; soon afterwards, a small settlement was established in Flying Fish Cove. The main reason behind this settlement was to provide timber supplies for the flatter and more habitable Cocos Island. Phosphate mining also began in the 1890's using indentured workers from Singapore, China and Malaysia.

British authorities in Singapore were responsible for providing a small section of the Police for Christmas Island. In 1901 one Sikh corporal and seven constables were added to the Sikh Contingent in Singapore to provide a small Police Force for Christmas Island. In 1910, Sikh policemen on the Island totalled 47. Postings for the Sikh Police Contingent generally happened on a yearly basis and continued right up to World War II.

Disruption occurred during World War II. In 1942 about 900 Japanese troops landed on the island and tried to take over the phosphate mining activities. On 10TH March, keenly aware of Japanese support for Indian independence, and possibly fearing death itself, the Indian troops mutinied, and were shipped off to Singapore with the option of joining the Indian National Army. The ones, who refused to join the INA, were either executed or sent to the labour camps, from where only few survived. In October 1945, Britain reoccupied Christmas Island. At Australia's request, the United Kingdom transferred sovereignty of the island to Australia in 1957.

Sikh police officers on Christmas Island

FIJI

Fiji Police 1900

The early Sikh migrants were mainly from the Jullunder and Hoshiarpur districts, although some also came from Ludhiana, Amritsar, Ferozepore, Lahore, Ambala and Rohtak districts of Punjab. They were all young and mostly younger sons of the family. The early migrants were mostly single men and those who stayed in Fiji married Hindu women and eventually became prosperous farmers. They maintained close ties with their families in the Punjab and remitted money back to their families. From 1900, Fiji authorities recruited Sikh police officers from Hong Kong and Shanghai, to police their growing Indian population. In 1916, C. F. Andrews and W. W. Pearson, in their report on Indian indentured labour in Fiji, expressed high regard for the Indian Police Force in Suva, which was made up of Sikhs. They noted that unlike in India, these police officers did not take bribes. They wrote that:

'We found an extremely well conducted Indian Police Force in Suva. These Indians, who were Sikhs, were paid a good monthly wage, and expressed themselves, on the whole, contented with their position. They had come out under an agreement, but there was nothing about it that was servile. Their passage was quite different from that of the ordinary coolies. They were treated well by their senior officers, who spoke highly of their men'. (Andrews and Pearson, 1918)

Walter Gill, who served as an overseer for the Colonial Sugar Refining Company in Lautoka during the final years of indenture has also written about significant numbers of Sikhs employed in the Western Division of Fiji to police the Indian population.

A Sikh police officer checks permits of Fijian vendors. (Suva)

PERSIA

Great Britain's interest in Persia began early in the nineteenth century. This interest led to friction with Russia, Persia's northern neighbour. The Anglo-Russian Agreement of 1907 helped to stabilize nearly a century of intermittent conflict between them. This agreement provided for a Russian sphere of influence in northern Persia, while a neutral zone separated it from Britain's sphere of influence in south-eastern Persia. For Russia, Persia represented an area for future territorial annexation. Great Britain, on the other hand, sought no territory in Persia. Britain's primary concern was the oil fields and the military security of India, its jewel in the East. The British Army intervened in Persia almost from the outset of the First World War, to prevent the loss of its oil supplies to pro-German factors in the Persian Government and, later, to the Turks.

The story of the operations undertaken in Persia during the period of the Great War is rather complicated, involving a number of different regions, local tribal disturbances, and a Persian mutiny and, in the end, activities against the Bolsheviks during the Russian Civil War.

Bushire, 1914

Bushire was used as a base by the British Royal Navy in the late 18TH century. In the 19TH century, Bushire became an important commercial port. It was occupied by British forces in 1856, during the Anglo-Persian War of 1856–1857. Bushire surrendered to the British on 9TH December 1856. In November 1914, a small Indian force was landed at Bushire to protect British interests. The 96TH Infantry put down an anti-British rising near Bushire by Tangistani tribesmen on 12TH July 1915. A larger Indian force temporarily occupied the port of Bushire on 8TH August. The 96TH were in action again on 13TH August when they and 16TH Cavalry attacked and destroyed the fort of Dilwar. On two further occasions, 20TH August and 9TH September, Tangistani tribesmen sought to attack Bushire across the Mashilah strip, but were again defeated by 96TH Infantry and 16TH Cavalry. Indian forces left Bushire on 16TH October 1915. Subedar Dhan Singh, Sepoy Mehar Singh, 96TH Infantry. Lieutenant Balwant Singh, Risaldar Prem Singh won the Indian Order of Merit at Bushire. Sowar Kirpal Singh and Sowar Atma Singh of 16TH Cavalry were awarded the Indian Distinguished Service Medal for their conspicuous gallantry at Bushire.

Muscat, 1915

In October and November 1914, it had appeared that enemy propaganda was likely to cause trouble at Muscat and at Chahbar. The Sultan of Muscat was under British Protection and when, after the war with Turkey, it was reported that Turkish agents were instigating a rebel force to attack the Sultan, the British had no option but to assist him. The 95TH Infantry from Bombay and 102ND Grenadiers from Bushire, were accordingly sent to reinforce the half a battalion of 102ND already at Muscat. The threatened rebel attack on Muscat took place on 11TH January 1915.

Persia

Muscat, January 1915 (Cont.)

The British garrison at Muscat consisted of about one thousand rifles, under the command of Colonel Edwards, who had received instructions from India that he was not to take the offensive but that, if he was attacked, he was to inflict severe punishment on his assailants. To cover the three coastal towns of Matrah, Muscat and Sidab, as well the residence of the Sultan at Bait-al-Falaj, Colonel Edwards held, with a line of piquet posts, the hill ridges to the southward and westward. These rose to a height of 300 to 800 feet and commanded the main approaches at distances of one to four miles from Muscat, at the centre of the three towns. The total length of the line that should have been held was about eight miles. But, owing to a considerable reduction in the strength of his force through sickness, Colonel Edwards was only able to operate widely extended Piquets for about three-quarters of this distance. Moreover, he could obtain little or no assistance for the Sultan's local troops, who declined to fight beyond the walls of the town. On the 11TH, the enemy's force, estimated at about 3,000 tribesmen, started its main attack against the right centre of the British outpost loin on a frontage of about two miles. Close fighting ensued, but the Piquets held their own, with the exception of one on the extreme right, held by twenty-five rifles, which was forced to retire about 4 a.m., when the enemy occupied its position. As soon as it was light, Colonel Edwards launched a counter-attack with his main force, 102ND advancing westwards towards the British right centre and 95TH, who were about mile and half to the south, advancing northward after clearing their immediate front. By noon, the tribesmen were in full retreat having suffered about five hundred casualties, while one of the British force only totalled twenty. As the enemy remained in the vicinity, arrangements were made to send British naval and military reinforcements. But it was soon seen that these would not be required, as the tribesmen proved to be so disheartened by their losses that they dispersed to their homes, abandoning all idea of further hostilities. Clear proof was obtained that the Turco-German influence had caused the attack, which had been carried out in an unusually determined fashion, under the stimulus of the Turkish declaration of *Jihad.* During the operations, the Indian Army casualties were one Officer and 29 Other Ranks killed or died of wounds.

Persia

Ahwaz, January 1915

In the third week of January, the Turks violated Persian neutrality by sending troops into Arabistan with the avowed intention of making a flank attack on the British at Basra and of injuring the British by destruction of the oil-pipeline. At first, it was hoped the Shaikh of Mohammerah and the Bakhtiaris would he able to protect Ahwaz, the oil-pipe and the oil field. But the Turkish bribes and cry of Jihad proved to be too strong for some of the Shaikh of Mohammerah's tribesmen, who threw off their allegiance and joined other Persian Arab tribes who were assisting the Turks. At the same time, they destroyed portions of the pipeline. Up to this period, the British had been very careful, in their operations against the Turks in the Basra vilayet, to respect Persian neutrality. But, as the Shaikh of Mohammerah now said that he could no longer control his tribesmen or guarantee the security of foreign property, the British were obliged to detach a small body of troops from Shatt-al-Arab to proceed up the Karun to Ahwaz, which the foreign colony had been forced to withdraw. However, the force was forced to retire before superior numbers of Turks and Arabs. The Indian troops from Mesopotamia were ordered to Ahwaz to deal with the Turks and Arabs, which they did. They also arrested all Germans agents, within their reach, who were in communication with the enemy.

Jask and Chabbar, April 1915

In November 1914, because of threats from local tribesmen, thought to have been stirred up by enemy agents in Shiraz, two companies of 95TH Infantry were sent from Bombay to Jask and Chabbar in the Persian sector of Mekran. On 16TH - 17TH April 1915, 95TH Infantry defended the coastal town of Jask against a tribal raid and attack was made against Chabbar on 3RD May. Although the enemy tribesmen were repulsed on both occasions, it was felt that they still posed a threat to the area and additional troops were sent to Jask and Chabbar from Muscat at the end of April 1915.

Bushire; May 1915

The Persian governor of Bushire, hearing that the headman of a neighbouring village was collecting armed men to attack the British Residency, despatched a force, which included some gendarmerie, to apprehend this headman. But the defection of the gendarmerie forced the governor to apply for British military assistance. This was at once afforded. On 7TH May, a detachment of about two hundred rifles of the 96TH Infantry moving to carry out the Governor's request and meeting with resistance, rushed the village and captured the headman, dispersing his following. Twenty-eight of them were killed, wounded, or captured. Bushire was then reinforced from India by the remaining half-battalion 96TH Infantry, which dropped fifty men en route to strengthen the post at Chahbar.

Persia

Seistan Field Force, 1916

The Russians and the British decided to establish a cordon in East Persia along the Afghan Persian border. The Russians did so in the Northern provinces and the British cordon in the south to the north of Birjind, in the general area known as Seistan. A 'Seistan Field Force' of Cavalry and Infantry was to establish a East Persian Cordon along the Persian- Afghan border, with a view to destroying or capturing any parties engaged in activities detrimental to the interest of the Allies and to maintain British prestige in the area by a show of force among wavering Persian tribes. The Seistan Field Force was to operate in the Karakoram desert in Russian Turkistan for four and half years.

In 1916, the incidence of raids against the line-of-communication of the Seistan Field Force gradually increased. In the middle of March, Brigadier Dyer, commander of the Field Force, tried to negotiate with the tribes. Brigadier Dyer's efforts to negotiate having failed, he assembled a small mobile column consisting of 28TH Cavalry, 2 mountain guns and 65 rifles from 19TH Punjabis, to deal with the raiders. The column made contact with chief Jiand's men and opened fire. Jiand Khan mounted his camel and fled, followed by his men who scattered and were soon out of sight. Jiand Khan came in and made his submission on 17TH April. At Lirudik on 13TH April 1916, a detachment of 19TH Punjabis defeated a tribal Lashkar and at Kalamas on 26TH September, 26TH Cavalry captured a party of gunrunners with a considerable quantity of arms. The Seistan Field Force was increased with another two cavalry troops. It managed to take a few forts and subdued various tribes. August 19TH, brought the end to a campaign carried out under extremely adverse weather conditions, on rough and waterless terrain, with much hardship for the men as well as the animals in the column.

Burma Mounted Rifles

During January 1917, arrangements were made in India to send a reinforcing column, to consist of about 230 mounted infantry rifles from the Burma Military Police. In 1886, the Government of India sanctioned the raising of the Military Police to facilitate the withdrawal of the main part of the regular forces in Burma. The military police battalions were organized like regular army regiments, and their duties were entirely military. The Military Police at the end of 1888 included 3,937 Sikhs. During the First World War, the Burma Military Police Battalions were milked dry for volunteers to serve in Persia and Mesopotamia. In 1916, the Burma Police Battalions were bodily formed into three squadrons of Burma Mounted Infantry for service in Trans-Caspia. Eventually the squadrons were renamed Burma Mounted Rifles. Sir Percy Sykes expressed his high appreciation of the discipline, gallantry and soldiery spirit of the Burma Mounted Rifles.

Persia

Dehbid, June 1917

On 1ST June, a squadron of the Burma Mounted Infantry, on their way to Dehbid, came into collision with a band of robbers belonging to a Khamseh tribe and pursued them for some miles, inflicting casualties without loss to themselves. On 18TH and 19TH June part of the Burma Mounted Infantry detachment at Dehbid were engaged in that vicinity with a robber band that had looted a donkey caravan. The action was most effective, nine of the robbers being killed or wounded and eighteen captured, while part of the lost property was recovered. This affair had an excellent effect in the neighbourhood.

Qashqais, July 1917

On 4TH July, a column composed of the Burma Mounted Infantry, under Jemadar Partab Singh, moved out from Dehbid to deal with a band of robbers belonging to a tribe section of the Qashqais. There was a long list of robberies by these particular men and they were held in greater dread than any others in the area. The enemy's encampment was near an old fort, whose walls had been reported as having fallen to a height of only two or three feet from the ground. It was now seen to be a much more formidable defence than had been reported. Perched on the top of a small steep isolated hill, rising two hundred feet above the plain, its high walls were intact on all but the eastern side and were well loopholed. Moreover, it was closely surrounded by the roofless walls of an old village, so located on the hill slopes that the enemy could fire in tiers from the loopholes in them. Major Williams, with two troops of Burma Mounted Infantry, took up position about one thousand yards east-south-east of the fort, under a desultory but continuous fire from the enemy. Major Williams decided to isolate the fort from all the communication with the hills, and then, if necessary, to assault the fort. In furtherance of this plan, he sent a troop of Burma Mounted Infantry, under Jemadar Partab Singh, to clear a large camp just south of the fort and to cut in between the latter and the hills. Jemadar Partab Singh's troop, having driven the enemy back sufficiently, joined Major Williams, whose detachment was still engaged in a firefight with the fort. The Indian troops, having been under arms for over fifteen hours and having marched distances varying from thirty-three to forty-six miles, were at this time very tired and hungry. But they responded with spirit to assault the fort. Some of the Qashqais and Bassari tribesmen attempted to assist the fort garrison by advancing from the hills. But these were ineffectual, and the tribesmen in the fort, discouraged by the steady determination of the advancing Indian infantry, started to flee when these arrived within one hundred yards and fixed bayonets. Streaming away through the hills to the south-west, the discomfiture of the 500 tribesmen was effectively completed by the Burma Mounted Infantry's fire.

Persia

Khwaja Jamali, September 1917

Sir Percy Sykes urged the necessity for punishing the robber tribes, who had been guilty of a long series of depredations on the Kerman – Yezd, Shiraz – Isfahan, and Shiraz – Saidabad roads. The first tribe to be dealt with was the Lashanis, who inhabited the country between Niriz and Arsinjan, immediately to the north of Lake Niriz. A small column, termed Dehbid Column, with one squadron of Burma Mounted Infantry, marched off from Qawwamabad on 20TH September. Having destroyed several forts and having captured or destroyed a considerable amount of forage, the column halted at Abadeh Kaleh on 25TH September to destroy several more forts. Starting on its march again on the same day, the column found its way blocked by a body of some five or six hundred Lashanis, who were holding a position round the village of Khwaja Jamali. There was a strong, well-built fort in the village, as well as six separate loopholed towers. Two troops Burma Mounted Infantry were sent to attack and turn the enemy's left flank, which they did, and ten minutes later the tribesmen in this part of the position were seen to be fleeing northwards. The enemy had fled at a great pace, and the nature of the country prohibited pursuit. The excellent work of the Indian troops had enhanced their prestige locally and a great step forward had been made in the direction of the restoration of law and order on the main caravan routes.

Gumun, January 1918

On 21ST January, on learning that the robber band was in the hill to the northeast of Saadatabad, Burma Mounted Infantry marched off in pursuit. The robber band had moved on via Arsinjan to the vicinity of Gumun. Burma Mounted Infantry encountered them there on 24TH January; they attacked and killed about 25 of them. They destroyed two of their camps and recovered a considerable number of plundered animals. They completely routed the robbers, burning their remaining camp, and recovering many more animals they had plundered. The weather was extremely cold and the men had covered from twenty-four to forty miles that day. On 27TH January, Burma Mounted Infantry, displaying considerable dash and spirit, completely routed the robbers, killing or wounding about 80 of them. After an uncomfortable return march in intensely cold and snowy weather, the squadron reached Shiraz on 3RD February. The complete success of the expedition and the well-deserved, severe punishment inflicted on the robbers had immediate and excellent effect.

South Persia, March 1918

The performance of the Sikh soldier for gallantry was so high that the authorities sought for another squadron of Burma Mounted Infantry for service in Persia. On arrival of the third squadron, the title of the contingent was changed to Burma Mounted Rifles.

Persia

Northern Fars, May 1918

The operations against the Chah Haqis and the Labu Muhammadis included two squadrons of Burma Mounted Infantry. Reaching and surrounding the camp at Buru -i- Heart early on 10TH May, Colonel Grant found that the bulk of the tribe had already moved off to a camp at Chenar -i- Naz, in which vicinity a large band of Chehar Rahi robbers were also said to be encamped. Colonel Grant advanced on Chenar -i- Naz, guided by one of the few men he had just captured. From a point about a mile to the northeast of Chenar -i- Naz, the Labu Muhammadi camp was seen, and Major Dyer with five troops of Burma Mounted Infantry and four Lewis guns was at once detached to move against it. Meanwhile, Major Dyer encountered some opposition from the Labu Muhammadi, but two troops with him advanced boldly and charged with bayonets fixed. They drove the tribesmen into the high hills to the west, and pursued them for some distance. In the meantime, Colonel Grant had been engaged with the Chehar Rahis. Menaced by Colonel Grant's column, the Chehar Rahis were forced to abandon the bulk of the animals and plunder they had recently taken from caravans on the Yezd road. Retiring in small groups towards Chehar Rah plain, they made a stand on a pass about nine miles south-west of Chenar -i- Naz. Burma Mounted Infantry's two troops drove them from here in a final attack, which coming after sixteen hour's fighting, and having covered about fifty miles, was a fine effort. It was estimated that the tribesmen, whose numbers had amounted to about 350, had sustained over 60 casualties, while the Burma Mounted Rifles, who recovered a large number of animals and much plundered property, had only two men wounded.

Ahmadabad, June 1918

On 16TH June, Colonel Orton, with the greater part of the Indian troops, moved on Ahmadabad, where the Kazeruni tribe was the strongest. The Burma mounted Rifles secured Ahmadabad as the Kazeruni fled headlong before their advance. They then confronted and attacked considerable bodies of mounted tribesmen, whose increasing numbers betokened Qashqais reinforcement. By this time the 2,000 tribesmen, for the most part Kazeruni, had retired with a loss of about 250 casualties. On the Burma Mounted Rifle's retirement on Ahmadabad, the Qashqais displayed great bravery and in places got within two hundred yards of the Burma Mounted Rifles, but the increasing volume of fire they encountered was too much for them, and they had fallen back, having sustained heavy losses. Colonel Orton had achieved his object most successfully, it being estimated that of about 3,200 tribesmen engaged, 200 had been killed and 300 wounded. Next day Sir Percy Sykes telegraphed to India expressing his high appreciation of the discipline, gallantry and soldierly spirit of the Burma Mounted Rifles.

Persia

Following the collapse of the Russian Army after the 'October Revolution', the Turks increased pressure on the Caucasian front, heading towards Baku and the Caspian Sea. The British were already supporting 'White' Russian elements against the Bolsheviks in North and South Russia, so further intervention along the Persian frontier was inevitable, following the establishment of Bolshevik rule in Trans-Caspia early in 1918.

Bairam Ali August 1918

In August 1918, the Trans-Caspian force had been driven back by the Bolsheviks to Bairam Ali, on the eastern edge of the Merv oasis, on which the Trans-Caspian Government were largely dependent for Turkoman work force and supplies. Its loss, moreover, would probably also induce the garrison of Kushk, with its large amount of war material, to declare definitely for the Bolsheviks. The two machine guns of 19TH Punjabis left Muhammadabad on 11TH August and, moving by railway from Artik, reached Bairam Ali on 12TH. Next, the Bolsheviks attacked. The Trans-Caspian force, consisting of about 1,000 men, largely Turkoman, was lacking in organisation and discipline. It had only one gun and five machine guns and, though commanded by an efficient Turkoman officer, had useless Russian staff. The Bolshevik attacking force was composed of about 1,000 men, with a number of field and machine guns, with another 2,000 men held in reserve. The Trans-Caspian force, making only half-hearted resistance, was defeated and the retirement would have resulted in a decisive disaster, but for the gallant behaviour of the Punjabi machine gun detachment. These men fired their guns until they became too hot to handle and, according to the Trans-Caspian account, inflicted 350 casualties on the enemy. Two of the Punjabi detachment were wounded, and one of its machine guns had to be abandoned, after two men had been burnt trying to carry it out of action. The Trans-Caspian force, thoroughly demoralised, fell back to Merv, after damaging the bridge over the Murghab River, retiring before Bolshevik advance without attempting any resistance past Tejend Dushak. The Punjabi machine gun detachment, every man ill with influenza, returned to Muhammadabad.

Kaahka, August 1918

The Trans-Caspian commander, with bulk of his troops, had taken up position in the village of Kaahka. The enemy advance on Kaaka met with only slight resistance from the Turcoman detachment. They were checked for some time by gallant resistance offered by few Punjabis. Arriving here simultaneously with the enemy, a company of Punjabis charged with the Bayonet and drove him back, eventually putting him to flight and capturing five of his machine guns. This ended the fighting, for the Bolshevik force hastily retreated in front of the Punjabis.

Persia

Armistice, October 1918

On 31ST October, the armistice with Turkey had come into force. Under its terms, the Allies obtained free access to the Black Sea. Turkish troops were to withdraw immediately from North-West Persia and from part of Trans–Caucasia. The portions of the Trans-Caucasia railway under Turkish control were to be placed at the free and complete disposal of the Allies, who would also occupy Batum; and the Turks were to raise no objection to an Allied occupation of Baku.

Dushak, October 1918

The Tran-Caspian and British force started on 13TH October to attack the Bolshevik's force at Dushak. The Infantry, deploying at once, advanced to the attack; Russians and Armenians on the right, the three Punjabi companies in the centre and Turcomans on the left. When the infantry attack arrived within about one thousand yards of the Bolshevik's position, a heavy gun and machine gun fire, and all the Russians and Armenians, except the small body of ex-regulars, met it and Turkomans ceased to advance. The Punjabis pushed on with speed and determination, but incurred heavy casualties. The British guns, firing with great accuracy, did much damage to the enemy trains and to the station, which, just as the Punjabis reached it, was totally wrecked. The Bolshevik losses had evidently been considerable and the Russian, Armenian, and Turcoman infantry now came on and indulged in an orgy of massacre and plunder, which the Punjabis, with their British officers all casualties, were unable to stop or restrain. The enemy had lost the station, but some of the enemy had moved to the west of it and started a counter-attack, at the same time as the enemy reinforcements from the Tejend direction commenced attack from the east. By this time, the Trans-Caspian soldiery had gone off with their plunder. The enemy attack had to be met by about 150 Punjabis. A retirement became necessary and withdrawal in a north-westerly direction was ordered. The 28TH Cavalry and the British and Russian guns carried this out coolly and in excellent order. Halt was made at Arman Sagad, where most of the Trans-Caspian soldiery again disappeared. The British casualties had been considerable. Those in 19TH Punjabis had 47 killed and 139 wounded and had lost about 50 percent of their strength. The Trans-Caspian casualties only totalled 30, practically all among the small body of ex-regulars. The enemy's casualties are unknown, but prisoners' and subsequent reports estimated that at least 1,000 of them had been killed or wounded. As the Trans-Caspian Chief of Staff said in his official report, only the heroic conduct of the Indian troops and of a few of their own men had saved them from complete disaster. General Malleson also reported that the Russian circles were filled with the greatest admiration for the part played by the British and Indian troops, whom they regarded as being equal to ten times their own number of any of the other combatants.

Persia

Firuzabad, October 1918

A British force, commanded by Colonel Orton, left Shiraz on 20TH October with a column composed of three squadrons of Burma Mounted Rifles, two sections of 36TH Mountain Battery and 124TH Baluchis to take action against the Qashqais at Firuzabad. On 24TH October, it was evident that the enemy intended to stand and fight and about 250 of them were seen in occupation of a ridge westward of Ibrahimabad village. Meanwhile, Colonel Dyer, with two squadrons of Burma Mounted Rifles, their advance supported by the fire of the Mountain guns, had secured a minor ridge some 1,200 yards north of the enemy's main position. The Baluchis were sent forward to secure the left flank about Ibrahimabad and to attack this position. The remaining Burma squadron and a Baluchi company were retained as a reserve. Two of the Baluchi companies gained a knoll about 1,000 yards north-west of the enemy's position without difficulty; the third company, securing the left flank about Ibrahimabad. These movements had brought the enemy's main position under accurate gun fire and a cross fire from the Lewis guns and rifles of the Burma Mounted Rifles, with a result when an attack was launched it attained complete success within twenty minutes. So far, the British casualties had been only seven, all among the Baluchis, but the enemy had lost about eighty killed and wounded. In the meantime, Colonel Dyer had inflicted severe loss on the Qashqais. He had reached Deh -i- Barm unobserved and taken up a concealed position in front and in the village, while sending some scouts towards the enemy's camp. These scouts afterwards came galloping back to the village, pursued by some five to six hundred Qashqais horsemen. The Burma Mounted Rifles then opened fire with their Lewis guns and rifles, with devastating effect, before the Qashqais could wheel off and get out of range. Nevertheless, and in the face of this heavy fire, the tribesmen made two or three gallant attempts to gallop in again to recover their wounded men and rifles. But as they only sustained further casualties without succeeding, they finally abstained, and at dusk, Colonel Dyer withdrew to Gilak without molestation. After dark, the Qashqais returned and carried off their wounded, subsequently estimated at 100, leaving 103 dead where they had fallen. The Burma Mounted Rifles had sustained no casualties.

Qashqais on the march

Persia

Annenkovo, January 1919

On 16TH January 1919, a Bolshevik force, subsequently estimated at several squadrons of cavalry, eight guns and four thousand infantry made a sudden attack on the Trans-Caspian position at Annenkovo. Besides the Trans-Caspian force there were at Annenkovo half squadron of 28TH Cavalry and one company 19TH Punjabis. The nearest British supports were at Bairam Ali, some thirty odd miles away. At the Bolshevik attack, the Punjabis experienced little difficulty in maintaining their position, but the Armenians, who were unexpectedly fighting very well, were greatly outnumbered and had be reinforced by a Punjabi platoon. The enemy, however, continued to push in fresh troops and under a heavy enfilading machine-gun fire, the Armenians broke and fled. Fortunately, at this critical juncture, the train carrying a company of Punjabis from Bairam Ali steamed up and came on right into the hail of bullets. The men jumped out of the carriages, formed into lines and advanced straight against the enemy's right flank. The Bolsheviks held their ground till the Punjabis were within 50 yards and then broke and fled in disorder, losing heavily as they crossed the front of the other Punjabi company. In the meantime, about three squadrons of Bolshevik cavalry and 1,500 infantry had driven back 28TH Cavalry and the Turkomans and one of the armoured trains had been surrounded. The train's crew of Russian ex-officers, however, jumped out and charged the enemy with gallantry and vigour, just as the platoon of Punjabis came up to their assistance, and brought the attack to a standstill. By this time, the main Bolshevik force was in full flight across the desert and seeing this, those attacking the Trans–Caspian right also broke and fled. In their flight, the enemy managed to save his guns, although he lost seven machine-guns. His casualties had been severe, nearly 200 corpses being found next morning, his total loss being subsequently estimated at 600. The Trans-Caspian casualties totalled 70 and those of the Punjabis 46. It was subsequently ascertained that the Bolshevik plan had been to surprise and overwhelm the Annenkovo detachment by simultaneous attacks against both flanks; that against the left being carried out by 2,500 infantry and the one against the other flank, by 1,500 infantry.

Fin, 1919

Indian troops evacuated Trans-Caspia in 1919, leaving behind them a reputation for discipline and gallantry, which any troops might be proud of and which they well deserved. One of their last exploits is worthy of narration as exemplifying the fighting spirit with which they were imbued. A reconnoitring patrol of 28TH Cavalry, fourteen strong, finding itself cut off by a body of about 150 Bolsheviks cavalry, had charged through them and had then turned and charged through them again, killed or wounded 21 of the Bolsheviks, at a loss to itself of one wounded and two made prisoner.

Persia

Subedar Bal Singh
19TH Punjabis

Subedar Bal Singh was awarded the Indian Order of Merit for conspicuous gallantry in fighting against the Bolsheviks in Trans–Caspia on 14TH October 1918. In an attack on the enemy, Subedar Bal Singh led his platoon with great dash and bravery under very heavy machine-gun fire. He took command of the company when the British Officer had been wounded and by his coolness and power of command ensured the retirement being conducted in an orderly manner.

Subedar Hukam Singh (Posthumous)
19TH Punjabis

Subedar Hukam Singh was awarded the Indian Order of Merit for conspicuous gallantry against the Bolsheviks in Trans–Caspia. This Sikh officer led his platoon into action on 19TH January 1919 with the greatest gallantry and inspired all his men by his fearlessness. He was killed while encouraging and leading his men.

Sepoy Dalel Singh
19TH Punjabis

Sepoy Dalel Singh was awarded the Indian Order of Merit for conspicuous gallantry in fighting against the Bolsheviks in Trans–Caspia on 14TH October 1918. Sepoy Dalel Singh carried messages throughout the day for his company commander, regardless of personal safety, and finally delivered an important message after being severely wounded.

Indian Distinguished Service Medal
19TH Punjabis

The following Sikh soldiers were awarded the Indian Distinguished Service Medal for their conspicuous gallantry in Trans-Caspia.

Sepoy Bal Singh, Sepoy Ganga Singh, Sepoy Udham Singh, Sepoy Surjan Singh, Sepoy Waryam Singh, Lance Naik Gurdit Singh, Lance Naik Sohan Singh Lance Naik Gian Singh Lance Naik, Asa Singh, Naik Sher Singh, Naik Karam Singh, Naik Jowala Singh, Havildar Asa Singh, and Jemadar Nihal Singh.

Subedar Karam Singh
36tTH Mountain Battery

At Abadeh fort in South Persia, about 180 miles from Isfahan, a small garrison of British and Indian troops had been beleaguered since 28TH June 1918 by Qashqais tribesmen and mutineer levies. The garrison had held out against enormous odds. It was relieved on 17TH July by a section of Mountain Artillery and Burma Mounted Rifles, which had made a forced march of 180 miles in seven days in intense heat. Subedar Karam Singh was awarded the Indian Order of Merit.

Persia

Risaldar Gulzar Singh
Burma Mounted Rifles

Risaldar Gulzar Singh was awarded the Indian Order of Merit for conspicuous gallantry on 25TH May 1918 in South Persia. He extricated his squadron from a very difficult situation in excellent order. Having done so, returned to the open to help bring in the bodies of an officer and wounded men, under heavy enemy fire. He was conspicuous for his skilful leadership in every action in which he was engaged.

Jemadar Kishen Singh
Burma Mounted Rifles

Jemadar Kishen Singh was awarded the Indian Order of Merit for conspicuous gallantry on 23RD October 1918 in South Persia, in an action in which two of his troopers were wounded, about three hundred yards from the enemy's position. Jemadar Kishen Singh gallantly led his troop to their rescue and brought them in. In another action, Jemadar Kishen and two troopers were severely wounded and lay out exposed to the enemy fire from 4.15 pm until dusk, when it became possible to rescue them.

Sowar Uttam Singh
Burma Mounted Rifles

Sowar Uttam Singh was awarded the Indian Order of Merit for conspicuous gallantry on 23RD October 1918 in South Persia.

Indian Distinguished Service Medal
Burma Mounted Rifles

The following Sikh soldiers were awarded the Indian Distinguished Service Medal for their conspicuous gallantry in Trans-Caspia:
Sowar Saudagar Singh, Sowar Man Singh, Sowar Uttam Singh, Lance Daffadar Basta Singh, Lance Daffadar Meja Singh, Daffadar Ralla Singh, Daffadar Hukam Singh, Daffadar Chanan Singh, Daffadar Wariam Singh, Daffadar Mohar Singh, Risaldar Gulzar Singh, Jemadar Wariam Singh, and Jemadar Partab Singh.

Hon. Lieutenant Balwant Singh
(Unit untraceable)

Lieutenant Balwant Singh was awarded the Indian Order of Merit for conspicuous gallantry and devotion to duty at Bushire, Persia in 1917.

Indian Distinguished Service Medal
1ST (Kohat) Battery

The following Sikh soldiers were awarded the Indian Distinguished Service Medal for their conspicuous gallantry in Trans-Caspia:
Gunner Kishen Singh, Jemadar Munsha Singh, and Havildar Jaggat Singh.

NYASALAND

Nyasaland (now named Malawi) is a landlocked country in Southeast Africa. It is bordered by Zambia to the northwest, Tanzania to the northeast and Mozambique surrounds it on the east, south, and west. The name Malawi is thought to be a derivation of the word Maravi. The Amaravi people founded a dynasty known as the Maravi Empire in the late 15TH century and began to decline during the early 18TH century. The downfall of the Maravi Empire correlates to the entrance of two powerful groups into the region, the Angoni and the Yao. The Angoni and their chief Zwangendaba arrived from the Natal region of modern day South Africa. The Angoni were part of a great migration, known as the *mfecane*, of people fleeing from the head of the Zulu Empire, Shaka Zulu. While fleeing from Shaka, the Angoni had adopted many of his military tactics. They made use of these tactics to attack and conquer the people of the Maravi Empire. The Angoni would conduct annual raids on their neighbours, to take both food and slaves.

In Nyasaland, young Angoni men were often formed en masse into a new regiment known as a *Libandla*, of which each village or prominent chief might have severeral regiments. Each *Libandla* was divided into companies called *Libuto*, which varied in strength up to 100 men or more and were allocated to one of the two major divisions of the army, the younger men, or *amajaha*, and the veteran *amadoda*. An officer known as *Induna*, was responsible to the overall leader or 'war Induna' appointed by the *nkosi* or chief, led each regiment and company. An independent army of any size continued to be known by the Zulu term *Impi*.

The Yao were a Bantu people originating in the north of Portuguese East Africa and upon migrating to Nyasaland set themselves as rulers over the indigenous tribes. They soon began attacking both the Achewa and Nyanja inhabitants to capture prisoners, who they later sold as slaves. The Yao were the first, and for a long while, the only group to use firearms in conflict with other tribes. They were also different in religion from their neighbouring tribes, choosing in 1870 to follow Islam like their Arab trading partners, rather than the traditional Animism practiced by surrounding tribes.

Using their strong partnership with the Yao, the Arab traders set up several trading posts along the shore of Lake Nyasa. An Arabic trader from the coast, Jumbe Salim Bin Abdalla, founded the largest of these posts in 1840 at Nkhotakota. During the height of his power, Jumbe transported between 5,000 and 20,000 slaves through Nkhotakota annually.

The slaving practice of the Yao and the Arabs brought them into contact with the British, to whom they were determined and troublesome enemy.

Nyasaland

Slave Trade

Arabs carried out the slave trade in Central Africa in cooperation with some African tribes. The Arabs had various ways of obtaining African slaves. Armed gangs of Arabs and Muslim Africans would conduct raids and simply seize Africans. This might be done surreptitiously or by outright attacks on villages, often done with great brutality. According to a Muslim account, the Arabs "are the most savage human beings that exist. Compared with sedentary people, they are on a level with wild, untameable animals and dumb beasts of prey." Slavers would often raid villages at night and simply kill those who resisted or tried to run away. The Arab slavers might also use trade goods such as cloth trinkets and metal goods to barter for captives from local chiefs. African tribes and kingdoms were commonly involved in warfare with neighbouring groups. Thus, they often acquired captives taken in war. In some cases, knowing that there was a ready market for these captives, helped to promote raids and attacks among African groups. Arab slavers would play African tribes against each other. The tribal wars helped to weaken the Africans kingdoms and made it easier for the slavers to operate.

Tattoo of the Sikhs at Fort Lister, Nyasaland 1896.

The Horror of Slavery

Nyasaland

The motives of Britain's imperialist activities in Africa from 1869 to 1912 were to colonize, to search for new markets and materials, and to convert natives to Christianity. As its free trade and influential relationship with Africa was threatened, Britain began to turn trade agreements into stronger and more formal protectorates and even colonies. In order for British colonies to stay competitive economically, it was in the interest of the British government to suppress the slave trade.

'At this time slave trading was the main and flourishing industry of Africa and it has been estimated that up to 100,000 East African natives were killed or captured each year. The entrepreneurs of this trade were Arabs and half-breeds with the enthusiastic co-operation of the local African chiefs.' (Magor, 1993, p131)

David Livingstone was a Scottish pioneer medical missionary with the London Missionary Society and explorer in Central Africa. During his explorations, he reported on the extent and evils of the slave trade in Central Africa and died near Lake Bangweulu in 1873. Two years later the Free Church Mission became the pioneer of permanent British settlement in Nyasaland, with the foundation of Livingstonia Mission on Lake Nyasa. Trade followed the missionaries, when in 1884; the African Lakes Company built a trading station at Karonga. The arrival of the British at Karonga was a threat to the slavers' livelihood and the three Arab slavers, Mlozi, Kopakopa and Msalema, living in the area, built themselves stockades about seven miles from Karonga to consolidate their hold on the slave route. In 1887, Mlozi massacred a number of Wakonde tribesmen, and because of his threat, Karonga station had to be abandoned. In 1888, the British returned to Karonga with a force of five hundred tribal levies, who having defeated the Arab slavers, disappeared back to their villages with the plunder. An attack with a force of about 220 tribesmen against Kopakopa's stockade was repulsed, in which one European and five natives were killed. As at that time, the British were not powerful enough to capture the slavers stockades, they made a treaty with the slavers, allowing them to retain their stockades. The arrangement, however, was more of temporary truce than a peace.

In May 1891, when British Protectorate over Nyasaland was proclaimed, Harry Johnston was appointed Her Majesty's Commissioner for British Central Africa. Harry Johnston obtained Sikh volunteers from the Indian Army to bulwark his regime. This Sikh contingent was to form the first armed force of the new Protectorate. It was commanded by Captain C.M. MacGuire of the Indian Army and designated as the Central African Rifles.

'During the initial period of pacification, the Sikhs performed the role of shock troops, leading attacks against various chieftains. By 1895, as the country became more settled, the Sikhs undertook garrison duty at a half dozen forts scattered across the protectorate.' (Metcalf, 2008, p.120)

Until the slaver's final defeat in 1896, a number of expeditions were mounted against them.

Nyasaland

Fighting the Slavers

A. J. Swann, a contemporary writer, describes the situation in Central Africa thus: 'The whole of the East African Coast and the Interior was either in the hands of native chiefs, Arabs, or marina half castes. They all had one objective. Their ambition was to sell and transport to the coast as many of the inhabitants as they could possibly capture. Besides those actually captured, thousands were killed or died of their wounds and famine, driven from their homes by the slave raiders. Thousands perished in internecine wars, waged for slaves, with their own clansmen or neighbours, slain by the lust for gain, which was stimulated by the slave purchasers. The many skeletons that have been found amongst the rocks and woods all testify to the awful sacrifice of human life which must be attributed directly or indirectly to this trade of hell.'(Swann, 1910)

For nigh on seven years the Sikh soldiers fought the slave hunters in steamy jungles of Central Africa and prevailed in stopping the 'trade of hell.' During this period seventeen Sikh soldiers made the supreme sacrifice, they were killed in action. Twelve Sikh soldiers were awarded the Indian Order of Merit for their conspicuous gallantry against the enemy. The Sikhs also trained and put together a native force, which in due course met all the requirements of the Protectorate. Subsequently, because of the cost factor, the Sikh contingent was phased out.

A Sikh Sentry Fort Johnston Nyasaland

"Guardian over all stands the Sikh, who being immune to local influence of all kinds, constitutes the 'motor muscle' of Imperial Authority as he stands erect beside his rifle on guard over British Interests 6,000 miles from the Punjab. He is a picked volunteer from all the Sikh Regiments. If at any time considerations of expense or desire to obtain homogeneity in the military forces of the Protectorate should lead to the disbandment of these companies, those who take the decision will have incurred responsibility which few would care to share with them.' (Churchill, 1908)

Nyasaland

Expedition against Chikumbu, July – August 1891

The first expedition against the Yao slaver Chikumbu took place in July 1891. He had settled amongst the peaceful Nyanja people of Mlanje, whom he had been gradually subjugating. In 1890, the Nyanja appealed to Mr. John Buchanan, the acting British Consul for Nyasaland, for protection. The old Nyanja chief, Chipoka, had died in 1890, and on his deathbed had, with the consent of all his sub-chiefs, and subjects, transferred the sovereign rights of his country to Queen Victoria, in order to pledge the British Government for protection against Yao attacks. At the same period, some English planters had just begun to settle in the Mlanje district, and although they had paid relatively large sums to Chikumbu, he continued to extort larger and larger payments from them. Eventually upon their refusing to give him any more money, he committed various acts of violence on them. He also stopped the natives working for the planters. Chikumbu was a very great slave trader and kept up a direct communication with the East Coast of Africa at Angoche, whither his caravans of slaves were generally forwarded. Accordingly, Captain MacGuire was dispatched with a force of fifty Sikhs to bring Chikumbu to reason. As the Sikhs advanced, they were repeatedly attacked by the Yaos, but went on to defeat Chikumbu's force and capture his town. As Chikumbu fled, his brother was taken prisoner. A large number of slaves found in the town were released.

Expedition against Mponda September -October 1891

Commissioner Johnston and Captain MacGuire, with seventy-eight Sikh Sepoys, ten Zanzibaris and eighty Makua tribesmen with a 7-pounder gun, decided to take action against Mponda, a powerful Yao chief, who was an active slave raider. One of the reasons for Johnston's desire to deal with Mponda was that a local chief, Chikusi, had appealed to him for protection against the slave raider. As a gesture of defiance, Mponda had beheaded fourteen of Chikusi's people and had stuck their heads on posts round his stockade, which was already decorated with the skulls of a hundred other victims. On the opposite bank of the Shire Lake to Mponda's stronghold, Captain MacGuire built a fort and named it Fort Johnston. From this base, he moved off to attack Mponda's stronghold. Meanwhile when a slave caravan bound for Kilwa arrived, a Yao chief Chindamba, arranged to sell all his slaves to the Kilwe traders. MacGuire immediately attacked Chindamba, drove his people into the hills, and destroyed his town. Mponda welcomed the opportunity and had no difficulty in capturing Chindamba's people in the outlying villages to be sold as slaves. Johnston issued an ultimatum to Mponda that unless the slaves were freed he would attack the town. At Mponda's refusal to comply Captain MacGuire and the Sikhs drove the Yaos out of town and destroyed the stockades. On October 22ND, Mponda handed over Chindamba's people and a large number of other slaves who were to have been sold to the Kilwa traders. Three days later, he came over to Fort Johnson and signed a treaty abolishing the slave trade in his territory.

Nyasaland

1ST Expedition against Makanjira, October – November 1891

Harry Johnston next turned his attention to the slave raiders near Lake Nyasa and Lake Shirwa. Here again the Yao chiefs were the culprits, encouraged by the Arab and Swahili ivory merchants, wanting slave porters. The principle villain in this region was Makanjira. On October 28TH 1981, Harry Johnston, Captain MacGuire and the Sikhs embarked on the steamer, *Domira*, (Domira was a single crew steamer, length 89 feet, beam 13 feet and displacement 67 tons) to sail up the Shire and attack Makanjira's town. Makanjira's men opened fire on the steamer as soon as it approached the shore and MacGuire replied with incendiary shells from the 7-pounder, which set the town alight in four places. Johnston and thirty-four Sikhs boarded the barge, which had been towed behind the steamer, and landed on the west side of the town, while MacGuire bombarded the eastern side. When it became too dark to serve the gun, MacGuire landed ashore in the Domira's boat with six Sikhs and made straight for the guns in the hands of the slavers. He captured the guns and before withdrawing, set fire to a slaver's new dhow that was almost ready for launching. Next morning MacGuire renewed his attack on the town, defeated the Yaos in a pitched battle in which several Sikhs were severely wounded, and saw to it that the town was completely burnt to the ground and destroyed another two dhows. Four Sikh soldiers earned the Indian Order of Merit for their conspicuous gallantry in this action.

Expedition against Yao Chief Kawinga, November 1891

The expedition against Chief Makanjira had hardly returned to Zomba when news came of depredations by Kawinga, a powerful Yao Chief. He was a notorious slave trader and lived on the northwest shore of Lake Shirwa, and commanded an important route to the coast. In 1889, he was reputed to have sent as many as a thousand slaves to the markets of Kilwa and Quinlimane. When MacGuire tried to storm Kawinga's stronghold he was wounded in the chest and his attack was repulsed, but Kawinga was forced to sue for peace. Kawinga was duly repentant and paid a fine of five tusks. In return, Johnston sent him wheat, oats, barley, and twelve different kinds of vegetable seeds and urged him to go in for agriculture. Sixty-nine Sikh soldiers had taken part in this expedition. They had suffered several casualties and four of them were awarded the Indian Order of Merit for their conspicuous gallantry.

A Sikh NCO in British Central Africa, 1896

Nyasaland

Reporting to the Foreign Secretary on the results of four months continuous campaigning against the slavers in Southern Nyasaland Johnston wrote. 'It will soon become patent to the unscrupulous rascals of the East African littoral, from Kilwa to Quinlimane that slave trading in the Shire province is a dangerous and unprofitable pursuit. We have also brought the powerful Yao chiefs to accept British domination, except the irreconcilable Makanjira who will probably remain an implacable but I hope impotent foe for the rest of his days. But appearances tend to show that there will be important defections from his rule and it is not unlikely that in time his own people may eject him from power when they find friendship with the British more profitable than enmity.' (Gale, 1958, p.116.)

2ND Expedition against Makanjira, 15TH – 21ST December 1891

Captain MacGuire returned to complete the building of Fort Johnson, which was to be permanently garrisoned. Makanjira possessed a fleet of slaving dhows and information came that two of them were hidden in a small cove. The chance was too good to miss and MacGuire embarked with a small force in the *Domira.*

'MacGuire set off in the Domira with a few Sikhs. Landing with a small force of 28 Sikhs, on 15TH December, he was about to demolish the dhows when Makanjira, with 2,000 followers, attacked him and forced his party back to the beach. There he found his boat had been wrecked by a storm which had arisen, and the *Domira* herself in endeavouring to come as close as possible inshore, had stuck on a sandbank, not far off the beach. After three Sikhs had been killed, MacGuire told the others to wade out to the *Domira* whilst he and a few men as rearguard kept off the Yaos with the bayonet. As MacGuire withdrew and was pulling himself aboard the *Domira,* he was shot dead. The Sikhs struggled on board with the loss of three killed and defended the stranded steamer against all comers for three days. Makanjira then enticed the doctor and chief engineer on shore with a promise of surrendering MacGuire's body, and treacherously murdered them. Once again the stranded *Domira* was besieged, this time for five days and owing to the efforts of the second engineer and the Sikhs, who behaved splendidly throughout, the *Domira* escaped, firing her gun into Makanjira's hordes as she drew away.' (Moyse-Bartlett, 2002, p18.)

Nine Sikhs were killed during this operation. The following Sikh soldiers were awarded the Indian Order of Merit for their conspicuous gallantry during the operation: Havildar Nand Singh, Naik Ishar Singh, and Naik Jhanda Singh.

Nyasaland

Expedition against Zarafi, January – February 1892

Another chief who had to be brought to book was Zarafi, who dominated the territory to the east of the Upper Shirè and had long been an active Slaver. Soon after MacGuire's death, Zarafi attacked Fort Johnson. The commissioner, Harry Johnston, hurried north to its relief with some British volunteers and the remaining Sikhs. Siege was raised and some of Zarafi's villages were raided and burnt in revenge. For the time being, however, his subjugation could not be attempted. The Sikhs, who had actually wept over MacGuire's death, were at this time reduced to 63 effectives, of whom ten were suffering from wounds. Mr. J.G. King, who had been left in charge at Fort Johnson, with the help of one hundred Angoni and an inadequate force of thirty-five Sikhs and thirty Zanzibaris, set off to attack Zarafi. At the foot of the slavers' fortress, King was seriously wounded, losing six of the Sikh soldiers killed and losing a 7-pounder gun in the bush. Johnson was obliged to remain on the defensive until the arrival in June 1892 of Captain C. E. Johnson, the new commander with a draft of 60 Sikhs. During 1893, the armed forces of the Protectorate were reorganized and strengthened. The original contingent of Sikh soldiers, who had given valiant service, returned to their homeland at the end of their three–year engagement. Captain Johnson asked in future only Jat Sikhs should be sent and it was decided to increase the number. Soon a draft of 100 Sikhs arrived under command of Lieutenant C. A. Edwards and a second draft of the same strength of Sikhs under Lieutenant W. H. Manning arrived from India. The military force now numbered 3 British officers, 200 Sikhs, and 150 native regulars. Though the Sikhs were still the mainstay of the force, the need to train local troops was at last realized, for the Government of India were growing disturbed at the frequent requests for Sikh soldiers to serve in Africa, as it was anxious to preserve the recruitment of Sikhs for its own use.

Expedition against Liwondi, January – February 1893

The Yaos on the Upper Shirè, inspired and led by Chief Liwondi, were another thorn in the Commissioner's flesh. In the campaign against him, the plucky little *Domira* again found herself in an unenviable position when she went aground in the Shirè opposite one of Liwonde's towns and the crew was trapped in the fire between defenders and attackers. The arrival of reinforcements for the Administration's forces relieved the position and Liwonde's capital town was captured and burnt down. The Chief Liwondi himself escaped and gave occasional trouble for the next few years.

Nyasaland

Expedition against Nyassera and Mkanda, November 1893 to January 1894

Lieutenant Edwards led a punitive expedition and after a brief campaign subdued Yao chief Nyassera. Soon afterwards, trouble arose with the Mlanje chief Mkanda. By that time, the second draft of 100 Sikhs had arrived. An expedition was organized and after several days hard fighting among the crags and precipices, Mkanda's strongholds were captured as he fled into exile.

2ND Expedition against Makanjira, November 1893 to January 1894

The main trouble spot during 1893 was Kota Kota, on the western shore of Lake Nyasa, ruled by an independent potentate called the Jumbe. Puffed up by his victory over Captain Maguire, the troublesome Makanjira attacked Chief Jumbe, who was friendly to the British. By the middle of 1893, Makanjira had captured most of the territory until Jumbe was penned in Kota Kota itself. Johnston decided that the time had come to settle accounts with Makanjira. The first step was to deal with a rebel called Chiwauru, who had overthrown Jumbe and established his stronghold at Kisamba. Johnson and Edwards marched with 113 Sikhs and some Makua tribesmen and attacked Kasamba's fortified village, which was surrounded by an eight-foot high wall. Covering fire from a 7-pounder gun had little effect and eventually Johnson ordered the assault. The Sikhs charged gallantly for the eight-foot high wall. The first to scale the wall was shot dead, but his comrades soon reached the top and had the mass of natives below at their mercy. Chiwauru was killed, the town taken and hundreds of captured slaves released. The expedition then crossed the Lake and meted out similar treatment to Makanjira's town and a number of smaller towns and villages, including the village where Maguire, Boyce, and MacEwan had met their deaths. Fort Maguire was erected on the Lakeshore and garrisoned by Sikhs. Early in 1894, Makanjira attacked the fort but was defeated with heavy loss. His power at last was broken and he sought refuge in Portuguese territory. Havildar Bulaku Singh was awarded the Indian Order of Merit for conspicuous gallantry in this action.

Sikh contingent, 1894

In November 1894, Johnston obtained permission to negotiate in India an agreement for two more drafts of Sikhs to serve in Central Africa for a period of three years. He expressed the highest admiration for the services rendered by the previous drafts. Johnson was allowed to select up to twenty from any of the Sikh or Punjabi units: no less than 500 of the 900 men in one regiment alone (45TH Sikhs) offered themselves as volunteers and Johnson considered that he had obtained 'the very cream of the Sikh regiments.'

Nyasaland

2ND Expedition against Zarafi, Matapwiri and Kawinga, September - November 1895

Early in 1895, trouble again arose with the Yao chiefs, Kawinga, Zarafi, and Matapwiri, as they decided that the time had come to drive the British out of the Shire Highlands. Kawinga began operations with a raid near the Scottish Mission. A force of six Sikhs and a few Atonga sent against him fortunately took the precaution of constructing a strong *boma* (an enclosure) around their post, for within a few days Kawinga attacked it with 2,000 warriors. The handful of men held on grimly and when reinforcements of Atonga arrived, sallied out with the last few rounds of ammunition, and routed the enemy with a spirited charge. Meanwhile Captain Manning, with a force of 55 Sikhs and about 200 Africans, attacked Kawinga's stronghold and captured it after two days siege. Matapwiri was tackled next. In September, a mixed force set out from Forts Lister and Anderson and approaching Matapwiri's village at night, achieved complete surprise and easy victory. In the following month, with a punitive force of five officers, 65 Sikhs and about 230 native troops, Lieutenant Edwards took Zarafi's upland villages by storm, and the lost 7-pounder gun was recovered. Zarafi fled to the Portuguese territory.

Expeditions against Mlozi, Msalema and Kopakopa, December 1895

Mlozi and his confederates were again threatening Karonga and raiding the countryside for slaves. An attempt at negotiation failed completely. A force of 6 officers, 100 Sikhs, and 300 native troops was therefore assembled at Fort Johnston and taken by steamer to Karonga. On 1ST December, Lieutenant Smith posted detachments round Mlozi's stockade. Next morning a force of Sikhs and sailors from the gunboats bombarded Msalema's stockade, the nearest to Karonga and captured it with little difficulty. Kopakopa's stockade was similarly captured and then the forces started bombarding Mlozi's stockade. A shell was dropped on Mlozi's hut and he was wounded. Rumour spread among his followers that he had been killed. Desperate and angered by this news, the defenders made a furious sortie, which was met by the Sikhs, who fought their way over the walls of the stockade. About 200 of the enemy were killed for the loss of one Sikh, three others killed, and six wounded. Mlozi was tried and hanged the next day, and the Arab stockades were then systematically destroyed.

'A parley was held with Mlozi the chief under a flag of truce, and he was offered his life if he would surrender; but he refused, choosing to fight to a finish. The earthworks were at last blown down by artillery and Sikhs let go. They stopped at nothing in their mad rush to victory. All the stockades fell in rapid succession. Mlozi was captured, tried, and executed for the brutal massacre of those grand Wakonde in the lagoon.' (Swann, 1910)

Nyasaland

Expedition against Mwazi, December 1895

Immediately after Mlozi's defeat, Lieutenant Edwards began further expeditions against disaffected chiefs. His first move was to send Lieutenant Alston with 149 Makua and 40 Sikhs to join A. J. Swann, the political officer at Kota Kota, in an expedition against the Chewa chief Mwazi, an ally of the Arabs. Swann had brought 2,400 auxiliaries, who were kept in reserve while Aston attacked with the regular troops. At the sight of Mwasi's warriors brandishing their spears behind the stockades the Makua hung back, so the Sikhs stormed the stronghold. Mwazi escaped, but Saidi Mwazungu, the ringleader in the treacherous Makanjira murders of 1891, was captured, tried, and hanged.

"The country was open, the people were quarrelsome, and they had been of Zulu extraction, there were enough of them to give considerable trouble. Several chiefs protesting neutrality, and to them were given white flags to hoist over their towns. At 4 a.m. in a downpour of rain, we marched towards Mwazi's headquarters. As we approached the mountain, stray shots were fired at us from the slopes, and we could see a host of half-wild creatures brandishing their spears in the neighbourhood of their stockades. A detachment of Makua soldiers was ordered to extend into skirmishing order, to drive in the outposts of our enemy; but they showed the white feather, and refused to march into the high grass. These cowards did not relish the wily native and his spear. It was not a task to attempt with my armed rabble, so they were ordered to remain under the mountain and not to take part in the fight until they saw us take the first village. My detachment, consisting of Sikhs, was marched across to the right. As we took up position the natives fired, wounding several men, but they refused to retire. The people shouted at us:

"We'll send you back to the lake to eat fish"

"Junglee, Junglee, plenty know how to fight."

The Sikhs called all Africans Junglees, and thoroughly despised them. Alston occupied the centre position, a sergeant- major the left. At the sound of a bugle, we were to fire five volleys, fix bayonets, and charge. How eager those splendid Sikhs were, and as steady as on parade. They needed no leading, for at the first note of the bugle their rifles rang out, bayonets were fixed, and with a shout, they were off, straight for those loopholed walls. The other detachment charged simultaneously, making such a deafening noise as had never been heard on the plain before. The heavy fire from rifles and arrows checked us several times, as we got closer, but the Indian blood was up. No native could face their wild looks, as, with a final shout, they flung themselves over the stockade and rallied inside, breathless, perspiring, and dirty, but victorious! The same process was repeated with several other large towns, some taking longer to capture than others, but they all went under in the end." (Swann, 1910 p166)

Nyasaland

Expedition against paramount chief Tambala of the Angoni, January 1896

Living in an area of Northern Rhodesian land, lying just west from the border and approximately level with the southern end of Lake Nyasa, was a branch of Zulu descent that had migrated northwards from southern Africa. The Angoni had established and maintained itself by conquest, as its military skills and organization were superior to those possessed by its neighbours. Their warriors were organized into regiments, and carried a heavy stabbing spear, smaller throwing spears, a club or axe and an oval hide shield for protection. Their villages were not fortified but were located in hilly sites that were difficult to suddenly attack. A branch of Angoni had crossed the Zambezi River in 1835, from where they had moved northwards, raiding, looting, and adding to their wealth of cattle and slaves until they settled in the area west of Lake Nyasa.

In January 1896, Edwards sent an expedition against the paramount Angoni chief Tambala. Tambala's village was perched on the flat of a hill with three precipitous sides and a fourth covered with large boulders. The village was bombarded by artillery from another hilltop and the stronghold captured. The operation met only with partial success, for although Tambala's stronghold was captured, the chief escaped and joined the Chewa raider Odete.

Expedition against Chewa chief Odete, October 1896

To break the Tamabala – Odete alliance, Manning left Kota Kota on 6TH October and five days later, was climbing the mountain slopes by a little-used track, with a force of 24 Sikhs and about 80 Africans. One by one, the raiders' villages were surprised and rushed and finally, against a hail of spears and stones, the main stronghold on the mountain peak was stormed, where Odete and other chiefs submitted. Manning was then free to punish the Angoni chief Chikuse for a number of raids south of the lake.

Expedition against Chikusi, October 1896

Captain Stewart led the expedition against Chikusi, which included 4 military and political officers, 58 Sikhs, 198 African troops, and a 7-pounder gun. Marching by way of Liwondi, through country thoroughly devastated by the raiders, he reached Chikusi on 21ST October. Manning's force arrived next day, and on 23^{RD,} the village was taken. Chikusi and a party of his warriors attempted to breakout, but the chief was captured, tried, found guilty and shot.

Nyasaland

End of the Slaver's War 1896

At the end of the Slaver's War, the armed forces of the Protectorate consisted of a Commandant, a Second in Command and a Staff Officer, a Third Officer and a Quartermaster, six Company Officers, a Sergeant Major of Artillery, the Sikh contingent and about 300 native troops. These forces were now reorganized and expanded as the Central African Rifles, comprising six companies of 120 rifles each: three of Atonga, two of Yao and one of Marimba. In view of this increase in local enlistments, when applying for another Sikh contingent in the following year the Commissioner asked only for 80-100 men, saying that within a few years he hoped to be almost independent of Sikhs, provided a few could be secured as drill instructors and N.C.O.'s to command small stations. The Sikhs had prevailed in stopping the traffic in human flesh and blood in Central Africa.

Expedition against Serumba, August 1897

In August 1897, Manning led an expedition, consisting of 4 officers, 51 Sikhs, and 4 companies of Africans to punish the Anguru tribe living in the region south of Lake Chilwa, following a number of highway robberies. Serumba the Anguru chief was primarily responsible for the robberies. Little resistance was met; Serumba was captured, his village burnt and a fine imposed.

Sikh soldiers manning Fort Loangweni, 1898.

(Source: 'The Soldiers burden')

NORTHERN RHODESIA

Northern Rhodesia was a territory in Central Africa initially administered under charter by the British South Africa Company and formed by it in 1911 by amalgamating North-Western Rhodesia and North-Eastern Rhodesia. Although it had features of a charter colony, the territory's treaties and charter, gave it Protectorate status. From 1924, the United Kingdom government administered it as a British Protectorate. Northern Rhodesia became independent in 1964 as Zambia.

The Angoni people who feature in this work are descended from the Ngoni tribe in South Africa. They had adopted the fighting tactics of Shaka Zulu. They conquered indigenous tribes with ease as they wandered as far north as Lake Tanganyika, and subsequently settled on the plateau of eastern Zambia and adjoining areas of Nyasaland, between 1850 and 1870.The Angoni ruled this area until the British with the Sikh troops coming in from Nyasaland, conquered it in 1897.

Angoni Spearman of Northern Rhodesia
(Harry Johnston)

The terrain of Northern Rhodesia

Northern Rhodesia

Angoni Rebellion. 1898 (Northern Rhodesia)

Across the Northern Rhodesian border, the Angoni tribe were living around the area of Fort Jameson, where a trading company tried to expropriate a large tract of Angoni land by a fraudulent concession. Consequently, the Angoni threatened the Company. The Company frantically appealed for help. British Central Africa Protectorate had undertaken to provide military support for Northern Rhodesia when that was requested.

A military force was despatched across the border to reach Fort Jameson. Captain H. E. J. Brake was in command and he had with him six rifle companies of Africans, 118 Sikhs, Maxim Guns, and two 7-pounder field guns. A British officer assisted by a Sikh Colour Sergeant and three Sikh sergeants commanded each African company. The guns were crewed by Africans under Sikh instructors. The remainder of the Sikhs formed their own rifle company. On 19TH January, Brake marched 30 miles north to Fort Loangweni in heavy rain and relieved the small garrison. Next day he moved his force to occupy commanding ground nearby, whilst the Angoni were observed concentrating a force of around 10,000 warriors in the villages. The tactics used by the Angoni regiments were based on making sudden rushes of overwhelming strength, from concealed positions on enemies armed only with spears. These tactics could not be used against an enemy with rifles, who knew how to seize the vital ground before offering battle.

Brake's use of Maxim guns, 7-pounders, rifle volley-fire, and finally a silent advance with the bayonet destroyed the Angoni will to fight. The tribesmen did not lack courage but they would not attack into the British rifle volleys. The few firearms that the Angoni possessed were used ineffectively. Then a new body of at least 500 warriors in full wardress approached, having come from Chief Mpeseni's capital. Four artillery shells, a Maxim burst, and a bayonet charge that was not faced up to caused the rapid dispersal of the survivors of this 500.

Another factor that was observed was that although the Angoni had up to 25,000 warriors, the tribe could never concentrate a very large force for any one battle. They had so roughly handled all their neighbours that the other tribes were always on the lookout for signs of Angoni weakness, so that revenge could be taken. Therefore, all Angoni villages throughout the tribal lands had to be strongly garrisoned at all times. This kept many warriors out of the fight, unless it was occurring near their own villages.

During the next few days, Brake's men patrolled the area, skirmishing with and completely dispersing the Angoni fighters. The old Chief Mpeseni could no longer control his son Singu and the younger warriors. On 30TH January Lieutenant J. S. Brogden captured Singu. After a trial by Drumhead Martial, (a swift military trial held in the field), Singu was summarily shot in front of a collection of chiefs on 5TH February. On 9TH February, Chief Mpeseni surrendered and was exiled for a year to Fort Manning. With his banishment, resistance to the British halted.

Northern Rhodesia

Operations against Yao chiefs Nkwamba and Mataka, October 1899

1ST Battalion Central African Rifles continued its task of pacification even beyond its borders. On the eastern frontier, two chiefs named Nkwamba and Mataka kept raiding both sides of the border, which culminated in killing two European traders. The punitive force led by Captain Pearce left Zomba with 9 officers, 119 Sikhs, and 269 Askaris and after very little resistance destroyed Nkwamba's village in the Namweras Hills. However, Mataka proved more troublesome and escaped to the Portuguese territory.

Operations to aid chief Kazembe, September-November 1899

In September 1899, an expedition was authorised in aid of chief Kazembe, who lived near Lake Mweru in North East Rhodesia. Kazembe had previously refused to enter into treaty with the British, but now sought aid against the last remaining Arab Slavers in his district. A force of 12 Sikhs and 60 Askaris with a 7-pounder gun marched from Karonga to Abercorn and struck southwest to Kazembe's district. At their advance, the slavers fled into Belgium territory and Kazembe then entered into a treaty with the British. In the space of two months, the troops taking part in this expedition marched nearly a thousand miles.

Operations against the Angoni, November-December 1900

In November, renewed operations took place in Central Agoniland under Captain Stokes, who was in command at Fort Mlangeni. During these operations, over 300 villages were destroyed and twenty tribesmen killed. In spite of these reprisals, a mail runner was murdered and a strong force was, therefore, sent out to avenge his death. More villages and stockades were destroyed and Chief Tambola, who had escaped in 1896, was captured. Like Sikhs and Gurkhas, the Angoni had won praise for their resistance to the British. The admiration of Angoni's courage took the form of their recruitment into the kings African Rifles.

Angoni warrior 1900

(Harry Johnston)

ASHANTI

The Ashanti Campaign, 1900

The Ashanti were a powerful and highly organized group of tribes living in the north of the Gold Coast Colony (now Ghana). The consciousness that the Ashanti were a great people was aroused by their wise man Anoky, who affirmed that the spirit and the strength of the nation were enshrined in the Golden Stool. All chiefs were 'enstooled', not crowned, for in Ashanti it was the symbol of royal authority. The British had conducted operations against the Ashanti in 1873-74 and in 1895-96. After the last occasion, King Prempeh was deported and a treaty was drawn up with the remaining chiefs. In March 1900, the British Governor visited Kumasi, held a meeting with the chiefs, and asked why, as representative of the paramount power, the Golden Stool had not been brought from its hiding place for his use. This demand was a serious blunder and precipitated a rebellion among Kumasi, Ofinsu, Ejisu and Adansi sections of the tribe. To put down the rebellion, troops were ordered to the Gold Coast, which included 1ST Battalion, Central African Rifles with four British officers, seventy-three Sikhs, 276 African Askaris and a machine gun detachment. They left Zomba for the Gold Coast, under the command of Major Cobbe, with half of 2ND Battalion to follow from Berbera. Cobbe and his men were in action in August and suffered heavy casualties in thick bush. 'All ranks, especially those fine soldiers the Sikhs, behaved admirably' wrote Colonel Wilcocks, the commandant of the West African Frontier Force in his despatch, 'and if it were not for this impossible bush we should soon wipe out most of the Ashantis'. Lieutenant Colonel Brake and four companies of 2ND Battalion arrived on 13TH August and were in action a week later. At the battle of Obassa on 30TH September, the Ashanti held firm and continued to fire volley after volley at close range, so the assault could not be pressed. It was plain that the undertaking was beyond the capacity of the advance guard and its supporting troops. Colonel Wilcocks himself came forward. As a former officer of the Indian Army, he placed great reliance on the Sikhs and telling them that he would watch the charge, he ordered them to attack the centre of the stockade in the teeth of the Ashanti fire. As the bugles sounded, the Sikhs dashed down the slope, followed by the rest of the line. This charge decided the issue of 'a somewhat doubtful day.' The Ashantis still fought on but gave way before the Sikhs, as they came under devastating enfilading fire that rapidly spread panic and completed the rout. Obassa was a hard fought victory over a most courageous enemy.

The Sikhs fought several actions in conjunction with the West African Frontier Force. When the campaign ended, they earned high praise from Colonel Wilcocks for their discipline, drill, and shooting. They returned to Nyasaland via the Mediterranean, having gone around the cape, so they circumnavigated Africa.

Naik Hira Singh, a volunteer attached to the Central African Rifles, was awarded the Indian Order of Merit for conspicuous gallantry in action. He was foremost in the attack as the Ashanti fled to the bush.

Ashanti

Sikh soldiers of Central African Rifles

Ashanti Warrior

GAMBIA

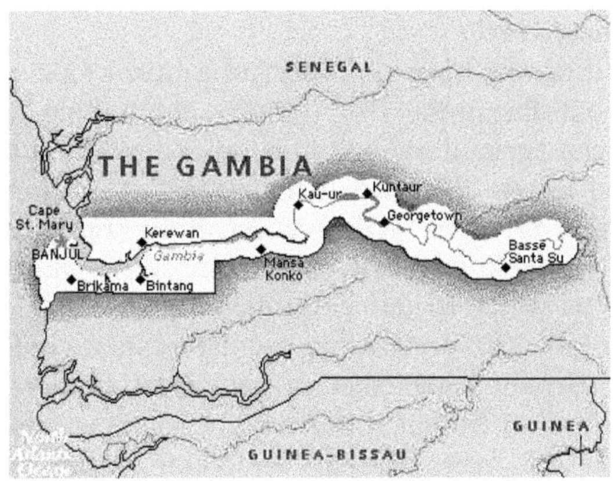

Gambia

Gambia is a country in Western Africa. It is the smallest country on mainland Africa. It is bordered to the north, east, and south by Senegal, and has a small coast on the Atlantic Ocean in the west. Its borders roughly correspond to the path of the Gambia River, the nation's namesake, which flows through the country's centre and empties into the Atlantic Ocean. Its size is almost 10,500 km² with an estimated population of 1,700,000. On 18TH February 1965, Gambia was granted independence from the United Kingdom. Banjul is Gambia's capital, but the largest conurbation is Serrekunda. The Gambia shares historical roots with many other West African nations in the slave trade, which was key to the establishment of a colony on the Gambia River, first by the Portuguese and later by the British.

Mandinka Warrior of Gambia 1900
(Lamutamu)

Gambia

The Gambia Expedition, 1900

The West African coastline had been an important source of slaves for European and American traders, but during the 19TH Century, the trading emphasis moved towards obtaining African agricultural and mineral commodities in exchange for European manufactured goods. This led to European expeditions methodically exploring the hinterland of the West African coast. Both France and Britain were interested in the territory now known as The Gambia, and eventually an amicable agreement was reached by which Britain controlled a strip of land on each side of the navigable course of the River Gambia, whilst France controlled the land surrounding the strip. Britain established a capital at Bathurst (now named Banjul) on the coast, built Fort Bullen at Barra Point on the north side of the river mouth and Fort James 19 miles further upstream on James Island. They suppressed slavery and administered Gambia from a headquarters in Sierra Leone. The agreement with the French had settled the boundaries of Gambia in 1889, but this meant little to the native slave raiding chiefs, who were accustomed to operate indiscriminately on both sides of the frontier. One of these chiefs, Fodi Kabba, had been driven out of the colony in 1892 and had settled at Medina, beyond the frontier in French territory, whence he raided impartially in all directions. On 14TH June 1900, two travelling commissioners were murdered with their police escort of six constables, as many chiefs refused to recognize British authority. In 1901, a military expedition was authorized against the rebellious chiefs, which was afterwards prolonged to settle matters with the slavers. As Gambia possessed an armed police force of only 100 men, it was decided to employ four companies of 2ND Battalion, Central African Rifles and four companies of West India Regiment from Sierra Leone. The command of this Field Force was given to Lieutenant Colonel Brake of 2ND Battalion, Central African Rifles, who travelled to Bathurst on the *SS Dwarka.* At Bathurst, with the rest of the Field Force, including four companies of West India Regiment, they sailed up the river and eventually landed at Tendaba. Their objective was the stockaded town of Dumbutu, which they reached after a three-hour advance through long grass. Two companies of 2ND Battalion, Central African Rifles, under Major Plunket, moved round to the left flank to get between the village and the French border. Surprise was complete and when the defenders finally surrendered, more than forty were dead and over 200 men and women were captured. Losses on the British side were one carrier killed and four men wounded. There were some sweeping–up operations, including tax collection and capture of over 200 rifles. Brake and his men went to the Gold Coast next, to put down mutiny in the West India Regiment.

On 3RD June a detachment of Central African Rifles, including a Sikh Havildar Jaimal Singh, embarked for England. On 26TH June King Edward V11 inspected them at Marlborough House and presented medals for both the Ashanti and the Gambia campaigns.

EAST AFRICA

East African Rifles

The Imperial British East Africa Company (IBEAC) received a royal charter in 1888 to exploit the region of the Great Lakes in Central Africa and take over the British concessions negotiated with the Sultan of Zanzibar. The British also occupied Kismayu in Jubaland. They wanted a Cape to Cairo route. When the Company collapsed in 1895, Britain declared a Protectorate over the company's East African territories. It covered present day Kenya and the land west of the Juba River. The Protectorate's soldiers, consisting of Sudanese, Swahili, Sikhs and locally recruited tribesmen in equal number, were formed as the East African Rifles. They were based on the Company's own body of armed guards which had been formed earlier from Sudanese, Somalis and the Swahilis. The first commandant of East African Rifles was Major Hatch, with headquarters at Fort Jesus, Mombasa. Major Hatch suggested that in view of the troubled state of the coast, 300-trained troops from a Punjab Regiment be recruited for East Africa. The establishment, authorised in 1895, allowed for 300 Sikhs, 250 Sudanese, 300 Swahilis, and 200 'mixed' men. The force included fifteen Sikh gunners and some hospital attendants recruited in India. Their first sortie in 1896 was against the Wakamba tribe, who had burned some police posts set up to prevent slave trading. A large collective fine was imposed, villages were burned, and a barracks constructed in the heart of Wakamba territory to discourage recurrence. In late 1897, East African Rifles were ordered to put down a mutiny in Uganda. Eighty men marched 360 miles in nineteen days to get to the scene and the railway line, although incomplete, was pressed into service to transport the remainder of the force. By the end of January 1898, 4 officers and nearly 400 Sikh and Sudanese troops from East Africa were in Uganda. The regiment lost 1 officer and 17 native officers and men killed, and 1 officer and 16 other ranks wounded during the operations. After the Uganda mutiny, the battalion was reorganized into five Sudanese and three Swahili companies. The Sikh contingent remained until their contracts expired in 1900, when a fourth Swahili Company replaced them.

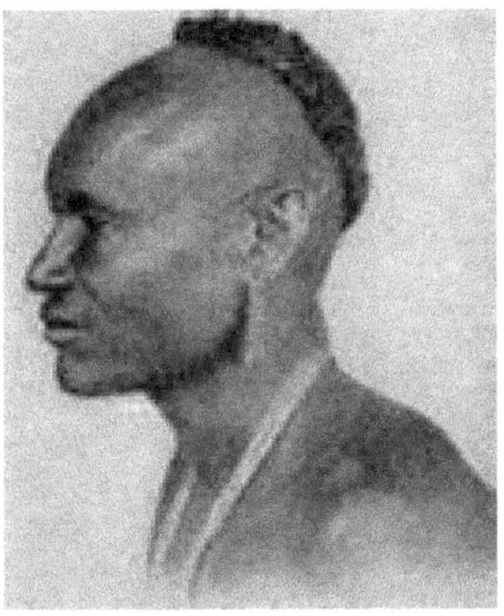

Wakamba Warrior

East Africa

At the outbreak of the First World War, the Germans in East Africa did not only cut the vital line of British communication from the Cape to Cairo but also provided Germany with a naval base from where the German ships could operate in the Indian Ocean and destroy British ships on route to and from India. Consequently, the British Government decided to capture German East Africa. The Indian Government was given responsibility for this. India despatched its army to East Africa and so began the East African campaign. Other British imperial, colonial and South African troops also came to join the campaign in East Africa. However, the Indian Army maintained a force to at least brigade strength throughout the fighting, and a total of 17,500 Indian soldiers served in East Africa during the war. The topography of the country, the climate and the heavy rain were an onerous handicap to the allied soldiers. Malaria, dysentery and other tropical diseases took their toll of unacclimatised troops. General Paul Emil von Lettow-Vorbeck, Commander-in-Chief of German Forces in East Africa during First World War is, by military standards, a legendary character. For over four years during war, he kept a large allied army chasing him, but always succeeded in repulsing attacks and threatening further guerilla action. The main actions took place over a stretch of East Africa then known as Kenya, Tanganyika and Uganda. At one time the Germans were operating south of the present Mozambique border. Von Lettow finally surrendered on 25TH November 1918, days after the official armistice of 11TH November, at Abercorn in present day Zambia. At most, the German forces numbered approximately 3,000 white troops and 11,000 Askari. At the time of the surrender 155 white troops and 1,168 Askari laid down their arms and were allowed the Honours of war.

Tsavo River, September 1914

On August 15TH, Taveta, a place situated at the south-eastern foot of Kilimanjaro, in British East Africa, which was weakly held by the British, was taken by German force under Captain Von Prince. The first Indian contingent to see action in East Africa was 29TH Punjabis. The Regiment had disembarked at Mombasa and was at once sent up the country by rail. On September 4^{TH,} the British received information that a German force was advancing on Tsavo. This German force had compelled a small British detachment on upper Tsavo to withdraw, after an encounter near Mzima. Two companies of 29TH Punjabis were ordered to attack the German force in the flank and rear, driving it to the other two companies of Punjabis, who were in a position astride Tsavo River, five miles west of Tsavo. However, the German force of 300 men with two Pompoms and three Maxim Guns, took the rear guard unawares with heavy fire. After the encounter, the German force retired, receiving a severe mauling. In this action, Jemadar Pala Singh and Jemadar Bhagwan Singh won the Indian Distinguished Service Medal.

East Africa

Gazi, October 1914

On 7TH October, 29TH Punjabis and the Jind Infantry defended Gazi area against a German force about 300 strong. In the counter-attack, one company of 29TH Punjabis hit the German force's right flank, while one company of Jind Infantry attacked the left flank successfully, and two companies of Jind Infantry attacked the front of the German force. This double enveloping movement, combined with the frontal attack by the Indian units, compelled the Germans to retreat. Captain Bihara Singh, Havildar Gujar Singh, Subedars Bahal Singh, Bishan Singh and Sepoys Sadhu Singh, Lakha Singh, Jagta Singh, and Khiwan Singh of Jind Infantry won the Indian Distinguished Service Medal for their conspicuous gallantry at Gazi.

Tana, November 1914

The most famous and tragic action of the East African campaign was the attack on the German port of Tanga. The battle was a disaster for the Indian force engaged, and led to humiliating withdrawal and the unnecessary loss of huge quantities of equipment, which was of great value to the German forces. The plan of attack had been over-ambitious, in trying to cut off the enemy's retreat by railway with so small a force. Subedar Bakhtawar Singh of the Jind and Subedar Randhir Singh of Kashmir Rifles won the Indian Order of Merit on this occasion.

Longido, November 1914

Longido is an isolated hill situated to the northwest of Kilimanjaro Mountain. About 800 to 1,200 German soldiers garrisoned Longido. On November 3RD an attack was made on Longido, in which 29TH Punjabis captured three enemy positions in succession. Subadar Major Kesar Singh won the Order of British India. The Kapurthala Infantry, who had arrived on 3RD October and been employed at kajiado, Bisal, and Menga Hills, also took part in the fight. However, the British forces retired without achieving their object. The total loss of the British force was 19 killed, 33 wounded, while the German losses were 118 killed and wounded.

Jassin, January 1915

On 16TH December, a general advance from British East Africa pushed the Germans back across their frontier in the Umba Valley. Jassin was occupied on 2ND January 1915, and the Jind Infantry took up an advanced entrenched position. A German counter-attack was made on 12TH January but was successfully driven off. On 18TH, however, the enemy made a more determined effort on Jassin. The Jind Infantry made a very plucky effort to support the Garrison, but were driven back by vastly superior numbers and had to retire. Major-General Natha Singh was wounded and it would have gone harder with the Regiment but for a gallant counter-attack by Subedar Harnam Singh, who was taken prisoner after all his men were killed. Subedar Harnam Singh was awarded the Indian Order of Merit.

East Africa

East Africa, 1915

For most of 1915, British and Indian forces remained on the defensive, concentrating on safeguarding the frontiers of British East Africa, as well as the Mombasa – Nairobi railway, the rail centre at Voi, and the shores of the Great Lakes. This extensive defence commitment, and the terrible problems of communication and transport, over-stretched the available forces and there were constant cross-border raids by the Germans.

Bukoba, June 1915

In June 1915, Major General Tighe decided to take action against Bukoba town, situated on the western shore of Lake Victoria. This town had a powerful wireless station and it was thought that its capture would dislocate the German line of communication. The attacking force included 28TH Mountain Battery, escorted by 29TH Punjabis. The Faridkot Sappers and Miners and the British section were behind 25TH Fusiliers. The German force, consisting of 200 rifles and Maxim guns, was holding a very strong position. On June 22ND, the guns of 28TH Mountain Battery started firing on men seen digging entrenchments around the Rest House. The German force replied to this fire from a position at Bukoba where they had a gun. The 28TH Mountain Battery soon knocked out this gun. The German force had to retire under pressure of the fire of 28TH Mountain Battery. The 25TH Royal Fusiliers then entered the wireless station and the German flag was hauled down. The victory in this engagement was due to the superior number of the British force and the accurate fire of the Mountain Battery.

Mbuyuni, February 1916

Early in 1916, General Tighe began to take the offensive, as far as his scanty force permitted. The enemy were driven out of Serengeti and Mbuyuni and had to withdraw their garrison at Kasigau. On 12TH February, a reconnaissance in force was made at Salatia, which resulted in 130TH Baluchis being surrounded for a time. The Rhodesians, seeing their danger, asked to be sent to their assistance. The Baluchis managed to cut their own way out, but the incident gave rise to feelings of very warm mutual regard between the two regiments. Later in the month, South African General Smuts took command of the forces in East Africa and began operations against German forces around Kilimanjaro on 6TH March.

East Africa

Kilimanjaro, March 1916

With the coming of General Smuts to East Africa, the offensive was resumed. The first step was to capture the Kilimanjaro area. The German force in the Kilimanjaro area consisted of 4,000 rifles. To defeat this force Smuts sent a force of 18,400 men, 57 guns, and 99 Machine Guns, which included 1ST and 2ND Divisions. The 1ST Division started from Longido Hill towards its first destination, Vie Bomaja Ngombe on March 5TH, 1916. The following morning, a German detachment met this force at Ngaserai and was driven off by the two companies of 29TH Punjabis and a section of 27TH Mountain Battery. On 8TH March, 1ST Divison reached Gerarague from where it advanced and took Ngombe by the night of March 12TH. While 1ST Divison was thus engaged, 2ND Division advanced towards Salatia Hill. A frontal attack was delivered with the help of aeroplanes on March 8TH at Salatia, which drove away the Germans and the next day the Salatia Hill was occupied by 2ND Division. During the advance towards Salatia, the road and the railway line from Voi to Maktau, which was constructed by Faridkot Sappers, had proved very useful. On the enemy side, the Germans were concentrated around Reata and the Latema Hills. The British advance, under pressure of the heavy fire of the Germans, had to retire. Later they decided to push forward and endeavour to clear the Ridge with a bayonet charge. In the fight which ensued, the German forces were driven back. The following morning, the Germans evacuated their position at the Latema Hills. Consequently, the British forces occupied these positions on Mach 13TH. “Thus the conquest of the Kilimanjaro-Meru area, probably the richest and most desirable district of German East Africa, was satisfactorily accomplished.” General Smuts wrote enthusiastically about the conduct of the British troops, “All these hardships were endured with unfailing cheerfulness and a chance of dealing a blow at the enemy seemed to be the only recompense required.” Gunner Havildar Bhan Singh and Lance Naik Natha Singh of the 27TH Mountain Battery, and Subedar Bhagwan Singh and Sepoy Sadda Singh, won the Indian Order of Merit for their conspicuous gallantry against the Germans in the Kilimanjaro area. Havildar Bachan Singh and Naik Sundar Singh of the same regiment were awarded the Indian Distinguished Service Medal. (Soldiers Burden, undated)

Kilimanjaro Area

East Africa

The attack on Kisangire, September 1916

Fearing that the Germans might be tasked with operating against the Central Railway, the British decided to attack Kisangire. Major General Natha Singh, the commander of the 240-man strong Jind Infantry, was ordered to march from Dar es Salaam with his Sepoys and his two machine guns. The Ruler of the Sikh Princely State of Jind had supplied the Jind Infantry to the war effort as part of the Indian Imperial Service Scheme. The Jind Infantry had been fighting in East Africa since 1914 and had gained a reputation for professionalism and bravery in action. Already operating around Kisangire and observing the enemy's movements were 40 Scouts under the command of Lieutenant G. D. Howarth of the Intelligence Department. Howarth reported that the German post was in a building on top of a steep conical hill, around which two lines of trenches had been dug. The easiest line of approach was from the west and south-west. Moving off before dawn on 9TH October 1916, the Sikhs marched around the rear of the conical hill, and at 0930 hours, they were ready to attack. Nathan Singh placed three of his companies and the machine guns in the first line and kept his fourth company as a reserve in a second line. He had 183 Sepoys deployed. The Sikhs worked through the bush towards the hill until enemy outposts engaged them and then they rushed forward and captured the first trench line. From there a bayonet attack was mounted that captured the inner trench line. But now problems arose because of the lack of artillery support for the Jind troops. The building was engaged with machine gun and rifle fire but these rounds had no effect on the strong stonewalls of the post. In retaliation, the enemy shot down both Sikh machine gun crews. Sepoy Sadha Singh displayed conspicuous gallantry, for which he was awarded a posthumous Indian Order of Merit. He proceeded forward under a hot fire along a communication trench and removed a number of dead bodies, which were impeding the advance, when he was severely wounded, and died of his wounds. After losing 13 men dead or mortally wounded, 27 others wounded, and eight wounded and missing, Nathan Singh broke off the action, and withdrew to Maneromango and re-grouped.

Rufiji, December 1916

On December 22ND, an attack was launched across the Rufiji River near Ruaha, with flanking columns attacking near Duthemi, Wiransi, and Dakawa. In the process of these advances, 130TH Baluchis were heavily attacked on 1ST January, 1917 near Wiransi but drove off the Germans. Mkalinso Bridge was successfully secured on 3RD January and 1ST Brigade endeavoured to surround the Germans as they fell back across the Rufiji near Kibembwe on 4TH. The Germans continued to retire slowly southwards throughout January, fighting a continuous series of rearguard actions, with Kissingiri and Kibata falling to the British and the area north of the Rufiji being cleared. The capture of Utete on January 21ST concluded these operations.

East Africa

Behobeho Chogwali, January 1917

During 3RD January, 1ST East African Brigade made an exhausting cross-country march culminating in a 60-metre descent over a field of huge boulders. The Brigade Commander halted his exhausted men for the night a few kilometres short of the destination. The following morning, Behobeho Chogwali was reached without incident and the advance turned north to Behobeho Kwa Mahinda. At about 1030 hours, contact was made with the enemy and two companies of 30TH Punjabis came up in support, as the Kashmiris extended the left flank. Ninety minutes later Wangoni Company came into view from the north. The Wangoni Askaris, relatives of the Zulus, immediately attacked the British-held ridge. A lively and lengthy action then developed but the Punjabis held their ground, efficiently using their two Maxim machine guns and two Rexer light machine guns. The Punjabis lost Naik Gurdit Singh killed and three Sepoys wounded in the desperately fought action.

The Last Push November 1917

By the end of April 1917, the Germans had been forced to evacuate the whole of the area north of the Matandu River. Advancing from Kilwa on 5TH July, one column pushed the Germans back on Narungomba, from where they were driven by 33RD Punjabis and 40TH Pathans after fierce fighting on the 19TH. Perhaps the hardest and the most costly action of the campaign was fought from 16TH to 19TH October 1917 at Nyangao, where four days solid fighting were necessary to defeat the Germans and force them southwards once more. German troops, exhausted and short of supplies of all kinds, surrendered at end of 1917.

Captain Nand Singh, Faridkot Sappers, Jemadar Sundar Singh and Subadar Labh Singh, 30TH Punjabis, with Jemadar Sarup Singh of the Kashmir Mountain Battery, won the Indian Order of Merit for their conspicuous gallantry. The following soldiers were awarded the Indian Distinguished Service Medal for their conspicuous gallantry: Assistant Surgeon Bir Singh, Subedar Amar Singh, and Havildar Mehar Singh, 33RD Punjabis; Jemadar Hakam Singh, Havildar Lal Singh, Subedar Thakur Singh, Havildar Gurdit Singh, and Havildar Dalel Singh, 30TH Punjabis; Sepoy Puran Singh and Subedar Udham Singh, 29TH Punjabis; Havildar Pala Singh and Jemadar Mangal Singh, Faridkot Sappers; Gunner Narain Singh, Havildar Sant Singh, and Driver Santokh Singh, 20TH Mountain Battery; Naik Narain Singh, Havildar Narain Singh, and Naik Natha Singh, 27TH Mountain Battery.

At the fall of German East Africa, mainland Tanganyika was placed under the control of British Colonial authority in 1919. On 9TH December 1961, Tanganyika gained independence from Great Britain. In 1964, Tanganyika united with several islands in the Indian Ocean, including Zanzibar and Pemba, to form the United Republic of Tanzania.

East Africa

The Sikh Princely States troops in British East African Campaign.

Faridkot Sappers and Miners

The Faridkot Sappers were in Africa from November 1914 to February 1918. In the advance to Moshi, they were divided, half going from Longido with General Stewart, and half from Taveta with General Smuts. From March to May 1916, they were road making for General Van Deventer in a ceaseless downpour of rain. In June and July, they were at Mkalama. In August and September, they continued to work well in spite of rain and half rations. In December, they bridged the Rufiji River for Beve's Brigade, and later for General Sheppard at Kibambawe. They then returned to Morogoro and were kept on road repair throughout the rains. In October, they were with the Belgians in the Mehenge area. In January 1918, they bridged the Rovena for the Lindi Force. In February, they returned to India. Lieutenant Colonel Nand Singh was awarded the O.B.I. and the I.O.M. Lieutenant Colonel Bishan Singh was awarded the O.B.I.

Kapurthala Infantry

The Kapurthala Infantry were in Africa from October 1914 to December 1917. They were employed on outpost duties until August 1915, after which they served at Msambweni for three months. They were then kept on Railway duty in the Kiu District. Thereafter they were employed on reconnaissance and outpost duties until October 1917. For the last two months of their stay, they were at Tanga and Lindi. Major General Sardar Puran Singh was awarded the O.B.I., as well as C.I.E. Lieutenant Colonels Nihal Singh and Moti Singh and Major Maya Singh, and Captain Rur Singh were awarded the O.B.I.

Jind Infantry

The Jind Infantry were in Africa from October 1914 to December 1917. They earned the highest opinions of all the generals under whom they served, especially their fighting at Jassin. Major General Natha Singh, who commanded with great gallantry, was awarded the O.B.I., as well as C.I.E. Lieutenant Colonel Baldev Singh was awarded the O.B.I.

General Natha Singh with officers of the Jind Infantry

East Africa

Faridkot Sappers and Miners

Faridkot was a Sikh Princely State in the Punjab. The ruler, on the outbreak of war, supplied a company of his Sappers and Miners for British use. The unit was about 130 men strong, with over 90 percent of them being Jat Sikhs. They were despatched to British East Africa with Indian Expeditionary Force "B" in October 1914. Fewer than 25 died during the campaign, and this low figure is a tribute to the hardiness of Jat Sikhs. The unit was awarded the Battle Honours: Kilimanjaro, Behobeho, and East Africa 1914-1918.

The following Sikh soldiers were awarded gallantry awards for their conspicuous gallantry during the East African Campaign:

Captain Nand Singh
Faridkot Sappers and Miners

Captain Nand Singh was awarded the Indian Order of Merit for conspicuous gallantry and devotion to duty in the field. He served in East Africa from 1914 to 1918, and ended the campaign as Lieutenant Colonel.

Indian Distinguished Service Medal

The following Sikh soldiers of Faridkot Sappers and Miners were awarded the IDSM for their conspicuous gallantry in East Africa: Subedar Raghbir Singh, Jemadar Moti Singh, Jemadar Chet Singh, Havildar Harnam Singh, Naik Sawan Singh, Naik Thana Singh, and Lance Naik Kishen Singh.

Subedar Harnam Singh
Jind Infantry

Subedar Harnam Singh was awarded the Indian Order of Merit for his gallant conduct at Jasin in East Africa, on 18TH January 1915. He rallied a small party to cover a retirement and held the enemy in check until all in his party were killed, and he was severely wounded himself and taken prisoner.

Naik Kehar Singh
Jind Infantry

Naik Kehar Singh was awarded the Indian Order of Merit for the exemplary, cool manner in which he worked his machine gun under heavy fire on 16TH and 17TH December near Masanga, while serving with the Indian Expeditionary Force in East Africa.

Sepoy Sadda Singh (Posthumous)
Jind Infantry

Was awarded posthumous Indian Order of Merit for conspicuous gallantry in action on 9TH October 1916 in East Africa. He proceeded forward under hot fire, along a communication trench and removed a number of dead bodies, which were impeding the advance. He died of his wounds.

East Africa

Indian Distinguished Service Medal

Jind Infantry

The following Sikh soldiers of Jind Infantry were awarded the IDSM for their conspicuous gallantry in the battle of Jasin: Captain Bihara Singh, Subedar Bahal Singh, Subedar Bishan Singh, Havildar Gujar Singh, Sepoy Sadhu Singh, Sepoy Lakha Singh, Sepoy Jagta Singh, and Sepoy Khiwan Singh.

25TH Cavalry (Frontier Force)

During the First World War, 25TH Cavalry went to German East Africa and joined in the pursuit of the German general Von Lettow Voreck to the Mozambique border. They were withdrawn from cavalry operations in the face of the depredations of the tsetse fly on their horses. The following Sikh soldiers were awarded the Indian Distinguished Service Medal for their gallantry in East Africa and on the North West Frontier of India: Lance Daffadar Sohan Singh, Kot Daffadar Suba Singh, and Sowar Budh Singh.

24TH Hazara Mountain Battery (Frontier Force)

The 24TH (Hazara) Indian Mountain Battery served in East Africa from 26TH April 1917. A typical extract from their War Diary reads: "Ndundwala 2ND July 1917. One section came into action and fired 87 rounds shrapnel at enemy holding river crossing place at range 750 yards. Forward observer reported three direct hits on his breastworks." (Ferndale, 1988) They returned to India in November 1918. The following Sikh Gunners were awarded the Indian Distinguished Service Medal for their conspicuous gallantry in East Africa: Gunner Gehna Singh, Gunner Ram Singh, Gunner Nar Singh, and Subedar Sant Singh.

27TH Mountain Battery

The 27TH Indian Mountain Battery, with six guns, formed part of Indian Expeditionary Force 'C', from 27TH August 1914 to 2ND January 1918 in East Africa. The Mountain Battery was divided between the Magadi and Voi-Tsavo areas and spent a few months countering enemy raids on the railway. A succession of actions took place in which the regiment proved invaluable, but the enemy never stood to fight for any length of time. Havildar Bhan Singh and Lance Naik Natha Singh were awarded the Indian Order of Merit and the following Sikh Gunners were awarded the Indian Distinguished Service Medal for their conspicuous gallantry: Havildar Bachan Singh, Havildar Bhan Singh, Havildar Narain Singh, Naik, and Naik Narain Singh.

29TH Punjabis

During the First World War, the regiment served in Palestine, Egypt and East Africa. The following Sikh soldiers were awarded the Indian Distinguished Service Medal for their conspicuous gallantry in East Africa: Subadar Udham Singh, Jemadar Pala Singh, Jemadar Bhagwan Singh, and Sepoy Puran Singh.

East Africa

28TH Mountain Battery

The 28TH Indian Mountain Battery with six guns arrived in German East Africa with Indian Expeditionary Force 'B' on 30TH October 1914, returning to India in December 1916. The 28TH Battery's first engagement occurred with the guns tied to the deck of HM Transport ship Bharata, firing in support of the unsuccessful British attempt to capture Tanga, on 3RD and 4TH November 1914. A succession of actions took place in which the regiment, with its sister regiment 27TH, proved invaluable, including their actions in defending Jasin on 18TH January 1915. The following Sikh Gunners were awarded the Indian Distinguished Service Medal for their conspicuous gallantry: Havildar Sant Singh, Gunner Narain Singh, and Driver Santokh Singh.

30TH Punjabis

The 30TH Punjabis arrived at Dar-es-Salaam in German East Africa on 11TH December 1916. They fought a major battle on the Rufiji River and suffered severe losses. In a desperately fought battle at Tandamuti Hill, the German Askaris cut one of the companies to pieces. The Askaris charged home again and again. In this desperate fighting 255 rank and file were killed, wounded or missing.

Subadar Labh Singh
30TH Punjabis

Subadar Labh Singh was awarded the Indian Order of Merit for conspicuous bravery and initiative in action on 18TH October 1917 in East Africa. Subadar Labh Singh's skilful control of fire, and fearless example, enabled determined enemy counter-attacks to be repulsed by the company he commanded.

Jemadar Sundar Singh
30TH Punjabis

Jemadar Sundar Singh was awarded the Indian Order of Merit for conspicuous gallantry and skill in handling a machine-gun section on 3RD August 1917 in East Africa. The enemy was attacking from both flanks and the front at very close quarters. The Machine Gun Officer was severely wounded. Jemadar Sundar Singh took command of the Machine Gun Section, succeeded in withdrawing all the machine guns except one, and brought them safely back.

Indian Distinguished Service Medal
30TH Punjabis

The following Sikh soldiers were awarded the Indian Distinguished Service Medal for their conspicuous gallantry in Jungle fighting: Subedar Thakar Singh, Jemadar Hakam Singh, Havildar Lal Singh, Havildar Gurdit Singh, and Havildar Dalel Singh.

East Africa

33RD Punjabis

The 33RD Punjabis disembarked at Kilwe on 8TH May for service in German East Africa. One of the patrols advancing on Wungui was ambushed and wiped out. On 12TH June they suffered another catastrophe, when a patrol proceeding in the direction of Kilwe was ambushed, suffering more casualties. After some small engagements, the regiment was engaged in heavy but successful battles at Kihunburu and Narugombe.

Indian Distinguished Service Medal
33RD Punjabis

The following Sikh officers were awarded the Indian Distinguished Service Medal for their conspicuous gallantry in Africa: Subedar Amar Singh and Havildar Mehr Singh.

57TH Wilde's Rifles (Frontier Force)

The East African Campaign was a series of battles and guerrilla actions, which started in German East Africa and ultimately, affected portions of Mozambique, Northern Rhodesia, Kenya, Uganda, and the Belgian Congo. The 57TH Rifles were engaged in long months of hard trekking and stiff fighting against a determined enemy. The German colonial forces fought for the duration of World War 1 and surrendered only after that war had ended.

Indian Distinguished Service Medal
57TH Wilde's Rifles

The following officers and men of 57TH Rifles were awarded the Indian Distinguished Service Medal for their gallantry during the East African Campaign: Havildar Kapur Singh, Havildar Bhagwan Singh, Havildar Udham Singh, Havildar Sundar Singh, Jemadar Hira Singh, Naik Amir Singh, and Naik Amar Singh.

A sketch of an Askari of the German East African Schutzrupp, 1914

East Africa

East African Campaign

The East African Campaign was a series of battles fought in East Africa during World War II by the British Empire, the British Commonwealth of Nations and several allies against the forces of Italy from June 1940 to November 1941. Fighting began with the Italian bombing of the Rhodesian air base at Wajir in Kenya and continued pushing the Italian forces through Somaliland. Eritrea and Ethiopia until the Italian surrender after the Battle of Gondar in November 1941.

While the Kingdom of Egypt remained neutral during World War II, the Anglo-Egyptian Treaty of 1936 allowed the military forces of the United Kingdom to occupy Egypt in defence of the Suez Canal. At this time, the Kingdom of Egypt included the Sudan. However, the Sudan was a condominium between Egypt and the United Kingdom known as the Anglo-Egyptian Sudan. On 10TH June 1940, when Mussolini led Italy into World War II against the British and the French, the Italian forces in Africa became a potential threat to British supply routes along the Red Sea and through the Suez Canal. While Egypt and the Suez Canal were Mussolini's obvious primary targets, an Italian invasion of either French Somaliland or British Somaliland were reasonable choices too. But Mussolini initially looked past both of these small, isolated colonies and, instead, looked forward to propaganda triumphs in the Sudan and British East Africa (Kenya, Tanganyika, and Uganda).

Italian Ground Forces

Amedeo, Duke of Acosta, was the Viceroy and Governor General of Italian East Africa. He had between 250,000 and 280,000 Italian troops available to him. Equipment for the Italian ground forces in East Africa was a mixed bag. The forces were equipped with about 3,300 machine guns, 24 M 11/39 medium tanks, a large number of L3/35 light tanks, 126 armoured cars and 813 pieces of assorted artillery. The most common Italian rifle was the Carcano Mod. 91. The Italians faced problems due the isolation of East Africa from Mediterranean supply lines, with very little opportunity for reinforcements or re-supply, leading to problems especially with ammunition.

Italian Soldiers in East Africa

East Africa

British Ground Forces

Initially, the British and Commonwealth forces in East Africa amounted to about 30,000 men under Major-General William Platt in the Sudan, Major-General Douglas Dickinson in British East Africa, and Lieutenant-Colonel Arthur Reginald Chater in British Somaliland. The British and Commonwealth forces were slightly better equipped than the Italians, and had access to re-supply and reinforcements. However, they were vastly outnumbered by the Italian forces available in Italian East Africa. Also, the Italians had at least another 208,000 men (fourteen divisions) available in Libya. On 10TH June 1940, in all of the Sudan, prior to the arrival of 4TH Indian Infantry Division and 5TH Indian Infantry Division, Platt had only three regular British infantry battalions (which were absorbed into the under-strength 5TH Indian Division when it arrived) and the 21 companies (4,500 men in total) of the Sudan Defence Force of which five (later six) were organized as small mobile machine gun companies.

Wajir

Starting in June 1940, the Italians tested the resolve of the British and Commonwealth forces along the borders of the Sudan and Kenya and in the shipping lanes of the Red Sea. On 13TH June, early in the morning, three Italian Caproni bombers appeared and bombed the Rhodesian air base at the fort located at Wajir in Kenya. The Rhodesian aircraft were still warming up and preparing to take-off on a dawn patrol. The Capronis bombed the fort, the landing-ground, and nearby housing. The King's African Rifles (KAR), then garrisoning the fort, lost four killed and eleven wounded. Two Rhodesian aircraft were badly damaged and a large dump of aviation fuel was set on fire. Following this, the air base at Wajir received regular visits from the Italians every second or third day and the Rhodesian pilots were made to realize the significant shortcomings in speed and fire-power of the Hawker Hardys they themselves flew. At dawn on 17TH June, the Rhodesians struck back and supported a successful raid by the KAR on the Italian desert outpost of El Wak in Italian Somaliland, some ninety miles northeast of Wajir. The Rhodesians bombed and set alight the thatched mud huts and generally harassed the enemy troops.

A British manned fort in Wajir

East Africa

Sudan

On July 4TH, 1940, Italian forces in Eritrea crossed the Sudanese border and forced the small British garrison holding the railway junction at Kassala to withdraw. The defenders lost 10 men, the attackers 117. The Italians also seized the small British fort at Gallabat, just over the border from Metemma, some 200 miles (320 km) to the south of Kassala. Even the villages of Qaysān, Kurmuk and Dumbode on the Blue Nile were conquered. Having taken Kassala and Gallabat, however, the Italians decided to venture no further in the Sudan - because of lack of fuel - and they proceeded to fortify Kassala with anti-tank defences, machine-gun posts, and strong-points. They were also disappointed to find the native population was not harbouring any anti-British sentiments. Ultimately, the Italians established a brigade-strong garrison at Kassala.

Kenya

In Kenya, after heavy fighting, the Italians occupied Fort Harrington in Moyale. At the end of July, Italian forces reached Dabel and Buna. These small villages, nearly one-hundred kilometres from the Ethiopian-Kenyan border, were to be the deepest points inside Kenya reached by the Italian army. Any further expansion was impossible because of the poor supply situation. Mussolini had laid claims to Kenya, but Hitler planned the dissection of the colony, with the southern part and the capital Nairobi forming a territory of the German Mittelafrika. Italy was also to replace the British administration in Sudan: Italian-Egyptian Sudan was to link Italian North Africa with Italian East Africa.

British Somaliland, 1940

On 3RD August 1940, approximately 25,000 Italian troops invaded British Somaliland. The Italians were commanded by General Guglielmo Nasi. The Italian force included five colonial brigades, three Blackshirt battalions, and three bands of native troops. They had armoured vehicles (a small number of both light and medium tanks), artillery, and, for the moment, superior air support. They were opposed by a British contingent, commanded by Brigadier Arthur Reginald Chater, of about four thousand men, consisting of the lightly armed Somaliland Camel Corps, 2ND (Nyasaland) Battalion King's African Rifles (KAR), 1ST Battalion Northern Rhodesian Regiment, 3RD Battalion, 15TH Punjab Regiment and 1ST East African Light Battery (four 3.7 inch howitzers). They were joined from Aden on 7TH August by 1ST Battalion, 2ND Punjab Regiment and on 8TH August by 2ND Battalion Black Watch. Chaters' force was not only critically short of artillery but it had no tanks or armoured cars nor did it have any anti-tank weapons to oppose the Italian medium and light tanks.

East Africa

Battle of Tug Argan

The Italians advanced in three columns, with the western column advancing towards Zeila, the central column towards Hargeisa, and the eastern column towards Odweina in the south. Lieutenant-General Carlo De Simone commanded the main central column. Chater used his Camel Corps to skirmish with and screen against the advancing Italians, as the other British and Commonwealth forces pulled back towards Tug Argan, to form defensive positions in the rugged Assa Hills overlooking the main road to the capital, Berbera. On 5TH August, within two days of the invasion, the towns of Zeila and Hargeisa were taken. The occupation of Zeila effectively sealed British Somaliland off from French Somaliland. Odweina fell the following day and the Italian central and eastern columns combined to launch attacks against the main British and Commonwealth positions at Tug Argan. At the end of the first week in August the British and Commonwealth forces in British Somaliland received reinforcements with the arrival of 1ST Battalion, 2ND Punjab Regiment, and 2ND Battalion, Black Watch. On 11TH August, a new, more senior, commander, Major-General Reade Godwin-Austen, reached Berbera. The Italians commenced their attacks at Tug Argan on 11TH August but, early on 15TH August, Godwin-Austen concluded that further resistance to the Italians would be futile as his troops were close to being cut off. He contacted the British Middle East Command headquarters in Cairo, Egypt. Godwin-Austen requested and received permission to withdraw his forces from British Somaliland. The determined effort of the Black Watch battalion, which covered the retreat, allowed the entire British and Commonwealth contingent to withdraw to Berbera with almost no losses. By 17TH August, most of the contingent was successfully evacuated from Berbera to Aden. On 19TH August 1940, the Italians took control of Berbera and then moved down the coast to complete their conquest of British Somaliland. The British colony was annexed to Italian East Africa. The British Prime Minister, Sir Winston Churchill, criticized General Archibald Wavell concerning the loss of British Somaliland. It was Wavell's Middle East Command which was responsible for the loss of the colony. Because of the low casualty rate, Churchill fretted that the British had abandoned the colony without enough of a fight. In response to this criticism, Wavell claimed that Somaliland was a textbook withdrawal in the face of superior numbers. He pointed out to Churchill that "A bloody butcher's bill is not the sign of a good tactician." According to Churchill's staff, Wavell's retort moved Churchill to greater fury than they had ever seen before. The conquest of the British Somaliland was the only campaign in which Italy achieved victory without the support of other Axis troops during World War II. British Somaliland was the first British colony to fall to enemy forces in World War II. (WW11 AT 70, 2010)

East Africa

Sudan

On 6TH November a surprise attack was staged to take back Gallabat. The attacking force comprised William "Bill" Slim's 10TH Indian Infantry Brigade. Slim was accompanied by a squadron of 12 medium and light tanks, a field regiment of artillery, and supported by the RAF. The attack began at 5:30 am and Gallabat was captured by 8:00 am. The planned follow-on assault on Metemma, on the other side of the ravine forming the border, had to be delayed because by this time nine of the tanks were out of action. Lieutenant-General Luigi Frusci, acting Governor of Eritrea and commander of the Italian forces there, was not prepared to relinquish the Italian-held positions in the Sudan. The Italian defenders occupied strong prepared positions with barbed-wire defences, which could only be broken by tanks. As Slim paused while his tanks were repaired, General Martini, the Italian commander at Gondar, sent a fierce onslaught from the counter-attacking Italian Royal Air Force. Italian aircraft appeared in great strength. The Italian airmen shot down seven RAF Gloster Gladiator biplane fighters whilst losing five Fiat CR-42s and, for forty-eight hours, proceeded to methodically bomb 1ST Battalion, Essex Regiment and 3RD Battalion, 18TH Royal Garwhal Rifles. The Italians did this until the British and Commonwealth troops were compelled to withdraw from the positions they had just won. The 10TH Indian Brigade re-occupied the ridge west of Gallabat three days later but the operation against Metemma was not continued. For the next two months, 10TH Indian Brigade and, after them, 9TH Indian Brigade (who relieved 10TH Brigade in December) simulated the activities of a full division. The brigades blazed lines of communication east from Gedaref and created dummy airfields and stores depots. The British forces did this to convince Italian Intelligence that Platt's main thrust would be towards Gondar rather than Kassala. Throughout November, December, and early January, Lieutenant-General William Platt continued to apply constant pressure on the Italians all along the border with the Sudan by continually patrolling and raiding with both his ground troops and his air force. On 6TH December, a large concentration of Italian motor transport was bombed and strafed by Commonwealth aircraft a few miles north of Kassala. The same aircraft then proceeded to machine-gun from low level the nearby positions of the Italian Blackshirts and colonial infantry. A few days later, the same aircraft bombed the Italian base at Keru, fifty miles east of Kassala. The Commonwealth pilots had the satisfaction of seeing supply dumps, stores, and transport enveloped in flame and smoke as they flew away.

East Africa

Wavell planned for Platt to advance southward from the Sudan, through Eritrea, and into Ethiopia and for Cunningham to advance northwards from Kenya, through Italian Somaliland, and into Ethiopia. While Platt advanced from the north and Cunningham from the south, Wavell planned for a third force to be landed in British Somaliland in an amphibious assault and to then re-take that colony prior to advancing into Ethiopia. According to the plan, all three forces were to ultimately join forces at the capital of Italian East Africa, Addis Ababa. The capture of Italian East Africa would remove land-based threats to supplies and reinforcements coming from Australia, New Zealand, India, South Africa, and British East Africa and passing through the Suez Canal for the campaign in North Africa and open the overland route from Cape Town to Cairo.

Eritrea, 1941

Lieutenant-General Platt's attack from the Sudan to take Eritrea could only begin once re-enforcements arrived from Egypt; in the meantime he continued to conduct harrying raids on Italian positions. The arrival of an Australian division in Egypt allowed General Wavell to release 4TH Indian Infantry Division from Operation Compass in the Western Desert. Further reinforcements in the form of a battery of 6-inch howitzers and a company of tanks were also forthcoming. The arrival of 4TH Indian Infantry Division, together with intelligence concerning the Italian plans, greatly aided Platt's plans. The main British attack on Eritrea, originally scheduled to start on February 8TH with an attack against the railway junction at Kassala, was brought forward to January 18TH. However, the aggressive skirmishing in the previous month had prompted the Italians, in late December, to withdraw from their northern flank back to Keru and Wachai. On January 19TH, 1941, Lieutenant-General Platt's two divisions, 4TH Indian Infantry Division, commanded by Major-General Noel Beresford-Peirse and 5TH Indian Infantry Division, commanded by Major-General Lewis Heath, entered Kassala, making for the heavily fortified town of Agordat to the east. On that first day, as the British and Commonwealth troops passed through Kassala and entered Sabdaret and Tessenei, the Italians were already dug in among the jagged foothills of the Eritrean Plateau on the approaches to Agordat.

Briggs Force

As the Indian divisions crossed the Eritrean border in the west, Briggs Force, operating independently from the main force, advanced eastwards from the Sudan and entered Eritrea from the north through the border town of Karora. After capturing Italian positions near Karora, Briggs Force fought its way to the northern defences of Keren and linked up with the main force in March.

East Africa

Agordat and Barentu

Advancing east from Kassala towards Agordat, 4TH Indian Division took the northern road via Wachai and Keru. Meanwhile the two brigades of 5TH Indian Infantry Division took the southern road via Tessenei, Aicota and Barentu. On 21ST January, 5TH Indian Division had occupied Aicota without opposition and Gazelle Force had reached the strongly defended position at the Keru Gorge, held by five Italian battalions. The Italian position at Keru was undone by a bold move by Major-General Heath, who sent 2ND Battalion Highland Light Infantry and 2ND Motor Machine Gun Battalion from 10TH Indian Brigade northeast along a track from Aicota to the rear of the Italian position at Keru. On 22ND January when 4TH Indian Division put in their attack, 5TH Indian Division detachment was across the Italians' rear line of communication. The Italian position, which should have been held for weeks, became untenable and while some elements of the Italian 41ST Brigade managed to escape across country in the night, General Fongoli with his staff and guns and 1,200 men were taken prisoner. By 25TH January the lateral line of communication between Agordat and Barentu had been cut, leaving these two strong points isolated from each other. Agordat was defended by four infantry brigades supported by 76 guns and a company each of medium and light tanks all under the command of General Lorenzini. The 4TH Indian Division's second brigade (5TH Indian Infantry Brigade) had by now concentrated from Egypt. Beresford-Pierse therefore paused to allow it, together with the first four tanks, to move into the front line. On the evening of 28TH January he sent 11TH Indian Brigade's 3RD Battalion, 14TH Punjab Regiment on a flanking move into the Cochen hills to the south. On 29TH January they were joined by 2ND Battalion, 6TH Rajputana Rifles. On 30TH January they were counter attacked by five Italian colonial battalions with mountain artillery in support. The Indian battalions came under intense pressure and were forced to give way but counter attacked on the morning of 31ST January and regained the lost ground. With Lorenzini's attention fully occupied by the events in the Cochen, Beresford-Pierse launched 5TH Indian Brigade in his main attack on the plain below, supported by four tanks. The tanks proved decisive and by the evening the road to Keren had been cut and the Italian defenders isolated. Once again the Italian forces attempted to get away in the hours of darkness but 1,000 prisoners were taken and 43 guns captured.

Meanwhile 5TH Indian Division had attacked Barentu and, despite facing 8,000 defenders with 32 guns, settled in prepared defences. They had prevailed without help from the tanks and occupied the town on 2ND February.

Within nine days, the forces of Beresford-Peirse and Heath had advanced 100 miles (160 kilometers) and broken through the Italian positions in the foothills, to capture Agordat on February 1ST. In total 6,000 prisoners had been taken and 80 guns, 26 tanks and 400 trucks captured.

East Africa

Metemma

On 31ST January, the Italian garrison at Metemma in northern Ethiopia, having been under increasing pressure for three weeks and realising that Platt's main thrust would not be coming from the Gallabat direction, withdrew towards Gondar. This withdrawal allowed 9TH Indian Infantry Brigade of 5TH Indian Infantry Division to occupy Metemma. Brigadier Mosley Mayne, 9TH Brigade's commander, sent units along the road towards Wahni to harry the retreating Italian forces and fought lively engagements 20 miles and 45 miles east of Metemma. Progress on the road was difficult because of the thickly laid minefields and it was during this period that 2ND Lieutenant Premindra Singh Bhagat of the Royal Bombay Sappers and Miners won the first Victoria Cross for the British Indian Army in World War II for a "...continuous feat of sheer cold courage" clearing 15 minefields and 55 miles of roads in 48 hours of unbroken effort.

Keren

Following the fall of Agordat, Gazelle Force set off in pursuit of the Italians. The key action took place at Keren, 60 miles further east of Agordat. On 5TH February, the Battle of Keren began. The battle started with assaults by elements of 4TH Indian Infantry Division on the Italian positions in the mountains leading to Keren. Initially the resolute Italian defenders prevailed with heavy casualties on both sides. Further heavy attacks took place over the next ten days, but the Italians held and there was no breakthrough. Platt decided to regroup and concentrate his forces before attacking again. On 14TH March, by the time the next assault on Keren commenced, Platt's force of about 13,000 men faced a re-inforced Italian defence of about 23,000 men. Once again, both sides fought with determination and both sides suffered heavy losses. It took until 27TH March for Keren to fall. In the account of the battle written in *Eastern Epic*, an official history of the British Indian Army in World War II, Compton Mackenzie wrote:

Keren was as hard a soldiers' battle as was ever fought, and let it be said that nowhere in the war did the Germans fight more stubbornly than those [Italian] Savoia battalions, Alpini, Bersaglieri and Grenadiers. In the [first] five days' fight the Italians suffered nearly 5,000 casualties - 1,135 of them killed. Lorenzini, the gallant young Italian general, had his head blown off by one of the British guns. He had been a great leader of Eritrean troops.
(Mackenzie, 1951)

Casualties at Keren were relatively high for both sides. The British and Commonwealth forces had more than 4,000 men killed, wounded or missing including 3,000 casualties from 4TH Indian Division. The Italians suffered about 3,000 men killed and several thousand men wounded, injured, or sick. Much of the Italian garrison was captured.

East Africa

Asmara

After Keren fell, Indian 5TH Infantry Division set off eastwards in pursuit of the retreating Italians and towards the Eritrean capital of Asmara, some 50 miles away. They left the Indian 4TH Infantry Division behind to mop up in Keren. After mopping up, the Indian 4TH Infantry Division returned to Egypt (leaving behind for a little longer the formations it had detached to Briggs Force).The retreating Italians fought minor skirmishes but mounted no major stand. A new defensive position was formed at Ad Teclesan, in a narrow valley on the route from Keren to Asmara. The 80TH Colonial Division was brought from Gondar and the remaining two battalions of the Savoia Grenadiers from Addis Ababa. However, the Keren defeat had shattered the morale of the Italian forces and when Heath's attack came early on 31ST March there was little fighting. On 1ST April, Asmara was declared an open town and 5TH Indian Division entered the town to take 5,000 more prisoners and capture the entire equipment reserve of the Italian East African armies, including 1,500,000 shells and 3,000,000 rounds of small arms ammunition. Three days later, after re-supply along the lengthening road to the Kassala railway junction on the Sudanese border, 10TH Infantry Brigade of Indian 5TH Infantry Division set off east again towards Massawa. Massawa was some 50 miles away, 7,000 feet lower, and on the coast. On 10TH Brigade's left flank was Briggs Force, which had advanced cross-country from Keren and was approaching Massawa from the north along the coast.

Massawa

The Italians had 10,000 troops and 100 assorted tanks and armoured cars to defend Massawa. About 1,000 of the defenders at Massawa were veterans from Keren and another bloody battle seemed likely. Elements of 5TH Indian Division coming from Asmara and Briggs Force, cutting across country from Keren, converged on Massawa. After some initial strong opposition, the Italian ground forces defending Massawa, lacking fuel, ammunition, and food, crumpled and resistance collapsed. In the week preceding capture, Massawa harbour was thoroughly wrecked by Italian sabotage of machinery in shore facilities, the sinking of two large floating dry docks, and the calculated scuttling of sixteen large ships in the mouths of the north Naval Harbour, the central Commercial Harbour and the main South Harbour, blocking access in and out. Scuttled, too, was a large floating crane. The harbour was rendered useless until repairs and salvage efforts could clear it thirteen months later.

East Africa

Berbera

On 16TH March 1941, Operation Appearance was launched. Staged from Aden, two battalions from the Indian Army and one Somali commando detachment were landed on both sides of Berbera by British naval "Force D". The two Sikh battalions (which had been part of the defending force evacuated in August 1940), made the first successful Allied landing on an enemy-held beach during World War II. When the Sikhs landed, an Italian colonel[] waited with the 60 men who constituted the Berbera garrison. The garrison had been low on food and water for weeks. The Italians stood in formation on the beach and waited to surrender to the arriving British force. The British promptly "secured" Berbera. A British officer present at the Italian surrender later wrote: "War can be very embarrassing".

Hargeisa

On 20TH March, Hargeisa was captured. The British and Commonwealth forces in British Somaliland spent the next months clearing the colony of the last remnants of its former invaders. The Somaliland Camel Corps was re-founded in mid-April and, in addition to looking for Italians, re-acquired its job of rounding up local bandits. From British Somaliland, British and Commonwealth forces advanced westward into eastern Ethiopia. In late March, they linked up with advancing forces from the Southern Front around Harar and Diredawa in Ethiopia.

Amba Alagi

Wavell's strategic priority was for Platt to push southwards from the Sudan to Addis Ababa and for him to meet up with Cunningham pushing northwards from Kenya. A major obstacle for Platt was located at Amba Alagi, a 12,000-foot high mountain between Asmara and Addis Ababa. The Italians decided to defend the area around Amba Alagi in force. They drove galleries into the solid rock to protect their troops and to hold ample ammunition and stores. In this mountain fortress, the defenders, under command of the Duke of Aosta, thought themselves to be impregnable. Platt gave Major-General Mosley Mayne and the Indian 5TH Infantry Division the task of taking Amba Alagi. Mayne was only able to deploy a single expanded brigade, the Indian 29TH Infantry Brigade, for this action. His attacking force was, therefore, inferior in numbers to the Italian defending force. Mayne's limited deployment was due to the demands on the British for internal security and for protecting their lines of communication. The supply route to Amba Alagi extended nearly 250 miles south of Asmara and some 400 miles from the main rail head at Kassala. On 3RD May 1941, Mayne sent in a feint attack from the east while, in the early hours of 4TH May, the main attack was made from the northwest over the hills. The hills were fiercely defended by the Italians.

East Africa

Amba Alagi (Cont.)

On 11TH May, Pienaar's brigade group arrived from the south and was put under Mayne's command. By 14TH May Amba Alagi was surrounded. With the arrival of Pienaar, the 7000 Italian troops of the Duke of Aosta were directly attacked by 9,000 British troops and more than 20,000 Ethiopian irregulars. A final assault was planned for 15TH May, but a fortuitous artillery shell hit an Italian fuel dump and ruptured a vessel containing oil. This caused oil to flow into the remaining drinking water of the Italian defenders. The lack of drinkable water then forced the Italians to surrender. On 18TH May, the Duke of Aosta surrendered his embattled forces at Amba Alagi. General Mayne agreed to surrender with "full military honors" (allowing the troops to march off the battlefield in formation and then surrender their arms) in exchange for the Duke's agreement to hand over the battlefield 'clean'. This put the Duke on his honour to identify all mines and booby-traps to the troops taking over the area and included his agreement that the Italians' remaining equipment and stores should not be sabotaged or destroyed. Mayne later wrote:

'The Duke of Aosta was delighted with my concession and, as he told me, gave a rigid and unmistakable edict that the hand-over was to be complete and clean, making it quite clear that any breach of his orders would mean that he had broken his own word. So the Italians did pay up. We got everything intact and no one, save Abyssinian patriots who broke all bounds in their search for loot and deserved their fate, suffered so much as a scratch from a hidden mine, although there were plenty of them about.

'The enemy was granted "honours of war". The fortress, with all its stores complete, was handed over and the Italians, under arms, marched down the long winding road. While the victorious troops watched from the hill tops, the defeated army came down in a long column, eight abreast past the point where General Mayne took their salute. A few hundred yards further on was a guard of honour, composed of one platoon from each battalion, British, Indian, and South African, which presented arms as the tired Italians marched by. A pipe band playing "The Flower of the Forest" added to the pathos of the scene, as the vanquished troops filed into the village of Medani Alem and laid down their arms. It had been a very complete victory and a glorious end to a campaign, which will remain famous for its speed and the magnificent fighting of always outnumbered Imperial forces. The 5TH Indian Divison had advanced over 500 miles across deserts, up mountains, in burning heat and drenching rain, had taken part in the fearful battle of Keren, had won the fights at Barentu, Ad Teclesan and Massawa, and had taken prisoners more than twice its own numbers.'
(Government of India. 1942 p108)

East Africa

11TH Sikh Regiment

During the Second World War, all the Battalions of the Regiment served in several theatres of war against the Japanese, Germans and Italians. The 4TH Battalion was the first to be mobilised, and set sail for Egypt in September 1940. After a short spell at Sidi Barrani, it joined the 'Gazelle Force' for the drive into Eritrea. The Battalion kept in pursuit of the Italians at Kassala and Agordat, as they kept slipping away before the attack. Finally the Battalion was in the Brigade attack on Aqua Col, a strongly held feature; in early 1941.The fighting was so fierce, that of the two companies that went into the assault, one had 87 casualties. "Naik Ujagar Singh, moving ahead of his section, attacked a machine gun post single handed. He shot down two of the enemy with his rifle, and then, after throwing grenades into the post, rushed to the position and bayoneted the remainder of the detachment, and captured the machine gun". On 15TH March, the Sikhs stormed the 'Samana Ridge' of the Keren Hills. In this action, Naik Nasib Singh, who had six Italians to his score, won an Indian Distinguished Service Medal. Another Indian Distinguished Service Medal was awarded to Naik Daulat Singh for fine and resolute leadership. On 30TH November, the Battalion was involved, with the help of 1ST Punjab Regiment in desperate fighting at Omars. They overran the garrison of 3,000 men, at a combined cost of 336 casualties. Jemadar Gurbaksh Singh was awarded a posthumous Indian Order of Merit for outstanding gallantry, and an Indian Distinguished Service Medal was awarded to Havildar Karam Singh for great personal courage and leadership.

12TH Frontier Force Regiment

During the Second World War, the Battalions of 12TH Frontier Force Regiment, served in several theatres of war against the Japanese, Germans and Italians. The 1ST and 3RD Battalions served in North Africa, Syria, Iraq and Iran against the Axis forces. During September 1941, 1ST battalion arrived in the Sudan and was moved to the frontier. On November 6TH, it joined a small mixed force and attacked the enemy position at Fort Gallabat. The Fort was captured after fierce hand-to-hand fighting. After the action the battalion was occupied in constant offensive patrolling, and causing further casualties to the enemy. From November 6TH to November 11TH an action was fought near Jebel Serobatib, some thirty miles northeast of Kassala, over very difficult rocky country. One company of the Battalion assisted in the attack, in which 262 prisoners were taken and considerable damage inflicted. The Battalions were heavily involved in the fighting at Agordat, Keren, and Amba Alagi and then moved on to fight at Gazala, Bir Hacheim, and El Adem. Finally, 1ST Battalion was ordered to Italy in 1943. The following Sikh soldiers were awarded the Indian Distinguished Service Medal for their gallantry in action in 1942: Naik Dalip Singh, L.D. Chanan Singh, and Jemadar Sant Singh.

East Africa

13TH Frontier Force Rifles

The 13TH Frontier Force Rifles served in North Africa, Egypt, Syria, and Iraq. During September 1941, 4TH Battalion arrived in the Sudan and became part of a special independent force to watch Kassala, and greatly distinguished itself both in the preliminary offensive patrolling and during the advance into Eritrea. This small body operated from Gash Delta. Small parties of the enemy were frequently captured, telephone lines were cut, and convoys of lorries bringing supplies were shot up. The battle for Barentu was a grim soldier's battle, in which the better men won by sheer fighting ability. On January 21ST, 13TH Frontier Force Rifles evicted a Colonial Brigade from a strong position astride the road and the fighting continued for three days, the enemy resisting most stubbornly, and finally Barentu fell on February 2ND. Another position considered impregnable by the Italians was captured, after some hard fighting in which the 13TH Frontier Force Rifles particularly distinguished themselves. Finally, the Italians fell back on Amba Alagi; it was a very strong position on a 3,350 metre high mastiff. After some fierce fighting, the Italians surrendered ceremonially on 19TH May 1941. After an incursion into Syria, where they captured Deir ez Zor and Raqqa, they were back in North Africa and fought at the battles of Gazala, Sidi Razegh, and Gambut Mersa Matruh. The resistance in North Africa ended on 12TH May. The following Sikh soldiers were awarded the Indian Distinguished Service Medal for their gallantry in action in the Middle East:
Havildar Babu Singh, Naik Indar Singh, Naik Nika Singh in 1941, and Havildar Kehar Singh in 1943.

Jemadar Dhera Singh
2ND Punjab Regiment

"The success of the attack of 'B' Company on an enemy strong point on 25TH November 1941 was very largely due to the courageous and cool headed leadership of Jemadar Dhera Singh. Directing the centre and the right hand platoons in broad daylight, in full view of the enemy and under considerable fire, he coordinated their attack, and by his example of coolness and daring, led them into the final charge with such dash and determination that the position was taken, resulting in the capture of two Italian Officers, 42 other ranks, a 20 mm gun and other weapons and war materials.There is no doubt that risking his life, so that his men could see him, was a great factor in preventing any hesitation, which at that point might have been fatal. On many previous occasions, Jemadar Dhera Singh led his platoon successfully against enemy positions, showing utter disregard for his own personal safety. For continuous good work and exhibition of sterling qualities of leadership throughout the Eritrean campaign and the operations in the Western Desert, Jemadar Dhera Singh was awarded the Indian Order of Merit."

KENYA

Kenya Police (with Diljit Singh Bahra)

In 1888, Imperial British East Africa Company (I.B.E.A.C.) took over the British concessions negotiated with the Sultan of Zanzibar, which also included Kenya. In the early stages of British occupation, I.B.E.A.C set up a police force, primarily to buttress the occupying power. This force drew armed African guards - known as Askaris - into its rank and file under the command of Somali and Sikh officers, with a few Europeans filling its uppermost echelons. By 1897, the I.B.E.A.C had set up a police headquarters in Mombasa and command stations in Vangu, Rabai, Malindi, Lamu, and Kismayu. By 1902, police units had been set up in Nairobi, Mombasa, and Kisumu. These units were soon brought under a single command named the British East Africa Police that would later, in 1920 with the emergence of Kenya Colony, be renamed the Kenya Police.

Inspector Kapur Singh

The first Sikh Police Officer recruited was Kapur Singh, an Inspector from Punjab, who was brought over from India in 1895 to join the ranks of Kenya Police. His sons Satbachan Singh and Laxman Singh followed him. Satbachan joined in the early 1920s, served in Nairobi, Kisumu, Lamu, and Voi, and retired as a Chief Inspector in 1945/46. They were followed by a galaxy of Sikhs, who had served in the Indian Army with honour in Central Africa and Uganda, before transferring to the Indian Police and then immigrating to Kenya, where they joined Kenya Police. Until 1948, Asians and Africans were prevented from rising above the position of Inspector. At that time, there were only 5 Asian Chief Inspectors and 34 Inspectors and Assistant Inspectors. In contrast, the Europeans had 154 officers of that rank. That year the 43 colonial police forces came under the umbrella of the Colonial Police Service, under the Command of an Inspector General and conditions of Service for the Asians improved. Many Sikhs joined the newly created Kenya Police Reserve (KPR). The Mau Mau emergency in the 1950's attracted more Sikhs to the Police. In the early years, until 1948, Asians joined the police service in the rank of Assistant Inspectors.

Kenya

Kenya Police (Cont.)

Notable Sikh Officers who joined around this period and raised to the Superintendent rank were Bhajan Singh Bohi, Gurbax Singh Kehar, and Hazara Singh. Whilst a Chief Inspector in 1950, Bhajan Singh attended the Colonial Police Course in Hendon, London.

Superintendent Kartar Singh Bharaj

Kartar Singh Bharaj joined Kenya Police in the late twenties/early thirties and served for 30 years. His four sons followed in his footsteps. Mohinder Singh Bharaj joined the force in 1945 and retired as a Superintendent of Police in 1975. Nirmal Singh Bharaj joined the force in 1948 and was in the Fingerprints department based at CID Headquarters in Nairobi. He served for 30 years. Parminder Singh Bharaj and Parlad Singh Bharaj were both uniform officers in Kenya Police and retired as Inspectors. Inderjeet Singh Geddi joined in late twenties/early thirties. He retired as a Chief Inspector. Rajinder Singh Kehar joined the force in late 40s. He served in General duties and special branch in Nairobi.

Superintendent Karam Singh Panesar

Karam Singh Panesar, joined Kenya Police in September 1946, and served in Thikha, Nanyiku, Thomson Falls, Nakuru, Kapasibat, Kisumu, and headquarters in Nairobi. He attended the Colonial Police Course at Hendon, London, England in 1958, and Bramshill Staff College in Hampshire, England in 1962. He retired in April 1974 as Senior Superintendent of Police and was Acting Assistant Commissioner of Police for six months until his retirement. He was the most senior Sikh Police Officer in Kenya and was the senior investigation officer in the high profile murder investigation of Kenya's Cabinet Minister, Tom Mboya in July 1969.

Kenya Police (Cont.)

Avtar Singh Matharu joined the force after leaving school in January 1953 as a constable and rose to the rank of Assistant Superintendent of Police when he retired in 1967. He served in Nairobi, Nyanza Province, and Kisumu. He attended the Colonial Police Course at Hendon, London, England in 1961. Inderjeet Singh Kehar also joined in January 1953. He attended Bramshill Staff College in Hampshire, England in 1963. He retired as ASP in 1967. Joginder Singh Sokhi, who also joined in 1953 and rose to the rank of Senior Superintendent of Police (CID) when he retired in the eighties. Tarsem Singh Rumpal joined the force in 1953, initially as a civilian. He transferred to regular uniform police in 1956. He served at several stations, including Nakuru, and then in CID HQ. He retired as Chief Inspector.

Chief Inspector Hardev Singh Kular

Hardev Singh Kular joined the civil department of the police in 1953 and then the regular force in 1955 as Assistant Inspector. He became the Chief Prosecutor in Nairobi and retired in 1969 as Chief Inspector. He served as a prosecutor in Nairobi, Mombasa and Thika. He represented Kenya at the 1956 Melbourne and 1960 Rome Olympic Games as a hockey player and in 1972 Munich Games as Kenya's Team Coach. He was Kenya's Team Manager at the 1988 Seoul Olympic Games. Balbir Singh Sidhu, a member of the police civil staff also represented Kenya at hockey at the 1956 Melbourne Olympic Games. Jagnandan Singh was another notable personality who worked in the fingerprint department and represented Kenya at hockey at the Rome Olympic Games in 1960.

Kenya

Kenya Police (with Harjinder Singh Kanwal)

The Kenya Police was founded approximately at the beginning of the 20TH century. Around 1890, the Uganda Railway line started its mammoth journey from the coastal town of Mombasa, Kenya, towards the hinterland, to reach Port Florence (Kisumu, then in Uganda – the reason why the railway line was called Uganda Railways). Towards the end of the century, about 32,000 Indians worked on the Uganda Railway at one time or another. Mr. A. M. Jeevanjee, who had previous experience in successfully recruiting men for the Imperial British East Africa Company, including a 300-strong police force, recruited most of them under contract from the North West Province (Punjab) of India. During the strenuous laying of the railway line, ample difficulties were encountered by the contractors and the labour force. Wild animals, especially lions, the man-eaters of Tsavo, were a terror to the humans plus the marauding African tribes who were a considerable hindrance to the work being carried out.

A Sikh soldier with son employed by the Uganda Railways around 1890 for policing the railway line

Kenya

Kenya Police (Cont.)

The British hired professional hunters to deal with the lions and other wild animals. During this traumatic period, a police force was formed to safeguard the property and the lives of the labourers, by keeping regular watch during the construction work. The armed guards, who were called the 'Askaris', were on regular beats. The wild plains of Kenya were turned into a law-abiding region by this small group of police, who patrolled day and night to create an atmosphere of safety and tranquillity.

An excerpt from 'Cuckoo in Kenya' by W. R. Foran depicts the exploits of the Police around 1904. He was sent to Nairobi Police Station to relieve Inspector Basant Singh and to make him serve under him. In the book, he writes:

" . . . *The Sikh Inspector accepted being deposed with a friendly smile, which I thought did him immense credit and seemed anxious to prove helpful to the stranger within their midst . . . . All the records were kept in Urdu by the Indian police-writers; and Basant Singh seemed the only man of the staff with more than a superficial knowledge of English. The handicap confronting me made my heart sink into the pit of my stomach. I felt like a lamb among wolves. . . . Still more agitated now than when I entered the police station, I transferred my interest to a hefty stack of police files and criminal investigation reports. Basant Singh had quietly placed them on the table, speaking in rapid and fluent Hindustani far too fluent for me to understand all he said. . . . . I glanced up sheepishly at the smiling, watchful Sikh Inspector, seeking inspiration from his non-committal face. There glowed no ray of hope for me behind those bright brown eyes and the carefully trimmed black beard. My heart slumped down into my boots. . . . . I much question if he realised how great was the chasm of my ignorance. If he did grasp this, he was gentleman and sportsman enough to conceal the fact. I owe Basant Singh much for steering me safely through those trying days of noviciate. . . . . The splendid Sikh had served with the Railway Police from the very beginning of construction work on the railway, and for the past two years had been in full charge of Nairobi Police Station. He was a great 'Shikari' (hunter), a brave man and worthy of the highest traditions of the gallant Sikh Units in the Indian Army in which he served with honour before transferring to the Indian Police and then coming to British East Africa. Basant Singh had killed twenty-four lions during the advance of the railway to Nairobi, making a habit of hunting them with a .303-rifle, for which he possessed only .256 calibre ammunition. To make these cartridges fit his rifle, he wrapped them around with paper. This intrepid Sikh sportsman was a first-class shot, but there are not many who would have dared tackle lions with ammunition that did not fit the rifle. Certainly I would not.* "

(Foran, 1936)

Kenya

Kenya Police (Cont.)

A small town, Machakos, 43 miles from Nairobi was supposed to be the capitol of Kenya but later on Nairobi took preference over it and the building of one of the charismatic cities of the world began. Pioneers like Lord Delamere and General Grogan were the backbone of the Kenya governing body and they had a big hand in the development of Nairobi and the rest of the country.

The British are known as great organisers and in view of that a proper police force was established with the help of Indians from India, especially the Punjabi Sikhs, who were well known for their valour and loyalty, which the British had envisaged during the Punjab battles and during the First World War, which was second to none at the time. The British were aware of the potential of the Sikhs. These sturdy men, who were skilled and semi skilled artisans, were a great help in building the country. The British were aware of the faithfulness and the bravery of the Sikhs, thereby giving them the jobs, which were suitable to their character. The skilled and semi skilled labour force was one aspect and the administration side the other, where the more educated ones were employed to do the clerical work of the East African railways. The Police force grew from strength to strength with plenty of Asians serving diligently and reaching top posts. With the steady growth of Nairobi as the capitol city of Kenya, the Kenya Police also grew into a force worth reckoning. The Asians were an integral part of it, with the Africans on lower ranks. At that time, the inhabitants of Kenya were divided into three communities, Europeans, Asians and Africans. The 'Asians' (collectively Hindu, Sikh and Muslims) being the inhabitants of India. Initially the police chiefs were the British white men, who eventually gave way to Asians, especially Sikhs, who were considered loyal and proficient officers. After the first Sikh Inspector Kapur Singh, the police force was infested with Punjabis who did an excellent job in keeping the law intact in the country.

Sikh Police officers around 1945

Kenya

Kenya Police (Cont.)

Sergeant Harnam Singh at Kisumu 1905

Channi Singh - personal bodyguard to President Mzee Jomo Kenyatta from 1963-1969

Kenya

Some Sikh and African Police Officers with European Chiefs around 1960

Kenya Regiment 1962
With European, African and Sikh members

The NANDI

The Nandi is a Kenyan ethnic group or tribe living in the highland areas of the Nandi Hills. The Nandi Hills are lush green rolling hills at the edge of the Great Rift Valley. There is also a small town named Nandi Hills. It was a battle ground against the Luo and Luhya communities and the burial site of the renowned Nandi seer Koitalel Arap Samoei. He is buried under a symbolic tree, on top of Nandi Hills with its red earth. When Koitalel was killed by British officer Richard Meinertzhagen the ground turned red on the spot of his death. Nandi form a sub-group of the Kalenjin people. Before British colonization, they were sedentary cattle-herders, sometimes also practicing agriculture; their settlements were more or less evenly distributed rather than being grouped into villages. Like other Nilotic peoples, they were noted warriors. In pre-colonial times, they enjoyed a fearsome reputation as fighters; Arab slave-traders and ivory-traders took care to avoid the area.

Nandi Warrior
(A. C. Hollis)

The caravans for Uganda or for the European settlers, which consisted of parties of porters, for everything had to be carried by humans on their heads or on donkeys, passed within sight of the Nandi Escarpment and such easy pickings were a considerable temptation to the Nandi, to which they often succumbed.

The Nandi

1ST Expedition, October 1895

On 20TH August 1895, the Nandi attacked the caravan bound for Uganda. A wounded Swahili reported that the mail party had been attacked, the mail burnt, and the boxes broken. On 7TH October, another attack on a caravan was reported, in which nine men were killed, six wounded and 40 head of cattle stolen. These and similar aggressive acts were the cause of the first military expedition against the Nandi, designed to safeguard the route between Uganda and the coast. On 14TH October 1895, Major Cunningham of the Uganda Rifles led a punitive force of 1,000 against the Nandi. Cunningham divided his force into two columns, the larger under himself to march east on Kapiyet, and a smaller of about 100 men under Captain Sitwell to approach from the south. The main column set out through the villages of Kabaras, which the Nandi had recently attacked. While thus engaged his patrols reported that the column was being watched by large concentration of Nandi. In the valley of the River Kimondi, Cunningham stood to face a sudden attack, delivered by about 500 tribesmen, who advanced rapidly through the long grass in a formation resembling three-sided square. It was the first time that the Sudanese had faced the tossing skin headdresses and flashing, long-bladed spears of the Nandi warriors, but they stood firm and their fire checked the attack before it reached close quarters, though the enemy scored a minor success by cutting off and annihilating a party of fourteen men. After this action, Cunningham resumed his march to the southeast. In the early morning, darkness of 17TH November the Nandi again attacked, creeping up in large numbers towards the boma. The sentries were alert and the attack was beaten off.

2ND Expedition, February 1897

'Peace' was established with the Nandi in February 1896 and a post set up at Nandi Fort, about four miles west of Kapsabet. By the end of the year, due to further raids and murders, a further punitive expedition was launched. The field force-marched first to Eldama Ravine, where it was split into two columns, one to operate against the Kamasya tribe and the other against the Elgeyo tribe. On 20TH June, the columns passed into friendly country. The proceeds of the expedition totalled 238 cattle and 7,838 sheep and goats. These were distributed to the accompanying Masai and the troops. While the second Nandi expedition was in progress, despatches from Buganda, reported some kind of political mischief was brewing and ordered the force to get back to Entebbe as soon as possible. The Nandi operations were therefore broken off, rather sooner than was desirable, as the expedition returned to Buganda.

The Nandi

3RD Expedition, July – October 1900

In 1900, persistent looting and attacks necessitated another expedition. Lieutenant Colonel J. T. Evatt commanded this expedition. In June, Captain Parkin and a small expedition of 25 soldiers and some Masai spearmen killed 25 Nandi and captured 229 cattle and 1,800 sheep and goats. However, they were followed up by the Nandi and lost two killed and one wounded. The action precipitated an expedition, which absorbed virtually all the resources of the Uganda Rifles. The Nandi dispersed and refused to fight, but cut up a number of small parties, even annihilating 20 Sudanese in one skirmish. Evatt's camp was attacked and might well have been overwhelmed if the Nandi, who fought with great courage, had not been driven off by fire from the Maxim gun. Casualties had been heavy on the Nandi side with 74 killed, 1,039 cattle, 3,100 sheep captured, while the Army and auxiliaries' casualties had been 13 killed, and 111 wounded. The troops that carried out these operations were from 1ST Battalion Uganda Rifles (4TH Battalion, Kings African Rifles). There were also 20 police officers from Kisumu and 225 Indian troops. As was usual at the time, Indian troops in the Uganda Rifles came from virtually every Sikh infantry unit in the Indian Army.

Kibigori Station

Owing to the temporary arrangement of dual occupation of the former Eastern Province of Uganda, the fourth series of operations against the Nandi group of tribes involved the 3RD, 4TH, and 5TH battalions of the Kings African Rifles. The province was officially transferred to East Africa on 1ST April 1902. Five days later, the Nandi raided Kibigori Station and stole thirty steel sleepers. It was the first time the tribe had attempted to carry off such weight of metal, and Hobly, the Assistant Commissioner, wiring O.C. Troops at Muhoroni to pursue the thieves, left for Nandi with 30 police. On arrival, he heard that Captain Lindesay of five K.A.R. had reached Kaptumo with 50 Sikh Sepoys, and that the Nandi had just stolen another sixty sleepers. On 10TH April, Hobly left Kaptumo with and escort of 110 rifles for a meeting with several hundred Nandi warriors, including representatives of every section of the tribe. After a long palaver, the Nandi admitted the thefts, saying that they were hungry and had taken the iron to cut up and sell for food. Hobly warned them that "this was practically tantamount to an act of war, for the railway was as precious to us as their cattle were to them", and the missing sleepers were recovered.

The Nandi

4TH Expedition, April 1903

Early in February Captain Nicholson made a second visit to the Kamelilo, with an escort of 30 rifles 4TH K.A.R. and 30 rifles 5TH K.A.R. with a maxim gun. Their leader frankly acknowledged the thefts and the murder of two Indian coolies, and was given ten days to restore the material and surrender the murderers. The Kamelilo made no attempt to honour their promises. Kamelilo continued their thefts and attacked a Somali trader. Another visit by the civil authorities failed to obtain a reparation or guarantee of future good behaviour. The tribesmen were again entreated to listen to reason, but on this occasion met all accusations with absolute denial. All efforts at a peaceful settlement having failed, on 14TH April Hobley formally instructed Nicholson to inflict upon the Kamlilo a compulsory fine of livestock and not to leave the country until the elders unanimously sued for peace. Nicholson's intention was to concentrate first on capturing cattle and prisoners, sending them back to Muhoroni under guard. He would then be free to continue burning huts and destroying crops until the Kamelilo sued for peace. The fourth expedition against the Nandi set out on 28TH April and its operations lasted for five weeks over a tract of country bordering twenty miles of the railway line. The Kamelilo could not be tempted into open attack, but were constantly on the wait for stragglers and shot poisoned arrows into the camps at night. Rain fell daily and all streams were flooded, but the columns forced their way across steep mountains and through ravines, practically living on the country and destroying all the crops they did not consume. At length, on 1ST June, when 300 head of cattle and about 4,500 goats and sheep had been captured, and the Nandi had lost a hundred warriors, their envoys sued for peace. The expedition had cost two Sepoys and two porters killed, and one Sepoy wounded.

5TH Expedition, October 1905

As before, the tribe committed further raids and murdered more Europeans. In July 1905, the Commissioner delivered an ultimatum. When this expired he ordered an expedition on a scale that was intended to settle matters for once and for all. The Nandi expedition of 1915 was the largest punitive expedition ever to be assembled in the Protectorate. The final campaign against them was over in December 1905. The Nandi had 750 killed and 30,000 cattle and goats captured. The Nandi were moved into a smaller reserve and thereafter no further trouble occurred.

UGANDA

Uganda has a rich and varied military history. Many of the country's pre-colonial societies possessed complex military organizations. One of the most powerful traditional leaders, Kabarega, king (*omukama*) of Bunyoro from 1870 to 1899, transformed his personal guard into a standing army. This force used a variety of modern weapons, including Remington rifles, and percussion muskets, breech and muzzleloaders. Mutesa I, king (*kabaka*) of Buganda from 1852 to 1884, also raised a standing army, led by a general and several captains. At the height of its power, Mutesa's army of several thousand warriors had more than 1,500 rifles. After Britain became interested in Uganda's economic potential in the nineteenth century, a group of British merchants created a small military force to protect their interests. In 1890 the Imperial British East Africa Company, which administered the territory that would become Uganda, established an army to defend British investments there. This force of 300 included Sudanese soldiers (most of whom were recruited in Egypt) who were organized into a Zanzibar Levy. The following year, Selim Bey, who commanded a military unit for the German explorer Emin Pasha, agreed to allow about 100 of his Sudanese troops to join the British force in East Africa. After Britain declared a provisional protectorate over Uganda in 1893, the colonial authorities formed a military unit of 600 regulars and 300 reservists, most of whom were Sudanese. Four Arabic-speaking British officers assumed responsibility for their training. In December 1893, Colvile led a force of several thousand Buganda fighters and 420 Sudanese in a campaign against Bunyoro, Buganda's arch-rival. This "pacification" succeeded in subduing Bunyoro and secured for Buganda a politically dominant role in the protectorate. Sudanese soldiers provided the mainstay of the Ugandan army, whose task was to preserve British interests and to launch punitive expeditions against those who rebelled against the crown. In 1895, the colonial authorities organized these soldiers into rifle companies, which became known as the Uganda Rifles. Despite the good reputation they achieved at riflery, many Sudanese became disillusioned with the rigors of military service in a foreign country under British command. Their grievances included loneliness, low pay, poor food, bad officers, and frequent reassignments, often to remote areas. When the colonial government failed to resolve these problems, the Uganda Rifles mutinied in 1897, killing the commander of the force and five other European officers. Discontent spread rapidly through Uganda's Muslim community, which was sympathetic to the Sudanese soldiers, and violence erupted in several regions. Finally, Britain dispatched troops from India to suppress the mutiny. To prevent another revolt, the colonial government diversified the composition of the military. It reduced the number of Sudanese recruits, increased recruiting among the Indians and Ugandan Africans, and increased the overall ratio of European officers to soldiers. The government also granted a 400 percent military pay raise. But by December 1900, military expenses were eroding the profitability of the colonial enterprise, so Special Commissioner Sir Harry H. Johnston organized a lower-paid constabulary of 1,450-armed natives.

Uganda

The following year, to further reduce costs, British officials consolidated all military forces in East Africa and British Somaliland into the King's African Rifles (KAR). In 1903, the Uganda Armed Constabulary Ordinance and the Uganda Prisons Ordinance separated the police and prisons from the KAR. The colonial authorities maintained racial separation in the military by assigning Africans to 4TH Battalion and Indians to 5TH Battalion. In 1913, the authorities disbanded 5TH Battalion and supplemented the Ugandan unit with the Uganda Volunteer Reserve and Uganda Rifles Corps, both auxiliary forces that could be used to quell domestic disturbances. The Uganda Rifles took part in several punitive expeditions and armed patrols in Uganda and neighbouring territory. The best documented among these were against the peoples of western Kenya between 1902 and 1906. The campaigns against Sheikh Muhammad Abdullah Hassan (dubbed the "Mad Mullah" by foreigners) in British Somaliland in 1909 and 1910, and an expedition into southern Sudan (then Jubaland) are both covered in the articles on Somaliland and Jubaland.

Review of Sikh troop at Entebbe, Uganda, 1906

Uganda

Buganda 1890

In 1890, Captain Lugard arrived with a few soldiers to impose the Imperial British East Africa Company's rule on Buganda. The country was on the verge of civil war. The Muslim party, with its Arab allies, was preparing an attack on Buganda from Bunyoro. Lugard's aim was to compose the differences between the hostile factions and to instruct Mwanga (King of Buganda) in the art of impartial kingship, but it soon became plain to him that little progress could be made without some independent means of upholding his own authority and maintaining the Company's prestige. He had left Mombasa with 70 Sudanese, and by the time he reached Buganda, he had about 50 Sudanese and Somali 'troops' in whom a semblance of discipline had been inculcated. 270 porters, most of whom were quite useless for fighting, eleven rounds of ammunition per man, and a worn-out maxim gun. In January 1981, Captain W. H. Williams joined him with 75 Sudanese, 100 Swahili and another maxim gun. While Lugard devoted his energies to political affairs, Williams took in hand the training of the force on which so much depended. Another safari reached Buganda from the coast in March, and the best of the men were taken to strengthen the little military force. The fort, which had been considerably enlarged, now housed 7 Europeans and 650 men.

The Kabarega, 1891

It was not long before the force was in action. Kabarega of Bunyoro had joined hands with the Muslim party, and Lugard went west with the Buganda army to meet him. His troops marched in the centre of a vast throng of 25,000 Buganda Levies, advancing cross-country in parallel column, with its chief at the head. On 7TH May, with Lugard's force in the centre of the attack, the Muslims were met and scattered. Lugard wanted to pursue, but his allies refused and the levies broke up.

Selim Bey, 1891

Lugard decided on a course that had long been in his mind. Captain Williams was sure that no more Sudanese could be recruited in Egypt. But Emin Pasha's troops, under the command of Selim Bey, had the reputation of being the 'best material for soldiery in Africa', and Lugard thought that with their aid the Company might hold both Buganda and Bunyoro. Selim Bey agreed that he would serve in alliance with the British, but retaining for the time being the Egyptian flag. Lugard held a parade to explain the new agreement, and afterwards the two regiments marched past, headed by their drums, bugles and tattered flags. About 600 were armed with rifles.

Uganda

Stocked forts, 1891

Lugard planned to split the Sudanese into garrisons of manageable proportions in a line of stockaded forts along the southern boundaries of Bunyoro. Before returning to Buganda, he built and garrisoned five forts with the whole of 1ST Regiment and part of 2ND Regiment. From 2ND Regiment Lugard selected 89 men under Selim Bey to augment the garrison at Kampala.

Civil War, 1892

Within a few weeks, civil war was raging in Buganda. Eventually a division of the country was made between the three parties, six provinces being allotted to the Protestants, three to the Muslims and one, the province of Buddu, to the Catholics. Complaints of Lugard's actions during the mutiny, had been raised in Europe by the missionary societies, and in this critical situation, he decided to leave for home.

"Local allies were essential, and for this reason Lugard was driven to support the Protestant interest, to the detriment of the impartial role he sought to maintain. His introduction of the Sudanese troops created many problems for Uganda in the years to come. They may have been 'the best material for soldiery in Africa', but only if properly disciplined and led. Lugard's line of forts looked formidable on a map, but in practice, they were merely a handful of isolated, earth-banked stockades, not even defensible in design, with palisades too high to fire over and without loopholes. As an effective barrier to Kabarega and the gunrunning caravans of the Arabs, they were of little use, except as bases for mobile patrols. But the Sudanese officers had neither the incentive nor the initiative needed, and in fact were soon hard put even to maintain themselves, especially in the forts 3 and 4, which were situated in a foodless area. Political motives caused by the aspirations of other European nations, the importance attached to the Nile, the desire for economic expansion, the zeal of the missionaries and their supporters at home, were all factors impelling the attempt to do too much with too slender means. There was no time for consolidation. The hand full of soldiers and administrators, who laid foundations of the new protectorate in the early 1890's, had to rely upon such military resources as lay at hand. The result was an exhausting succession of campaigns that culminated at last in unexpected disaster." (Moyse-Bartlett, 2002 p. 53)

Uganda

Uganda protectorate, 1893

Sir Gerald Portal, the British Agent and Consul-General at Zanzibar, was sent to examine the situation and report on the best means of dealing with the country. Portal thought that the declaration of a protectorate would be the simplest course. He recommended that the Imperial British East Africa Company's jurisdiction should cease, and that a commissioner should be appointed over Buganda, Busoga, and Kavirondo. In 1893, the Imperial British East Africa Company transferred its rights to the British Government, and a Protectorate was proclaimed, to which effect a treaty was signed in 1893. The British government decided to declare a protectorate only over the area covered by Buganda and its provinces, bounded by Koki, Ankole, Bunyoro, and Busoga, territories in which arrangements were to be limited to agreements with the local chiefs. Such was the intention, but even before the protectorate was declared, a series of campaigns had begun that led inevitably, during succeeding years, to the extension of the protectorate boundaries.

Bunyoro, November 1893

In November 1893, Colonel H. Colvile, the new British representative, reached Kampala with two other officers. From now on, other military officers continued to be seconded for service in Uganda. A threatening situation was developing in Bunyoro, for Kabarega was rumoured to have an army of 8,000 men equipped with firearms and 20,000 spearmen. Captain Owen reported that an attack was expected on the forts in Singo, and Colvile decided to take the initiative. On his instructions, Captain Owen made a night march with 200 men. On discovering his enemy awaiting him in a well-concealed position, he attacked with small arms fire for three hours, and eventually drove the Banyoro from the long grass and bush in a headlong flight. This action had a salutary effect on Owens's Sudanese and Buganda allies, who had expected such a small force to be overwhelmed. The effort to crush Kabarega was continued with greater intensity. However, regular troops were so few that they had nearly always to be supplemented by levies from friendly tribes, who fought under their own chiefs. The campaign often differed but little from the inter-tribal warfare of former times. Moreover, rival forces were by no means always ill- matched, as many years elapsed before the illicit sale of firearms could be stopped. The fighting tribes of Africa often showed considerable military skill and Kabarega in particular was an outstanding tribal commander.

Uganda

Lubwa Hill, October 1897

A mutiny in 1897 of the Sudanese troops used by the colonial government led Britain to take a more active interest in the Uganda Protectorate. An exploring expedition was projected, and Major J. R. L. Macdonald chosen to command it. The government of India had seconded two British officers and Jemadar Bhagwan Singh with 30 men of 14TH and 15TH Sikh Regiments as an escort for Macdonald's party. Six other officers came direct from England, and Macdonald engaged a caravan of 350 Swahili porters, increased later by another hundred. Meanwhile a mutiny had broken out among the Sudanese regiments, who were joined by the men from Njemps, and the whole party made for Mumia's. After threatening to attack the fort and demanding rations, they eventually withdrew. The mutineers next made for the fort at Lubwa, hoping to raise the garrison and join forces with the disaffected Muslim elements in Buganda. The whole force, numbering about 600 Sudanese and 200 Buganda Muslims, was admitted to the fort. Major Macdonald followed and occupied a hill dominating the fort with 10 Europeans, 17 Sikhs, and 340 half-trained Swahilis. On the following day, the mutineers attacked Major MacDonald's force for five hours, but were defeated and driven back into the fort. This was a remarkable feat by the Sikhs, who with their Maxim guns had performed prodigies of valour, and the half- trained Swahilis and by the fact, the mutineers were led by experienced native officers. Another force, crossing a swamp supposed to be impassable, attacked the rebel stockade at Kabagambi, and carried it with great gallantry.

Writing about the Sikhs, Major Macdonald stated. 'This detachment fully maintained the great reputation of the Sikhs, and fought with such gallantry that they secured the admiration of all'. Ten Sikh soldiers were awarded the Indian Order of Merit for conspicuous gallantry during these operations. (Sikh Cyber Museum, 2003b)

Action at Lubwa Hill

Uganda

Uganda, 1897

In October, the Foreign Office was warned that the local forces were unable to cope with the situation, and advised to order to Uganda the 300 Sikhs of the East African Indian Contingent, then at Mombasa and to arrange for a battalion from India to replace them. In November, the Sikh Contingent began to move inland. 150 Sepoys, under Lieutenant Scott, going forward from the railhead on 23RD and another 70 Sepoys following soon afterwards. The garrison of East African Rifles at Machakos was also relieved and sent to Uganda.

Operations at Lubwa Fort, October-December 1897

From October 18TH to the beginning of December, when reinforcements began to arrive, the Government troops consisted of 17 Sikhs and about 350 partly trained Swahilis. During this period, two engagements and seven skirmishes had taken place, in which 19 Government troops were killed and 45 wounded. The Sudanese mutineers still numbered between 400 and 500 men and were occupying a very strong position on the margin of the lake. As soon as reinforcements arrived, an advanced fort on the peninsula was constructed, 1,000 yards from the enemy's fort, the working parties being protected by covering parties. The main work was completed and held by 90 regular soldiers and 140 Swahilis, who beat off a night attack the same day. On 9TH and 10TH the cutting down of the enemy food supply by the Waganda tribesmen commenced, covered by parties of Swahili soldiers. Whilst these operations were in progress, the enemy made a desperate attack on the left flank with some 150 men, who crept up to within a few yards, concealed by the long grass and the thick vegetation. The left flank of 100 Swahilis, under Lieutenant Macdonald, was driven back and he, whilst trying to rally his men in the most gallant manner, was shot and died almost instantaneously. The Sikhs and the soldiers of the East African Rifles beat off the attack after most desperate fighting at close quarters.

Kabagambi

On February 23RD Captain Harrison led an attack on the rebel stockade of Kabagambi, when, 500 yards from the fort, the mutineers came out to meet them. Severe fighting took place and the mutineers were driven back into their fort. After some desperate fighting at close quarters for two hours, the Sikhs captured the fort. After one of the stiffest fights of the campaign since the first attack on Lubwa Hill of October 19TH, Sikhs had gained a most brilliant victory over the mutineers. The latter fled in utmost confusion, leaving all their belongings behind them and bolted, some into the Swamp, but the majority along the road leading to Mruli, which is densely wooded with bush. Harrison followed to Mruli, to find the mutineers on the opposite bank of the Nile. The immediate danger to Bunyoro had been averted, and the defence of the province was in the hands of the Sikhs and the East African Rifles.

Uganda

Buddu

In December, the Mujasi Gabriel made strenuous efforts to persuade the Sudanese garrison to join him. Macdonald left for Buddu with a force of 200 men, including Harrison's contingent of East African Rifles. Hearing on way that Gabriel's men had been dispersed, he was about to return when news came that Mwanga had escaped from German territory and was in Ankole with 1,300 – 1,400 rifles. Sitwell was ordered to guard the Bwera while Macdonald continued his march, disarmed the Buddu garrisons, and on 15TH January defeated Mwanga's army at Kisalira.

The Armed Forces

Realizing that after the mutiny the armed forces would have to be completely reorganized, Ternan submitted proposals to the Foreign Office without further delay. He suggested that 400 Indian troops should be enlisted, as the backbone of the forces. That 700 Sudanese, not directly implicated in the mutiny, should be retained, and that 700 Swahilis should be recruited. The African troops were to be incorporated in two mixed battalions, comprised of six companies, three Sudanese and three Swahili, with an establishment of 13 officers and 702 rank and file per battalion. Asked for an opinion, the War Office agreed in principle with these proposals, though considering them if anything too modest. The Foreign Office, therefore, lost no time in asking the Viceroy of India whether 400 men, Sikhs or Punjabis preferred, could be recruited for Uganda on the same terms as those supplied for British Central Africa. The government of India had become increasingly reluctant to provide troops for service in Africa, especially from Punjab regiments, as it was feared that recruitment for the Indian Army might suffer in those provinces nearest to the North-West Frontier. The Viceroy informed the Foreign Office by cable that his Commander-in-Chief could not spare any more Sikhs or Punjabis, and thought it inadvisable to recruit Pathans. The news of Mwanga's escape was regarded as so alarming that pressure was placed upon the India Office to order the recruitment of a contingent for Uganda without further delay. The 27TH Bombay Infantry was accordingly followed to East Africa by a wing of 4TH Bombay Infantry, and in March, 1898, Captain J. T. Evatt was appointed to raise the first Indian Contingent, 400 strong, for service in the Uganda Protectorate.

Uganda

Bunyoro

Throughout June and July, operations continued in Bunyoro against those chiefs who supported the rebellion, though Mwanga and Kabarega still eluded capture. In July, the mutineers who had built another stockade near Mruli, showed fresh signs of aggression. To prevent their escape across the Nile a force assembled in secret on the further bank. On 3RD August, the advance began in two columns. The first under Major Price consisted of four officers and 237 men of 27TH Bombay Infantry and one officer and 24 men of the Uganda Rifles. Under the cover of darkness, Price surprised and overcame an enemy piquet on a hill overlooking the mutineer's fort, and then waited for dawn to combine his attack with that of the second column. The second column consisted of two officers and 159 men of the Uganda Rifles, one officer and 53 men of the East African Rifles, three maxim guns manned by Sikhs and a 7-Pounder gun. At daylight on 4TH August, the stockade was bombarded and stormed by the two columns, 40 mutineers being killed and two men of the Uganda Rifles slightly wounded. This ended the main operations against the mutineers; Macdonald reported that they had fought five major and seven minor engagements, and 35 skirmishes. Altogether, some 2,000 troops had been employed and 3,000 Buganda auxiliaries equipped with firearms. Supported by a hastily raised body of several thousand carriers, these troops made many arduous marches throughout an area exceeding 40,000 square miles. Seven Europeans and 280 Indians and Africans were killed and five Europeans and 555 Indians and Africans were wounded during the mutiny operations.

In his final despatch, Major Macdonald stated, 'The detachment of Sikhs, men selected from 14TH and 15TH Sikhs, fought with such determined and conspicuous gallantry as to add to the already high reputation of these regiments.'

Uganda Rifles

By 1900, the Uganda Rifles consisted of 1,952 men, organized in 16 companies; there was an Indian contingent of 402 soldiers with British officers, known as 1ST Battalion, Uganda Rifles. In 1902, the Uganda Rifles became part of the King's African Rifles and the Indian contingent became 5TH Battalion, King's African Rifles. (As was usual at that time, the Indian troops in the Uganda Rifles came from virtually every Sikh infantry unit in the Indian Army.) *

* The author growing up in Jinja, Uganda, remembers two Sikh Nco's of the Kings African Rifles, marching through Jinja in 1956.

Uganda

Uganda in 1902

At the start of 1902, the Uganda Protectorate was considerably larger than the state of Uganda is today, as the map of subsequent boundary changes illustrates. In April 1902, Uganda's large Eastern Province was transferred to British East Africa (now Kenya) with some border adjustments; however, the railway line from Mombasa on the Indian Ocean to Kisumu on Lake Victoria, although now terminating in British East Africa, continued to be called The Uganda Railway. Lake steamers sailed from Kisumu to ports on the Ugandan shore of the lake and the railway continued to be the lifeline of the Uganda Protectorate for imports and exports, as the alternative route down the River Nile from Egypt was long and difficult. On Uganda's southwestern border was German East Africa (now Tanzania), and German troops, civilians and trade goods began using the Uganda Railway to reach Kisumu. The Germans then took steamers and landed at German ports on the southern and western shores of the lake.
Politically Uganda had established borders with British and German East Africa, but the border with the Belgian Congo was disputed, and the border with British Sudan needed surveying as a prelude to demarcation. In the north of Uganda, the course of the River Nile was occupied by British garrisons and posts, and civilian administrators were being appointed. However the remainder of the vast isolated area, up to the assumed Sudan border, was un-mapped and unknown, although illegal Swahili elephant hunters and Abyssinian rifle traders were very active there. For the time being Britain did not wish to impose administrative procedures on the Africans living in the north, and these tribes carried on with their traditional pastoral way of life, which included raiding each others' villages.

Kings African Rifles

At midnight on 31ST December 1901, the military force in the Protectorate, the Uganda Rifles, had ceased to exist; the formation of the King's African Rifles (KAR) began a moment later. Uganda then had two KAR battalions:

• The 4TH (Uganda) Battalion, consisting of nine companies of African infantry

• The 5TH (Uganda) Battalion, consisting of four companies of Indian (Sikh) infantry, recruited with the permission of the Government of India.

In the early days of British colonial activity in Uganda, Sudanese soldiers had been recruited, but after the suppression of a mutiny in 1897 recruits were obtained from other ethnic groups. Bagandans from the kingdom on the shores of Lake Victoria were enlisted along with other local tribesmen.

Uganda

In 1902, Lieutenant Colonel James Hayes Sadler moved from being Consul General in Somaliland to become High Commissioner in Uganda. On the instructions of the British Foreign Secretary in London, Hayes Sadler stated: 'The policy of the Administration is rather to avoid conflict with the wilder tribes, such as those inhabiting the large tract of country to the north of Elgon and between the Nile and Lake Rudolf, and trust to the principles of our rule becoming known to them through the intervening tribes until such time as the permanent occupation of their country becomes a necessity'.

The Mount Elgon region

But in 1902, military action in support of the civil authority was needed to check the activities of recalcitrant tribes living in the forests and ravines that surrounded the 4,321-metre high Mount Elgon in the Central Province. The belligerent tribesmen lived in small separate communities on the northern and western slopes of the mountain. They did not combine to confront the British but they mounted small ambushes on traders' caravans and government messengers, before withdrawing onto the flanks of the mountain, where there were many hiding places amongst the crags and gullies. An irritant to the tribesmen was the presence of a Bagandan former administrator (appointed by the British after the mutiny), the Kakunguru. He, whilst at first doing a sound job for the British in fighting back the tribal raids, built up a following of his own Bagandans to whom he offered 'free' land. The land belonged to the Mount Elgon tribes and this resulted in a prolongation of the conflict. The British solution was to appoint a European political officer to be stationed at Budaka and to settle the Bagandans near Mbale. However, the Kakunguru and his men were always welcome when British military expeditions went onto Mount Elgon, as the Bagandans were useful at locating hidden herds of cattle, which were then seized as a punitive measure. In January 1904, Mbale became an administrative station, as it had developed into a thriving commercial centre. In August, two Indian traders were killed with spears and their caravan was plundered on the road from Mbale to Mbai. The culprits were identified as a tribe living to the north of Jackson's Falls that had been attacking intruders since the British moved into Uganda, and so the local acting sub commissioner, A. G. Boyle, decided to offer a sharp disciplinary lesson. One of Boyle's aims was to demonstrate to neighbouring tribal chiefs the advantages of accepting British administration.

Colonel A. H. Coles, formerly of the Buffs and the Egyptian Army, was Commandant of 4 KAR and his No 4 Company was based at Jinja. Coles ordered an expedition to be mounted under Captain A. H. C. MacGregor (Royal Irish Fusiliers) against the guilty tribes.

This force left Jinja on 21ST September and marched north-north-east through grassland and banana groves up into the Elgon foothills. Around 1,000 warriors armed with spears and bows and arrows awaited the British. War horns had been blown over the previous few days to assemble the fighting men. During the next fortnight MacGregor and his men spent day after day, sometimes in pouring rain, climbing up to crests to find huts stripped and empty. The tribesmen were always somewhere on the mountain slopes ahead of them. The huts were burned and the Bagandans seized some cattle, but the tribes did not possess much stock, and that fact made the infliction of punishment more difficult. On one occasion, a hostile gathering was observed over a kilometre ahead but a few Maxim bursts dispersed it. The rearguards covering the withdrawal of the seized livestock took the most punishment, as poisoned arrows from tribesmen following behind targeted them. On 4TH October, most of the local chiefs came into MacGregor's camp to ask for peace. Only 50 cattle and 692 sheep and goats had been seized but 25 warriors had been killed and that was enough. The blame for the killing of the Indian traders was placed on a drunken chief named Songoro, who was believed to be suffering from dementia. Boyle decided to move the government boma (fortified compound) at Mbai nearer to the disaffected area.

Fighting the Yobos

Boyle had another task for MacGregor and that was to teach the belligerent Yobo tribe a sound lesson, and authority was received by telegraph for the mounting of a second operation. On 18TH October, MacGregor marched out with roughly the same number of men, but this time it was estimated that 5,000 hostile warriors would confront the British. The Yobos were ready and had boasted that they would kill at least one European. When he entered the Yobo heartland, which was enclosed by high cliffs and ridges on which the enemy could be seen until the Maxim gun reached out to them, MacGregor built a boma. He then sent the Kakunguru and his men round the right flank, whilst the Askari advanced towards an occupied ridge. As the troops came up to an enormous banana plantation about 100 warriors emerged and charged whilst waving spears and chanting war cries. The Askari were ordered into fire positions and a couple of volleys stopped the attack. Another volley was needed to stop another assault when entering the plantation, and then the Askari advanced in extended line until they heard firing to their front signalling that the Bagandans were bringing in a herd of cattle.

Uganda

Fighting the Yobos (Cont,)

For the next few days skirmishing and stock seizures continued, until British scouts reported that the remaining herds were being moved eastwards out of the area. MacGregor decided to repeat his previous tactic and sent the Kakunguru's Bagandans and 30 police to outflank the herds and make a surprise attack. Two hours later Lieutenant S. W. H. Rawlins followed the same route to give support and collect stray cattle. Before long Rawlins heard heavy firing to his front and observed the police fighting a steady withdrawal action over a spur, along with 110 cattle. The previous owners of the cattle were agitated and in hot pursuit and were closing onto the police, who were running short of ammunition. Rawlins' bugler signalled the Askari presence on the battlefield and the Yobos fell back, to the relief of the police. These close-quarter fighting tactics were not usual, as most of the time the Yobos preferred to stand well back under deep cover, firing poisoned arrows into the air to land on tracks that the British were using. However, losing cattle reduced a tribesman's personal wealth and social standing, and so village herds were not surrendered easily. More stock was collected over the next few days and MacGregor marched back to Mbale herding 1,027 cattle and 1,604 goats. A portion of the animals would have been distributed amongst the levies, and the Askari and police would have been eating meat for some time. The political officer would also have used the offer of a return of a percentage of the seized herds as an inducement for tribal leaders to accept British administration. About 100 Yobo warriors had been killed, whilst the British had suffered negligible losses. British firepower had made a deep impression on tribesmen whose principal weapons were spears.

A punitive operation in Budama

In late 1905, Chief Bwino Kiko led an uprising in the Budama area south-west of Mount Elgon. The government boma at Peta was destroyed and 40 Bagandans were massacred. Captain L. E. S. Ward was ordered to lead an expedition against Chief Bwino Kiko. Ward marched from Jinja to Peta and established base camp there. Then each day two columns went out into the disaffected area, each column splitting into three parties. Huts and agricultural plots were destroyed and cattle and sheep seized. Again the primitive tribal weapons were no match for British firepower and around 70 dissidents were killed at a cost of one Basoga levy wounded. Bwino Kiko surrendered on 24TH September after his own village had been destroyed.

Uganda

Chief Eseme

The Political Officers then decided to break the power of Chief Eseme, who had rejected British authority and was disturbing the nearby Kileu area. Ward marched out on 4TH October but he had to exercise more caution now, as the dissidents were believed to have 300 rifles. A British attempt at surprise failed, when local guides on a night march proved unreliable. Eseme's and other villages were burned and stock was seized but Ward could not disperse his men too widely because of the threat of enemy rifle fire. The Maxim gun was often in use, clearing areas of vegetation where tribesmen lurked. Eseme waited for an opportunity and when it came he, armed with a Mauser rifle, and about 15 of his men with Martini Henrys, attacked a small group of police. The Askari had to move quickly to support the police who were hard pressed. Eseme's party then split up and withdrew, leaving one corpse behind. The Political Officers had been presumptuous in thinking that Eseme's power could be easily broken, and when Ward was ordered to return to Jinja, the tribe had not submitted and the warriors were still fighting against intrusions into their area. A change in policies and tactics now occurred on both sides in the Central Province, doubtless helped by economic development. British Political Officers became more acknowledged and respected by the tribal chiefs, who were prepared to discuss matters before taking up arms. Meanwhile the police became strong enough to mount small expeditions on their own.

The Northern Patrol

During 1910, the Uganda Government was forced to re-assess its policy of non-intervention in the north of the Protectorate. One of the reasons cited for not getting involved had been the revenue that was collected from ivory, brought out of the north by licensed traders; in other words, the government was extracting revenue from the north without having to pay the administrative cost of occupying the area. But by now, a large number of firearms had been sold illegally in the north, and the tribes used these weapons to both raid each other and to decimate the vast herds of elephant that roamed in the area. There was now far less potential ivory revenue for the Government to collect, and unlicensed Swahili and Abyssinian traders had become adept at exporting tusks in other directions, to avoid the Ugandan authorities. However, the most critical factor affecting the north of Uganda was the discovery of Abyssinian troops in the Turkana and Karamoja regions in the northeast. Abyssinia was staking a claim to tracts of land west of Lake Rudolph.

Uganda

Nimule

In mid-1911, the civil authorities in the Nile Province wished to enforce the 1909 Collective Punishments Ordinance against two hill tribes, the Eiyerri, and Gimorreh, who lived about 80 kilometres northeast of Nimule. 'A' Company 4 KAR was sent up the Nile by steamer from Hoima to Nimule. Lieutenant W. I. Webb-Bowen was the company commander and he had with him Lieutenant W. P. Baldock, 80 Askari carrying 100 rounds, one Maxim gun, and five porters. Captain P. S. H. Tanner, Uganda Police, and 35 men were to follow later when the supply situation at Nimule had been organised satisfactorily. These troops were referred to as the Northern Patrol. 'A' Company reached Nimule on 13TH July and the District Commissioner briefed Webb-Bowen. As the rains were coming, a prompt start was made two days later, before the rivers in the region flooded. The Askari marched through Lokai and Parajok, noting that most tribesmen possessed a Snider or Le Gras rifle, and reached the Eiyerri country on 18TH July. The Eiyerri and Gimorreh villages were seen on the tops and sides of steep hills that were often covered with dense bush. Caves and enormous boulders were dotted around the hills. Outposts on high ground observed the Askari and swiftly reported the British movements to the villages. On July 20TH, 'A' Company reached the foot of a hill, which was 600 metres high. A forward screen of Askari ascended, followed by the remainder of the company; shooting started when the troops were half way up the ascent. 10 of the dissidents were shot, but the remaining warriors withdrew in good order. At the summit, Webb-Bowen burned the village, cut down the grain crops, and drove off 100 sheep and goats. The Eiyerri re-occupied the village when 'A' Company withdrew but the Maxim gun dispersed them. The following day a similar operation took place on another hill but this time there were no goats and sheep in the village when the Askari arrived. For the next 48 hours 'A' Company searched caves and burned villages but could not come to grips with the Eiyerri and Gimorreh warriors. Around 20 tribesmen were killed, whilst four of 'A' Company's porters were severely wounded by spear attacks in the tall grass that grew at the base of the hills. Webb-Bowen then withdrew to Nimule and the rains fell. Although not much impact seemed to have been made on the Eiyerri and Gimmorreh, the group of Lokoya tribes in the region had taken notice of the devastation that a Maxim gun could cause, and this group talked with the Uganda civil authorities and offered a voluntary fine in compensation for their own depredations.

Uganda

Operations in the Opei and Nangiya Hills

Tanner and his police officers had now arrived and on 7TH September, the Northern Patrol went into the field again to operate in the Opei and Nangiya hills that lay due east of Nimule. The aim was to clear the hills of illicit traders and to punish the tribesmen who had sheltered them, and who had acquired weapons to use in attacks on other tribes. Sites were to be reconnoitred for military posts, as British garrisons were being planned for the region. The Northern Patrol arrived at the 750-metre high, heavily wooded Mount Opei on 15TH September. Tanner and his police were left there with some Askari, whilst Webb-Bowen marched straight on for 48 hours to Kiteng Hill, as he had been informed of the murder there of 14 Swahili traders. A camp was established at Kiteng but a message arrived from Tanner at Akol Hill near Opei requesting support. Tanner's group had been confiscating cattle from the Madi tribe when attackers killed a KAR Askari and wounded another. A camp was left at Kiteng and Webb-Bowen retraced his steps to Akol Hill, where he found Tanner guarding 211 head of cattle. Baldock was sent on in advance with 35 Askari to Mount Opei, where the hostile Madi villages were located, whilst a heliograph-signalling link was established between Akol and Kiteng. Webb-Bowen gained the assistance of a local friendly chief named Akowo, who supplied porters to carry the supplies, but as these men had elaborate hair styles loads could not be carried on heads but were suspended on poles between the shoulders of two men. At Mount Opei Baldock found the Madi village, running along the base of the hill for a kilometre. The next morning he started burning the village but his Askari were fiercely attacked and he withdrew. When the main body arrived with Webb-Bowen a group was sent up on the hill to cover the destruction of the village, but this group received a warm welcome from Madi rifle and spearmen and from rock throwers. The vegetation was very dense on the hill and the cliffs were honeycombed with concealed caves. One Askari was shot through the chest. That night Webb-Bowen used his Maxim gun and war rockets (possibly 9-pounder Hale Mark VIIc rockets) against the Madi campfires on the hill. The use of these weapons at night turned the battle, and on 21ST September Chief Aluru and one of his headmen approached the British camp asking for peace. A rocket had killed three men sitting around a fire. Although Aluru was detained, the warriors on the hill remained defiant and would not surrender their firearms, but the Askari could now complete the destruction of the village and standing crops. The rockets were used again for a second night, before Webb-Bowen marched his men and Chief Aluru back to Kiteng camp. The Northern Patrol then based itself at Kiteng and started to establish British authority in the region. Skirmishes were fought with recalcitrant tribes and rogue Abyssinians, and when necessary more villages were burned and livestock and caches of illegal ivory were seized. At Mount Rom on 5TH November, aggressive Nangiya tribesmen attacked the Askari using accurate breech-loading rifles, but the warriors received a surprise when the Maxim gun was efficiently brought into action.

Uganda

The Lango Detachment, 1911-1912

In 1911, it was decided to send 'B' Company 4 KAR into the Lango region north of Lake Kioga, where the Askari would support the authority of the District Commissioner (DC) there. The company commander, Captain R. H. Johnston, marched his 125 men the 320 kilometres from Bombo, accompanied by another 175 wives, children, and porters. The party arrived on 12TH September. The DC was extremely unhappy, complaining that far too many people had arrived for the food resources in the region, and he insisted on half the company returning to Bombo. This example of a lack of effective communications between the civil and military authorities was all too prevalent at that time, straining relationships on the ground. The unwanted half of the company returned to Bombo in October with its families and porters. At Ngetta Johnston's men constructed grass-roofed huts with mud walls for accommodation and stores, and the Askari built a mosque in their after-duty hours. As the local tribes were friendly, Johnston wished to push further north to link up with the Northern Patrol, but he was forbidden from leaving the area administered by the DC. He was also instructed to only patrol in the administered area after receiving the DC's permission, and that his escort was limited to a maximum of 12 Askari. On querying with his own HQ as to why he was in Lango, Johnston was told that he was there to be at the disposal of the DC. During the next few months, tension eased between the DC and Johnston, who started patrolling further north and in due course opened up a good well-watered route to the Northern Patrol. In mid-1912 a decision was made to send the Lango garrison, now commanded by Lieutenant H. A. Lilley and 58 Askari of 'D' Company, up to join the Kiteng garrison. However, sleeping sickness spread along the north bank of the River Nile west of Lango and the Askari were needed to deal with this situation. Captain Tanner of the police had been depopulating the affected areas and cutting down the vegetation that harboured the tsetse fly, but he died of blackwater fever before the job was completed. A detachment of the Lango Askari was now employed on this task. On 30TH October 1912, Lilley marched the Lango garrison, minus the families who returned to Bombo, up to Madial where the Kiteng base had been re-located. Lilley's Askari had skirmished in Lango with a few tribesmen who had attacked government or military messengers, but it had been the presence of the Askari in Lango rather than their actions that had settled the area so that the DC and the police could administer it effectively.

Uganda

The Northern Garrison, 1912 – 1914

By the end of 1912, the Northern Patrol was being referred to as the Northern Garrison, as that title-inferred permanence. Major J. K. Clothier was appointed to command the Garrison. However, the proposed Sudan-Uganda boundary line was being surveyed and Uganda was hopeful that its more troublesome mountainous regions in the north would be transferred to Sudan. This resulted in a reluctance to spend money on punitive expeditions in those regions, as it was unlikely that a permanent Ugandan administration would be put in place afterwards. However, a ball was rolling now that could not be easily stopped. As the Northern Garrison dealt with raiders, the tribes that had been the victims of those raiders now expected British protection to continue. As this usually involved more operations to totally disarm the raiders, more territory then came under Ugandan administration with a consequent need for security. The former administrative headquarters of the Nile District at Nimule was moved to a more central position in Gulu and a new post was opened at Kitgum. In March 1912, the Northern Garrison seized 2,000 cattle from the Morongole tribe. During the next two months, 16 Nakwai villages were destroyed and punitive measures were taken against the Lokoya. The Logire Mountains lay 30 kilometres northeast of the new base at Madial and the tribes living on the slopes of the mountains continually raided the herdsmen on the plains below. 'A' Company 4 KAR operated against the raiders on the easterly spur of the mountains from the 21ST to 29TH of October 1912, marching onto the hillside by night. Initial surprise was gained and herds of goats and sheep were seized, but two Askari were killed by dissident spearmen. Two sections of Askari then climbed to the summit where Dongotono warriors suddenly and fiercely attacked them. Up to that moment, it had not been known that the Dongotono existed. Using only spears and poisoned arrows the warriors pushed the two sections back down the hill, killing one Askari and wounding two others. 'A' Company withdrew but sporadic skirmishing continued against the various tribes in the Logire area for several months, with British firepower gradually convincing the recalcitrant tribes to discuss terms. In early 1913, 'A' Company marched back to Bombo, having been relieved by 'E' Company. Captain W. T. Brooks replaced Clothier. Meanwhile Lilley and 75 Askari were detached for a few months to accompany the Sudan-Uganda Boundary Commission that was commanded by Captain Harry Kelly, Royal Engineers. Dissidents occasionally harassed the Commission and although it had an escort of Sudanese Infantry and Camel Corps soldiers, Lilley and his Askari were welcomed.

Uganda

The Didinga Expedition

The Didinga tribe lived in the north of the Logire Hills; they were hostile to neighbours and they were accomplished raiders. It was believed that traders had never visited them and so it was expected that they would not possess firearms. The Dodo tribes around Morongole now disarmed and under British protection, were suffering from Didinga depredations. Strong warnings issued from Madial were met with Didinga taunts and jeers. The Didinga territory lay north of the Boundary Commission line but the Sudanese Government gave permission for the Northern Garrison to mount an expedition. Captain Brooks led the expedition, which consisted of 190 Askari from 'D', and 'E' Companies divided into three columns. Each Askari carried 100 rounds of ammunition and six days' rations. An equal amount of ammunition was carried in reserve. Not much was known about the Didinga country and a reconnaissance would have compromised the expedition. The first day's activity, on 19TH June 1913, consisted of a night march by No 1 Column to block the Laroma valley, followed by the other two columns sweeping through the area from different sides. Surprise was achieved, 20 tribesmen were killed, and 623 head of cattle seized. An assessment could now be made of Didinga territory, which was found to cover about 40 square kilometres. The country was fertile and well wooded, with villages positioned on heights and accessible only by steep and narrow paths. All three columns now began to sweep areas of the hills. After a week or so of watching the British tactics, the Didinga began to respond aggressively and effectively. Observation posts gave warnings of British advances that were met by short-range ambushes in the dense cover. Each tribesman carried up to six spears. One ambush at five metres range was delivered by up to 200 warriors, who killed three Askari and wounded four others. At night, the Didinga would raid the KAR cattle bomas to try to release the stock. In the thick vegetation, the columns could sometimes advance less than a kilometre in an hour, as patrols had to be constantly clearing the bush to the front and the flanks. On 7TH July, Brooks decided to halt the operations as he had secured enough stock to compensate the Dodo. But withdrawal was tricky as there were 2,000 cattle and 11 badly wounded men to be got out of the steep narrow valleys. Teams of up to eight men struggled with each stretcher, and in the end, the wounded were carried in blankets. The Didinga continued to aggressively attack the withdrawal, causing more Askari casualties. Finally, the expedition was concentrated in the Laroma valley by 28TH July, and was back in Madial by 7TH August. Three Askari had been killed and 11 badly wounded. Several porters were also wounded. Seizures amounted to 2,037 cattle, 1,660 goats, 62 donkeys, and seven tusks of ivory. The Didinga were not subdued, and Brooks believed that if the Madial garrison were withdrawn, then the Didinga would raid again and re-take the stock. But British attention was now focussing on the Turkana territory in the northeast of the Protectorate.

Uganda

Punitive Expeditions

Many colonial officials thought that punitive measures were unpleasant but necessary. These men appreciated that it was impossible to quickly break down the conventions and traditions that had been accumulated by tribesmen over centuries of internecine conflict. In contrast, a few officials considered that punitive measures were pointless as they "create a situation which is far worse than that existing prior to Government intervention. The punished parties have a habit of inflicting reprisals in the absence of visible signs of permanent government". The military officers who were the men at the sharp end, operating in uncharted, remote, and rugged territory, had few doubts about the necessity of punishing recalcitrant. They understood that the Government's prestige and authority rested upon its military superiority, and that above all else the tribes that had submitted had to be protected. When operating in a harsh and unforgiving environment kindness could easily be interpreted as weakness. Captain Leeke, writing from Madial, stated that the local tribes "were undoubtedly of an opinion that we were afraid of fighting the Didinga and, now that we had done so, are much easier to deal with".

Ugandan Sikhs and Belgian Congolese Askari on the disputed border

Uganda

Uganda Volunteer Reserve

In August 1914, Uganda, unlike the British East Africa Protectorate, had a Volunteer Reserve unit. This had started on 28TH April 1903 with the formation of a Uganda Rifle Corps based at Entebbe and was composed of European volunteers. On 25TH June 1914, a Kampala Corps was formed for Europeans, and two months later, another Kampala Corps was formed for Indian volunteers. In October 1914, a Jinja Corps was formed for Europeans.

The organisation became:

Entebbe – No 1 Company of the Uganda Volunteer Reserve (UVR).

Kampala – No 2 Company (European).

Kampala – No 3 Company (Indian).

Jinja – No 4 Company.

The companies were divided into four sections, each containing from 20 to 25 men. No.1 Company enlisted around a dozen Indian artisans who served as armourers, mechanics, and blacksmiths. Numbers 2 and 3 Companies held ballots to choose their officers. No.2 Company included French, Dutch, Afrikaner, Scandinavian, Greek and Armenian nationals, as well as British subjects. The Uganda Volunteer Reserve never fought as a formed unit but the variety of military employments that its members were deployed on illustrates the growth of Ugandan military forces in the early years of the Great War.

The Kagera Line

As Uganda shared a common border with German East Africa in the southwest, the British military priority was the defence of this border against possible German invasion. The Kagera River ran into Lake Victoria just inside Ugandan territory, but for the previous 90 miles, it meandered and looped to a distance of around 20 miles inside German territory before it touched Uganda again and ran along the border. The rough semi-circle of German territory within the loop was occupied by the British, but both sides quietly crossed the river in canoes to reconnoitre, ambush and raid each other's military patrols and posts. Nearly every military unit raised in Uganda was deployed at times along the Kagera Line, and many members of the Uganda Volunteer Reserve fought there. An early deployment of UVR Personnel to the Kagera Line was that of six Sharpshooters for sniping duties. Meanwhile those Volunteers who possessed motor cycles were formed into a Corps of Despatch Riders. Men with telegraphy experience were used on communications duties, and linguists in appropriate native dialects were used as liaison officers and interpreters. Most importantly, suitable UVR Non-Commissioned Officers were deployed into the Kagera Gun Teams, where they initially commanded machine guns and later also trench mortars, Hotchkiss guns and a field gun.

Uganda

Uganda Volunteer Reserve

No 3 Company

The Indian company had a majority of Sikh members, plus several Muslims and Hindus. About 30 of the men were ex-soldiers from the Punjab. When 13TH Rajputs were deployed on the Kagera Line, five men from No. 3 Company worked with the Rajputs as interpreters. Several other No. 3 Company men served in clerical appointments, both with the Field Force on the Kagera and in administrative units.

Duties behind the lines

The guarding of interned enemy subjects and of prisoners captured at the front became a UVR responsibility. These enemy personnel were escorted to Kisumu by boat and there handed over to the British East Africa authorities, who arranged for their shipment to camps in India. Other Volunteers were deployed on local defence duties and some made canoe patrols off Port Bell to secure the port.

Assistance to Belgian Forces

In order to assist the Belgian Congo forces move into German East Africa in 1916, Uganda agreed to supply transport units to aid the Belgian advance. The East Africa Transport Corps Congo Carrier Section (known as Carbel), the Bukakata-Lutobo Ox Transport Corps (known as Bukalu) and the Belgian Advance Ox Transport Corps (known as Belox) were formed and men from the UVR Served in all three units. It has to be said, however, that desertion rates from the carrier section were high, as it was widely believed, with some apparent justification, that when the Congolese troops ran short of food they chose a suitable-looking carrier to cook and eat.

Fin

In August 1916, the Governor of Uganda terminated the call-out service of the Uganda Volunteer Reserve. Many men served on as they were now members of units located deep in German East Africa, and a gruelling two years of active service lay ahead for those who survived. Without any doubt, the Uganda Volunteer Reserve had pulled its weight, having men with leadership potential available for service before war was declared. The operation of the Kagera line and the formation of new Ugandan units were helped considerably by the immediate availability of these Volunteers, both European and Indian.

Uganda

Uganda Police (with Diljit Singh Bahra)
Uganda police history began in 1900 when Special Commissioner Sir Harry Johnston established the Armed Constabulary with 1,450 Africans, under the command of British district officers. Eventually the Protectorate Police replaced the constabulary, and the colonial government appointed an inspector general as the commanding officer of all police detachments, including Sikh volunteers from Central African Rifles, who filled the middle ranks of the Police force. Although created as a civilian force, the police frequently carried out military duties. With the completion of the railroad in 1901, Uganda became a prosperous colony. The British colonists considered the Asians more "efficient" than the Africans. So, while Ugandans were more likely to own and profit from their land than was the case elsewhere in Africa, the British concentrated the trade and processing of the cash crops in the hands of the Asians. Mostly Asian-owned, large estates kept wages low by importing migrant workers from Uganda's less-affluent hinterlands. The years preceding independence, and the first years of the new government, were a time of "business as usual" for the Asian population. As the country gained experience of electoral politics, politicians found it useful to have a prosperous and visible minority to use as scapegoats. In 1971, Prime Minister Obote was overthrown by his handpicked protégé, Idi Amin. Amin's power rested in the army, but the army itself was deeply divided. Maintaining control of his troops was a difficult and expensive proposition, and Amin's own extravagance was a strain on the national budget. The obvious answer to his pressing economic problems was to confiscate the property of the Asian minority. The expulsion of the Asians from Uganda took place in September of 1972, and was propagandised by Amin as a victory for the "little man". The official line was that a pack of foreign exploiters had been run out, and the Africans would get back what was rightfully theirs. In practice, however, most of the proceeds wound up in the hands of the army. This sudden influx of wealth bought him a solid corps of loyal troops. As the African proverb says, "A dog with a bone in his mouth cannot bite you." The Ugandan economy, already in a tailspin, collapsed under the mismanagement of the expropriated property. Unmaintained equipment and inexperienced management brought most of these confiscated enterprises to a grinding halt within the first few years. A case could well be made that the Ugandan economy never recovered from this incident. The Asians of Uganda dispersed to many locations, mostly commonwealth countries. Some returned to their ancestral homelands of India and Pakistan. Others went to Canada, the U.K., or elsewhere in Africa.

Uganda

Superintendent Ajmer Singh Matharu

Uganda Police

Some of the Sikh police officers of the Uganda police were admitted to the United Kingdom, as in the case of Ajmer Singh Matharu, who had been a Deputy Superintendent of Police in Uganda. Ajmer joined Uganda Police as a sub-Inspector in 1956 and served in Kampala. Whilst a Chief Inspector, in 1961, he attended a 3 month CID Course in Wakefield Training Centre, West Yorkshire Constabulary, England. Ajmer was Uganda's national hockey captain from 1960–1964 and national Coach from 1964 to 1968. He retired from Uganda Police in 1968. He became the first turban wearing Sikh policeman when he joined Leicester and Rutland Constabulary on 6TH April 1970. Ajmer retired from the Leicester Police Constabulary in October 1989.

Manor Singh Sandhu joined Uganda Police in 1950 as a sub-Inspector and served in Kampala, Masaka, and the Northern Province. He was the most senior Sikh Police Officer in Uganda and retired as Superintendent of Police (CID) in 1969. He was a top class investigator and played hockey for Uganda Police.

Mohan Singh Ahluwalia joined Uganda Police in March 1953 as a sub-Inspector and served in Kampala, Jinja, Masaka, Mbale, and Lugazi. He attended Wakefield Training Centre of West Yorkshire Police, England in 1960 and served the last 12 years of his service in the CID. He retired as a Deputy Superintendent of Police (DSP) in June 1969.

Harbans Singh Bassan joined Uganda Police in March 1953 as a sub-Inspector and served in Kampala and Jinja. He died in a Road Traffic Accident whilst returning from a Police Conference in 1966. He was a DSP.

Jasbir Singh Mangat joined around 1963 and was an Assistant Superintendent of Police (ASP) when he retired around 1970.

TANZANIA

Tanzania Police (with Diljit Singh Bahra)

European colonists arbitrarily divided the East African region in the mid 1800's. Under the German-Anglo agreement of 1886, Tanganyika would become a German colony while Kenya came under British control. Germany ruled mainland Tanganyika, now known as Tanzania, from 1886 to 1919. The German colonialists did not establish a formal police force, as the Army and Para - military officers were used to maintain law and order. At the fall of German East Africa, mainland Tanganyika was placed under the control of British Colonial authority in 1919. The British set about establishing a number of institutions, including a police force. Senior ranks of the police force were filled with European appointments; middle ranks were made up of imported Asian officers from Kenya and local recruits completed the junior ranks. In 1930, there were 78 Europeans in senior positions in the police, 67 Asians made up the middle management and 1,719 Africans in the junior ranks. On 26.4.1964, Zanzibar merged with Tanganyika to form Tanzania.

Assistant Superintendent Niranjan Singh Sahota

Niranjan Singh Sahota joined the Tanganyika Police in 1947 as a sub-Inspector and served in Dar-es-Salaam, Moshi, Singida and Mwanza. He attended a fingerprints training course in Glasgow, Scotland in December 1958 and after that spent the rest of his service in the CID. He retired in April 1974 as Assistant Superintendent of Police.

Assistant Superintendent Arjan Singh Jagdev

Arjan Singh Jagdev joined the Tanganyika police in November 1952 as a sub Inspector. He served in Dar-es-Salaam, Tabora and Kibondo and retired as a Senior Assistant Superintendent.

JUBALAND

On 7TH November 1890, Zanzibar became a British protectorate and, on 1ST July 1891, ceded all its coastal possessions in continental East Africa to its protector. Together with Zanzibar's other former possessions in the area, Jubaland became part of the British colony of British East Africa. Jubaland was ceded to Italy on 29TH June 1925, purportedly as a reward for joining the Allies in World War 1 and had a brief existence as the Italian colony of Trans-Juba. It was incorporated into the neighbouring colony of Italian Somaliland on 30TH June 1926. In July 1960, Jubaland, along with the rest of Italian Somaliland and British Somaliland, became part of the independent republic of Somalia. The main city is Kismayo, on the coast near the mouth of the Juba. Bardera and Beled Hawo are the other principal cities of Jubaland.

Ogaden Warriors

Jubaland

Ogaden Somalis

From the time when the administration of Kismayu was taken over by the Imperial British East Africa Company in August 1891, Jubaland was the scene of frequent campaigns against the Ogaden Somalis. The Ogaden were a fierce and warlike tribe, estimated to muster about 6,000 warriors. They carried small round shields of giraffe hide and fought in pairs, with stabbing spear and knife, one man seizing his adversary while the other stabbed him. As they possessed few firearms their tactical preference was for ambushes and close fighting in thick country of their own choosing, through which they could spread with unusual speed.

Boran Galla, 1897

In 1897, in spite of a stern warning by the sub commissioner of the province, the Ogaden made an unprovoked attack on the Boran Galla, in the hope of securing cattle and slaves. As the Boran gave a good account of themselves, the matter was allowed to drop. A few months later, two Ogaden spies captured near Mfudu killed their escort of native police and escaped. Amad bin Marghan was warned that Kismayu and the coast would be closed to his people unless the murderers were surrendered or blood money paid. Ahamad pacifically inclined and paid an instalment of the fine, but his young warriors, anxious to 'wash their spears', were disgusted at such weakness and difficult to control. In April 1898, a Galla slave who had obtained British protection, was found by his Somali master, and killed. Police action followed in the Afmadu area, where the murderer's cattle and some of his relatives were seized. The Somali promptly retaliated by raiding toward Kismayu and killing two Arab traders close to the town. The time had clearly come for decisive measures, and a military expedition was authorised.

The Punitive Force, 1898

On the evening of 12TH March, it was reported that the police post at Yonti was in danger of attack. The following morning Lieutenant Ford marched to its relief with a force of twenty-six rifles and a maxim gun. On arrival at Yonti, he found that the enemy had already attacked and taken the post, killing eleven of the police and retiring on the approach of the troops. It was impossible to follow them up with his small force, so he withdrew his men to Turki Hill. A few days previously, a detachment of the East African Rifles had been ambushed along the road to Yonti. A reconnaissance on 13TH April found that the post there had been captured by Somalis, who had killed 15 of the police Askaris, before retiring into the bush. The punitive force assembled in May, included, in addition to the three companies of East African Rifles (with a Sikh contingent) already in Jubaland, two companies of 4th Bombay Infantry (with a Sikh company) and companies of the Ugandan Sikh Contingent, totalling 1,060 men.

Jubaland

Yonti Post

On 17TH May, Major Quentin transferred the headquarters of the force to Yonti, and built a stockade there, the garrison of Turki Hill being eventually reduced to seventy-five men. On 30TH May a large party of Ogadens was sighted close to Yonti post and pursued for some distance, their losses being reported as about twenty-five killed.

Helishid, 1898

Major Quentin now established an advance post at Helishid on Lake Wana, manned by 150 Sepoys. On 22ND June, a Sikh patrol of forty-one rifles went out from Helishid to reconnoitre the roads towards Malkhana and Kurkues. When the party had reached a point about two miles from camp, where the road passed through a hollow with thick bush on both sides, about 400 Somalis suddenly attacked them. The main body was marching in single file with an advanced guard fifty yards in front and a rear guard 100 yards in rear. The bush was very thick to within ten yards of the road and the first attack was made from the right. When the men turned to meet it, they were assailed in the rear by another part of the enemy. The attack was so sudden that the commander Jemadar Radha Singh and several Sepoys were killed before they could use their arms. The remainder retreated towards the lake, and when clear of the jungle succeeded in checking the enemy. Quentin redisposed his troops, reinforcing Helishid to 168 rifles, garrisoning Yonti with 151, and leaving only 91 rifles at Turki Hill. Two companies of Sudanese soldiers were in the Gosha district and 100 Sudanese and Swahili soldiers at Kismayu. On 14TH July, Somalis carried out a daring raid on Government cattle close to Kismayu. The Uganda Sikh Contingent reached the port a fortnight afterwards, to relieve Quentin's entire force for operations. On 3RD August the main punitive column, about 300 strong, marched from Helishid, forded the shallow lake, and surprised the Ogaden camp at daybreak, inflicting heavy casualties and capturing 450 head of stock. Ten days later Quentin made a second large capture in the same locality. This brought the Ogaden to their senses and the Sultan and his chiefs sued for peace, surrendering all captured arms, and agreeing to a fine of 500 cattle. Sultan Ahmad paid several visits to Kismayu, and for a time remained quiet.

On 1ST January 1902, the Kings African Rifles came into being, with the original forces of the protectorates incorporated as follows:

1ST (Central Africa) Battalion, (Formerly 1 C.A.R.)
2ND (Central Africa) Battalion, (Formerly 2 C.A.R.)
3RD (East Africa) Battalion, (Formerly 2 E.A.R.)
4TH (Uganda) Battalion (Formerly Uganda Rifles)
5TH (Uganda) Battalion (Formerly the Sikh Contingent of Uganda Rifles)
6TH (Somaliland) Battalion. (Formed from the local forces in British Somaliland)

NAIK BUTTA SINGH

INDIAN ORDER OF MERIT

Won for gallantry against the Ogaden Somalis in East Africa 1898.

For some years, the Ogaden Somalis had been causing trouble, which culminated in an extensive slave raid in Jubaland. It was decided to take punitive measures to bring the Somalis to order. On 22ND of June 1898 a patrol of 41 Sikhs, including Naik Butta Singh, under Jemadar Radha Singh, was sent out on reconnaissance from Helishid. They were ambushed by a large force of Somalis and suffered very heavy losses, with 27 killed, including the Jemadar, and four wounded. Apparently, the party was caught by surprise and the enemy got among them before they had time to fix bayonets. In this action, Naik Butta Singh, though twice wounded, showed great gallantry in carrying Rifleman Maya Singh, who was severely wounded, to safety and executed a very skilful retirement with his comrades, two of whom were also wounded. There is no doubt that these men were only able to return to Helishid due to Naik Butta Singh's quick and effective actions. He was at once promoted to Naik and subsequently received the Indian Order of Merit for his gallantry. The official citation for this award reads:

"Naik Butta Singh, 4TH Bombay Rifles, was granted the Indian Order of Merit for conspicuous gallantry in action near Helishid, on Lake Wama, East Africa, on 22ND June 1898, on which occasion, though twice severely wounded himself, he went to the assistance of Sepoy Maya Singh, who was mortally wounded, and after driving off several parties of the enemy, finally brought Maya Singh into camp with the assistance of two other Sepoys."

Butta Singh's richly deserved award was the only gallantry decoration granted for this campaign. It is not known how long Butta Singh had served with 4TH Bombay Rifles, but it is certainly a significant feat of arms that, as a rifleman, he had the composure, the leadership skills, and enough understanding of field tactics to execute this withdrawal against such overwhelming odds with such few men.

SOMALILAND

Somaliland in 1884

Somaliland occupied part of the African continent known as the "Horn of Africa" between the equator and 12TH degree of north latitude. It was bounded on the north by the Red Sea, on the east by the Indian Ocean, and on the west and southwest by Abyssinia and Jubaland, the latter a portion of the British East Africa Protectorate. The country formed a triangle: measuring 600 miles along the coast from the French port of Djibouti to Cape Gardafui; 1,100 miles from Cape Gardafui is Kismayu; and thence through Harrar to Djibouti, about 900 miles. The whole of this area, covering some 320,000 square miles was partitioned into spheres of influence among Great Britain, France, Italy, and Abyssinia.

Somali Warrior

'The Somalis comprise various tribes, occupying certain well-defined tracts and quite independent of each other, being often than not at feud among themselves. They are armed with spears of two kinds, a small and light one for throwing, and one of stouter make for thrusting. They also carry small round leather shields, about one foot in diameter; and some are armed with short straight double-edged swords and called *bilawas*. They also use a club, and carry a bow and poisoned arrows, and a knife. Rifles were scarce in the country before the Mullah's appearance.' (Beachey, 1990)

Sikh Soldier in Somaliland
(Illustrated London News, 1903)

Somaliland

Somaliland formed part of the Ottoman Empire, which came under Egyptian administration in 1866. In 1873, the Egyptian forces occupied the port of Berbera. Berbera was the principal port on the Somali coast and was the only one where vessels could anchor in all weathers. The British and Egyptian navies then cooperated for the suppression of the Slave trade in the Red Sea until the Egyptians abandoned Somaliland in 1884. The British, French, Italians, and the Ethiopians then divided the whole area into spheres of influence. The British occupied Berbera when four Somali tribes placed themselves under their administration for protection against the Ethiopians. The Protectorate of Somaliland was administered from India until October 1898, when control was taken over by the Foreign Office. In 1905, generally the British did not have much interest in the resource-barren region. They principally viewed the protectorate as a source for supplies of meat for their British Indian outpost in Aden. Hence the region's nickname of "Aden's butcher's shop". From 1899, the British were forced to expend considerable human and military capital in a bloody struggle to contain a decades-long resistance movement led by the Somali religious leader Sayyid Mohammed Abdullah Hassan, referred to colloquially by the British as the 'Mad Mullah'. Repeated expeditions were unsuccessfully launched against Hassan and his men before World War 1. The British finally managed to quell Hassan's twenty-year long struggles in 1920.

Sayyid Mohammed Abdullah Hassan, (The'Mad Mullah')

'Sayyid Mohammed Abdullah Hassan fought for a quarter of a century to keep Somaliland free of European and Ethiopian control and Christian influence. He was a master of desert warfare, and an able politician and negotiator, a man of cruel and merciless temperament indifferent to human suffering, driven and sustained by a religious fervour and an unshakable belief in his authority as a messenger of God. In his youth, a great athlete, in middle and old age, after disease had struck him, gross in body. To the end, he inspired his followers, the Dervishes, so that whatever the odds, however terrible the losses, however complete the defeats, in battle they were always willing to die for him and his cause. It is a fascinating and tragic story of unnecessary deaths and waste, occasions of great courage and self-sacrifice on both sides. The English called him the Mad Mullah. The British dead, like those of the later Greater War, may well have thought their own leaders mad as well'. (Beachey, 1990)

'The Somali Warrior, this bravest, vainest, and merciless fighter was capable of greatness, ready to spill his blood on the barren rocks of his country. He would die contemptuously, 'taking the sabre straight and laughing'. He was little concerned about wounds, which were plastered over with camel dung and left to putrefy and heal.' (Beachey, 1990, p.6)

Somaliland

In 1884, Britain declared a protectorate over northern Somaliland. The emergence in 1900 of Muhammad Abdille Hasan (the "Mad Mullah") and his band of dervishes represented a serious challenge to colonial rule in British Somaliland.

1ST Expedition, May-June 1901

The Mullah's repeated raids into British territory induced the Government, at the end of 1900, to sanction the raising of a local force for the defence of the Protectorate. At this time, the Mullah's force was reported to consist of some 1,200 horsemen and 6,000 foot, with about 300 rifles between them. A defence force under Lieutenant Colonel Swayne was raised, consisting of a Camel Corps of 100 men, Mounted Infantry of 400 and two corps of 500 Infantry each. With this force and with the co-operation of the Ethiopians in the east, the Mullah was driven into the Dolbahanta country. The enemy's strength at this time was estimated at about 5,000 men. In April 1901, Colonel Swayne moved to Burao, which was made an advance base; from there he advanced to Samala, where he built a *Zariba*` (an enclosure of bushes or stakes protecting a campsite) which he garrisoned with a force of 470 men. The main body then pushed on towards the Mullah's position, which side stepped the advance and delivered three determined attacks on the *Zariba* at Samala. The Mullah's forces were beaten off with the loss of 600 killed and wounded. As they retreated, they were intercepted at Odergoeh by the main column and their retreat became a rout as they fled over the border to Mudug. Swayne then abandoned the chase and turned his attention to the punishment of the Ali Gheri and other sections of the Dulbahante, who had always been the Mullah's chief supporters.

Battle of Ferdiddin, July 1901

In a short time, however, the Mullah's forces returned to the Nogal Valley, and were reported to be near Ferdiddin. In order to make a surprise attack, Colonel Swayne decided upon a night march with 75 mounted troops, and the rest on foot, accompanied by 16 baggage camels to carry the maxim guns. He sent his mounted force in advance, with the Infantry corps following on the right to crown the hills, and the second on the left across the plain. Heavy firing soon showed that the horsemen were engaged, and the reserve company doubled up in support. This part of the force bore the brunt of the action until the outflanking movement on the right and left brought sufficient fire to bear on the dervishes, and sent them scurrying into retreat. The Mullah's village was burnt and the enemy was followed in scattered parties for five miles through the dense bush. Over 60 dead dervishes were found on the scene of action. Swayne lost one officer and nine men killed, and one officer and 16 men wounded. Being short of water, Swayne was forced to discontinue the pursuit, and once again, the Mullah escaped into Italian territory.

Somaliland

2ND Expedition, May-October 1902

In December 1901, the Mullah once again entered the Protectorate, where his force was daily increasing. Caravans of rifles, smuggled into the country through Mijjarten ports, were reported to be reaching him at Mudug. A despatch from the Acting Consul-General Cordeaux reported that the Mullah had raised his following to 12,000-15,000 men, at least 600 of them armed with rifles. In Cordeaux's opinion, another expedition was imperative. Colonel Swayne, therefore, asked for reinforcements from the Kings African Rifles. With a force of 1,200 infantry and 70 mounted troops, reinforced by 300 men from 2ND Battalion, Kings African Rifles, and the secondment of Sikh signallers from 5TH Battalion, Kings African Rifles, and the Sikh Contingent of Central African Rifles, he moved to Burao, where he established a base and built a stockade fort. On 26TH May, he marched south from Burao with the largest force he could muster. A garrison of 150 men was left behind at Burao, and 100 men in a masonry blockhouse at Las Dureh. To defend these two posts Swayne asked for another six-guns. The authorities in British Central Africa were asked by the Foreign Office to dispatch an officer and 60 Sikhs, with a maxim gun to garrison Berbera and other posts on the line of communication. Then he moved east into the Nogal Valley to check the raids from the Mijertein, where he detached a column under Lieutenant Colonel Cobbe to attack the Mullah's fort at Halin. The fort, which contained a number of rifles and large quantities of stock, was captured.

Battle of Erigo, October 1902

In October, Swayne commenced his advance on Mudug, and while advancing through the thick dense bush at Erigo, the Mullah's Dervishes attacked his force. They were attacked from all sides by riflemen and spearmen and some of the Somali Levies panicked, but the Sikhs and companies of Kings African Rifles stood firm. When the enemy had been driven off, most of the scattered camels and their loads were recovered, but the Dervishes carried off a maxim gun, which had been dropped by its bearers during the action. After the fight, Colonel Swayne retired to more open country, and on 11TH October fell back towards Bobotle, as the Levies were too much shaken to allow him to continue his advance. The news of fighting at Erigo reached the Foreign Office on 18TH October, in the form two telegrams. The first message reported that the enemy had been driven off with heavy loss, and the intention was to renew the attack on the Mullah. The second stated the fighting had been very severe; that the Somali Levies were much shaken; that the Mullah was ' bringing up reinforcements from all sides'; and that Swayne was retiring immediately and wanted 600 reliable troops and the remainder of the Reserve Battalion to be dispatched to Berbera.

Somaliland

3RD Expedition, 1902-1903

The check at Erigo left the advance force concentrated at Bohotle, with the Mudug oasis still in the possession of the Mullah, against whom a third campaign was now undertaken. Colonel Swayne was recalled and the direction of operations was entrusted to Brigadier General W. H. Manning. His first step was to replace the Somali Levies, who no longer could be relied on for close fighting. Accordingly, reinforcements from British Central Africa, East Africa, Aden, and India were ordered to embark for Somaliland. By the end of 1902, British forces totalled 2,674 ranks. As soon as a flying column could be ready, Bohotle, which was surrounded by hostile piquets, was relieved and garrisoned by Bombay Grenadiers from Aden and the British Central African contingent of Sikhs. Consent was given by the Italians to operate in their country and the plan was to land a force on the east coast at Obbia, march northwards, and drive the Mullah out of the Mudug oasis area. The column was further strengthened by two guns of a battery of 7-pounders loaned from Aden. 21 Sikhs of the Indian Contingent, who proved themselves excellent gunners, served them, and the unit was known as Kings African Rifles Camel Battery.

Sikh Gunners
(Kings African Rifles Camel Battery)

Somaliland

Battle of Gumburu, April 1903

The Somali Field Force to land at Obbia consisted of 86 British officers and 2,256 other ranks, including one section of the Lahore Mountain Battery, 2ND Regiment of Sikhs, Punjab Mounted Infantry, and 1ST, 3RD, and 5TH Kings African Rifles (with 102 Sikhs). The Berbera column consisted of 78 British officers and 2,297 other ranks including the Indian Contingent of British Central Rifles (105 Sikhs).

On 17TH April, Lieutenant Colonel Cobbe was commanding a Flying Column ahead of the main body moving against the Mullah. He had orders to secure the water supply at Wardair. Having established a *Zariba*, a camp fortified with a thorn hedge near Gumburu, he had cause to send forward 'A' Company 2ND Battalion Kings African Rifles, 48 men of 2ND Sikh Regiment and two maxim guns under Lieutenant Colonel Plunkett to secure the return of a small scouting party. Colonel Plunkett, in his eagerness to engage the enemy, was drawn on to a distance of four miles from the *Zariba* where he was attacked by the whole of the Mullah's force, numbering perhaps some 14,000 men. The British column of 224 of all ranks had apparently formed three sides of a square in single rank on the march out, with the Sikhs in the front face. Afterwards a half company was thrown across the rear face. The troops were attacked by about 4,000 horsemen and 10,000 warriors, apparently commanded by the Mullah in person. With the fanatical contempt for death that they always showed in his presence, the dervishes swept from all sides upon the square, first horsemen, then riflemen on foot, and finally hordes of spearmen who broke into the square with the weight of their headlong rush, heedless of the devastating fire of maxims and rifles. All were successfully repelled until the ammunition ran out. The Sikhs had taken with them 100 rounds per rifle in their pouches. There was no reserve ammunition. Moreover, the Sikhs used solid bullets not suited to stop a charging savage. When the ammunition started to run out the order was given to breakout with the bayonet and charge back to the *Zariba*. Plunket was killed and the little force was borne down and overwhelmed. No European or Sikh survived the fight.

Battle of Gumburu (Rai England)

Somaliland

Battle of Daratoleh, April 1903

On 22ND April, a column of 213 all ranks, which included 85 Sikhs of the Central African rifles, under the command of Major Gough, advanced and established a base at Danot. From Danot Major Gough decided to push on to Daratoleh, which was held by a strong force of the enemy. The column had not marched far before the mounted infantry fought an action against the Mullah's scouts and reported a large enemy force in front. Gough at once dismounted his men and formed a square with the Camels in the centre. The ground was dead flat; with thorn bush 15-20 feet high. A short period of extreme tension followed and then the attack broke in a sudden uproar of rifle fire from the long grass and thorn bush, at a range of 20-50 yards. Gough afterwards estimated the Mullah's force at 300 mounted riflemen and 500 spearmen. The attack continued for three hours, while the square remained steady and the Maxim guns were moved by the Sikhs from point to point to counter each threat as it developed. As the ammunition was running short, Gough decided to retire. Just then, the Dervishes were apparently reinforced as their assault, which had gradually slackened, was suddenly renewed. Throughout the afternoon the retirement continued, the Dervishes continually harassed the flanks and the rear. They were driven off by repeated bayonet charges. During the retreat, at a time when the rearguard had fallen some distance behind, Captain Bruce fell shot through the body. Major Walker, Sergeant Nderamani, and a Corporal of 2ND Battalion K.A.R., Lance Naik Maieya Singh of the Central African Rifles and Sowar Umar Ismail of 6TH Battalion K.A.R remained behind to fight off the Dervishes pressing around them. For the parts they had played in this action, Rolland and Walker and later Gough were awarded the Victoria Cross, the men of the K.A.R., the African D.C.M. and Lance Naik Maieya Singh the Indian Order of Merit. British casualties were six officers and 38 other ranks killed or wounded, whilst the Dervishes lost about 150 killed or wounded.

Battle of Daratoleh (Rai England)

Somaliland

4TH Expedition, 1903-1904

After these reverses, British prestige was at stake and forces were increased to divisional strength of 6,389 all ranks and placed under the command of Major General Sir Egerton, K.C.B., D.S.O. The reinforcement included 2ND, 4TH and 6TH Battalions Kings African Rifles, Sikhs of Central African Rifles, Camel Corp Battery (Sikhs), 1ST Battalion Hampshire Regiment, 27TH Punjabis and 52ND Sikhs. Kirrit was made the advanced base from which to strike at both Nogal Valley and the Bohotle area and by the end of October one brigade was concentrated at Bohotle and the other at Eil-Dab. A reconnaissance party of Mounted Infantry discovered the enemy in force at Jidbali.

Battle of Jidbali, January 1904

His Majesty's Government now decided on a further increase to the force in Somaliland, in view of the Mullah's position in the Nogal and its proximity to the British sphere. More than 8,000 troops, of which 1,000 were British, were employed, in the hope that the Mullah's power would be permanently shattered. The enemy's force, which numbered between 6,000 and 8,000 Dervishes, was concentrated at Jidbali, where the Mullah, deciding to make a stand, received a most crushing defeat. Egerton described the disciplined fire of the Sikhs and K.A.R. as 'terrific'. The Mullah's casualties in the actual fight at Jidbali must have been very large, but far greater were his losses during the course of his subsequent flight northwards to Jidbali, and thence eastward into Italian territory. It appears that the Mullah only sought sanctuary in Italian territory after receiving solemn assurances of a safe passage from Osman Mahmoud, the Sultan of the Mijertein. Thus, this fourth expedition was completely successful in all but bringing the Mullah himself to bay, and so putting an end to his movement. The morale of his Dervishes as a fighting body had been destroyed, and their numbers, estimated at 6,000 to 8,000 before Jidbali, could not have exceeded 800 on the conclusion of the campaign. Above all, the Mullah's personal prestige was temporarily shattered, and the discredited refugee in Italian territory must have made a poor figure. In March 1905, the Illig or Pestalozza Agreement was concluded between the Italian Government and the Mullah, whereby peace was declared between the Dervishes on the one hand and the British and Italian Governments on the other. The Mullah was assigned a port and certain territories in Italian Somaliland, beyond which he and his Dervishes undertook not to encroach. The Mullah also agreed to become an Italian protected subject. This agreement was, however, nullified soon after it was concluded, as the Mullah left Italian territory, and by 1907 had re-established himself on the British side, raiding and looting everywhere.

Somaliland

Operations at Shimber Berris, November 1914-15

The Mullah had built a series of forts on the plateau of the Burao range, each capable of holding 50 men. Fields of fire had been cleared around the forts and the area was full of caves. Lieutenant Colonel T. A. Cubbit rendered the following report to the Commander in Chief on the operations at Shimber Berris:

'I left Burao on 17TH November with a self-contained mounted column of 14 officers and 540 rank and files, composed partly of Indian contingent and partly of Camel Constabulary. The neighbourhood of Shimber Berris was reached on 19TH without the dervishes being aware the column had left Burao. The column had ascended the Burdab range of hills and found the enemy to be in occupation of three forts on the top of the hill. The attack on the two nearest forts commenced at 11 a.m.; a party of the Indian contingent under Lieutenant Howard rushed one, but the other, although charged repeatedly by the Camel Corps, was firmly held by the Dervishes. During one of these charges Captain Simmons of The King's Own Yorkshire Light Infantry, was killed within one yard of the door. Machine guns were brought into action at close range, but to no avail. Realising that the force was too strong to be rushed, I broke off the action at 3 p.m., the withdrawal being affected in good order and almost without molestation. The column camped eight miles south of the Burao. Reinforced by a gun from Burao, the column advanced against the forts again on the morning of 23RD November. One fort offered no resistance and the next fort attacked on 19TH was speedily captured. Captain Dobbs was then dispatched with two companies and the gun to attack a third fort, 1,100 yards away, but necessitating a detour of four miles owing to the presence of precipitous ravines. The attack was well executed; 60 to 70 dervishes fled out of the fort and down the hill, suffering some casualties. A fort in the Valley near the wells and 800 feet below my position was shelled, whereupon the enemy evacuated the forts and caves in the valley and fled eastwards.

In view of the fact that there were a number of severely wounded officers and men in my camp, I deemed it imperative to return to my camp in Burao as soon as possible. Moreover, without explosives, it was impossible to affect anything more than very partial demolition of the forts; therefore, I decided not to attempt any demolition in the valley. The column was accordingly assembled at 3 p.m. and Burao was reached on 25TH.

The terrain at Shimber Berris is extremely difficult; the Burao range rises a sheer 1,100 feet out of the plain and is intersected with deep ravines covered everywhere with boulders and thick scrub. The forts are remarkably well sited and very strong. The walls are 9 to 12 feet thick at the base, 16 to 20 feet high, and 24 feet wide, provided with well made machicouli galleries, but badly constructed loopholes, and each fort is capable of holding between 50 and 70 men. The sides of the cliffs are honeycombed with caves, some of which are capable of containing 100 men and animals.

Somaliland

Operations at Shimber Berris, November 1914-15 (Cont.)

'The troops were not in sufficient strength to leave a post at Shimber Berris, and, as I anticipated, the Dervishes returned in about a fortnight. The General Commanding Officer Aden placed an officer with thirteen men, of 23RD Sikh Pioneers at our disposal. So I was enabled to concentrate a force, partly mounted and partly dismounted, of 15 officers, 570 rank and file, (Sikhs and Somalis), six machine guns and two guns in the neighbourhood of Shimber Berris on 2ND February. On 3RD February, I advanced in two columns against the forts of the Burao. Although the Dervishes had commenced construction of new forts, the hilltop was unoccupied and the Sikh Pioneers blew up the forts. The following morning, 4TH February, the column was transferred from south to north of the Burao by a pass seven miles west of Shimber Berris and was concentrated on the plain close to that place by noon. The enemy were holding two forts overlooking and flanking a deep Nullah and a fort at the far end of the Nullah, also in occupation of the numerous caves in the hillsides.

The two flanking forts were captured after two hours fighting, but the enemy developed a heavy fire from the caves, and from the middle and the vicinity of the fort. The guns were brought forward and with machine guns engaged the middle fort and the caves at close range. The enemy's fire slackened, and the Dervishes were observed to be evacuating the fort and retiring southwards up the ravine. I despatched a company against this fort, but, although unable to affect an entrance, the company remained round the fort and enabled the Pioneers to place a charge of guncotton against the door, under a hot fire from the occupants inside. The fort and its defenders were blown up, hand grenades were thrown into caves, known still to be occupied, and the two flanking forts were blown up. I then withdrew the column, reaching my *Zariba* at 6.15 p.m., fighting having lasted continuously for more than five hours. The next morning all the caves were found to be evacuated. Leaving a tribal post at Shimber Berris, the column returned to Burao on 7TH and 9TH February.'

The following Sikh Pioneers were awarded the Indian Order of Merit for their conspicuous gallantry in this action. The citations for the awards read:

Naik Sher Singh: *For bravery in action on 4TH February at Shimber Berris, Somaliland. In placing a charge of gun cotton against the door of the fort, he was knocked over and rendered practically insensible by the discharge of Dervish rifles through the door, but after getting clear, he returned and placed the box in the correct place.* (Duckers, 1999, p.220)

Havildar Teja Singh: *For bravery in action on 4TH February at Shimber Berris, Somaliland. He followed Naik Sher Singh to the door of a fort and coolly placed a charge of gun cotton; arranged fuses correctly, fired the charge and enabled the demolition to be carried out successfully.* (Duckers, 1999, p.221)

Somaliland

Fifth and final expedition, 1920

'The Mullah withdrew towards his major fort at Taleh and the Governor, Sir Geoffrey Archer, consolidated the political situation in the areas he vacated, but the war in Europe then claimed many officers and a holding policy became necessary. Archer improved his control of the west of the Protectorate, while the Camel Corps became increasingly effective against the Dervishes, as they could advance rapidly and strike hard. Several hundred scouts strung out across the territory on the line of the de facto frontier with the Mullah, helped the Camel Corps, while infantry garrisoned the towns. The Camel Corps was reorganized into three camel–mounted companies (two Somali and one Indian) a Camel Battery manned by Sikhs, a Pony Company and an Indian contingent of 400 men. Its name was changed to Somaliland Camel Corps. The effects of drought and an epidemic of dysentery reduced the Mullah to desperate measures in attempts to restore his fortune and reputation and he raided close to Burao and then against the Dolbahanta, with little success. The Camel Corps made a major sortie on 5TH October, after 500 men raided the area of Eil Dur Elan. Lieutenant Colonel Ismay pursued the Dervishes to the northeast and trapped them in two narrow passes. Six machine guns were very effective against the 300 Dervishes on the crests and in the caves, and forced them to withdraw. The Mullah had lost eighty per cent of his force since Dul Madob and he withdrew into his last redoubt of forts, Taleh, Jilib, Baran and Wardair; then 1914-18 war ended.' (Malcolm Page, 1998, p.21*)*

'The campaign was opened by a bombing attack on the Mullah's forts. The attack on Baran Fort was mounted from Las Khorai. The fort was a square building with corner towers 40 feet high. It was solidly constructed and was defended by about 100 men. The fort was mortared but it was decided that it was insufficiently damaged, as there were only six direct hits out of 321 rounds fired. The attack resumed on 23RD at a shorter range with more effect and in the evening, a demolition party exploded 100 lbs. of gun cotton against one of the towers. On attacking at first light the following morning, the fort was found to be unoccupied. The destruction of Baran and the other forts then took only a few days. In this last and final round against the Mullah, the British had the advantage of communication by wireless and the use of aircraft. One by one, the Mullah's forts and strongholds were captured and destroyed and even the maxim guns lost at Erigo and Gamburu were recovered. Nevertheless, the Mullah still managed to elude his pursuers. He fled to his fort at Tale, a gigantic fortification that dwarfed any other in Somaliland. Lieutenant Colonel Ismay set out with the Camel Corps in pursuit and chased him southwards to the border, where he crossed the Hud to Galadi. In the process, most of his sons and relations were killed, captured, or surrendered, but the Mullah fled on into the Ogden country. He died at the age of 56 in November 1920 and thus ended the life of a man who for twenty years had fought great odds and managed to elude all the forces the British and Ethiopians could deploy against him.' (Magor, 1993, p.183)

Somaliland

The Sikh contingent 150 strong leaving Garrero for the front. 1903

Somali Dervish

ADEN

A ship under British colours was wrecked near Aden. The crew and passengers were badly treated by the Arabs and the Indian government demanded an explanation for the outrage. Sultan Mahsin of Lahej undertook to make compensation for the plunder of the vessel, and agreed to sell Aden town and its port to the British. Commander Stafford Butterworth Haines of the Indian Navy was sent to complete these arrangements but the Sultan's son refused to fulfil the promises that his father had made. A combined naval and military force was thereupon despatched from Bombay, which captured Aden and annexed it to the British Empire in the name of the East India Company on 16TH of January 1839. Aden became the gateway to India (the jewel in the Empire's crown). As Gibraltar guarded the entrance to the Mediterranean, so Aden guarded the entrance to the Red Sea, and - most important - the Suez Canal. In the days before efficient air transport, the shipping routes between Britain and the Sub-continent of India were vital and Aden was the major port between the two. Britain established protectorate over Aden and the British military was responsible for keeping the peace. Any tribal insurrection in the area was crushed as Britain maintained control of her supply routes. There was normally one British and one Indian infantry battalion stationed in Aden. The latter was usually at full strength (about 800 all ranks) strong. At this time, Indian battalions had few British officers, the number varying between five and nine, plus around 15 Indian officers. The Indian battalions came to Aden for two years and had to find a number of detachments: 50 men on Perim and for many years a sizeable detachment in British Somaliland.

Shaikh Sa'id, November 1914

Shortly after the outbreak of war with Turkey, on October 31ST, 1914, it became clear that the Turks, in co-operation with a number of the Arab tribes, were preparing an advance against the Aden Protectorate. The Turks had gathered in some strength on the Shaikh Sa'id Peninsula, which runs out to the south of the Red Sea towards the Isle of Perim. 29TH Indian Infantry Brigade, then on its way from India to Suez, was ordered to interrupt its voyage to capture Shaikh Sa'id and destroy the Turkish works, armaments, and wells there. On November 10TH, transports conveying three battalions of 29TH Indian Infantry Brigade and 23RD Sikh Pioneers arrived off the coast of the peninsula. They stormed the Turkish positions and compelled the enemy to retreat, leaving his field guns behind. The Sikh Pioneers then carried out demolitions at Turbah Fort and guardhouses, which included the destruction of two 6-inch guns, and four field guns of sorts, large quantities of shells and cordite. Having accomplished its task, the Pioneers re-embarked and sailed for Aden. It was not considered advisable at this time to push an expedition into the country to attack the Turks there. The Turks, consequently, remained in some force on the northern boundary of the Aden Protectorate.

Aden

Perim, June 1915

When the Sikh Pioneers arrived at Aden from Shaikh Said, a company was sent to Perim, which was threatened by the Turkish activity on the mainland. The Turks had reoccupied Shaikh Sa'id and endeavoured from there to effect a landing on the north coast of the Isle of Perim. The garrison of the island, a Company of the Sikh Pioneers, successfully repulsed this attack. As the Turks had put out the lights in the Red Sea, the British took these over and the Pioneers put guards on the lighthouses. Havildar Kehar Singh captured a dhow bringing an angry letter from Turkish authority to know why a light was burning (the British occupation not having been realised!)

Lahaj, July 1915

During May 1915, the enemy was reported to be becoming more active. During the latter half of June, reconnaissance discovered a strong Turkish force beyond Lahaj, supported by a large number of Arab tribesmen, which indicated a possible Turkish advance on Lahaj from Mawiyah. Consequently, the Camel Troop fell back on Lahaj, and was reinforced by the advance guard of the Aden Movable Column, numbering two hundred and fifty rifles, with two ten-Pounder guns. This advance guard had moved up under most trying conditions. The heat was intense, there was a great shortage of water, and it was difficult to make any progress over the heavy, sandy plains. The main body of the Aden Column was so delayed by difficulties of transport and by shortage of water that it did not reach Lahaj at all. The force in the Sultan's capital found itself faced by several thousand Turkish troops, with twenty guns. In addition, Arab tribesmen had rallied by the thousand to help the Turks. A few hundred men, the Sultan of Lahaj's little native army, backed the British. The troops were suffering terribly from the climate and from the shortage of water. To add to the difficulties, the Arab camp followers of the Aden Troop deserted them in a body at the most critical hour and took with them all their camels. Fighting opened on the evening of Sunday, July 4TH. Time after time, the enemy attacked the front and were driven off each time. The Turkish artillery was much stronger, but the men of the Royal Artillery strove, by courage and skill, to make up for the inequality in numbers. They showed a devotion to duty, which afterwards drew a warm tribute from the general commanding the Aden Brigade. Before long the Turkish artillery had kindled fires in different parts of Lahaj and the men were in danger of being outflanked and cut off by the flocks of Arab horsemen. The Sultan was killed with many of his men. The troops struggled to defend the capital as long as they could, hoping every hour for the arrival of the main body of the Aden Column. Hour after hour, they waited in vain. Relief did not come. Next day there was nothing to be done but to fall back from Lahaj towards Aden. The men at Lahaj had fought splendidly, but their task had proved beyond their strength.

Aden

Shaikh-Othman, July 1915

The British force fell back on the Kaur, immediately outside the Aden Peninsula. The Turks followed them up and occupied Shaikh-Othman, a town about two miles inland from Aden Harbour. This place was formerly part of the Sultanate of Lahaj and was now within the British Protectorate. The Turks at this stage held practically the whole of the Aden Hinterland, except immediately around the peninsula. They had reoccupied Shaikh Sa'id and had destroyed Lahaj. Some appreciation of the real perils of the situation apparently reached the Indian authorities and it was decided to increase the Aden garrison. On July 20TH 1915, troops from Aden, 28TH (Frontier Force) Brigade, a battery of Royal Horse Artillery and a detachment of Sappers and Miners, under the command of Lieutenant Colonel Elsmie, surprised the Turks at Shaikh-Othman, completely defeated them and drove them out of the place. Between fifty and sixty Turks were killed and wounded, and several hundred men, mostly Arabs, were made prisoners. This success was followed up in the following month by an attack by a small column on a Turkish post between Lahaj and Shaikh-Othman. The Turks were driven from the town. Another attack in a different direction was equally successful. Reports reached Aden that the Turks were preparing to retire from Lahaj itself, and in September, a column under Colonel Elsmie set out in the direction of Waht. Here it surprised a force of seven hundred Turks, with eight guns, who were supported by about a thousand Arabs. The Turks were driven back, and Waht fell into British hands. The remainder of the year saw a series of cavalry skirmishes and the defeat of a Turkish advance towards Imad.

Movable Column, January 1916

In January 1916, the Aden Movable Column defeated a large Turkish force near Subar and in March again defeated the Turks near Imad. The Turkish outposts at Jabir and Mahat were attacked in December and 200 casualties inflicted. On 5TH January 1917, Hatum and Jabir were occupied and a Turkish counter-attack successfully repulsed. The continuation of a policy of active defence saw Turkish forces and outposts being harassed whenever possible throughout 1917 and 1918. The vital port of Aden remained safely in British hands and was never seriously threatened by an enemy, which simply could not pierce its defensive cordon.

Aden remained under British rule until 1967. It then became the capital of the People's Democratic Republic of Yemen on November 30TH, 1967.

Aden Troop

Aden Troop was a small cavalry unit specially raised in India for service in Aden. One of the least known reverses suffered by the British Army in the First World War was that which happened at Lahej in early July 1915. The intense heat and insufficient preparations resulted in the repulse against the Turks. Lance Daffadar Hira Singh was awarded the Indian Distinguished Service Medal for his gallantry in this sorry affair.

Aden

Malay States Guides

The Guides, Infantry and a battery of Artillery were raised in 1875, with class composition of Sikhs and Punjabi Mussalmans, being ex-Indian Army soldiers. During the First World War, the Battery and the Infantry joined the Aden Defence Force from October 1915 onwards. The Battery at the strength of three Indian officers, 54 Gunners, 50 Drivers and five followers, the Infantry numbering 788 all ranks, predominantly Sikhs. They continually clashed with the Turks and had a great deal of marching under very hot sun.

Jemadar Gurdit Singh
Malay States Guides

Jemadar Gurdit Singh was awarded the Indian Order of Merit for conspicuous gallantry in action on the night of 15TH and 16TH February 1918, in Aden. This Sikh officer commanded a platoon in an attack against an enemy piquet. He personally volunteered to go forward and exactly locate the piquet and by doing so materially assisted the success of the operation. Subsequently in the attacks, he led his platoon with great gallantry and determination.

Havildar Kehar Singh and Sepoy Sarwan Singh
Malay States Guides

The above soldiers were awarded the Indian Order of Merit in Aden for conspicuous gallantry on 5TH August 1916, in dashing out to within 400 yards of the enemy's position and bringing in a wounded Indian officer under heavy shell and rifle fire.

Naik Sawan Singh
Malay States Guides

Naik Sawan Singh was awarded the Indian Order of Merit for gallantry and devotion to duty in Aden in 1915.

The following officers and men of Malay States Guides were awarded the Indian Distinguished Service Medal for their conspicuous gallantry against the enemy in Aden:
Havildar Wir Singh, Havildar Bagga Singh, Jemadar Bogh Singh, Naik Santa Singh, Sepoy Surian Singh, and Sepoy Lal Singh.

Sepoy Sohan Singh
23RD Sikh Pioneers

Sepoy Sohan Singh was awarded the Indian Order of Merit for conspicuous gallantry and devotion to duty in Aden on 4TH July 1915. He also showed the greatest pluck and determination when he escaped from captivity. He made his way through 350 miles of strange country and after undergoing many privations, due to lack food and water and a bad climate, rejoined the British forces.

EGYPT

The importance of Egypt to Britain rose dramatically after the opening of the Suez Canal in 1869. At a stroke, there was a new route from Europe to the Far East that halved the journey time between Britain and India. At this point Egypt was developing rapidly along western lines, but the following decade saw increasing tension between Britain and Egypt.

From 1805, Egypt had been nominally part of the Ottoman (Turkish) Empire, but it was effectively ruled by a dynasty established by the strong and modernising ruler Muhammad Ali. By 1869, it had benefited from years of investment (much of it British and French) in irrigation, railways, cotton plantations and schools. By 1876, however, its ruler Khedive Ismail Pasha had run up debts of almost £100 million. In spite of the Khedive's sale of his 45 percent holding in the Suez Canal to Britain for £4 million in 1875, Egypt was heading for financial ruin. The crisis led to heightened French and British intervention in Egypt. Khedive was forced to accept Anglo-French control of his treasury, customs, railways, post offices, and ports. This amounted to an erosion of Egyptian sovereignty, which provoked a nationalist mobilisation in the form of a demonstration by unpaid army officers under the leadership of Ahmad Arabi Pasha Al-Misri (also known as Arabi). By September 1881, Arabi and his followers were powerful enough to force the new Khedive, Tawfiq, to replace his government with one more favourable to the nationalist movement. In January 1882 Arabi himself, who commanded huge personal popularity, became Minister of War. The appearance of a popular nationalist movement inside Egypt and a defiantly independent government alarmed both Britain and France, who were concerned about access to the Suez Canal and their financial investments in Egypt. In the hope that a show of force would help to undermine the nationalists, they sent a small joint fleet under the command of Admiral Sir F. Beauchamp Seymour (Commander-in-Chief of Britain's Mediterranean fleet) to Alexandria, on Egypt's Mediterranean coast. The fleet arrived at Alexandria on 19TH-20TH May. Meanwhile, Egyptian forces had been busy shoring up Alexandria's defences in anticipation of an attack. As relations between Britain and Egypt broke down, Arabi ordered the strengthening of Alexandria's defences with modern Krupp cannon. On 10TH July, Admiral Seymour demanded that the Egyptians remove these guns, but the Egyptian government refused. With the Egyptian government refusing to remove the guns, Seymour gave the order for the bombardment of the gun emplacements in the forts around Alexandria. At 07:00 on 11TH July 1882, the first shell in the bombardment was fired by HMS Alexandra and aimed at Fort Adda (or Ada). The whole fleet was engaged by 07:10 and the bombardment lasted until 17:30, a total of 10 and a half hours.

Egypt

Alexandria

British landing parties entered Alexandria (in what was described as a policing action) on 13TH July, two days after the bombardment. The city had been partially destroyed by fire and, following the departure of Arabi's soldiers, law, and order had collapsed. That same day Khedive Tawfiq sought British protection leaving, Arabi as leader of the Egyptian government. Arabi's troops were encamped outside Alexandria and the British feared for the security of the Suez Canal.

Suez Canal

To secure the Suez Canal and safeguard British interests the British Prime Minister, Gladstone, sent an expeditionary force to restore order and install a new administration in Egypt. Between 13TH July and 6TH September 1882, two armies, one from Britain and the other from India, converged on Egypt under the command of Lieutenant-General Sir Garnet Wolsley.

Kassassin

Since the army, on its march to the Delta would have to depend entirely on the canal for its water supply, and this could easily be drained between Kassassin and Ismailia by shutting the Kassassin lock, the first object of the British was to seize Kassassin, which was reached and occupied on 30TH August. On the morning of 9TH September as the Indian Cavalry brigade was furnishing the outposts at Kassassin, a large number of the enemy attacked a piquet of 13TH Bengal Lancers. The piquet charged down on the attackers and drove them back with loss. About the same time, the enemy was observed advancing in considerable force and on receipt of this information a cavalry regiment was at once sent to the front and the infantry brigade turned out. It was observed that the enemy was advancing in two bodies, from the north and the west. The cavalry was manoeuvred so as to keep these two bodies separated. As the Indian Brigade threatened the left of Tel-el-Kebir column, 1ST Brigade moved against the right of the column from Es Salahiyeh. The Egyptians made no stand against the cavalry advance and the infantry had followed them up to within 5,000 yards of the Tel-el-Kebir position, while the Es Salahiyeh force had retreated with equal haste before 1ST Cavalry Brigade. It is possible that had an attack now been made on Tel-el-Kebir it would have succeeded. It would not, however, have been the decisive success for which Sir Garnet Wolsley wished; therefore, it was decided not to push the advantage any further that day. The period 9TH–12TH September was taken up by the march to the front and by the successive arrival in camp of those portions of the army, which had not yet been concentrated at Kassassin. Throughout this action, the Indian cavalry attracted attention by their steadiness. During these operations, Trumpeter Surain Singh earned the Indian Order of Merit for conspicuous gallantry against the enemy and Lance Daffadar Aussan Singh specially brought to notice for his gallant conduct.

Egypt

Tel-el-Kebir

At Tel-el-Kebir, the Egyptian army had prepared defences consisting of a number of deep ditches and embankments constructed out of the desert sand. The defence lines that had been under construction for six weeks, started from a point on the fresh water canal about two miles east of Tel-el-Kebir Bridge and extended northwards for about four miles. The desert around Tel-el-Kebir was extremely flat, so any approach by the British would easily be spotted. Further, it had been noticed that the outposts and piquets of the enemy were only sent out beyond their entrenchments at daybreak. For these reasons, it was decided to advance up to the enemy's position at Tel-el-Kebir by night and attack the entrenchments at the first gleam of dawn. In pitch darkness, the troops moved forward in silence followed by the cavalry in rear. The force had marched about three miles when the warning shots, which heralded the attack of the Highland Brigade, were heard. The Highlanders then pushed forward over the open ground against the guns, which were protected by some pits and covered by some trenches with about 400 men in them. 20TH Infantry at the same time taking the flank. The 7TH Infantry supported the Highlanders, while the 29TH Infantry followed in the rear of the 20TH Infantry. The mountain battery came into action on the canal bank, firing at the flashes of the guns. The Infantry advanced by rushes, drove the enemy from their entrenchments on the south bank, and captured four guns. The whole line now advanced, driving the enemy before it and capturing his guns. The cavalry were pushed forward to cut off the fugitives who were soon pouring into the village of Tel-el-Kebir from the northern side. Once Tel-el-Kebir was in British hands, a number of infantry and cavalry divisions moved off to secure other positions. These included a triumphant march on Cairo on 14TH September. It was soon seen that the Egyptians had decided to capitulate. A small party of cavalry occupied the citadel; 10,000 of the enemy had surrendered their arms and started for their own homes. Arabi and his associates were taken prisoner, court-martialled, and exiled to Sri Lanka; Khedive Tawfiq was restored to power. The war was effectively over. Egypt became a British protectorate in 1914.

Bengal Lancers at the Battle of Tel- El-Kebir.

Egypt

The Suez Canal was a vitally important supply route for the British Empire. During the First World War, troops and equipment of the Australian, New Zealand and Indian forces passed this way en route for the Western Front, in addition to millions of tons of foodstuffs, minerals and other provisions bound for Britain and her Allies. In order to maintain security, look after British interests in the protectorate and to defend the strategically critical Suez Canal, there were 70,000 British troops in Egypt by January 1915. Many of these were in units of the Indian Army. During the war, British forces stood on the defensive along the Suez Canal, defeating various attempts by the Turks to capture or damage the canal. The most important features affecting the fighting were the narrow coastal plain from the Suez Canal area stretching northwards past Gaza and Jaffa.

Suez Canal, January 1914

14TH Ferozepore Sikhs arrived at the Suez Canal on 2ND of December. The troops were employed in routine defence duties and in extending and improving the defences of the Canal. In the early morning of 28TH of January, about two hundred of the enemy attacked the Sikhs' outpost held by "E" Company. The Turks were repulsed and suffered heavy casualties, leaving a number of killed and wounded on the battlefield. The Sikhs captured some prisoners, who were in a sorry state after their march from Palestine across the Sinai Desert. A strong Turkish force attacked Qantara early on the morning of 3RD of February. These attacks were beaten back by the double companies of 14TH Sikhs.

Bir-en-Nuss, November 1914

A Sikh Princely States unit, Patiala Lancers, extensively patrolled the Suez Canal during the First World War. Their first clash came in north Sinai when they encountered a force of some 200 Bedouins and Turks near Bir-el-Nuss. The Patrol lost one Indian officer, twelve other ranks killed, and three Sepoys wounded but inflicted some sixty casualties on the enemy. The Lancers reached Patiala on 27TH January 1919, after more than four years active service overseas.

Serapeum, January 1914

92ND Punjabis were given the task of defending the Serapeum section of the Suez Canal. Early in January, the Turks raided Kantara. Supported by rifle and machine gun fire, they succeeded in approaching Serapeum. 92ND successfully charged the attackers, taking many prisoners. On the morning of 4TH the Turks were still in strength, entrenched on the East Bank of the Canal. 92ND Punjabis were ordered to attack and round up the Turks in this position. The Punjabis stormed the entrenchments and compelled all the Turks to surrender.

Egypt

Kantara, January 1915

In January 1915, the Turks assembled a force of two Divisions and took the central route across the Sinai desert. Carrying pontoons and rafts, they approached the east bank of the Suez Canal in the early hours of 3RD February 1915. Indian machine-gunners cut swathes through those on the water and through men massing in the gullies on the east bank. The enemy panicked and many Arab troops on the Turkish side surrendered. The enemy renewed their attack at dawn, with additional diversions launched at Kantara and near Ismailia. Shelling from the British ships, and continued staunch resistance by the Indian troops in the defensive posts, stemmed the Turkish attack. The entire Turk force withdrew, back across the Sinai towards Beersheba. The Turks lost 1,500 troops in this action.

Tussum, February 1915

On 3RD February 1915, the Turks made a serious attempt to cross the Suez Canal near Tussum with planned attacks on five other points. None of these efforts came to anything, the attackers being defeated at Tussum and at another action fought at Kantara.

Katia, April 1916

On 23RD April 1916, the Turks raided a British outpost at Katia, with two infantry battalions, one mountain howitzer battery and one camel cavalry regiment. It was a successful attempt and the British cavalry unit in Katia was taken prisoner, together with its commander, 23 officers, and 257 troopers. Katia was one of the outposts built on the east side of the Canal. There was no British existence there during the first Turkish attempt to take the Canal the previous year.

Romani, August 1916.

At the start of 1916, the British defensive line ran along the line of the canal. It was felt that that line needed too many men to operate it. So it was decided to move to a new position further east, along the northern coast of the Sinai desert, from where a smaller force could block the routes to Egypt from the east. Work then began on a defensive position at Romani. Eighteen infantry redoubts, each with 100 rifles and two machine guns, were built on a line of sand hills along a seven-mile front south from Mahemdiva on the coast, ending at Katib Gannit. A ridge ran west from Katib Gannit, protecting the southern flank of the British position. A branch line was built from Romani to Mahemdiva, and a narrow gauge railway from Mahemdiva along the coast to Port Said. This ridge was given the name Wellington Ridge. In early July a Turkish army 16,000 strong, commanded by Kress von Kressenstein, began an advance across the Sinai. This force contained 3RD (Anatolian) Division and Pasha I, a force of German machine guns, artillery and anti-aircraft guns. Kress' intention was to establish a base within artillery range of the Suez Canal and bombard the shipping.

Egypt

Romani, August 1916 (Cont.)

On 19TH July, the British discovered the Turkish army and quickly reinforced the Romani position. On 24TH July, the Turks reached a position ten miles east of Romani and then stopped for ten days while their heavy artillery crossed the desert. Early on the morning of 4TH August, the Turks were finally able to attack Wellington Ridge. The pressure was relieved by the arrival of the New Zealand Brigade and 5TH Mounted Brigade. By the end of the day, the Turkish attack had failed all along the line. The Turks capitulated and the armistice was signed on November 1918, ending the First World War.

Britain had unilaterally recognized the independence of Egypt in 1922, but continued to occupy the country militarily, and dominate its political and economic affairs. Subsequent to the Anglo-Egyptian Treaty of 1936, the British occupation was limited to the Suez Canal Zone; however, a treaty provision allowed British troops to re-occupy the rest of the country in time of war.

The following Sikh soldiers were awarded gallantry awards for their conspicuous gallantry during the First World War in Egypt:

Sowar Hukam Singh
14TH Cavalry (Scinde Horse)

Sowar Hukam Singh was awarded the Indian Order of Merit for conspicuous gallantry and devotion to duty in Egypt on the morning of 23RD September 1918. When his squadron, with a troop from 29TH Lancers, was attacking an enemy position, the objective of his troop was two houses, from the top of which heavy machine-gun fire was being directed on the troop. Sowar Hukam Singh and two other Sowars, without the slightest hesitation and with the greatest gallantry, charged through to the enemy under heavy machine-gun fire. By their dash and gallantry, these men helped to capture seven machine-guns and 500 infantry.

Sowar Balwant Singh
14TH Cavalry (Scinde Horse)

Sowar Balwant Singh was awarded the Indian Order of Merit for conspicuous gallantry and devotion to duty in Egypt on the morning of 23RD September 1918, when his squadron, with a troop from 14TH Cavalry, was attacking an enemy position. The objective of his troop was two houses, from the top of which heavy machine-gun fire was being directed on the troop. Sowar Hukam Singh and two other Sowars, without the slightest hesitation and with the greatest gallantry, charged through to the enemy under heavy machine-gun fire. By their dash and gallantry, these men helped to capture seven machine-guns and 500 infantry.

Egypt

Jemadar Prem Singh (Posthumous)
34TH Pavo Poona Horse

Jemadar Prem Singh was awarded a posthumous Indian Order of Merit for conspicuous gallantry and devotion to duty in Egypt on 28TH July 1918. Jemadar Prem Singh organised and carried out a successful attack, with his troop, on a hostile party. Owing to his dash and perseverance, 15 of the enemy were killed, one officer and four men being made prisoners. He personally killed two of the enemy. The example of fearlessness, which he set, was magnificent. Jemadar Prem Singh was killed in action.

Jemadar Amar Singh
34TH Pavo Poona Horse

Jemadar Amar Singh was awarded the Indian Order of Merit for conspicuous gallantry on 23RD September 1918 in Egypt. During an action with the enemy, Jemadar Amar Singh was sent out with a troop to endeavour to get round the enemy's flank, as the regiment was being held up frontally. He located six machine-guns, which he promptly charged and captured taking several prisoners, thus enabling the regiment to advance.

Resaidar Dayal Singh
34TH Pavo Poona Horse

Resaidar Dayal Singh was awarded the Indian Order of Merit for conspicuous gallantry on the night of 21ST–22ND September 1918 in Egypt. The regimental outpost line was attacked by an unknown number of the enemy. Resaidar Dayal Singh was sent with his troop to reinforce the advance squadron. On arrival at the outpost, he immediately led a charge on the enemy. With great dash, Resaidar Dayal Singh and his troop killed a number of the enemy and captured over 150 prisoners.

Havildar Wazir Singh
1ST KGO Sappers and Miners

Havildar Wazir Singh was awarded the Indian Order of Merit for conspicuous gallantry and devotion to duty in Egypt during the operations of September and October 1918, especially on 19TH September 1918, when in charge of party of Sappers advancing with the infantry against the enemy's trenches. He was particularly noticeable for his dash and courage and set a fine example to his men. He had previously done good work and behaved with great bravery, particularly on the night of 28TH–29TH May, when in charge of a party erecting a wire entanglement, he was wounded but refused to leave his party until he personally saw the work was completed.

Egypt

Havildar Mangal Singh
47TH Sikhs

Havildar Mangal Singh was awarded the Indian Order of Merit for conspicuous gallantry whilst serving with the British forces in Egypt in 1917.

Lance Naik Thaman Singh
47TH Sikhs

Lance Naik Thaman Singh was awarded the Indian Order of Merit in Egypt for conspicuous gallantry during the attack on 19TH September 1918. Although wounded in two places, he carried his Company Commander, who was seriously wounded, back to the shelter under heavy machine-gunfire. He then rejoined his company and carried further operations, setting fine example of endurance.

Subedar Mehar Singh
47TH Sikhs

Subedar Mehar Singh was awarded the Indian Order of Merit Egypt for conspicuous gallantry and devotion to duty in the operations on 19TH and 20TH September 1918. On 19TH, with skilful handling of his company, he greatly contributed to the successes of the operations. On 20TH September, he collected a few men at a critical time and rushed the enemy automatic rifle, which was enfilading the advance of the rest of the company, and destroyed it.

Havildar Wazir Singh
47TH Sikhs

Havildar Wazir Singh was awarded the Indian Order of Merit in Egypt for conspicuous gallantry and devotion to duty in the operations on 19TH and 20TH September 1918. On 19TH September, he took command of his platoon when the commander was wounded and showed great ability and judgment. On 20TH September, when the company was held up by heavy rifle fire, with a few men he rushed the enemy automatic rifle which was enfilading the advance and caused the enemy to abandon two other automatic rifles by his skilful use of the captured weapon.

Lance Naik Dalel Singh
53RD Sikhs

Lance Naik Dalel Singh was awarded the Indian Order of Merit in Egypt for conspicuous gallantry and initiative on the night of 6TH and 7TH May 1918. Lance Naik Dalel Singh accompanied a patrol of two platoons, which was surprised by a large body of the enemy, coming under fire of rifle, and machine-guns at close range. He repulsed the attacks and systematically withdrew his platoons. He had previously done excellent work and obtained accurate and valuable information.

Egypt

Naik Phaga Singh
1ST KGO Sappers and Miners

Naik Phaga Singh was awarded the Indian Order of Merit in Egypt for conspicuous gallantry on 9TH September 1917. On the night of 8TH September, Naik Phaga Singh was in command of a section of a raiding party. On finding that a wounded man had been left behind, Naik Phaga Singh immediately led out men in the moonlight, in the face of heavy machine-gun fire, to rescue the wounded man. In the process of safely bringing the soldier back to the line, he was seriously wounded.

Havildar Suba Singh
56TH Punjabi Rifles (Frontier Force)

Havildar Suba Singh was awarded the Indian Order of Merit for conspicuous gallantry and devotion to duty when in command of a patrol of nine men on the Suez Canal on 22ND March 1915. Havildar Suba Singh surprised and engaged a strong raiding party of Turks, estimated at 400, under German officers. In the fight that ensued, he showed a determined front and fought with great gallantry. Although severely wounded, Havildar Suba Singh continued to lead and encourage his men and extricated his patrol from a very difficult situation, with the loss of two killed and three wounded, whilst the losses to the enemy were estimated at 12 killed and 15 wounded.

Jemadar Phuman Singh
72ND Punjabis

Jemadar Phuman Singh was awarded the Indian Order of Merit for conspicuous bravery during the raid on enemy Sangars on 16TH August 1918 in Egypt. The British officers and two Indian officers of the assaulting and clearing parties had become casualties and Jemadar Phuman Singh, under heavy shell-fire, reorganized the few remaining men and attempted with great gallantry to penetrate the enemy Sangar. This gallant officer managed to get within twenty yards of the enemy Sangars. However, his party had become too small to be of any avail and he ordered a retirement, which was carried out successfully, under heavy enemy machine-gun and high explosive shellfire.

Lance Naik Jagat Singh
72ND Punjabis

Lance Naik Jagat Singh was awarded the Indian Order of Merit for conspicuous gallantry and devotion to duty in the raid on enemy Sangars on 16TH August 1918 in Egypt. Although wounded himself, he remained with his British officer, who had a broken leg and had been left about one hundred yards from the enemy Sangars, when the assaulting party had withdrawn owing to heavy casualties. Lance Naik Jagat Singh, under heavy fire, attended to the British officer and dressed his wounds.

Egypt

Sepoy Kishen Singh
72ND Punjabis

Sepoy Kishen Singh was awarded the Indian Order of Merit in Egypt for conspicuous bravery and devotion to duty. In the raid on enemy Sangars on 16TH August 1918, an Indian officer was wounded in the leg, within a few yards of the enemy Sangar. The party had been compelled by casualties to withdraw but Sepoy Kishen Singh remained with the officer and, although under fire, managed to drag him back under cover of rocks some two hundred yards away.

Sepoy Dasunda Singh
89TH Punjabis

Sepoy Dasunda Singh was awarded the Indian Order of Merit for conspicuous gallantry in the operations on the Suez Canal on 3RD February 1915. Sepoy Dasunda Singh brought up ammunition to his comrades under heavy fire and each time on the return journey carried back a wounded man to the ambulance, which was about 800 to 1,000 yards in rear. He also carried Sepoy Hakim Singh, who was killed and Sepoy Sucha Singh, who was wounded, from the firing line, removing his boots in order to perform the journey quicker.

Sepoy Nard Singh
91ST Punjabis

Sepoy Nard Singh was awarded the Indian Order of Merit for very conspicuous gallantry and coolness on 4TH July 1919, with the Egyptian Expeditionary Force. About 40 of the enemy in the hills attacked a party of 15 signallers and an escort, under a British officer who was severely wounded in the leg. Sepoy Nard Singh immediately went to his assistance and dragged him under cover, remaining with him while the enemy searched the ground in the vicinity and killed a wounded Sepoy lying close to their hiding place.

Naik Nihal Singh
92ND Punjabis

Naik Nihal Singh was awarded the Indian Order of Merit for conspicuous gallantry at Tussum during operations on the Suez Canal on 3RD February 1915. As his company moved out to counter–attack the enemy, Naik Nihal Singh worked his way to a point from where he shot and killed one of the enemy, while the remainder of the group rushed back to their trench. He kept firing on the enemy in the trench and enabled his company to get to a point from which they could infiltrate the enemy trench. This they did and compelled the enemy to surrender. During the remainder of the day's fighting, Naik Nihal Singh led his squad with coolness and pluck.

Egypt

Rifleman Sukh Singh
125TH Rifles

Rifleman Sukh Singh was awarded the Indian Order of Merit for conspicuous gallantry and initiative on 19TH September 1918 in Palestine. During the attack on the enemy position, Rifleman Sukh Singh and a British officer had got some distance ahead of the rest of the company. While so advancing, Rifleman Sukh Singh managed to capture two enemy horses. He gave one to his officer and mounted the other himself. Continuing to press forward in this manner, they caught sight of an enemy battery in retreat. Without the slightest hesitation, they galloped in pursuit and on coming up on the guns; Rifleman Sukh Singh held ten of the enemy, whilst the officer compelled the surrender of the battery officers and the guns.

Havildar Wasakha Singh
152ND Punjabis

Havildar Wasakha Singh was awarded the Indian Order of Merit in Egypt for conspicuous gallantry during the operations in September and October 1918. Particularly on 19TH September 1918, during an attack when his company commander fell wounded in the open. Havildar Wasakha Singh, with another man, at once advanced from a captured enemy position to bring the officer into cover, under heavy machine-gun fire. Whilst doing so, the other man was severely wounded but Havildar Wasakha Singh succeeded in bringing the officer and the other man under cover of rocks.

Sepoy Kartar Singh (Posthumous)
152ND Punjabis

Sepoy Kartar Singh was awarded a posthumous Indian Order of Merit in Egypt for conspicuous gallantry on 19TH September 1918. After the first attempt to take the enemy trenches had failed, and the men were falling back to their original position, Sepoy Kartar Singh rushed forward under heavy fire from the second line, throwing bombs until the supply was exhausted and he was killed. He displayed great courage and devotion to duty.

Sepoy Jai Singh
Burma Military Police

Sepoy Jai Singh was awarded the Indian Order of Merit for conspicuous gallantry in action at Khan Abu Malul, Egypt, on 19TH September 1918. Several times he was forced to withdraw with his Lewis gun by grenade attacks by the enemy. He displayed great determination and courage in coming into action in different places.

Egypt

Captain Bhagwan Singh
Patiala Infantry

Captain Bhagwan Singh was awarded the Indian Order of Merit in Egypt for gallantry and devotion to duty on the night of 29TH–30TH April 1918. When in command of the advance guard they were held up by a party of the enemy with machine-guns concealed in thick scrub. Captain Bhagwan Singh led his men in such a prompt and fearless manner that the enemy were forced to retire hastily.

Subedar Kala Singh
Patiala Infantry

Subedar Kala Singh was awarded the Indian Order of Merit for conspicuous gallantry in action at Gallipoli in 1916. Subedar Kala Singh served with 14TH Sikhs. A Double Company of the Patiala Infantry was attached to 14TH Sikhs and they stayed with them after the Gallipoli campaign. They served in Egypt, Persia, and Mesopotamia.

Subedar Dharm Singh
Patiala Infantry

Subedar Dharm Singh was awarded the Indian Order of Merit for gallantry and devotion to duty on 30TH April 1918 in Egypt. His platoon came under very heavy shell and machine–gun fire. An order was issued for the company to withdraw to a more sheltered position but Subedar Dharm Singh remained where he was, as he had two seriously wounded soldiers with him whom he could not remove. He remained there for over two hours, until stretcher–bearers could go out and bring them in.

Jemadar Indar Singh and Havildar Ganda Singh
128TH Pioneers

Jemadar Indar Singh and Havildar Ganda Singh were awarded the Indian Order of Merit for conspicuous gallantry in charging a number of the enemy who had landed at Tussum on the Suez Canal on 3RD February 1915.

Sikhs of the 62ND Punjabis in action during the Battle of Suez Canal

Egypt

15TH Ludhiana Sikhs

In 1914, 15TH Ludhiana Sikhs went to fight in France with 3RD Lahore Division, but in late 1915, the Regiment was posted to Egypt, where it operated against a much more traditional and tribal enemy.

The Senussi

Working from eastern Libya, Sayed Ahmed, known as the Senussi, was the leader of a sect of devout Muslims. His men had been fighting the Italian occupiers of Libya with considerable success. They were trained and assisted by a group of Turkish military officers led by Nuri Bey, half-brother of the Turkish War Minister, Enver Pasha. During 1915, German submarines began supporting the Turkish effort with the Senussi's army by transporting Turks and weapons to Eastern Libya and attacking shipping along the Egyptian coast. The Senussi was at first reluctant to fight Britain, but in the end Nuri Bey persuaded him to join the Turkish Holy War and to invade Egypt. The Allied reverses at Gallipoli doubtless influenced the Senussi's thoughts and actions. In early November 1915, a German submarine sank the British ships Tara and Moorina off the western Egyptian coast. The British survivors of these attacks were handed over by the submarine to the Senussi, who arranged their captivity. The Senussi's troops then harassed and fired upon the British outposts at Sollum and Sidi el Barrani. British Headquarters in Cairo decided that a withdrawal was necessary, and all British troops west of Matruh were ordered to move to that location. At Sollum, the most westerly British post, the withdrawal was effected rather too hastily, as the Egyptian Army garrison of the fort was left behind. During the withdrawal, many Egyptian Coastguards deserted to the Senussi with their weapons and camels. The Senussi's followers now occupied and pillaged all the abandoned British locations.

Western Frontier Force

On 20TH November 1915, the British formed the Western Frontier Force (WFF). The commander was Major-General A. Wallace and he assembled his force at Matruh. A light railway moved the men and mounts from Alexandria to Dabaa, and from there the men marched or were shipped the seventy-five miles to Matruh. The WFF contained an infantry brigade composed of three partially-trained British battalions, 6TH Royal Scots and 2ND Battalion, 8TH Middlesex Regiment, plus 15TH Ludhiana Sikhs. The other main component of the WFF was the cavalry brigade consisting of three composite British Yeomanry regiments and a composite regiment of Australian Light Horse. Brigadier-General the Earl of Lucan commanded the infantry, and Brigadier-General J. D. T. Tyndale-Biscoe commanded the cavalry. The 15TH Ludhiana Sikhs was the only regular major unit. The one artillery battery, the Nott's Battery Royal Horse Artillery, was to perform very well in the forthcoming actions.

Egypt

Wadi Senab

By 3RD December, the British garrison at Matruh numbered 1,400 men. New arrivals included 'A' Battery, Honourable Artillery Company; two 4-inch guns manned by Royal Marines, two aircraft of 17TH Squadron, Royal Flying Corps, and a six-car detachment from the Royal Naval Armoured Car Division. Meanwhile, over 2,000 of the Senussi's men were believed to be moving south and west of Matruh. On 11TH December, General Wallace sent out a column to disperse a group of enemy, reported to be at Duwwar Hussein, sixteen miles west of Matruh. Lieutenant-Colonel J. L. R. Gordon was appointed Column Commander. The column consisted of 15TH Sikhs, less two companies, 2ND Composite Yeomanry Regiment, a section of guns of the Nott's Battery and a detachment of armoured cars. Lieutenant-Colonel Gordon took his infantry along a track that followed the telegraph line westwards to Sollum, while the cavalry, guns, and armoured cars used a road to the south-west, known as the Khedivial Motor Road, which also led to Sollum. The mounted column departed at 07.00 hrs on 11TH December, but the cavalry moved so quickly that the scouts could not keep sufficiently ahead of the main body. Around 300 of the enemy were waiting to the north of the road in the Wadi (valley) Senab, and they successfully ambushed the cavalry. Attempts made to turn the enemy's right flank were driven back by heavy fire, and a stalemate existed until a squadron of Australian Light Horse arrived from Matruh in the afternoon. Then, using artillery support, the cavalry forced the enemy group out of its position. Eighty dead and seven prisoners were left behind by the Senussi troops. British losses were sixteen killed and seventeen wounded. During this action, Lieutenant-Colonel Gordon continued along his track and established a firm base at the Umm Er Rakham wells. The cavalry joined him there during the night. As the cavalry mounts were exhausted, 12TH December was spent in resting and in rounding up nearby enemy stock. The 6TH Royal Scots, less two companies, joined Gordon during the night of 12TH December, as did a convoy of stores. On the following morning at 08.30 hrs, Gordon marched west to Wadi Hasheifat, planning to turn south up the wadi towards Duwwar Hussein. As the track was expected to be unfit for heavy wheels, the sixty 1ST Line Transport pack mules of 15TH Sikhs were loaded with reserve ammunition and extra water for the column. One company of 15TH Sikhs was left to guard the camp. As the British column approached the Wadi Hasheifat from the east, the cavalry was forward and dispersed, No. 2 Company of 15TH Sikhs was the advance guard, and two platoons of the Royal Scots formed the left flank guard. Lieutenant-Colonel Gordon heard heavy firing on his left and observed his left flank guard running very swiftly towards the shore, pursued by an equal number of uniformed and well-drilled soldiers, who used formations and cover as they followed up the fleeing Royal Scots.

Egypt

The Senussi

The British soldiers were not attempting to engage the enemy, who were troops of the Muhafizia, the Senussi's regular army trained by the Turks. The Sikhs' two machine guns came into action to halt the enemy advance. Many more of the enemy now appeared and Lieutenant-Colonel Gordon decided to fight on the edge of the plateau that rose from the coastal plain. The Royal Scots were ordered to move forward and to the left, and the cavalry were brought back to man the right of the line; however, the cavalry took some time to reorganize, and the Royal Scots appeared unwilling to advance. This left the advanced guard, which had occupied some mounds, in an exposed position and Gordon ordered it to withdraw towards the headquarters. The 15TH Sikhs' company commander, Captain C. F. W. Hughes, replied that he could not comply with the order unless he abandoned his wounded, and that he was therefore obliged to hold his ground. The enemy increased the pressure around 10.00 hrs by bringing 4-inch guns into action and by effectively deploying machine guns. Lieutenant-Colonel Gordon radioed back to the camp at Umm Er Rakham ordering forward all reinforcements that could be spared, and the machine gun section of the Royal Scots and seventy-five men of the Australian Service Corps, armed with rifles, were sent forward. As these reinforcements approached the main body, an enemy machine gun engaged them. This induced the Royal Scots machine gun section to break and run for cover with their guns into the sand dunes on the beach, but the Australians stayed and fought well. Finally, two squadrons of Australian Light Horse came forward from Matruh and escorted two Royal Horse Artillery field guns onto the beach, where they engaged the Senussi's warriors. Also, HMS Clematis, a newly built submarine trawler mounting two 4-inch guns, appeared offshore and fired at the enemy positions. A lucky British shell exploded amongst one of the largest groups of enemy, scattering it, and that was the turning point of the action. The enemy began to withdraw, and as his machine-guns ceased firing, the Royal Scots advanced to their nominated objective. The 15TH Sikhs advanced guard regrouped and evacuated its four dead and nineteen wounded. Knowing he could not achieve a decisive result and aware of the fatigue felt by men and mounts, Lieutenant Colonel Gordon withdrew his men to their camp and on the next day the column returned to Matruh. British casualties amounted to nine killed and fifty-six wounded, whilst enemy casualties were around 100 killed and wounded. *

* The Official History comments:
'The enemy had been driven off, but had been able to retire unmolested, and must be given credit for the surprise and the vigour of his attack. Had the standard of training and the experience of the whole column been equal to those of the 15TH Sikhs, the Senussi might have been heavily defeated.'
(from *Frontier and Overseas Expeditions)*

Wadi Majid

Bad weather now prevented operations for ten days and during this time 1ST Battalion, New Zealand Rifle Brigade arrived to join the Western Frontier Force. Meanwhile British aerial reconnaissance reported that the enemy was concentrating 900 Muhafizia in three battalions, plus four mountain guns and two machine guns, six miles south-west of Matruh where Jebel (mountain) Medwa dominated the road to Sollum. General Wallace hoped to surprise the enemy force, and at 05.00 hrs on 25TH December, two columns moved out from Matruh. The southern composite cavalry column under Brigadier Tyndale-Biscoe detoured on a southern loop through Wadi Toweiwa, attempting to position itself to prevent an enemy withdrawal. The infantry column, comprising 15TH Sikhs, 1ST N.Z. Rifle Brigade and 2ND Battalion, 8TH Middlesex Regiment, plus supporting arms, advanced down the Sollum road. General Wallace's headquarters followed the infantry column. The only effective signalling sub-unit in the force was 15TH Sikhs' signals platoon. Lieutenant-Colonel Gordon, who had asked to command his battalion rather than do a job that General Wallace could easily manage, was ordered to command the infantry column. Major G. Pennefather-Evans commanded 15TH Sikhs. As dawn broke, an enemy outpost spotted the British advance and gave the alarm by lighting a huge bonfire. Observing that Jebel Medwa was not occupied, Gordon sent one of the two 15TH Sikh companies forming the advanced guard to seize the Jebel, and this was achieved without opposition. At around 08.00 hrs, an enemy mountain gun began to shell the road from a ridge west of Jebel Medwa where the enemy battalions were forming up. This caused 15TH Sikhs to open out into artillery (i.e. dispersed) formation, astride of but well clear of the road. With Lieutenant-Colonel Gordon using his telescope and acting as an observer, the Nott's Battery engaged and silenced the enemy gun from a range of 2,000 yards, whilst shells from HMS Clematis also fell on the enemy-occupied ridge from a range of 10,000 yards. Lieutenant-Colonel Gordon requested General Wallace to relieve the Sikh company on Jebel Medwa, and a company of the Middlesex did this. The 15TH Sikhs now advanced on the enemy ridge on a frontage of 200 yards, with 1ST New Zealand Rifles following. Companies of New Zealanders were placed as guards on each flank as the Sikhs moved briskly across an open plateau. The advance was halted 800 yards from the enemy, to allow the cavalry to appear and take up position. As the cavalry did not appear, the advance continued but now with both New Zealand companies on the right flank. As the British troops moved onto the ridge the enemy broke and fled, some of them hiding in caves and gullies where they were shot or bayoneted. The whole of the ridge was secured by 10.00 hrs. Gordon now brought the guns forward onto the plateau, where they fired into the retreating enemy. Regrettably, the cavalry was not in position to complete the destruction of the Muhafizia battalions.

Egypt

Wadi Majid

The southern column had first been delayed by moving its guns over difficult terrain, and then had been engaged at around 08.00 hours by enemy camelry and horsed cavalry, who had anticipated the British cavalry move. Although machine gun fire finally dispersed the enemy, this contact disrupted the column's advance. At 15.00 hrs, the cavalry column appeared but by then the battle was nearly over. The enemy had retreated into Wadi Majid, followed by the Sikhs and New Zealanders. The enemy camp in the wadi was set alight and the Muhafizia rearguard, demoralized but still fighting effectively, was driven onto the beach. Some of the enemy feigned death or wounds, but then opened fire at close range. This so enraged the Sikhs that any of these men taken alive were thrown into the burning tents. The light was fading and at 17.00 hrs, Colonel Gordon broke off the infantry pursuit, ordering the battalions to bivouac on Jebel Medwa. The mounted troops returned to Matruh that night, followed by the infantry early the next morning, 26TH December. British losses had been thirteen killed and fifty-one wounded. The Senussi's force lost between 300 and 400 dead, and eighty prisoners were taken.

Halazin

The 15TH Sikhs were now involved in two minor operations because of aerial observation of enemy encampments. On 28TH December, a column marched out to Bir Gerawla, twelve miles southeast of Matruh, and on 12TH January 1916, another column marched to Jebel Howeimil, thirty-five miles in a similar direction and fifteen miles south of the coast at Baqqush. In both cases, the camps were found to be deserted and were burned down. Livestock in the immediate vicinities was seized. On 19TH January, an aeroplane located the main enemy camp at Halazin, twenty-two miles south-west of Matruh. Over 300 tents were observed, one of them belonging to the Senussi himself. General Wallace left Matruh at 04.00 hrs on 22ND January, with an infantry and a mounted column. A South African battalion now joined the WFF. The right-hand infantry column was commanded by Lieutenant-Colonel Gordon and the left-hand mounted column by Brigadier Tyndale-Biscoe. The force bivouacked in bad weather at Bir Shola, just over half way to Halazin. On 23RD January, Gordon's column advanced on a compass bearing directly towards the enemy, whilst the mounted column echeloned to the left front of the infantry. Motor transport experienced extreme difficulty on the sodden ground, and the armoured cars returned to Matruh. By 09.25 hrs, the cavalry were in action against parties of the Senussi's men and Brigadier Biscoe requested the infantry to attack, whilst the cavalry manoeuvred against the enemy's right flank. At 10.00 hrs, 15TH Sikhs advanced with No. 1 Company leading, No. 2 Company 200 yards behind, and No. 3 and No. 4 Company 300 yards further to the rear. Each company echeloned its platoons to the left. Support was provided by 2ND South African Infantry, 1ST New Zealand rifles and the covering fire of four guns of the Nott's Battery.

Egypt

Halazin

The enemy displayed considerable skill in withdrawing to prepared defences and made good use of mountain guns and machine guns, causing attrition amongst the British troops. Seeing that his right flank was being aggressively turned by parties of the enemy, Gordon reinforced that flank, first with two companies of South Africans, then with a company of New Zealanders with machine guns, and finally by a company of Royal Scots. Meanwhile, on the British force's left flank the cavalry was also outflanked and receiving effective enemy machine gun and artillery fire. Despite receiving reserves, the mounted troops were gradually driven in. Two companies of New Zealanders were sent to stabilize the left flank, which they did, and the remaining New Zealand Company advanced on the left of the Sikhs. The shape of the British advance now resembled a horseshoe with the Sikhs in the centre of the curve. The British infantry did not flinch, despite the open ground it crossed and the punishment it took. By 14.45 hrs the Sikhs, New Zealanders, and South Africans were through the enemy camp and into the entrenchments. The enemy defenders broke and retreated into the desert, abandoning their position. The British cavalry mounts needed water and were not in a condition to pursue, so again the Senussi's men escaped. The British had lost one British officer, twenty men killed, ten British and three Indian officers, and 278 other ranks wounded. The 15TH Sikhs suffered eighteen men killed and two British and three Indian officers and 115 men wounded. The Senussi escaped, but he had lost around 200 men killed, including Turkish troops, and up to 500 wounded. General Wallace camped two miles to the east, and the non-walking or riding wounded had to be carried through the wet ground on stretchers. The British force took two days to complete its withdrawal to Matruh.

Jemadar Basant Singh, 15TH Sikhs, received the Indian Order of Merit for gallantry at Halazin, the only I.O.M. granted for this action. In addition, eight other ranks of 15TH Sikhs were awarded the Indian Distinguished Service Medal.

The Senussi and his followers continued to present a security threat in the Western Desert for a further twelve months. But the participation of 15TH Sikhs in the campaign was over, as the regiment now received orders to proceed to India. The 15TH Sikhs had withstood the worst of the fighting so far, and had provided the backbone for a very untrained, inexperienced, and under-staffed Western Frontier Force. The regiment had acquitted itself with distinction, and for its services in this theatre, it received the honour 'Egypt 1915-17.' Because of the post-war reforms of the Indian Army, it became 2ND Battalion, 11TH Sikh Regiment.

SUDAN

The Sudan Campaign was fought between a radical group of Moslem dervishes, called Mahdists, who had over-run much of Sudan, and the British and Egyptian forces who nominally controlled the government of the region. The Mahdi, also known as Muhammad Ahmad, was a self-proclaimed prophet whose base of support was Arab traders, who were angry over the efforts of the Egyptian-British government to abolish slavery. They had long held most of the population in subjugation, and now either made alliances with or massacred the native tribes in the region. In a short time, the Mahdists, who opposed not only the infidel British, but also the secular Egyptian government, controlled much of Sudan. The Sudan region had long been a bastion of slavery. Principally slave-trading Arab tribes, who gained dominance and enslaved much of the Negro population, controlled it. As Britain gained ascendancy over Egypt, it pressured the Egyptian khedives to prohibit slavery, and eventually General Charles Gordon, a British war hero, was installed as the Governor of Sudan. He worked tirelessly for nearly a decade in Sudan, doing everything possible to break up the slave trade, and finally returned to Britain exhausted. The Mahdist movement was not at first taken seriously by the Egyptian governor until late 1883, when the Mahdists massacred two Egyptian armies sent to restore order. The Mahdist warriors were fanatical, brutal, and nearly fearless, and much of Sudan fell under their influence out of sheer terror. The British government, had no desire to contend for Sudan and ordered the Egyptian and British garrisons in the region to retreat, and left Sudan in the hands of the Mahdists. In 1896, the British resumed their war upon the Mahdists of Sudan, but in the interim, several important things had happened. Mahdi himself had been murdered by one of the women in his harem, and the Khalifa, one of his Generals, took his command. The Mahdists themselves were troubled with internal disputes, and the Italians in the east, and the French in the west had hindered their expansion. Most importantly for the Britain, the Egyptian government itself, which had been in a precarious state during the first war against the Mahdi due to financial troubles and the recent rebellion in the army, was now on a much more solid footing, under the administration of Lord Baring. The Campaign was led by Kitchener, who built a railroad through the Nile valley before leading the British and Egyptians to a decisive victory over the Mahdists. The decisive battle was fought at Omdurman. Following defeat of the Mahdists at Omdurman, an agreement was reached in 1899, establishing Anglo-Egyptian rule, under which a governor-general appointed by Egypt, with British consent, governed Sudan.

Battle of Kashgal, November 1883

On November 3RD 1883, an Egyptian force, 11,000 strong, under Hicks Pasha, with several British officers, was led by a treacherous guide into a defile, where they were attacked by the Mahdists, and after fighting for three days, were massacred almost to a man.

Sudan

Battle of El Teb, February 1884

The Battle of El Teb was fought on February 4TH, 1884, when a column of 3,500 Egyptian troops under Baker Pasha, marching to relieve Sinkat, was overwhelmed, and practically annihilated by 12,000 Sudanese under Osman Digna. The Egyptians lost 2,360 killed and wounded.

Battle of Tamai, March 1884

The Battle of Tamai was fought on March 13TH, 1884, when 4,000 British, under General Graham, attacked and defeated the Mahdists, under Osman Digna, destroying their camp. The British fought in two squares, one of which was shortly broken by the Mahdists, who captured the naval guns. The second square, however, moved up in support, and the Mahdists were repulsed and the guns recovered. The British lost 10 officers and 204 men killed and wounded; the Dervishes over 2,000 killed.

Battle of Trinkitat, March 1884

The Battle of Trinkitat was fought on March 29TH, 1884, when the British, 4,000 strong, under General Graham, totally defeated 6,000 Mahdists, under Osman Digna, after five hours' severe fighting. The British casualties amounted to 189 killed and wounded; the Mahdists lost about 2,000. This action is also known as the Battle of El Teb.

Battle of Khartoum, January 1885

This city, defended by an Egyptian garrison under General Gordon, was invested by the Mahdi in the early part of 1884, and, after a gallant defence, was stormed and taken by the Mahdists on January 26TH, 1885.

Battle of Abu Klea, January 1885

The Battle of Abu Klea was fought on January 17TH, 1885, between a British force, 1,500 strong, under Sir Herbert Stewart, and 12,000 Mahdists, of whom about 5,000 actually attacked. The British square was broken at one corner, owing to the jamming of a Gardner gun, and the Mahdists forcing their way inside. A desperate hand-to-hand conflict followed. Eventually the assailants were driven off, and the square reformed. The British loss was 18 officers, among them Colonel F. Burnaby and 150 men. In the immediate vicinity of the square, 1,100 Arab dead were counted.

Battle of Abu Kru, January, 1885

The Battle of Abu Kru was fought on January 19TH, 1885, between 1,200 British troops under Sir Herbert Stewart, and a large force of Mahdists. The Mahdists attacked a short distance from the Nile, and the British square moved towards the river, repelling all assaults successfully till they reached the Nile. The British losses were 121, including Sir Herbert Stewart, mortally wounded. This action is also known as the battle of Gubat.

Sudan

Battle of Kirbekan, February, 1885

The Battle of Kirbekan was fought on February 10TH, 1885, when the British, about 1,000 strong, under General Earle, stormed the heights of Kirbekan, which were held by a strong Mahdist force, and totally routed them, with heavy loss. The British lost 60 killed, among whom was General Earle.

Suakin, 1885

The British Government placed General Sir G. Graham in command of a strong force collected at Suakin, with instructions to destroy the power of the Osman Digna and to occupy the Hadendowa territory. Among the components of this force were Sikh troops, both the cavalry and infantry. The Sikhs bulked in the Bengal Cavalry regiments and of course, the infantry regiment of 15TH Ludhiana Sikhs.

Hashin, March 1885

To crush Osman Digna's power, first his force at Hashin had to be broken up. Accordingly, on 19TH March, as the cavalry brigade and Indian infantry advanced, a small force of the enemy was seen, which retreated, apparently upon the main body at Hashin. Later on, the whole enemy force retreated westwards, leaving a portion in occupation of Hashin Hill, whence it fired occasionally upon the cavalry. On the following day, a force of about 8,000 men, including the Indian contingent, advanced towards Hashin under the command of Sir G. Graham. A heavy fire was opened by the enemy, who were, however, driven from the summit. The Indian and Guards Brigades advanced and occupied the gorge between Bihilbat and the smaller hill. Considerable difficulty was encountered in moving through the bush. Two squadrons of 9TH Bengal Cavalry, while in pursuit of Arabs, were charged from the bush. One squadron dismounted and opened fire, but was driven back upon the Guard's square with the loss of nine men. On the right, 5TH Lancers and two squadrons of 9TH Bengal Cavalry charged with great effect and completely checked a body of the enemy, who were attempting to turn the British right flank. The whole force was then recalled to Suakin. The Indian losses amounted to one officer and eight non- commissioned officers and men killed, and three officers and thirty-six non-commissioned officers and men wounded. The enemy's strength was estimated at 3,000. The next step was to crush Osman Digna at Tamai. The advance on Tamai was difficult owing to the dense bush and frequent halts were necessary. The cavalry soon reported small bodies of the enemy retreating towards Tamai. At a distance of five miles from Suakin, the camel convoy was rapidly falling into confusion and it was considered impossible to carry on the advance. It was decided to form *Zaribas* (fortified bases) six miles from Suakin at the halting ground known as Tofrek.

Sudan

Battle of Tofrek, March, 1885

The British force and Indian Contingent marched from Suakin towards Tamai, to build three Zaribas at Tofrek. While still unfinished, they were heavily attacked by Arabs of the Hadendoa tribe. In one action 17TH Bengal Infantry broke and retreated. On the retreat of 17TH Bengal Infantry, the Arabs stampeded the animals collected to the left of that regiment and swarmed into the Berkshire Regiments *Zareba*, stabbing and cutting everywhere. Large bodies of the enemy rushed round in every direction, charging on the fence with the utmost courage, and intervening between *Zarebas* and the transport animals. They destroyed an enormous number of the latter. The Berkshires were pursued by the yelling Arabs. Fortunately the Sikh outposts kept their heads and retired steadily and in good order, which just gave the Berkshires time to reach safety. Even so, a few of the slower ones would have been overtaken, had not a very gallant Sikh Subedar turned back single handed, and killed several of their pursuers with his sword.

"Two soldiers of the Berkshires were saved from certain death by the magnificent daring of Subedar Gurdit Singh of 15TH Ludhiana Sikhs, who, placing himself between the pursuers and their prey, killed three Arabs in ||Asuccession by rapid sword cuts." (from *Frontier and Overseas Expeditions*)

The 15TH Sikhs and 28TH Bombay Infantry stood firm, maintaining an intact line and receiving and repelling successive attacks with a heavy fire. Hundreds of dead Arabs were afterwards counted in front of the Sikh position. Twenty minutes after the action commenced the "Cease fire" was sounded, yet in the short period 1,500 Arabs were killed, to take no account of the wounded.

The 9TH Bengal Cavalry enroute for Suakin, hearing firing at *Zareba*, returned with the two squadrons. About one mile from the *Zareba* they came upon a number camel drivers, some native infantry, a few British soldiers and a number of camels, all in full retreat from Suakin, closely pursued by the enemy in much greater force, who were cutting down and killing them in large numbers. Remounting and pressing on, they delivered more volleys within 300 yards of the enemy. The Arabs then dispersed, leaving many dead and wounded on the ground. On 24TH March, another convoy proceeded to the *Zareba,* escorted by 15TH Sikhs, 28TH Bombay Infantry, and 9TH Bengal Cavalry. Three miles from the *Zareba,* an escort of the Coldstream Guards and Royal Marines, who had come to take over the convoy, met the force. On its way back, it was attacked by the enemy in considerable force and in closing up the square more than one hundred camels were left outside and either killed or lost. On the following day, a water convoy reached the *Zareba* without mishap.

Sudan

Camel Corps

On 16TH April, orders were issued for the immediate formation of a camel corps, each of the Indian contingent regiments furnishing its quota for a combined company. On 6TH May the Camel Corps, two companies mounted infantry and 9TH Bengal Cavalry, marched soon after midnight form Suakin to attack a Shaikh who was threatening the line of communication. A force from Otao, comprising a company of mounted infantry and 15TH Sikhs, and 200 friendly natives who co-operated. The district was cleared of the enemy and his camp captured. In accordance with orders from England, the withdrawal of the expeditionary force began on 17TH May. Sir Graham in his despatch of 30TH May said: "The 15TH Sikhs on several occasions displayed their splendid marching powers". It should be recorded that on sailing from India the places of some fifty sick of the 15TH Sikhs were filled by volunteers from the 45TH Sikhs.

Suakin, 1885

9TH Bengal Cavalry

The 9TH Bengal Cavalry were highly praised for their operations around Suakin. The following Sikh officers and men were awarded the Indian Order of Merit in consideration of their conspicuous gallantry during these operations:

Resaidar Hookum Singh, Lance Daffadar Indhur Singh, Lance Daffadar Poourn Singh, and Trumpeter Kaiser Singh.

Sikh officers of the 9TH Bengal Cavalry.
Suakin Field Force 1885

Sudan

A Sikh unit in Cairo, on their way to Sudan, 1885.

Sikh Cameleers

Two Sikh members of the Camel Corps, one of whom is a Corporal, at a camp in Suakin. Other members of a Sikh regiment of the Indian Army look on. The Camel Corps was raised to overcome the difficulties of transport in the areas in which the force was operating. The camels were transported from India.

Sudan

Reconquest of Sudan, 1896

In 1892, Herbert Kitchener (later Lord Kitchener) became Sirdar, or commander, of the Egyptian army and started preparations for the Reconquest of Sudan. The British decision to occupy Sudan resulted in part from international developments that required the country be brought under British supervision. By the early 1890s, British, French, and Belgian claims had converged at the Nile headwaters. Britain feared that the other colonial powers would take advantage of Sudan's instability to acquire territory previously annexed to Egypt. Apart from these political considerations, Britain wanted to establish control over the Nile, to safeguard a planned irrigation dam at Aswan. In 1895, the British government authorized Kitchener to launch a campaign to reconquer Sudan. Britain provided men and materiel, while Egypt financed the expedition. The Anglo-Egyptian Nile Expeditionary Force included 25,800 men, 8,600 of whom were British. The remainder were troops belonging to Egyptian units that included six battalions recruited in southern Sudan. An armed river flotilla escorted the force, which also had artillery support. In preparation for the attack, the British established army headquarters at Wadi Halfa, and extended and reinforced the perimeter defences around Suakin. In March 1896, the campaign started; in September, Kitchener captured Dunqulah. The British then constructed a rail line from Wadi Halfa to Abu Hamad and an extension parallel to the Nile to transport troops and supplies to Barbar. Anglo-Egyptian units fought a sharp action at Abu Hamad, but there was little other significant resistance until Kitchener reached Atbarah and defeated the Ansar. After this engagement, Kitchener's soldiers marched and sailed toward Omdurman, where the Khalifa made his last stand. On September 2ND, 1898, the Khalifa committed his 52,000-man army to a frontal assault against the Anglo-Egyptian force, which was massed on the plain outside Omdurman. The outcome never was in doubt, largely because of superior British firepower. During the five-hour battle, about 11,000 Mahdists died, whereas Anglo Egyptian losses amounted to 48 dead and fewer than 400 wounded. Mopping-up operations required several years, but organized resistance ended when the Khalifa, who had escaped to Kurdufan, died in fighting at Umm Diwaykarat in November 1899. Many areas welcomed the downfall of his regime. Sudan's economy had been all but destroyed during his reign and the population had declined by approximately half, because of famine, disease, persecution, and warfare. Moreover, none of the country's traditional institutions or loyalties remained intact. Tribes had been divided in their attitudes toward Mahdist, religious brotherhoods had been weakened, and orthodox religious leaders had vanished. The condominium government of the Anglo-Egyptian Sudan was then established.

Sudan

Posed photographs of the 35TH Sikhs in Sudan, 1896

Sudan

Kassala.1940

At the outbreak of the Second World War, a mere 5,000 British troops were widely scattered across Sudan. On July 4TH, Italian forces in Eritrea crossed the Sudanese border and forced the small British garrison holding the railway junction at Kassala to withdraw. The defenders lost 10 men, the attackers 117. The Italians also seized the small British fort at Gallabat, just over the border from Metemma, some 200 miles to the south of Kassala. Even the villages of Qaysān, Kurmuk, and Dumbode on the Blue Nile were conquered. Having taken Kassala and Gallabat, however, the Italians spent time consolidating their positions in the captured areas and preparing for a further large-scale advance. The 5TH Indian Infantry Division started to arrive in the Sudan in early September, 1940. The 29TH Indian Infantry Brigade was placed on the Red Sea coast to protect Port Sudan, 9TH Indian Infantry Brigade was positioned southwest of Kassala and 10TH Indian Infantry Brigade was sent to Gedaref, accompanying the divisional headquarters. The 5TH Indian Division at once took the initiative. The raids on the frontier posts forced the invaders to pay heavily for their advance. The 5TH Indian Division, reinforced by the Sudan Defence Force, forced the Italian troops away from their aggressive design on the Sudan. The Axis powers were defeated and surrendered on May 2ND, 1945. The governments of Egypt and Britain signed a treaty guaranteeing Sudanese independence on 1ST January 1956.

Subedar Natha Singh, I.D.S.M., 1ST Punjab Regiment
(5TH Indian Division, 1945)

NORTH AFRICA

This section is titled North Africa instead of Egypt, as the battles also engulfed Libya and Tunisia. In 1937, anticipating global conflict, Britain made plans to send troops from India to Egypt, Iran, Burma, Singapore and Aden, should it became necessary to do so in the defence of British interests. In 1938, an infantry brigade group was earmarked for this purpose. In September of that year, the strength of troops to be sent to Egypt was doubled and a divisional headquarters added. 11TH Indian Infantry Brigade sailed for Egypt in August, a divisional headquarters, and 5TH Indian Infantry Brigade sailed in September. The divisional headquarters was designated to 4TH Indian Divison in Egypt. A Middle East Command, under General Sir Archibald Wavell, came into being in August 1939. Troops available in Egypt at that time were 7TH (British) Armoured Division consisting of two armoured brigades of two armoured regiments each, an armoured car regiment and a motor battalion, 4TH Indian Division consisting of two infantry brigades, a Royal Artillery Group, and eight British infantry battalions. The British and the French between them controlled a major part of the Middle East and had command of the sea and air in the Mediterranean.

In May, Hitler and Mussolini concluded a military alliance. On 1ST September, Germany invaded Poland with massive ground and air forces. On 3RD September, Britain declared war on Germany. India got automatically involved in the war and its forces fought in Africa, the Middle East, and Malay, Italy and in Burma.

The situation changed dramatically for the worse with the fall of France and the entry of Italy in the War in June 1940. After the fall of France on 20TH June 1940, French resistance in their colonies in North Africa, Syria and French Somaliland gradually collapsed. The Italians could now concentrate their efforts against the British in North and East Africa. Marshal Grazaini deployed the Tenth Italian Army in Cyrenaica. Its HQ was at Tobruk, with a motorised group, which had three tank battalions, plus 72 medium and 30 light tanks and two Libyan Divisions. The Italian XX111 Corps was at Badia with two Metropolitan divisions and one Black Shirt Division. XX11 Italian Corps with two divisions was on the line of communication. In the theatre, the Italians had a total of 415,000 troops, 215,000 in Libya, and 200,000 in East Africa. Wavell, on the other hand, had total o 85,000 men.

Sikh Gunners in Libya, 1941

North Africa

Nibeiwa, December 1940

On 9TH December a detachment of artillery commenced diversionary firing for an hour at the fortified Nibeiwa camp. At that moment 11TH Indian Infantry Brigade, with 7TH Royal Tank Regiment under command, attacked Nibeiwa from the North West, which reconnaissance had established as the weakest sector. The enemy, terribly shaken by the artillery bombardment and the invulnerable tanks, and having suffered heavy casualties, could not stand the sight of the bayonet. Through the dust and smoke they advanced, the bayonet a terrible weapon in the hands of these men from the plains of northern India. After some fierce fighting, Nibeiwa was taken; The Italian General was killed and 2,000 prisoners taken. Large quantities of supplies were also taken intact, while British casualties amounted to eight officers and forty-eight men. It was a magnificent victory. The thousands of prisoners were marshaled outside the camp, and were evacuated in captured transport. A few, very few, managed to get away to the Tummar Camps, but the surprise had been so complete and the attack so overwhelming that no organized defence could be made. Major-General Noel Beresford-Peirse, commander of 4TH Indian Division, ordered his 5TH Indian Infantry Brigade to move up with supporting field artillery and take positions for the attack on the Tummars.

The Tummars, December 1940

7TH Royal Tank Regiment and artillery had softened up Tummars defences for an hour. The tanks broke through the perimeter and were followed by the infantry. Tummar West was overrun, except for the extreme north east corner. The determination of the Indian soldiers was exemplified by the actions of Havildar Kalyan Singh of 1ST Punjab Regiment. When inside the camp, where there was still much resistance all around, his carrier was set on fire by a hand grenade. He wrenched his gun from its mounting, getting badly burnt as he did so, and at once went into action on the ground, silencing an enemy post. Not until his last round had been fired did he think of getting away and still under fire, saw his men packed into another carrier, before finding room for himself. Meanwhile 7TH Armoured Division's 4TH Armoured Brigade, while performing flank defence, had advanced to Azziziya where the garrison of 400 surrendered.

7TH Royal Tank Regiment in North Africa

North Africa

Sidi Barrani, December 1940

On the nights of 7TH December and 8TH December 1940, the Western Desert Force under the command of Major-General Richard O'Connor and comprising British 7TH Armoured Division and Indian 4TH Infantry Division reinforced by British 16TH Infantry Brigade, advanced a total of 70 miles to their start positions for the attack. The RAF made attacks on Italian airfields, destroying or damaging 29 aircraft on the ground. Selby Force, a mixed force of 1,800 under Brigadier A. R. Selby, moved up from Matruh and having stationed a brigade of dummy tanks in the desert as a decoy for the Italian air force, had by dawn on 9TH December taken position a few miles southeast of Maktila. In the meantime, the monitor HMS Terror and the gunboat HMS Aphis had bombarded Maktila, while the gunboat HMS Ladybird had shelled Sidi Barrani. On 10TH December, 16TH Infantry Brigade was brought forward from 4TH Indian Division reserve and with elements of 11TH Indian Brigade under command was sent forward in lorries to attack Sidi Barrani. Moving forward that morning across exposed ground, the force took some casualties but with support from artillery and 7TH Royal Tank Regiment it was in position, barring the south and south western exits to Sidi Barrani by 13.30. At 16.00, supported by the whole of the division's artillery, the attack, again with the support of 7TH Royal Tank Regiment, went in. The town was captured by nightfall and the remains of the two Libyan Divisions and the 4TH Blackshirt Division were trapped between 16TH Infantry Brigade and Selby Force. The 7TH Armoured Division tried to cut off the Sofafi garrison but the Italians had already withdrawn. Selby Force made an effort to cut off Maktila during the night 9TH–10TH December but was forestalled by the enemy's withdrawal. The Maktila garrison, finding its retreat cut off, surrendered. On 11TH December Selby Force supported by some tanks attacked and secured the surrender of 1ST Libyan Division. In the battle of Sidi Barani three Italian Divisions and a mobile group had been dispersed and 20,000 prisoners taken. The Italians were forced back again and again and further and further into Libya. Before what started as a raid was over, the whole of the Tenth Army had been destroyed. Egypt was clear of the enemy on 10TH December when Sidi Omar was captured.

Wrecked Italian tank at Sidi Barani, 1942 (Peter McIntyre)

North Africa

Afrika Korps, 1941

In early 1941, after the decisive British and Commonwealth victory in Cyrenaica, the military position was soon reversed. Wavell ordered a significant portion of O'Connor's XIII Corps to support Greece as part of Operation Lustre. While Wavell was reducing his forces in North Africa, German dictator Adolf Hitler responded to the Italian disaster by ordering Operation Sunflower. This was the deployment of the newly formed German "Afrika Korps" as reinforcements to the Italians, to prevent total collapse. The German corps included fresh troops with better equipment and a charismatic commander, General Erwin Rommel. When Rommel arrived in North Africa, his orders were to assume a defensive posture and hold the front line. Finding that the British defences were thin, he quickly defeated the Allied forces at El Agheila on March 24TH. He then launched an offensive which, by 15TH April, had pushed the British back to the border at Sollum, recapturing all of Libya except for Tobruk which was encircled and besieged.

Operation Battleaxe, June 1941

Operation Battleaxe was fixed for 15TH June. Its intention was firstly to destroy the enemy armour, and secondly to relieve Tobruk, invested by about two thirds of the enemy forces. The remaining third, 13,200 infantry, 70 field guns and 100 tanks, were strongly entrenched in positions north and west of the Halfaya Pass, and on the coastal plain. They must be defeated before Tobruk could be relieved. Wavell's forces were about equal to Rommel's, except in the vital arm, tanks, in which they were markedly inferior in quantity and, as it transpired, in quality. Operation Battle Axe was a total failure. Seventeen out of eighteen tanks supporting 4TH Indian Division's attack from Halfaya to the sea were ablaze in the first few minutes. They had suffered heavily from 88mm guns. It was the ultimate anti-tank weapon of its day, able to smash the heaviest tank at 2,000 yards. When the British rear was threatened by German armour, almost intact, while the British had lost in all ninety–six tanks, there was nothing for it but to call the attack a reconnaissance and withdraw to original positions.

Afrika Korps, 1942

North Africa

The Battle for Omars, November 1941

Before dawn on 18TH November, Eighth Army launched a surprise attack, advancing west from its base at Mersa Matruh and crossing the Libyan border near Fort Maddalena, some 50 miles (80 km) south of Sidi Omar, and then pushing to the northwest. Eighth Army were relying on the Desert Air Force to provide them with two clear days without serious air opposition but torrential rain and storms the night before the offensive resulted in the cancellation of all the air raids planned to interdict the Axis airfields and destroy their aircraft on the ground. However, initially all went well for the Allies. 7TH Armoured division's 7TH Armoured Brigade advanced northwest towards Tobruk with 22ND Armoured Brigade to their left. XIII Corps and New Zealand Division made its flanking advance with 4TH Armoured Brigade on its left and 4TH Indian Division's 7TH Infantry Brigade on its right flank at Sidi Omar. On the first day, no resistance was encountered as the Eighth Army closed on the enemy positions. The defences of Libyan Omar and Omar Nuovo had been very well prepared and were sited for all round defence.

Omar Nuovo, November 1941

The Royal Sussex drew Omar Nuovo as their portion and Libyan Omar was allotted to 16TH Punjab Regiment. The 11TH Sikh Regiment was ordered to mask, but not assault, Cove, four miles to the north. The Royal Sussex Regiment surged forward through the trenches and weapon- pits, taking 1,500 prisoners.

Libyan Omar, November 1941

The 16TH Punjab Regiment, with two tank squadrons, then passed through Omar Nuovo heading for Libyan Omar. In a few minutes, nearly all the tanks were ablaze, immobilized by mines, and smashed by the 88s. When the Punjabis debussed and formed up to attack, they had only five tanks instead of thirty. Nevertheless, they went in shoulder to shoulder with 1ST Punjab Regiment and 11TH Sikh Regiment, stalking, moving around, taking from the rear each weapon-pit and strong point, hurling hundreds of red Italian grenades they had brought from Keren. By evening, they had 500 prisoners and cleared the eastern part of the box. Next day, in many platoon and company actions, they took a thousand more prisoners and increased their hold to one third of the box.

2ND Punjab Regiment

North Africa

Qineiqina, November 1941

During this battle, 11TH Sikh Regiment was staging demonstrations to distract the enemy at Cova. During their demonstrations, platoons of the Sikh Regiment started across the open plain to capture a small Italian garrison at Qineiqina. Artillery, mortars, machine guns, and anti-tank guns pinned the platoons to the ground. There was a minefield round the post and the Sikhs had no supporting fire whatsoever. Ammunition would not last all day and when it was finished, the Italians would be able to pick off the prone attackers one by one. It looked as if two platoons would be wiped out. The only way out of the difficulty was to go forward. With a roar of "Wah Guru ji Ki Fateh" they swept up to the position and within minutes all was over. The Sikhs captured all the heavy guns and accounted for twenty-five of the enemy.

El Gubi, December 1941

The Axis had retreated and formed a defence line running south from the perimeter of Tobruk to El Adem and El Gubi. The next stage was the destruction of the remainder of the Afrika Korps, roaming about the front and the Italian divisions in the defences of El Gubi, El Adem, and round Tobruk. On the morning of 19TH November, the advance of 22ND Armoured Brigade was blunted by the Ariete Division at Bir el Gubi that continued to take a major toll of British armour in the opening phase of the battle. In the division's centre, 7TH Armoured Brigade and 7TH Support Group raced forward and took Sidi Rezegh airfield. Rommel withdrew with expert celerity behind the marshes of El Agheila, awaiting the arrivals of new tanks and reinforcements. They had not lost many Germans; only tanks which were replaceable, and Italians, which were expendable.

Relief of Tobruk, 1941

Tobruk was the site of a lengthy confrontation between Axis and Allied forces in North Africa during the Western Desert Campaign. The siege started on 10TH April 1941, when Tobruk was attacked by an Italian-German force under Lieutenant General Erwin Rommel and continued for 240 days, when the Eighth Army relieved it during Operation Crusader.

British '25 Pounder' artillery guns at the siege of Tobruk.

North Africa

Derna, December 1941

The 7TH Armoured Division moved across to the desert flank of 4TH Indian Division. The hunt was up. These two original desert formations set off in pursuit of Rommel. On 18TH Carmusa was reached. Leaving 16TH Punjabis to secure the Derna by-pass, the Royal Sussex raced back twelve miles along the road to Martuba. On the way, they captured an Italian tank complete with the crew, one heavy gun, some Italians and lorries. They threw themselves onto Martuba airfield, destroying three aircraft and securing huge dumps of bombs and stores. The 11TH Sikhs passed through the Royal Sussex, dropped two companies to block the road against forces retreating from the east, while the Bren carriers and the remainder of the battalion scrambled down onto the plain. Then the carriers led the charge. The enemy columns were completely unprepared as the carriers and lorrried infantry swept down upon them, shooting up in Wild West fashion. Three hundred prisoners, five 88 mm guns and many vehicles were captured. The carriers poured onto the Derna airfields, and riddled planes, large and small. Transport planes, bombers, fighters, gliders, all were destroyed or captured in the wild scrimmage. In the midst of this action, twelve large JU 52 troop carriers appeared overhead, circled and settled in. The Sikhs, scarcely believing their luck, held their fire until the last plane glided down. Then all opened fire, as if on a single word of command. Rifles, machine-gun, mortars, anti-tank guns, field guns, and even pistols were used to pour a storm of shot and shell into the Junkers. Eight of these large aircraft were shot to pieces. Two got off the ground but crashed. Out of the dozen, only two managed to get away, with the Sikhs hoping that shortage of petrol would account for them also. The jubilant Sikhs found themselves in possession of tremendous booty. Halfaya and Bardia were being maintained from Derna and no less than 183 enemy aircraft, both sound and damaged, were captured on the landing grounds. Thousands of bombs were stacked round about, as well as large quantities of petrol, wine, and food. From contemplation of such an appetising scene, the Sikhs tore themselves away with reluctance and by nightfall had reached the edge of the escarpment. On the morning of December 19TH, 11TH Sikhs, disdaining the rather ineffective demolitions on the switchback road down the escarpment, pushed down to Derna and took possession.

Sikhs in the advance towards the capture of Derna in December 1941

North Africa

Benghazi, December 1941

The 4TH Indian Division commenced pursuit of the enemy along the coast while 7TH Armoured Division took a short cut across the desert route. Immense quantities of war material were captured, but in the main, it was a stern chase and the prisoners taken were mostly the administrative troops manning the dumps and airfields along the route. One squadron of divisional cavalry regiment, the Central India Horse, advanced on and occupied Benghazi on 24TH December 1941. By the end of 1941, the Eighth Army had won a famous victory. They had relieved Tobruk, driven the enemy out of Cyrenaica, and reduced him from eight divisions to the equivalent of two. In this victory, 4TH Indian Division had not played the lead, but a very strong supporting part, proving that the Indian Army of 1941 could fight the best troops that the best army in the world could put in the field. The Germans took the point. A captured note by a German staff officer read, "So long as 7TH Armoured Divison and the Indian Division are in the desert, we must watch out. They will be the spearhead of any attack."

Rommel attacks, January 1942

On 5TH January 1942 the Afrika Korps received 55 tanks and new supplies and Rommel started planning a counterattack. On 21ST January the attack was launched, which mauled the Allied forces, costing them some 110 tanks and other heavy equipment. The Axis forces retook Benghazi on 29TH January, Timimi on 3RD February, and the Allies pulled back to the Tobruk area and commenced building defensive positions at Gazala. The new British defensive positions ran southwest from the seacoast at Gazala for fifteen miles to Alem Hamza. From there it swung southeast to Bir Hakeim. The moment the Indian Division crossed this line enemy pressure ended. At once, 4TH Indian Division began to build defences. But the division was due for a rest, far overdue. Ever since August 1940, the division had been constantly in the desert or Eritrea. The casualties had to be replaced, new equipment and vehicles issued, and the whole trained up to the high standards of its predecessors. The 50TH Northumbrian Division took over, but it was not until early April that the whole of 4TH Indian Division at last reached Delta and comfort.

Sikhs, New Zealanders and South Africans at Mersa Matruh

North Africa

Eighth Army, 1942

From March to May 1942, there was stalemate in the desert, both sides hurriedly building up their forces for an offensive. More and more British troops flooded into Libya; Indian forces were particularly increased. The 4TH Indian Division was relieved in March, and its Brigades departed for three different destinations. The 7TH Brigade went to Cyprus, 11TH Brigade to Canal Zone and 5TH Brigade to Palestine. The 11TH Sikh Regiment was sent to Persia and Iraq Force, to show them how things should be done!

Gazala, May 1942

Following a lull in the desert war, which saw the Germans and British reinforce their armies, Rommel suddenly attacked British fortifications with an assault on the northern sector of the British line near Gazala. Pinning down the British in the north and outflanking 1ST Free French Brigade, Rommel succeeded in encircling the main British positions, trapping them in what became known as 'The Cauldron'.

The Cauldron, May 1942

The only coherent feature of the chaos in the area, known as the Cauldron, was the German armour, always concentrated, and knocked hell out of the British armour. About 800 British tanks were lost, most to the 88 mm and long-barrelled 50 mm anti-tank guns onto which they were lured by superior tactics. With only 50 cruisers and 20 tanks left, the infantry were helpless in the open desert. A whole brigade of 50TH Northumbrian Divison was overrun by panzers and destroyed, as were 10TH Brigade and half of 9TH Brigade and 5TH Indian Division. Saddest was the fate of 11TH Indian Brigade, which had stormed the Italian camps at Sidi Barani and Cameron Ridge at Keren, chased the enemy from the Jebel Achdar, and covered the retreat from Benghazi. Sent to Tobruk to help to defend the fortress, which no one decided to defend until it was too late. When the divisional commander surrendered, 11TH Indian Brigade had to surrender too.
Then it was back through Halfaya and Sidi Barani and Mersa Matruh to the place Auchinleck had chosen and prepared for Eighth Army's last stand, El Amein.

North Africa

El Alamein, June 1942

Alamein itself was an insignificant railway station on the coast. Some ten miles to the south lay the Ruweisat Ridge, a low stony ridge that nonetheless gave excellent observation for many miles over the surrounding desert. 20 miles (32 km) to the south of that lay the Qattara Depression. The line the British chose to defend stretched between the sea and the Qattara Depression, which meant that Rommel could outflank it only by taking a significant detour to the south and crossing the Sahara Desert. The British Army in Egypt recognized this before the war and had the Eighth Army begin construction of several “boxes” (localities with dugouts and surrounded by minefields and barbed wire), the most developed being around the railway station at Alamein. Most of the “line”, however, was just open, empty desert. Lieutenant General C. W. M. Norrie organized the position and started to construct three defended "boxes". The first and strongest, at El Alamein on the coast, had been partly wired and mined by 1st South African Division. The Bab el Qattara box, some 20 miles from the coast and eight miles southwest of the Ruweisat Ridge, had been dug but had not been wired or mined, while at the Naq Abu Dweis box (on the edge of the Qattara Depression), 34 miles from the coast, very little work had been done. The scattering of X Corps at Mersa Matruh disrupted Auchinleck's plan for occupying the Alamein defences. On 29TH June, he ordered XXX Corps (1ST South African, 50TH and 10TH Indian Infantry Divisions) to take the coastal sector on the right of the front and XIII Corps (New Zealand and 5TH Indian Divisions) to be on the left. The remains of 1ST and 7TH Armoured Divisions were to be held as a mobile army reserve. His intention was the fixed defensive positions should canalize and disorganize the enemy's advance, while mobile units would attack their flanks and rear. On 30TH June, Rommel's Panzer Army Africa approached the Alamein position. The Axis forces were exhausted and under strength. Rommel had driven them forward ruthlessly, being confident that, provided he struck quickly before Eighth Army had time to settle, his momentum would take him through the Alamein position and he could then advance to the Nile with little further opposition.

Sikh soldier with a souvenir at Benghazi

North Africa

Rommel Attacks, July 1942

At 03:00 on 1ST July, 15TH and 21ST Panzer Divisions were delayed by a sandstorm and then a heavy air attack. By the time they circled round the back of Deir el Abyad, they found the feature to the east of it occupied by Indian 18TH Infantry Brigade. After a hasty journey from Iraq, they had occupied the exposed position just west of Ruweisat Ridge and east of Deir el Abyad at Deir el Shein. On 1ST July, 21ST Panzer Division attacked Deir el Shein. 18TH Indian Infantry Brigade, supported by 23 25-pounder guns, 16 of the new 6-pounder anti-tank guns and nine Matilda tanks, held out the whole day in desperate fighting, but by evening the Germans succeeded in overrunning them. Meanwhile, 1ST Armoured Division had been sent to intervene at Deir el Shein. They ran into 15TH Panzer Division just south of Deir el Shein and drove it west. By the end of the day's fighting, the Afrika Korps had 37 tanks left out of its initial compliment of 55. During the early afternoon, 90TH Light had extricated itself from the El Alamein box defences and resumed its move eastward. It came under artillery fire from the three South African brigade groups and was forced to dig in. On 2ND July, Rommel ordered the resumption of the offensive. Once again, 90TH Light failed to make progress so Rommel called the Afrika Korps to abandon its planned sweep southward and instead join the effort to break through to the coast road by attacking east towards Ruweisat Ridge.

Ruweisat Ridge, July 1942

On 2ND July, Rommel ordered the resumption of the offensive. The British defence of Ruweisat Ridge relied on an improvised formation called Robcol, comprising a regiment each of Field artillery and light anti-aircraft artillery and a company of infantry. Robcol was able to buy time, and by late afternoon, the two British armoured brigades joined the battle with 4TH Armoured Brigade, engaging 15TH Panzer, 22ND Armoured Brigade, and 21ST Panzer. They drove back repeated attacks by the Axis armour, which then withdrew before dusk. The British reinforced Ruweisat on the night of 2ND July. The now enlarged Robcol became Walgroup. The Royal Air Force meanwhile made heavy air attacks on the Axis units. The next day, 3RD July, Rommel resumed the attack on the Ruweisat ridge. The combination of British artillery fire and constant air attacks halted the Axis advance.

4TH Armoured Brigade

North Africa

Rommel Digs In, July 1942

To relieve the pressure on the right and centre of the Eighth Army line, XIII Corps on the left advanced from the Qattara box (known to the New Zealanders as the Kaponga box). The plan was that 2ND New Zealand Division, with the remains of 5TH Indian Division and 7TH Motor Brigade under its command, would swing north to threaten the Axis flank and rear. This force encountered the *Ariete* Armoured Division's artillery, which was driving on the southern flank of the division as it attacked Ruweisat. The Italian commander ordered his battalions to fight their way out independently but the *Ariete* lost 531 men (about 350 were prisoners), 36 pieces of artillery, six tanks, and 55 trucks. By the end of the day, the *Ariete* Division had only five tanks. The day ended once again with the *Afrika Korps* and *Ariete* coming off second best to the superior numbers of the British 22ND Armoured and 4TH Armoured Brigades, frustrating Rommel's attempts to resume his advance. At this point, Rommel decided his exhausted forces could make no further headway without resting and regrouping. *Afrika Korps* had just 36 Panzers, his three German Divisions numbered just 1,200-1,500 men each, and his men were exhausted and operating at the end of their supply lines. On 4TH July, Rommel ordered the Axis forces to go on the defensive. Rommel was by this time suffering from the extended length of his supply lines. The Allied Desert Air Force was concentrating fiercely on his fragile and elongated supply routes, while British mobile columns moving west and striking from the south were causing havoc in the Axis rear echelons. Rommel could afford these losses even less since shipments from Italy had been substantially reduced (in June, he received 5,000 short tons (4,500 t) of supplies compared with 34,000 short tons (31,000 t) in May and 400 vehicles compared with 2,000 in May). Meanwhile, the Eighth Army was reorganising and rebuilding, benefiting from its short lines of communication. By 4TH July, 9THAustralian Division had entered the line in the north, and on 9TH July, 5TH Indian Infantry Brigade also returned taking over the Ruweisat position. At the same time, the fresh Indian 161ST Infantry Brigade reinforced the depleted 5TH Indian Infantry Division.

Sikh Gunners in the desert, 1942

North Africa

Tel el Eisa, July 1942

General Ramsden was to capture the low ridges at Tel el Eisa and Tel el Makh Khad and then to push mobile battle groups south towards Deir el Shein. Meanwhile XIII Corps would prevent the Axis from moving troops north to reinforce the coastal sector. Ramsden tasked 9TH Australian Division, with 44TH Royal Tank Regiment under command, with the Tel el Eisa objective and 1ST South African Division with eight supporting tanks, Tel el Makh Khad. Following a bombardment, which started at 03:30 on 10TH July, 26TH Australian Brigade launched an attack against the ridge north of Tel el Eisa station along the coast. The bombardment was the heaviest barrage yet experienced in North Africa, which created panic in the inexperienced soldiers of 60TH Infantry Division Sabratha, who had only just occupied sketchy defences in the sector. The Australian attack took more than 1,500 prisoners, routed an Italian Division, and overran the German Signals Intercept Company. At 06:00 on 22ND July, 26TH Australian Brigade attacked Tel el Eisa and 24TH Australian Brigade attacked Tel el Makh Khad towards Mieirya (Ruin Ridge) the fighting for Tel el Eisa was costly, but by the afternoon the Australians controlled the feature. That evening 24TH Australian Brigade attacked Tel el Makh Khad with the tanks of 50TH Royal Tank Regiment in support. The tank unit had not been trained in close infantry support and failed to coordinate with the Australian infantry. The result was that the infantry and armour advanced independently and having reached the objective 50TH Royal Tank Regiment lost 23 tanks because they lacked infantry support. Once more, the Eighth Army had failed to destroy Rommel's forces, despite its overwhelming superiority in men and equipment. On the other hand, for Rommel the situation continued to be grave as, despite successful defensive operations, his infantry had suffered heavy losses and he reported that "the situation is critical in the extreme". The battle was a stalemate, but it had halted the Axis advance on Alexandria (and then Cairo and ultimately the Suez Canal). Eighth Army had suffered over 13,000 casualties in July (including 4,000 in the New Zealand Division, 3,000 in 5TH Indian Infantry Division and 2,552 battle casualties in 9TH Australian Division) but had taken 7,000 prisoners and inflicted heavy damage on Axis men and machines.

Indian Armour in North Africa, 1942

North Africa

El Alamein, November 1942

Eighth Army counter-offensives during July were unsuccessful, as Rommel dug in to allow his exhausted troops to regroup. At the end of July, Auchinleck called off all offensive action with a view to rebuilding the army's strength. In early August, British Prime Minister Winston Churchill and General Sir Alan Brooke, the British Chief of the Imperial General Staff, visited Cairo and replaced Auchinleck as C-in-C Middle East with General Sir Harold Alexander. Lieutenant-General William Gott was to command the Eighth Army. He was killed before taking command, when Luftwaffe fighters shot down the plane he was travelling in; Lieutenant-General Bernard Montgomery became Eighth Army commander. The Second Battle of El Alamein marked a major turning point in the Western Desert Campaign of the Second World War. The battle lasted from 23RD October-5TH November 1942. The First Battle of El Alamein had stalled the Axis advance. Thereafter, Lieutenant-General Bernard Montgomery took command of the British Eighth Army from General Claude Auchinleck in August 1942. During the campaign, half of Rommel's 100,000-man army was killed, wounded, or taken prisoner. He also lost over 450 tanks and 1,000 guns. The British and Commonwealth forces suffered 13,500 casualties and 500 of their tanks were damaged. However, of these, 350 were repaired and were able to take part in future battles.

The allied victory turned the tide in the North African Campaign. It ended Axis hopes of occupying Egypt, taking control of the Suez Canal, and gaining access to the Middle Eastern oil fields. El Alamein was the first great offensive against the Germans in which the Western Allies were victorious. Winston Churchill famously summed up the battle on 10TH November 1942 with the words, "This is not the end, it is not even the beginning of the end. But it is, perhaps, the end of the beginning." It was Montgomery's greatest triumph; he took the title "Viscount Montgomery of Alamein" when he was raised to the peerage after the war. Rommel, concerned that his army would be completely enveloped and destroyed if he once again halted to face the Eighth Army, withdrew all the way to Tunisia where the terrain would better suit a defensive action.

Indian Armour in North Africa

North Africa

Tripoli, January 1943

On 15TH January 1943, General Montgomery launched 51ST (Highland) Division against Rommel's defences while sending 2ND New Zealand Division and 7TH Armoured Divisions around the inland flank of the Axis line. Weakened by the withdrawal of 21ST Panzer Division to Tunisia to strengthen von Arnim's Fifth Panzer Army, once again Rommel was forced to conduct a fighting retreat. Tripoli, some 150 miles further on, with its major port facilities, was taken on 23RD January as Rommel continued to withdraw to the French-built southern defences of Tunisia, the Mareth Line.

Tunisia, January 1943

Rommel was by this time in contact with von Arnim's Fifth Panzer Army, which had been fighting the Tunisia Campaign against the multi-national British First Army in northern Tunisia since shortly after Operation Torch the previous autumn. Hitler was determined to retain hold of Tunisia and Rommel finally started to receive replacement men and materials. The Axis now faced a war in Africa on two fronts, with Eighth Army approaching from the east and the British, French and Americans of First Army from the west. Rommel's German-Italian Panzer Army was re-designated Italian First Army under General Giovanni Messe, while Rommel assumed command of the new Army Group Africa, responsible for both fronts. Similarly, the two Allied armies were placed under 18TH Army Group with Harold Alexander in command. However, the hope of an early conclusion to the campaign against the Axis forces was thwarted at the Battle of the Kasserine Pass, in the second half of February, when Rommel struck a costly blow against the inexperienced U.S. II Corps and destroyed their ability to make an early thrust east to the coast, to cut off the Italian First Army's line of supply from Tunis and isolate it from von Arnim's forces in the north.

General Alexander was in overall command of all the allied land forces in Tunisia. His plan to finish the campaign was for the Americans to take Bizerta and the British First Army to take Tunis from the west; while the Eighth army attacked from the south. By a quick change of plan, 4TH Indian Division and 7TH Armoured were transferred to the First Army, to strengthen the attack on Tunis from the west.

The Allies entering Tripoli, 1943

North Africa

Surrender, May 1943

In the last operation of the war in Africa 4TH Indian Division, on General Tucker's insistence and despite the misgivings of 4TH British Division on the left, attacked at night. They were supported by such artillery fire as they had never imagined, of 1917-18 dimensions, and by the morning of 6TH May 1943 they were through with very little loss. There was customary delay in sending through the armour; for once, it did not matter. Five days later Colonel General von Arnim, Commander-in-chief of all Axis forces in Tunisia, surrendered his own headquarters and Fifth Panzer Armee to Lieutenant Colonel L. C. J. Showers, commanding 2ND King Edward VII's Own Gurkha Rifles. A few weeks later General Montgomery, in a lecture to officers, made handsome amends for the past - I sent the First Army my best: 7TH Armoured and 4TH Indian Division (The Red Eagle Division).

The 4TH Indian Division came to the end of the long road. The road had led it from the Western Desert to Eritrea, from Eritrea to Syria, back to the Western Desert and two thousand miles across Africa. While its fame grew from battle to battle until the last campaign, the world came to know it from the lips of the Prime Minister himself, in glowing tribute to the only volunteer army in this world war. But there is no officer nor man in the Red Eagle Division who does not regard the fame showered upon him as an equal tribute to other Indian Divisions, who bore the heat and burden of other days and for whom the God of battles had decreed less fortune at the finish.

Indian Armour in North Africa

North Africa

The following Sikh soldiers were awarded the Indian Order of Merit for their conspicuous gallantry in North Africa during the Second World War. The citations of their awards read:

Subedar Fateh Singh (Posthumous)
1TH Punjab Regiment

"Subedar Fateh Singh was a veritable pillar of strength in his Company. His courage and leadership were outstanding and it is no exaggeration to say that whenever he led, no man ever hesitated to follow. His Battalion took part in many attacks and Subedar Fateh Singh was present at them all. He was always with his men encouraging them on and praising them in every way, doing his utmost to see that the Company did the job thoroughly. During a night march on 19TH June 1941 one platoon lost its way. Subedar Fateh Singh himself went in search of this platoon and managed to find it. He did not hesitate to go alone in the darkness of the night although fully aware that he may himself have run into enemy posts. Having found the platoon, he formed part of the reinforcements, which were being rushed to the aid of the others who were surrounded, and while on the way up he brilliantly led the platoon against a nest of machine-guns, completely routing the enemy. On 30TH November 1941, the Battalion was up against very stiff opposition. Subedar Fateh Singh's company was pinned down by extremely heavy machine-gun fire and was being heavily shelled, but seeing the necessity of immediate action, he stood up and cheered his men on and it was then that he was killed by a burst of machine-gun fire. His action was a tonic to the men; they no longer hesitated in going forward to their objective in spite of heavy losses."

Jemadar Aman Singh
Indian Armoured Corps

"During the night of 15TH and 26TH July 1941, Jemadar Aman Singh led a successful raid against an enemy machine-gun post and three other successive positions. All were attacked and stormed with hand grenades and bayonets and the defenders killed. Aman Singh showed the highest qualities of leadership and personal bravery, setting a splendid example to those serving under him. At the conclusion of his task, he brought all his men safely back in spite of heavy mortar and machine-gun fire. The raiding party suffered only a single causality, one man being slightly wounded. The success of this raid was not only due to his courageous leadership, but also to the zeal, energy, and skill, which he had shown during the preliminary reconnaissance of the enemy position."

North Africa

Jemadar Kartar Singh, (Posthumous)
14TH Punjab Regiment

"On 23RD July 1942 Jemadar Kartar Singh led his platoon forward in the face of intense medium machine-gun and shellfire. He was wounded and blown over by a shell-burst but rose and continued to lead and encourage his men. Soon after, he was again hit in the head by a bullet but he still attempted to rise but was unable to do so. Nevertheless, he encouraged his platoon from where he lay until he finally died from his head wound."

Jemadar Dhera Singh
2ND Punjab Regiment

"The success of the attack of 'B' Company on an enemy strong point on 25TH November 1941 was very largely due to the courageous and cool-headed leadership of Jemadar Dhera Singh. Directing the centre and the right-hand platoons in broad daylight, in full view of the enemy and under considerable fire, he co-ordinated their attack, and by his example of coolness and daring, led them into the final charge with such dash and determination that the position was taken, resulting in the capture of two Italian Officers, 42 other ranks, a 20 mm gun and other weapons and war materials. There is no doubt that, by risking his life so that his men could see him was a great factor in preventing any hesitation, which at that point might have been fatal. On many previous occasions, Jemadar Dhera Singh has led his platoon successfully against enemy positions showing utter disregard for his own personal safety. For continuous good work and exhibition of sterling qualities of leadership throughout the Eritrean campaign and the operations in the Western Desert, Jemadar Dhera Singh was awarded the Indian Order of Merit."

Jemadar Amar Singh
2ND Punjab Regiment

"On 25TH March 1941, Jemadar Amar Singh led his platoon against an enemy machine gun holding up the attack, and captured the gun and the crew. A few minutes later, his platoon was heavily counter-attacked and had to withdraw. He immediately re-organized his platoon, advanced and re-captured the position. Later he led a party against enemy hiding in some rocks and captured them. Throughout the night, though repeatedly counter-attacked, he maintained his position by personal example and encouragement. The bravery and coolness displayed by him under fire was of a very high order and an inspiration to his men."

North Africa

Naik Jagat Singh
2ND Punjab Regiment

"Whilst on patrol on 15TH June 1942, Naik Jagat Singh showed outstanding leadership. As Section Commander, he attacked an enemy armoured tractor mounted with an 88 mm gun, destroying the tractor and the gun with a stick bomb, and captured a prisoner. Later, on the night of 16TH-17TH June, Naik Jagat Singh, together with some of his section, was captured and placed in a truck under guard. Before the enemy had been able to totally disarm the party, this NCO knocked out his guard with a spare light machine-gun barrel, enabling thereby not only himself but also others of his section to escape. During the same incident he also helped to carry a wounded comrade."

Jemadar Gurbaksh Singh (Posthumous)
11TH Sikh Regiment

"During the attack on 27TH November 1941, Jemadar Gurbaksh Singh displayed outstanding gallantry and leadership. He was in command of 12TH Platoon, and personally led his platoon during the initial advance. Very heavy fire from all weapons caused the attack to waver somewhat. Jemadar Gurbaksh Singh, however, rallied his men and took them forward over open ground in the face of heavy fire to within 150 yards of the enemy position. There the fire was so intense that the platoon had momentarily to go to ground. Gurbaksh Singh was still not content and got up from cover to lead the platoon in the final assault on the enemy position. He had no sooner left cover than he was hit with a burst of machine-gun fire and a mortar bomb and was killed on the spot. The outstanding courage and leadership of Jemadar Gurbaksh Singh are worthy of the highest praise."

Havildar Natha Singh (Posthumous)
13TH Frontier Force Rifles

"During the night of 25TH-26TH March 1941, Havildar Natha Singh was commanding a forward platoon, which twice repulsed determined attacks. After the first attack, the platoon suffered casualties from our own artillery fire. After the second attack had been repulsed, the artillery fire again came down very heavily on the platoon's position. Havildar Natha Singh ordered his platoon back to another position about 100 yards in the rear and he remained in the original position. He was last seen alive throwing grenades at the enemy who were lying up in broken ground some thirty yards away. On the artillery fire ceasing, the platoon occupied its original position and found him dead. His very gallant conduct kept the enemy at bay and undoubtedly saved many lives in his platoon."

North Africa

Havildar Sadhu Singh
16TH Punjab Regiment

"Between 20TH and 22ND April 1943 the battalion had captured its objectives on the Djebel Garci feature. The adjutant had been wounded and relieved by the Signal Officer. The responsibility for all communications thus devolved on to Sadhu Singh as the Signal Havildar. Shelling and mortaring was continuous throughout the day and night, and communications by line were continually being cut. Sadhu Singh, showing the utmost resourcefulness and complete disregard for his personal safety, organized repair parties throughout the day and night. Casualties then became very heavy among the signallers and it became incumbent upon Havildar Sadhu Singh, apart from his other responsibilities, to carry out repairs himself, working over extremely difficult terrain and under enemy machine-gun and shellfire. This work he carried out again and again, showing unequalled example of devotion to duty. It was through his efforts that communications remained of a high standard throughout, resulting in the quick anticipation and neutralization of enemy counter attacks. Havildar Sadhu Singh showed extraordinary fortitude and courage, working unrelieved and unceasingly for 72 hours."

Subedar Major Sohan Singh OBI
13TH Frontier Force Rifles

"During an action on 28TH June 1942 when the Battalion's position was over-run by enemy tanks, Subadar Major Sohan Singh was instrumental in getting all the Battalion transport away to a place of safety. Later in the afternoon when he heard that his Commanding Officer had been captured, he proceeded alone in a truck to the scene of the capture in order to effect rescue. He was captured in the process. It was only through a ruse arranged by his Commanding Officer that he subsequently escaped, and it had been only with the greatest difficulty that he was persuaded to fall in with the plan, as he demanded to stay prisoner with the rest. His courage and demeanour during this episode was most praiseworthy. On this and many other occasions Subadar Major Sohan Singh, by cheerfulness and courage, set a high example to all ranks in the Battalion."

13TH Frontier Force Rifles

North Africa

Sepoy Saudagar Singh (Posthumous)
13TH Frontier Force Rifles

"During the attack on 8TH May 1941 on a hill, a high and difficult feature strongly held by the well-entrenched enemy, Sepoy Saudagar Singh was a member of the leading section. On nearing the summit, a heavy shower of hand grenades checked the advance of the section and Sepoy Saudagar Singh was wounded. In spite of his wound and utterly regardless of the very heavy rifle and machine-gun fire encountered, he led his section over most precipitous ground. He reached the enemy's trench, bayoneted two of the defenders, and was killed as he bayoneted the third. The remainder of the enemy then fled. His very gallant conduct in the face of heavy odds inspired his section to continue the advance and capture the position."

Jemadar Bhagat Singh (Posthumous)
1ST Punjab Regiment

"Jemadar Bhagat Singh led his platoon during an attack launched by a company on the night of 18TH-19TH June 1941. The company was under heavy machine-gun and rifle fire and casualties were heavy, but he inspired his men to advance, keeping up their spirit and maintaining the momentum of the attack. After about three hours of heavy fighting and rapid advance, the company came up against three strongly held machine-gun pillboxes. The fire was very heavy; the men were tired, and their number considerably depleted; nevertheless this officer led them forward with confidence and determination. His attack caused the enemy to run. In the very final stages, a fourth pillbox opened up rapid fire and Jemadar Bhagat Singh was killed."

Havildar Babu Singh (Posthumous)
Indian Engineers

"Havildar Babu Singh was Section Havildar to a Sikh section that was ordered to build a crossing over the Wadi Zigzao on the night of 22ND-23RD March 1943. The approaches to, and the Wadi itself, were subject to intense enemy shellfire and heavy machine-gun fire. During the night, this Havildar supervised the ramps on both sides of the Wadi to the stores area, finally driving down two lorry loads of stores to the site himself. His courage and leadership were beyond all praise and his magnificent example of personal bravery, a source of great inspiration to all his men. Towards the end of the operation, while manoeuvring a lorry-load of stores into position, an anti-tank shell killed him."

BRITISH POLICE

(with Diljit Singh Bahra)

As we have seen, the Sikhs were especially recruited by Britain to police various parts of the Empire. The Sikh police officers were pioneering Sikh immigrants to the far corners of Empire. Their descendants are keeping up the tradition and are serving in the police forces of their respective countries. Eventually the Sikhs came to serve in the heart of the Empire, the Police forces of Great Britain.

Senior police officers from East Africa and other British Colonies and dependencies attended the 'Colonial Police Course' (later known as Overseas Training Course) in England and the first Sikh Police officer wearing a turban known to attend a course at Metropolitan Police Training School at Hendon was Chief Inspector Bhajan Singh Bohi in 1950.

Assistant Superintendent Nasib Singh Kundra also attended this course and was in London when King George died in 1952. He was a member of the Colonial Police Force who guarded the King's body at Westminster Hall on the night before the state funeral.

It was the Independence of the East African countries of Kenya, Uganda, Tanganyika, and Zanzibar in the early 1960s that brought a large number of Asians to Great Britain. They mainly settled in London and the Midlands. Several of those who settled in the Greater London area were Sikhs who had served in the Police service in the East African Countries.

By 1965, a few of these former Colonial Police Officers had joined the Metropolitan Police Force in London as Civilian Support staff. There were also a couple of Sikh Special Police Constables in the Police Service.

The first known application by a Sikh, wearing a turban, to join the Metropolitan Police Force was in January 1969. He was a former senior Police Officer in Kenya. The decision whether to allow a Sikh to wear a turban in the police service took rather a long time and the applicant took employment elsewhere. In April 1969, James Callaghan, the Home Secretary gave authority for Sikhs wearing turbans to join the British Police Service.

Harbans Singh Jabblal

The first Turban wearing Special Police Constable in England was a former Kenya Police Officer, Harbans Singh Jabblal. He joined the Metropolitan Police Force Civil Staff in 1966 and in January 1969 became the countries first turban-wearing officer.

British Police

Ajmer Singh Matharu

Ajmer Singh Matharu, who had been a Deputy Superintendent of Police in Uganda, became the first turban wearing Sikh when he joined Leicester and Rutland Constabulary on 6TH April 1970. Ajmer retired from the Leicester Police Constabulary in October 1989.

Inspector Diljit Singh Bahra

Diljit Singh Bahra was born in Kenya, came to Britain in 1967, and joined the British Army in 1968. He served in Germany, Northern Ireland, Cyprus and Kenya, before joining the Metropolitan Police Force on 1st April 1975. On promotion to Sergeant in February 1982, he served at Rochester Row, Marylebone, and Bexleyheath Divisions. He was promoted to Inspector in January 1992 and served at Bow Street, Canon Row, and Charing Cross until his retirement in January 2007. Diljit went on to manage the British Police Hockey Team in 1982 and was the Team Manager/ Coach for a period of 16 years. Currently Diljit is the Hon. Secretary of the Hockey Writers' Club (international membership) and the Media Overseers co-ordinator for the AIPS Hockey commission and the Hockey Writers' Club.

Currently Sikh police officers are serving in the regional police forces of England, Scotland, and Wales. Max Sahota, a Sikh, had risen to the rank of Assistant Chief Constable with South Yorkshire Police. Randeep Kohli, a Turban wearing Sikh, is a Superintendent of Police in the Metropolitan Police Service in London.

British Police

Chief Inspector Parm Kaur Sandhu

Chief Inspector Parm Kaur Sandhu joined the police service in 1989 as a constable and was promoted as a Sergeant in 1996, to an inspector in 2000, and to Chief Inspector in 2004. British-born Sandhu was awarded the prestigious Asian Woman of Achievement Award in the UK. Sandhu is a Chief Inspector with the Metropolitan Police (MET) and is the highest ranking female Asian officer in the Metropolitan Police.

Chief Inspector Shindo Kaur Barquer

The highest-ranking West Midlands Sikh police officer, Chief Inspector Shindo Kaur Barquer, joined the West Midlands Police Force at the age of 21. She progressively worked her way up the ranks, a journey that has been challenging but rewarding for this British Sikh born in West Bromwich. She has been honoured with 'The Police Long Service and Good Conduct Medal' which was instituted under the Royal Warrant by King George VI in 1951 and is awarded as a mark of the Sovereign's appreciation of long and meritorious service rendered by members of the Police Forces of the United Kingdom.

SOURCES

Allen, Charles. (2004) *Duel In The Snow.* John Murray: London.

Andrews, C. F. and Pearson W. W. (1918) *Indian Indentured Labour in Fiji.* Colortype Press: Perth.

Anon. (compiled by various officers). (1938) *History of the Guides 1846 – 1922.* Gale and Polden: Aldershot.

Beachey, Ray. (1990) *The Warrior Mullah, The Horn Aflame.* Bellow Publishing: London.

Bickers, Robert. (2003) *Empire Made Me.* Allen Lane: London.

Birdwood, F. T. (1950) *The Sikh Regiment in the Second World War.* Jarrod & Sons: Norwich.

Caroe, Olaf. (1964) *The Pathans.* Macmillan and Co. Ltd: London.

Chhabra, G. S. (2005) *Advanced Study in the History of Modern India (Volume 2 1813 - 1920).* Lotus Press: New Delhi.

Churchill, Winston. (1908) *My African Journey.* Hodder & Stoughton: London.

Duckers, Peter. (1999) *Reward of Valour, I.O.M.* Jade Publishing Ltd.: Lancashire.

Ferndale, Sir Martin. (1988) *History of the Royal Regiment of Artillery: The Forgotten Fronts and the Home Base*. Royal Artillery Institution: London.

Fleming, P. (1961) *Bayonets to Lhasa*. Rupert Hart-Davis:London

Foran, W. R. (1936) *Cuckoo in Kenya*. Hutchinson: London.

Gale, W. D. (1958) *Zambezi Sunrise*. Howard. B .Timmin: Cape Town.

General Staff, Army Headquarters, India. (1921) *Operations in Waziristan, 1919-1920*. Superintendent Government Printing: Calcutta.

Grant, Sir James Hope. (1875) *Incidents in the China War of 1860.* Blackwood and Sons: London.

Heath, I. (1999) *The North East Frontier.* Osprey Publishing Ltd.: Oxford.

Herbert, Christopher. (1978) *The Great Mutiny.* Allan Lane: London.

India Army Intelligence Branch (2006) *Frontier and Overseas Expeditions from India* (Vol.V1). The Naval and Military Press Ltd.: Uckfield.

Kaur, Arunajeet. (2003) *Sikhs in the Policing of British Malaya and Straits Settlements.* VDM Verlag Dr, Muller: Germany.

Sources

Khoo, Gilbert. (1982) *SINGA,The Lion of Malaya.* Eastview Productions: Malaysia.

Lopo, Malkiat Singh. (1979) *Sikhs in Malaysia Series (Volume Two)*. Lope Ghar Publication: Penang, Malaysia.

Mackenzie, Compton. (1951) *Eastern Epic*. Chatto and Windus: London.

Macmunn, Sir George. (1936) *The History of the Sikh Pioneers*. Sampson Low, Marston and Co. Ltd.: London.

Magor, R. B. (1993) *African General Service Medals.* The Naval and Military Press: London.

Metcalf, Thomas, R. (2008) *Imperial Connections.* University of California Press: London.

Moyse-Bartlett, H. (2002) *The King's African Rifles* (reprint). Naval and Military Press: London.

Nevill, H. L. (2005) *Campaigns on the North–West Frontier*. The Naval and Military Press: Uckfield.

Nutting, Anthony. (1994) *Scramble for Africa.* Constable & Co.: London.

Page, Malcolm. (1998) *K.A.R. A history of The Kings African Rifle.* Leo Cooper: South Yorkshire.

Punjabis.sg. (2012) *SWO Amar Singh Military Police Training School's new CO* (www document) <http://cyberraja.com/index.php?option=com_content&view=article&id=464:swo-amar-singh-military-police-training-schools-new-co&catid=77&Itemid=583>

Qureshi, Mohammed Ibrahim. (1958) *The First Punjabis.* Gale & Polden: Aldershot.

Renfrew, Barry. (2009) *Forgotten Regiments.* Terrier Press: Amersham.

Robson, Brian. (1986) *The Road To Kabul.* Arms and Armour Press: London.

Rollo, Dennis. (1991) *The Guns & Gunners of Hong Kong.* Gunner's Roll of Hong Kong: Hong Kong.

Rutter, Owen. (1922) *British North Borneo.* Constable and Co Ltd.: London.

Saul, David. (2002) *The Indian Mutiny.* Viking: London.

Sharma, Gautam. (1989) *Valour, and Sacrifice.* Allied Publishers Ltd.: New Delhi.

Sources

Shorey, Anil. (2005) *A Legendary Force: 1st Patiala*. Manas Publications: New Delhi.

Sikh Cyber Museum (2003a) *The Indian Mutiny - 1857* [www document] <http://www.sikhcybermuseum.org.uk/history/IndianMutiny1857.htm> (accessed 25 April 2012)

Sikh Cyber Museum (2003b) *The Indian Mutiny - 1857* [www document] <http://www.sikhcybermuseum.org.uk/history/SikhRegiments1859-1914.htm> (accessed 25 April 2012)

SikhiWiki. (2009) *The Sepoy Mutiny – 1857*. [www document] <http://www.sikhiwiki.org/index.php/The_Sepoy_Mutiny_-_1857> (accessed 25 April 2012)

Singh, Amarinder. (2010) *The Last Sunset.* Roli Books: New Delhi.

Singh, Harbans. (2004) *The Encyclopaedia of Sikhs.* Punjabi University: Patiala.

Singh, Inder. (1965) *History of Malay States Guides.* Cathay Printers Ltd.: Penang.

Singh, Karam. (2009) *The Police Contingent.* Lorong Pisang Bat: Singapore.

Soldiers Burden (undated) *Smutts: East Africa Dispatches* (www document) <http://www.trenchfighter.com/40117/165201.html> (accessed 11 May 2012)

Swann, Alfred, J. (1910) *Fighting the Slave Hunters in Central Africa*. Frank Cass and Co. Ltd.: London.

Government of India. (1944).*The Tiger Kills*. HMSO: London.

Government of India. (1946) *The Tiger Triumphs.* HMSO: London.

Government of India. (1942) *The Tiger Strikes*. Government of India: Calcutta.

WW11 AT 70, (2010) World War II Day-By-Day: Day 352 August 17, 1940 (www document) <http://worldwar2daybyday.blogspot.co.uk/2010/08/day-352-august-17-1940.html> (accessed 11 May 2012)

Younghusband, G. J. (1896) *The Relief of Chitral.* Macmillan & Co: London.

INDEX

Index

Index

Index

Index

Index

Index

ABOUT THIS BOOK

In the style which caused his ***Sikh Soldier: Battle Honours*** and ***Sikh Soldier: Gallantry Awards*** books to become mainstays of Sikh martial history since their publication, Narindar Singh Dhesi again brings his orderly thoroughness to the evaluation of colonial warfare and policing of the distant outposts of the British Empire. Narindar Singh has a masterly grasp of the most important elements of grand strategy, and the most vital but less studied aspects of the gallantry awards to the Sikh soldier. He provides the finest single-volume narrative reference on the subject with full coverage of events involving Britain, the Indian sub-continent, Africa, the Middle East, and the Far East, in addition to matters of battlefield action, the composition of the forces involved, and the outcome and effect of campaigns. ***Sikh Soldier: Policing the Empire*** also provides profiles of Sikh soldiers who served and are currently serving in the armed forces of their respective countries. Narindar Singh Dhesi's earlier books have been acclaimed as compendiums of information, vital components in the library of every Sikh household; these qualities are all present in this outstanding contribution to the study of colonial warfare and guarding the distant outposts of the British Empire by the Sikh Soldier.

Narindar Singh was born in 1940 at Eldoret in Kenya, where his father, Waryam Singh, an Akali freedom fighter, had migrated from the Punjab. He moved to England in 1957 and joined the British Army. After leaving the armed forces in 1964, he worked in the building and construction industry. He is married with four children and living in retirement at Southend on Sea, England.

He is the author of two books on Sikh Soldier i.e. ***Sikh Soldier: Battle Honours*** (ISBN 9781845748913) and ***Sikh Soldier: Gallantry Awards,*** (ISBN 9781845749057) and are available from The Naval and Military Press.

www.ingramcontent.com/pod-product-compliance
Ingram Content Group UK Ltd.
Pitfield, Milton Keynes, MK11 3LW, UK
UKHW051206260726
13967UKWH00011B/3130

9 781781 519851